FORGOTTEN WARS

Włodzimierz Borodziej and Maciej Górny set out to salvage the historical memory of the experience of war in the lands between Riga and Skopje, beginning with the two Balkan conflicts of 1912–1913 and ending with the death of Emperor Franz Joseph in 1916. The First World War in the East and South-East of Europe was fought by people from a multitude of different nationalities, most of them dressed in the uniforms of three imperial armies: Russian, German, and Austro-Hungarian. In this first volume of *Forgotten Wars*, the authors chart the origins and outbreak of the First World War, the early battles, and the war's impact on ordinary soldiers and civilians through to the end of the Romanian campaign in December 1916, by which point the Central Powers controlled all of the Balkans except for the Peloponnese. Combining military and social history, the authors make extensive use of eyewitness accounts to describe the traumatic experience that established a region stretching between the Baltic, Adriatic, and Black Seas.

WŁODZIMIERZ BORODZIEJ is Professor of Contemporary History at the University of Warsaw.

MACIEJ GÓRNY is Professor at the Tadeusz Manteuffel History Institute, Polish Academy of Sciences, Warsaw.

Studies in the Social and Cultural History of Modern Warfare

General Editor

Robert Gerwarth, *University College Dublin*

Jay Winter, *Yale University*

Advisory Editors

Heather Jones, *University College London*

Rana Mitter, *University of Oxford*

Michelle Moyd, *Indiana University Bloomington*

Martin Thomas, *University of Exeter*

In recent years the field of modern history has been enriched by the exploration of two parallel histories. These are the social and cultural history of armed conflict, and the impact of military events on social and cultural history.

Studies in the Social and Cultural History of Modern Warfare presents the fruits of this growing area of research, reflecting both the colonization of military history by cultural historians and the reciprocal interest of military historians in social and cultural history, to the benefit of both. The series offers the latest scholarship in European and non-European events from the 1850s to the present day.

A full list of titles in the series can be found at:
www.cambridge.org/modernwarfare

FORGOTTEN WARS

Central and Eastern Europe, 1912–1916

WŁODZIMIERZ BORODZIEJ
University of Warsaw

MACIEJ GÓRNY
Tadeusz Manteuffel History Institute, Polish Academy of Sciences, Warsaw

Translated by Jasper Tilbury

CAMBRIDGE
UNIVERSITY PRESS

University Printing House, Cambridge CB2 8BS, United Kingdom

One Liberty Plaza, 20th Floor, New York, NY 10006, USA

477 Williamstown Road, Port Melbourne, VIC 3207, Australia

314–321, 3rd Floor, Plot 3, Splendor Forum, Jasola District Centre, New Delhi – 110025, India

79 Anson Road, #06–04/06, Singapore 079906

Cambridge University Press is part of the University of Cambridge.

It furthers the University's mission by disseminating knowledge in the pursuit of education, learning, and research at the highest international levels of excellence.

www.cambridge.org
Information on this title: www.cambridge.org/9781108837156
DOI: 10.1017/9781108938495

© Włodzimierz Borodziej and Maciej Górny 2021

This is a translated and updated publication of *Nasza wojna. Tom 1. Imperia 1912–1916* written in Polish by Włodzimierz Borodziej and Maciej Górny and published by W.A.B. in 2014 (ISBN 9788328009417)

First published in English by Cambridge University Press in 2021

This publication is in copyright. Subject to statutory exception and to the provisions of relevant collective licensing agreements, no reproduction of any part may take place without the written permission of Cambridge University Press.

A catalogue record for this publication is available from the British Library.

ISBN 978-1-108-83715-6 Hardback

Cambridge University Press has no responsibility for the persistence or accuracy of URLs for external or third-party internet websites referred to in this publication and does not guarantee that any content on such websites is, or will remain, accurate or appropriate.

CONTENTS

List of Figures	*page*	vi
List of Maps		ix
List of Capsules		x
Introduction		1
PART I: The Fronts		11
1 The Road to War		13
2 Prelude: The Balkans 1912–1913		36
3 Before the Leaves Fall from the Trees ...		61
4 Breakthrough		138
PART II: The Rear		159
5 The Hinterland		161
6 The Hunger for Information		199
7 Loyalties		219
PART III: Occupation		243
8 The First Moments		245
9 New Orders		286
10 *Mission civilisatrice*		314
Afterword		349
Select Bibliography		352
Index		365

FIGURES

Unless credited otherwise, photographs are reproduced from the authors' collection.

Fig. 1   A demonstration in Sofia in support of the war with Turkey (1912).
Courtesy of Mr Peyo Kolev, lostbulgaria.com.   *page* 41

Fig. 2   Bulgarian soldiers and volunteers guarding the remains of a
bridge over the Arda River blown up by the retreating Turks.
Courtesy of Mr Peyo Kolev, lostbulgaria.com.   46

Fig. 3   A Bulgarian hospital unit next to the station in Stara Zagora, shortly
before heading to the front. Courtesy of Mr Peyo Kolev, lostbulgaria
.com.   48

Fig. 4   The triumphant entry of the Bulgarian cavalry into Edirne. Courtesy
of Mr Peyo Kolev, lostbulgaria.com.   52

Fig. 5   A Bulgarian widow with a child. Thrace. Courtesy of Mr Peyo Kolev,
lostbulgaria.com.   67

Fig. 6   The town of Lyck (today Ełk) destroyed during the fighting between
Germany and Russia in 1914. Courtesy of the Herder-Institut,
Marburg, Bildarchiv.   67

Fig. 7   Obituary of General Alexander Samsonov, published at the end
of August 1914 in the journal *Razvedchik*. Courtesy of Mariusz Kulik.   69

Fig. 8   A patriotic postcard from Neidenburg (today Nidzica). Courtesy of the
Herder-Institut, Marburg, Bildarchiv.   70

Fig. 9   Bulgarian soldiers on the Salonika Front in 1917 already had German
gas masks. Courtesy of Mr Peyo Kolev, lostbulgaria.com.   77

Fig. 10   Russian gunners in makeshift gas masks during the Brusilov Offensive.
Courtesy of Mariusz Kulik.   79

Fig. 11   Austro-Hungarian soldiers in the Carpathians.   82

Fig. 12   Polish peasants in the Congress Kingdom bowing before their
temporary new masters – the Hungarian Honvéd (1915).   89

Fig. 13   'The Arrest of Spies Dressed as Nuns', *Ilustrowany Kuryer Codzienny*,
a Cracow daily, 10 January 1915.   95

Fig. 14   'Warszawska Street in the town of Kalisz'. Courtesy
of the Herder-Institut, Marburg, Bildarchiv.   98

LIST OF FIGURES

vii

Fig. 15	Kalisz town centre in ruins. Courtesy of the Herder-Institut, Marburg, Bildarchiv.	99
Fig. 16	The stamp reads: 'Wrocławska Street in the town of Kalisz'. Courtesy of the Herder-Institut, Marburg, Bildarchiv.	100
Fig. 17	Wounded Russian officers in a military hospital in the depths of the empire. Courtesy of Mariusz Kulik.	105
Fig. 18	Red wine being dispensed on the first day of Orthodox Christmas, 1915. Courtesy of Mariusz Kulik.	108
Fig. 19	Christmas celebrations of the 1st (Sofia) Infantry Regiment in 1916. Courtesy of Mr Peyo Kolev, lostbulgaria.com.	109
Fig. 20	A 'domesticated' shelter for Bulgarian telephone operators on the Salonika Front. Courtesy of Mr Peyo Kolev, lostbulgaria.com.	110
Fig. 21	An Austrian trench in a village in the Stryj (today Stryi) district. Courtesy of Mariusz Kulik.	111
Fig. 22	Children greeting soldiers of the 3rd Austro-Hungarian Army with flowers.	113
Fig. 23	The shell-blasted Siedliska fort after the recapture of Przemyśl by the German and Austro-Hungarian armies.	118
Fig. 24	Russian prisoners of war marching along Piotrkowska Street in Łódź. Courtesy of the Herder-Institut, Marburg, Bildarchiv.	125
Fig. 25	Germans before the fortress of Dęblin (Ivangorod). Courtesy of the Herder-Institut, Marburg, Bildarchiv.	126
Fig. 26	The route of the Russian retreat was marked by villages in flames.	127
Fig. 27	The Russian evacuation affected a large part of the rural population. Courtesy of Mariusz Kulik.	128
Fig. 28	A cartoon comparing the military strengths of the Balkan states on the eve of the autumn campaign of 1915, *Ilustrowany Kuryer Codzienny*, a Cracow daily, 1 October 1915.	130
Fig. 29	Austro-Hungarian soldiers after the capture of Belgrade.	131
Fig. 30	The autumn and winter offensive in Serbia was a completely new experience for the Austro-Hungarian soldiers.	132
Fig. 31	Serbian peasants on their way back to an abandoned village (autumn 1915).	133
Fig. 32	Serbian troops crossing a river in Albania.	135
Fig. 33	The progress of the combined German and Austro-Hungarian offensive was hampered by extremely poor roads.	148
Fig. 34	Weapons and war materials captured by the Bulgarians in the Tutrakan fortress. Courtesy of Mr Peyo Kolev, lostbulgaria.com.	148
Fig. 35	A fallen Romanian soldier near the Tutrakan fortress. Courtesy of Mr Peyo Kolev, lostbulgaria.com.	151
Fig. 36	Mass being said for fallen Bulgarian soldiers. Courtesy of Mr Peyo Kolev, lostbulgaria.com.	152
Fig. 37	Austro-Hungarian prisoners of war eating dinner in Galicia. Courtesy of Mariusz Kulik.	154

viii LIST OF FIGURES

Fig. 38   French (colonial) soldiers in a camp accompanied by their
          former Bulgarian guards (1919). Courtesy of Mr Peyo Kolev,
          lostbulgaria.com. 158
Fig. 39   The manufacture of shells (1915). 166
Fig. 40   Russian graduates of nursing courses, autumn 1914. Courtesy of
          Mariusz Kulik. 179
Fig. 41   A Bulgarian propaganda postcard depicting Lance Corporal Donka
          Bogdanova. Courtesy of Mr Peyo Kolev, lostbulgaria.com. 182
Fig. 42   A Bulgarian pilot in front of his Albatros B.I aircraft, 1916. Courtesy
          of Mr Peyo Kolev, lostbulgaria.com. 206
Fig. 43   An ethnographic postcard of a Hasidic Jew in Hungary. 214
Fig. 44   Children from the Bulgarian part of Thrace (1916). Courtesy of
          Mr Peyo Kolev, lostbulgaria.com. 217
Fig. 45   East Prussia. A destroyed railway bridge in Darkehmen (now
          Ozyorsk in Kaliningrad province). Courtesy of the Herder-Institut,
          Marburg, Bildarchiv. 246
Fig. 46   A market in the town of Ortelsburg (Szczytno) abandoned by the
          Russians. Courtesy of the Herder-Institut, Marburg, Bildarchiv. 247
Fig. 47   Piotrków station in 1916. 250
Fig. 48   Refugees from Máramaros (Maramureș) on the north-eastern edge
          of Hungary returning home after the brief Russian occupation. 256
Fig. 49   Non-uniformed Serbian prisoners of war, the famous *Komitadjis*. 270
Fig. 50   Hungarian Hussars independently 'requisitioning' milk (1915). 273
Fig. 51   Damage to the cathedral basilica in Tarnów. 281
Fig. 52   The front page of a newspaper published by the Russians in occupied
          Lwów. Courtesy of Mariusz Kulik 288
Fig. 53   Austro-Hungarian soldiers visiting the throne room of the Skupština
          (Serbian parliament). 290
Fig. 54   The Kalemegdan monument shortly after the capture of Belgrade
          by the Austro-Hungarian and German armies. 292
Fig. 55   A railway bridge during an explosion. Courtesy of the
          Herder-Institut, Marburg, Bildarchiv. 296
Fig. 56   A street scene in occupied Šabac. 301
Fig. 57   The façade being installed on the Reichstag. 350

MAPS

Map 1	Central and Eastern Europe in 1914.	*page* xi
Map 2	Main Battlefields of the Balkan Wars.	xii
Map 3	The 1915 offensive.	xiii

CAPSULES

Kakania	*page* 16
The Friedjung Affair	20
The Offensive Doctrine	27
Franz Ferdinand d'Este	32
Chemical Warfare	76
Šabac and Kalisz	97
Faradization	102
The 28th Infantry Regiment at Esztebnekhuta (Stebnícka Huta)	118
Disease among the French in the Balkans	136
Anthropology	155
Black Cars Full of Gold	163
Ersatz	168
Ration Cards	171
Ecaterina Teodoroiu	181
The Armenian Massacre	187
The Occupation of Tarnów	280
Mitteleuropa	320
Handbuch von Polen	333
Bulgaria's Five Minutes	337
Germany Fights Typhus Fever	341

Map 1   Central and Eastern Europe in 1914.

Map 2 Main Battlefields of the Balkan Wars.

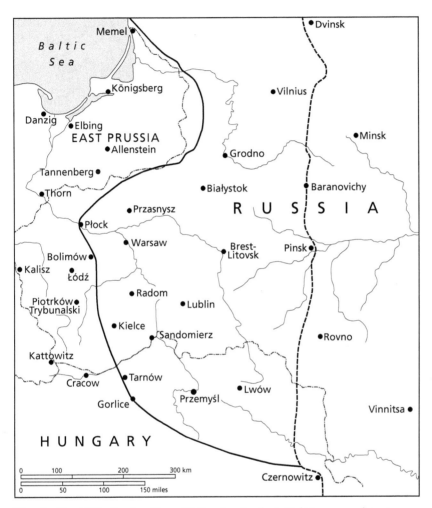

Map 3 The 1915 offensive. The solid line denotes the initial German and Austro-Hungarian positions; the dotted line shows the positions attained at the greatest extent of the offensive, in September 1915.

Introduction

How many people have heard of Przasnysz? Probably not many. In 1914, it was a small Mazovian town close to the southern border of East Prussia. Depending on the point of view, whether Russian or German, Przasnysz was situated on one of the main roads leading to East Prussia or, going in the opposite direction, to Warsaw.

In November and December 1914, and again in February and July of the following year, hundreds of thousands of Russian and German soldiers fought three great battles in Przasnysz. In the July 1915 engagement, the Germans suffered 16,000 killed or wounded, while the Russian losses amounted to nearly 40,000 men. The total number of dead, wounded, and missing is unknown, but it certainly far exceeded 100,000. Why is it, then, that so few people have heard of Przasnysz?

There are three answers to this question, and each has contributed to the genesis of this book.

Contrary to what a Russian or an inhabitant of Central and South-Eastern Europe might think, it is only to the east and south-east of Germany that the First World War has been all but forgotten. In Germany itself, it is not uncommon to see memorial plaques honouring soldiers from a particular village or city district who fought in the Great War. Certain words and symbols as well as the titles of novels and names of battlefields have also remained in the public consciousness. Germany is, therefore, a transitional zone between East and West, as has often been the case throughout its history, and in this instance it is a transitional zone between memory and oblivion. Indeed, for the French and British, the Great War is commemorated as such; 11 November remains an important date: in France it is a national holiday, while in Britain it is known as Remembrance Day, which continues to be solemnly observed. Anyone who has seen the museums in Ypres or Péronne should not be surprised, for it was here that legions of young Belgian, British, French, and German men perished. Far away, at Gallipoli, the soldiers of the Australian and New Zealand Army Corps were also massacred. The day they landed – 25 April (ANZAC Day) – is an unofficial public holiday in both former British colonies. These are European (in fact, global) places of remembrance that the Second World War has not overshadowed. The same could not be said of the museum in

INTRODUCTION

the Slovenian town of Kobarid, which commemorates one of the bloodiest massacres of the First World War, namely, the twelve battles of the Soča (Isonzo) River that continued almost uninterruptedly for twenty-nine months. Few have heard of the museum in Kobarid, but at least it exists. Just under 50,000 people visit it each year (a declining trend), whereas the museum at Ypres hosted nearly 300,000 visitors in 2013 (a rising trend).

In the places where the biggest battles of the Eastern Front were fought and where the trench warfare lasted longest – located in present-day Poland, Ukraine, Belarus, Lithuania, Latvia, and the Russian Federation – the only extant reminders of the conflict are the war cemeteries (if at all preserved). For the inhabitants of those places, the First World War is prehistory, irrelevant to modern times. The difference is thus fundamental: for the French and British, the war is an element of their identity, and for this reason they commemorate 11 November, visit museums, and read books about it. For the inhabitants of our part of Europe, George F. Kennan's famous phrase that the First World War was 'the great seminal catastrophe of this century' sounds as if the American diplomat was barking up the wrong tree.

These fundamental differences in remembrance have their counterpart in historiography. As we were working on the Polish edition of this volume in 2013, the landscape of research in that area was almost completely barren. The most significant work on the subject was Norman Stone's study, by then almost forty years old.[1] Anniversary commemorations between 1914 and 1918 altered the image to the extent that a substantial amount of interesting books and articles on the eastern theatre of the Great War came out through imprints located roughly within the Helsinki–L'viv–Freiburg im Breisgau triangle. Aside from Jörn Leonhard's monumental study on the 1914–1918 period,[2] which returned the eastern fronts to their rightful place, historians from our region contributed huge amounts of new knowledge on states as far apart as Finland and Ukraine.[3] Many studies also considered Austria-Hungary through that lens,[4] but in this context the perspective did not change as significantly after 2013: the Habsburg monarchy collapsed under the concurrent blows of hunger, national aspirations, and the actual incapacity to manage the crisis

---

[1] Norman Stone, *The Eastern Front 1914–1917*, New York, NY 1975.

[2] Jörn Leonhard, *Die Büchse der Pandora. Geschichte des Ersten Weltkriegs*, Munich 2014.

[3] One example: Tuomas Tepora and Aapo Roselius (eds.), *The Finnish Civil War 1918. History, Memory, Legacy*, Leiden 2014. As for Ukraine, the extent of new writing makes any listing of titles a pointless exercise. The same applies to studies concerning the Jews as citizens of Russia and Austria-Hungary.

[4] Manfried Rauchensteiner's *Der Erste Weltkrieg und das Ende der Habsburgermonarchie 1914–1918* (Vienna, Cologne, and Weimar 2013) was published while the Polish edition of our book was being typeset. For Rauchensteiner's latest publication, see his chapter in Helmut Rumpler (ed.), *Die Habsburgermonarchie und der Erste Weltkrieg*, vol. XI of *Die Habsburgermonarchie 1848–1918*, Vienna 2016.

INTRODUCTION 3

exhibited by rulers who lost the necessary credibility following the failures of 1914 and the human losses in the battles at the Isonzo or in far-off Volhynia. That Austrian and German historians played a significant part in the process of civilizing the desert is not at all surprising.

Meanwhile, between 1914 and 1917 people across Europe were well aware of the existence of the Eastern Front, and it was not entirely forgotten during the inter-war period either. Austrians were told stories about a fortress with an unpronounceable name – Przemyśl; Germans recognized the name Tannenberg; and everyone remembered the hunger and ration cards. Only in the next generation did the Eastern Front vanish from readers' and historians' minds; it became the 'Unknown Front', something from a far away place, where – with the exception of the revolutions in Russia – nothing important happened to alter the outcome of the war.

For decades, thus, Western historians hardly ever mentioned the Russian Front, let alone the fighting in Serbia, Romania, or Greece. When, in the 1990s, modern studies on the First World War began to emerge, the East remained slightly exotic, slightly marginalized, and still notably absent. In recent years the topic has attracted interest among a substantial group of mostly American and German historians, but the number of studies still pales in comparison with the body of literature about the Western Front. In Poland, the second-largest country of the region (after Russia), one could count on one's fingers the number of researchers currently working on the First World War. The same goes for the number of books written on the subject in the last forty years until very recently, when it increased to meet the demands of a string of anniversaries. Diaries and memoirs were an exception: usually written between 1914 and 1939 and often published during the inter-war period, they were for various reasons prohibited by the censors until 1989.

Censorship as a means of creating a socialist historical policy brings us to the third reason for writing this book. Already in the 1920s, interpretations of the recent past had a tendency to be ahistorical: although what happened before autumn 1918 was described by military historians, authors clung doggedly to the apparent logic of events and to the apparent infallibility of their protagonists. According to this logic, the war inevitably led to the final victory of Romania, to the creation of the Kingdom of Serbs, Croats and Slovenes, and to the realization of the national aspirations of the Finns, Estonians, Latvians, Lithuanians, Poles, Czechs, and Slovaks. Already before 1939, therefore, the First World War became a kind of lengthy prologue to the first chapter in the history of the nation-state. At school, children learned about the heroes of the struggle for independence, yet beyond its walls the people they usually met were veterans of the imperial armies. Czechoslovak and Polish Legionnaires were a small elite group with a disproportionally powerful influence not only on politics but also on the image of the recent past. In the mid 1930s, 80 per cent of Polish war invalids were former soldiers of the Russian,

Austro-Hungarian, and German armies, while the remaining 20 per cent had fought in the Polish Legions and in the Polish–Soviet war. If it were possible to measure the influence of these two groups in the public domain, the proportions would no doubt be reversed.[5]

After 1945, in turn, when the USSR assumed direct and indirect control over Central Europe and significant parts of South-Eastern Europe, the First World War was largely forgotten. It was written off as an episode that preceded the October Revolution, and the year 1918 was seen as a bizarre accident that ran contrary to the logic of history, for it was then that the communists should have assumed power in Bucharest, Riga, and Warsaw (and especially in Prague). Standing in the way of the communist project was the pernicious influence of the nationalistic elites, who aroused and then exploited the desire for independence while marginalizing the needs of the proletariat. After 1945, this narrative was promoted by institutionalized censorship, which replaced the self-censorship of the inter-war period. It played a major role in reducing the First World War to a history of betrayal by various non-communist political movements – reformist and ecclesiastical, bourgeois and peasant, fascist and nationalist – all of which ultimately led to a disastrous delay in the building of socialism in countries to the west of the Soviet Union.

After the collapse of communism, the year 1918 resumed the role it had played before the Second World War, although the process of recovering memory – even more so than in the inter-war period – did not encompass the entire First World War. On the contrary, the more the post-communist democracies built their national identities on the idea of a continuation of pre-war statehood, the less significant became anything that did not suit the narrative of a heroic nation fighting determinedly for four years to create or resurrect a nation-state.

Political manipulation, however, was not the only reason why the once 'Great' War was forgotten. This process is hard to imagine without considering another nightmare – the Second World War, which was even more ghastly for most countries of the region than the First, and its effects were even more dramatic. The massacres of Serbian peasants in 1914 and 1915 had little chance of remaining in the collective memory when juxtaposed with the ocean of blood that was spilled during the occupation of Yugoslavia between 1941 and 1945; the pogroms of the First World War were negligible when compared with the Holocaust. To the Greeks, the experiences of

---

[5] Jan Sobociński, 'Inwalidzi wojenni i wojskowi w Polsce według pochodzenia oraz przyczyn inwalidztwa', *Praca i Opieka Społeczna* 14, 3 (1934), pp. 313–324; data from Katarzyna Sierakowska, 'Niech się nasi bracia, ojcowie i matki dowiedzą [...], jakich se to wychowali bohaterów. Cierpienie w relacjach żołnierzy Polaków 1914–1918', in *Zapisy cierpienia*, ed. Katarzyna Stańczak-Wiślicz, Wrocław, 2011, pp. 267–282, here p. 281.

1914–1918 must have seemed very distant after the first winter under occupation (1941/1942).

There are many more places like Przasnysz, but, because they are hardly known, they cannot form even the kernel of a collective regional memory. Nowadays, Austrian and German secondary school pupils are unfamiliar with Przemyśl and Tannenberg, while to the French and Russians those names have never meant anything anyway. Polish schoolchildren, in turn, are certainly unaware that the most important battles of the Eastern Front in 1914 and 1915 took place almost exclusively within the borders of present-day Poland.

Hence our idea of writing a book that would restore people's memory of the horror that was the First World War in the lands between Riga and Skopje. Russians, Germans, Estonians, Latvians, Lithuanians, Jews, Poles, Belarusians, and Ukrainians fought in the uniforms of the Imperial Russian Army; Germans and Poles in the uniforms of the Imperial German Army; and Slovenes, Croats, Bosnians, Serbs, Austrians, Czech Germans, Czechs, Moravians, Silesians, Poles, Jews, Ukrainians, Slovaks, Hungarians, and Romanians all served in the Austro-Hungarian Army.

It was our war.

Contrary to legend, the battles on the Eastern Front were just as fierce as those in the West. It was in the East where most prisoners of war were taken and where the mortality rate in POW camps was the highest. Soldiers of the imperial armies and nation-states killed each other *en masse*; what set them apart was at times only their uniform – not their language, faith, or ethnicity. There is a place for heroism in this story, for the soldiers were capable of incredible bravery, but most of the situations and experiences we describe in this book were not part of the patriotic narrative: soldiers died for no reason, and without the sense that they were dying for a just cause. They marched into a battle only because they were told to do so by their lieutenants and corporals, who, statistically speaking, had even less chance of surviving the war than their subordinates.

When describing the fate of those men on the front lines, we refer to the debate that dominated historiography some twenty years ago. At that time, historians and psychologists asked the following question: how did the soldiers manage, for four years, to endure the hell in which they found themselves in the autumn of 1914? How could they cope with levels of stress that are unimaginable for Europeans today? The classic response pointed to the role of the nation-state and national identity: the idea of community generated a spirit of enthusiasm that made it possible to survive the trenches. On this interpretation it was easy to explain the collapse of the Russian Empire in 1917, where national identity was patchy and superficial, and even easier to explain the fragmentation of Austria-Hungary, where people's loyalty to their own national communities in the second half of the war proved to be stronger than their attachment to the multinational empire.

6   INTRODUCTION

A captivating debate on the issue took place among mostly French historians. Some, associated with the Museum of the Great War in Péronne, argued that national identification was central to the resilience of French troops. Meanwhile, their opponents stress coercion as a decisive factor: even French soldiers, who arguably fought for a modern nation-state, would have gone home without a second thought had it not been for the coercion they were under for four years. The debate continues to this day. Currently, the prevailing view is that the truth does indeed lie in the middle sometimes. The English term 'endurance' seems to reflect the reality of the trenches better than any other. While it is true that soldiers on all the fronts may have at times displayed great enthusiasm, they were at times also terrorized by their commanders, the military police, and the court martials. In general, however, they simply came to terms with the new situation in which they found themselves. They knew that there was no alternative, and on the whole they did their duty conscientiously – without great enthusiasm, but equally without the threat of summary execution.[6]

Civilians also died, went on strike, and suffered disease and starvation not for the national cause – as post-1918 historiographies often liked to claim – but simply because they lacked food, fuel, medicines, and basic sanitation. These privations were generally not due to the barbarous policies of the occupiers, however. Shortages and danger were, surprisingly, just as likely to be experienced by fellow citizens behind the front lines as by the inhabitants of conquered territories. This is another forgotten aspect of the story, since all historiographies after 1918 sought to prove the uniqueness of their own country's losses, which were caused by the exceptionally destructive, rapacious, and ruthless policies of the occupier.

The present authors are cautious with figures because the statistics often contain discrepancies. Much of the data contained in the literature is evidently false, yet such data are reprinted from earlier publications for the simple reason that no one could be bothered to check the information (or, less frequently, no one was able to). In other cases we are forced to rely on estimates, since no reliable data were produced at the time. Still other figures derive from propaganda, and their purpose from the outset was to convince rather than to inform. We try to select the most reliable data, where possible verified, and to present them in a proper context (without which their significance would be difficult to comprehend).

---

[6] See, among others, Arnd Bauerkämper and Elise Julien (eds.), *Durchhalten! Krieg und Gesellschaft im Vergleich 1914-1918*, Göttingen 2010; Julia Eichenberg, 'Consent, Coercion and Endurance in Eastern Europe: Poland and the Fluidity of War Experiences', in *Legacies of Violence. Eastern Europe's First World War*, ed. Jochen Böhler, Włodzimierz Borodziej, and Joachim von Puttkamer, Munich 2014, pp. 235–258.

INTRODUCTION   7

A while ago it became fashionable to use the term 'total war' in relation to the First World War, and at times one gets the paradoxical impression that the proof of its 'total' character was meant to augment the 1914 to 1918 period, raising it to the rank of a catastrophe as great as the period from 1939 to 1945. As the authors of this book, we do not feel compelled to elevate the subject of our research. We do not refer to the concept of 'totality' directly. Nevertheless, at this juncture, we owe it to our readers to mention the most commonly used elements of this definition. First, in terms of its intensity and geographical reach, 'total war' eclipses all previous conflicts. Second, the participants of that war do not feel bound by morality, common law, or international law; they are driven by hatred, which justifies crimes and coercion on a hitherto unprecedented scale. Third, the boundary between combatants and civilians becomes blurred. Civilians are treated as suppliers of goods and raw materials and as a reservoir of labour to be ruthlessly exploited. Their fate can be compared to that of the conscript, who is likewise milked for all he is worth. But the similarities go even further: civilians are exposed to the dangers of war whenever the military commanders consider it expedient. They face bombing and artillery fire, repression, including the death penalty, as well as starvation and epidemics. To a large extent, therefore, risk is equalized; in other words, the chances of survival are similar for soldiers and civilians alike. Finally, total war is about not just defeating, but annihilating the enemy. Readers will decide for themselves whether our narrative confirms this image of the eastern fronts and their hinterlands to the east and west.

We should warn readers who have chosen to start from the introduction, and not from any other chapter, that this book is not a typical work of military history. We try to find a happy medium between (not necessarily traditional) military history and social history, while taking into account the wartime history of science and culture in the broad sense. We thus describe the first years of the war in roughly chronological order, but what seems far more interesting to us than the sequence of events is processes and people's attitudes. In the subsequent two parts of the book, therefore, the narrative moves away from the chronology of events and focuses more on those two aspects. In wartime people kill and suffer, and each experience has a huge impact on them and their perception of the world. We are curious to know how our great-grandparents survived and how they were changed both by the war and by their experiences beyond the combat zone. Sometimes we feel as if we are describing things that are new or, to be more precise, things that have simply been forgotten. Wherever possible, we cite witnesses and participants of the events concerned. In our view, their voices exemplify the experience of a generation, social group, cultural community, or national community. We try to show that for many decades this experience was considered meaningless and interpreted as some sort of nightmare or even apocalypse. From our perspective, the fact that in 1918 an unforeseeable breakthrough was made,

INTRODUCTION

giving sense to all the previous suffering and sacrifice, is of no consequence whatsoever. In any case, that breakthrough led to the falsification of wartime memory, and that is what this book seeks to challenge: its purpose is to remind the reader, whether in Cracow, Riga, Sofia, or Zagreb, of the common traumatic experience that established a region stretching between the Baltic, the Adriatic, and the Black Sea. Meanwhile, the Anglophone reader will learn of events in that region that preceded the Second World War and the Holocaust.

The timeframe of our narrative and its key moments also diverge from the traditional approach. We are not interested in the history of international relations. Why? Let us cite the most spectacular example. Over the course of several decades there have been hundreds of books and articles written about the July crisis, and most of these have led readers up a blind alley by trying to convince them that the war was inevitable. In the Marxist interpretation this inevitability had to do with imperialist conflict, which was driven by the arrogance and greed of the economic and financial elites and by their fear of the labour movement. According to another interpretation, perhaps the most influential, the decisive factor was the German desire for world hegemony ('a place in the sun'). Sometimes the causes – and therefore the blame – were attributed to the eternal Russian ambition of conquering Constantinople or to the Viennese vision of seizing the Western Balkans; at other times, it was said that the war was deliberately provoked by the Serbs. Every theory that apportions blame to a single country can be supported by dozens, if not thousands, of documents, including those from July 1914 upon which historical descriptions of the July events are based. Yet none of these theories has stood the test of criticism. None has even attempted to explain the relationship between the origins of the war and its course, because no such relationship exists. It is for this reason that the July Crisis and other diplomatic events are, from our perspective, of scant importance. We encourage the reader to seek out great works on this subject published before ours.[7]

The timeframe of our book is 1912 to 1916: from the Balkan Wars until the death of Franz Joseph and the end of the Romanian campaign. Perhaps we shall be able to convince the reader that the conflict between the Ottoman Empire, Serbia, Montenegro, Greece, Bulgaria, and Romania is a prologue which, in our view, was more important than the diplomacy that took place in the summer of 1914. Indeed, one of the reasons why the whole 1914–1918 period was erased from national memories is that it was followed by events which – for Russians, Balts, Hungarians, Ukrainians, Poles, Greeks, and Turks – were far more important in shaping the inter-war period than Gorlice or Gallipoli.

---

[7] Christopher Clark, *The Sleepwalkers. How Europe Went to War in 1914*, London and New York, NY 2013; less well-known, but equally interesting: Sean McMeekin, *July 1914. Countdown to War*, New York, NY 2013.

INTRODUCTION

Until December 1916 the empires experienced difficult moments but they were still dominant. The Central Powers even seemed to be on the verge of victory, especially in the East. The first eastern empire to collapse did so in 1917, when new actors entered the scene.

The best book about the Great War in the East is, according to one of the present authors, *The Good Soldier Švejk* by Jaroslav Hašek; according to the other, it is *The Last Days of Mankind* by Karl Kraus. Our literary preferences have a certain connection with the structure of the present volume. The two aforementioned books belong to different national cultures, but they are both part of the legacy of the Habsburg monarchy. Although we try to treat the northern empires in the East in more or less the same way (we have no such ambition or capability in the case of the Ottoman Porte), we are principally interested in the Danubian monarchy. This is because, for decades, it encapsulated the problem of a multinational empire striving to maintain the primacy of the supranational idea over the growing national aspirations of its constituent peoples. Both Hašek and Kraus are aware of this tension, but this is not the reason their works have entered the European literary canon; in fact, they have done so for quite the opposite reason. While it is true that for both authors the brutality of the Great War often has an ethnic aspect, the reader soon realizes that national character is not the issue. These books are about the nightmare of our war, and the radically different perspectives they offer – the German–Austrian perspective, that of the empire's Czech capital and main city of one of its provinces, and finally the war as seen from the front – give an insight into the multifaceted nature of its forgotten cruelty.

Linguistic note: when we write about 'the Russians', we of course realize that a huge minority of soldiers in the Czarist army belonged to other nations. For want of better terms, we use the adjectives 'Russian' and 'Czarist' interchangeably, while being aware of their limitations. When we write about 'the monarchy', we mean the empire of Franz Joseph. This work uses the English names currently in use when appropriate. In other cases the name is given in the language of the given state at that time.

***

The idea of writing this book emerged in the spring of 2012 in Jena, or, to be more precise, in Wenigenjena across the Saale river, in the garden of the Friedrich Schiller University guest house at 23 Charlottenstraße. Three scholars of the Imre Kertész Kolleg were sitting at a table: the present authors and their younger Serbian colleague, Aleksandar Miletić. Aleksandar, an expert on the inter-war period, simply could not believe that his country had suffered such massive losses during the First World War. Maciej Górny was in the process of finishing the draft of his postdoctoral thesis on the attitudes of non-Western intellectuals during that period. Włodzimierz Borodziej was writing an article about the experience of the First World War in Central and South-Eastern Europe. During an evening conversation with our Serbian colleague we realized that it was not just in Poland that the subject of the Great War had been largely ignored by historians. As the privileged recipients of a scholarship awarded by the Imre Kertész Kolleg we decided that it would be a good idea to get to work on the topic. The first chapters of the book were therefore written in Jena and the remainder in Warsaw.

The conversations we had with other scholars and staff members of the Imre Kertész Kolleg were hugely beneficial to both of us. We would like to extend our special thanks to Viorel Achim, Jochen Böhler, Stanislav Holubec, Jurek Kochanowski, Ferenc Laczó, Elena Mannová, Lutz Niethammer, Joachim von Puttkamer, Stefan Troebst, Raphael Utz, and Theodore Weeks. During our stay in Jena, Daniela Gruber and Diana Joseph handled all the technical and organizational issues, for which we are very grateful. Finally, the help we received from the institute's junior staff as regards ordering books and dealing with the photocopiers likewise proved invaluable.

Also of great benefit to us were the meetings and discussions we had with colleagues we got to know thanks to the tireless efforts of two associations devoted to the First World War. We greatly appreciate both the International Society for First World War Studies and the Forum Österreich-Ungarn im Ersten Weltkrieg for remaining faithful to their calling even when there is no big anniversary looming on the horizon.

We would not have had access to some of the materials, and especially the illustrations, were it not for the selfless assistance of Grzegorz Bąbiak and Mariusz Kulik, who shared with us the intellectual fruit of their trips to Paris and Moscow.

The first readers of the parts of the manuscript were Joachim von Puttkamer, Timothy Snyder, and Philipp Ther. We would like to thank Piotr Szlanta and Theodore Weeks as well as the two other anonymous reviewers for their insightful suggestions, and everyone else for their comments and feedback. The authors bear full responsibility for the content of the book and for any weaknesses therein.

**

This publication was financially supported by the Ministry of Science and Higher Education – National Programme for the Development of Humanities.

PART I

The Fronts

1

The Road to War

The empires experienced the nineteenth century in different ways, and their experience was generally a bad one. The only empire to emerge in Central and Eastern Europe at that time – the German Empire – was also the only one that could regard the decades leading up to 1914 as a success.

Four powers figured on the map of Central and South-Eastern Europe in 1815: Prussia, Russia, Austria, and the Ottoman Empire. At the outbreak of war a century later, the northern borders appeared remarkably stable. Germany shared a border with Russia on Polish soil. Austria had evolved into Austria-Hungary, but its northern border had barely changed; only in the south, following the annexation of Bosnia-Herzegovina in 1908, did it extend much further than before. And indeed it was here, in the Balkans, that the changes were biggest, with the Ottoman Empire having lost its European foothold. The map of 1914 revealed six theoretically modern countries, i.e. self-styled or would-be nation-states: Serbia, Montenegro, Greece, Bulgaria, Romania, and Albania, the last of these having come into existence a year earlier. Along the borders of these countries lived ethnic and religious minorities; territories on the other side were, for a variety of reasons, often the subject of competing claims and a host of mutual grievances. In Western Europe, the Balkan nation-states were regarded as backward; it is true that in terms of life expectancy, infant mortality, literacy, industrialization, and urbanization they lagged far behind the Netherlands or Denmark.

Of the great powers, only Russia had comparable problems. For centuries it had been the biggest country in the world, stretching from Łódź, the 'Manchester of the East', to the Pacific. It had also been a long-standing member of the exclusive family of empires. At the same time, Russia was struggling with problems that were unique to that group: a lack of compulsory schooling, the still unresolved question of land ownership, and industrialization limited to islands in the centre, south, and west of the country. In theory it was a military superpower, yet it had suffered defeat on its own territory at the hands of a Western expeditionary force (the Crimean War of 1853–1856). In 1904–1905, it became the first European – in racialized terms 'white' – power to be not so much defeated as utterly humiliated by an Asian – in racialized terms 'yellow' – power, i.e. the Japanese. Then, in 1905 and 1906, the country was shaken by revolution, when the edifice of autocracy, in other words, the power of the Czar, which was not limited by a constitution, began to crumble. Everyone knew that the problems began at the top – the head of state was accountable to no one and far from infallible – but a cancer of inertia, corruption, incompetence, and stupidity had spread throughout the entire state administration; after the catastrophic war with Japan and the defeat of the 1905 revolution, a new phase of energetic internal reforms got under way. For most, the favourable economic situation did not obscure the fact that the state remained inefficient, parliament was a façade, and social tensions were rising at a time when part of the rural population was being transformed into an urban, industrialized one. The issue of national minorities was likewise intensifying. In one relatively small part of Western Russia conflicts escalated around the hitherto privileged Baltic Germans, their neighbouring Latvians and Estonians, and the more distant Lithuanians, Jews, and Ukrainians: in the late nineteenth century and early twentieth century, it was not just in the Balkans that the national idea became a source of inspiration for pastors and priests, teachers and clerks, who up until then had been considered the docile backbone of empire; not to mention the old Polish problem, which was the price Russia had paid for moving its borders under the Partitions of Poland in the late eighteenth century and the terms of the Congress of Vienna in 1815.

The situation in Germany at the beginning of the twentieth century was somewhat different. Unlike Russia, the Second Reich combined the features of an empire and a nation-state. Germans accounted for over 90 per cent of its population. The differences between the inhabitants of East Prussia and Baden remained considerable, but people from Königsberg and Freiburg expressed these differences in the same language, and with recourse to a common literature and similar values. They were members of a nation that many considered a model of modernity. German universities were seen as the best on the continent, and the country boasted the most innovative industries, such as chemicals, as well as an excellent state and local administration. The army, which had always been regarded as Prussia's foremost achievement, had won all of its recent wars. The picture was not so rosy in the colonies, which generated a deficit and were third-rate, providing neither prestige nor satisfaction. Under such circumstances, imperial ambition was focused on the south-east rather than on overseas territories. The planned railway to Baghdad was considered the most important project, for it would enable German economic expansion into the Balkans and Ottoman Empire and onwards into the Middle East.

Germany and Russia were similar in two respects. First, both experienced a rising tide of nationalism in the late nineteenth century and early twentieth century. In Germany, nationalism was symbolized by the army, right-wing political parties, associations, and newspapers, and above all by Kaiser Wilhelm II. The long-time chancellor, Otto von Bismarck, whom the young

Emperor ousted in 1890, was feared across Europe as a singularly devious and effective politician. Bismarck's successors lacked his charisma. Besides, the Emperor himself increasingly dabbled in foreign policy and loved to pose for photographs wearing a *Pickelhaube* (spiked helmet). Almost everywhere he went, Wilhelm aroused irritation as a posturing neurotic failure, offending all around him and provoking all manner of crises. In the history of modern Europe Wilhelm II will go down as one of the most incompetent monarchs with real power at their disposal. Nicholas II, who had ruled Russia since 1894, was the polar opposite of his cousin from Berlin in terms of temperament: his incompetence stemmed from his weakness. Russian nationalism thrived without any major contribution from the Czar.

Second, Russia and Germany were revered for their high culture, especially in the domains of literature and music, and foreigners were also attracted to Germany's outstanding universities. The superbly well-organized German working class was likewise considered worthy of imitation: Germany's Social Democratic Party (Sozialdemokratische Partei Deutschlands, SPD), which in the 1912 elections won almost 35 per cent of the vote, becoming the biggest parliamentary grouping, was supported by trade unions, educational and self-help organizations, and the most renowned left-wing intellectuals in Europe (which at that time meant in the world). But at the same time, the Reich, let alone Czarist autocracy, was a far cry from the soft power of Britain and France – the German lifestyle, from the aristocracy to the petite bourgeoisie, was not a model others wished to follow. During the Great War, knowledge of French remained the criterion by which cultured people – such as the mayor of an occupied city and its new commander – recognized each other.

Many were also repelled by the proverbial German arrogance and the equally proverbial Russian backwardness, which only reinforced the belief among German and Russian nationalists that their countries are disrespected and bullied by international public opinion.

The most complicated situation was that of Austria-Hungary. In 1867, the Habsburg monarchy was transformed into a dual monarchy with a single head of state (Franz Joseph ruled as King of Hungary and elsewhere as Emperor), foreign policy, army, and (in part) system of tariffs and finance. In the 48-million-strong Habsburg monarchy, Austrian Germans and Hungarians accounted for less than half the population (44 per cent; the various Slavic peoples accounted for 47 per cent). In theory, other nationalities enjoyed rights that were guaranteed under the constitution, which allowed them to develop local government, education, and culture; in practice, the situation varied and was much worse in Hungary than in the Austrian part of the Empire, popularly known as Cisleithania, the peculiar jumble of Habsburg countries extending from Vorarlberg in the west, at the border with Switzerland, to today's western Ukraine. The parliaments in Vienna and Budapest were beset with problems: conflicts escalated, parliamentary sessions were suspended, and the government's accountability to the legislature became a fiction. The left demanded universal suffrage, which was introduced for the male population of Cisleithania in 1907.[1] Hungary retained its existing electoral system that benefited both the ruling nationality and the propertied classes, which amounted to more or less the same thing. Austrian Germans in Bohemia and Moravia felt that they had been abandoned to the ever-more-powerful Czech national movement and, increasingly, looked to the thriving German Reich as a potential, if not ideal, guardian.

We are in no position to explain the distinctions between 'nationalities', ethnolinguistically defined, and 'nations' pretending to represent one general or particular nationality. Yet, East Central and South-Eastern Europe did not differ significantly from Ireland or Catalonia. The common denominator was the tendency towards secession from a former empire, in which those living at the centre cannot speak the language of those from the peripheries. Similarities abound in biographies of the aristocracy and the financial class: the former, universally suffered as a timeless and necessary evil around 1900; the latter, a foreign body. In the part of Europe under consideration here, both elites would be wiped out between 1918 and 1945, accounting for the distinctions between Barcelona, Belgrade, Budapest, and Dublin, but this falls outside the purview of this study.

To explain the peculiarities of the region, it might prove useful to turn to literary classics rarely revisited in the twenty-first century. The fragment in question concerns 'Kakania' – a garbling of the official name of the Habsburg monarchy after 1867, when it became the Austro-Hungarian Empire, 'kaiserlich und königlich' (the imperial and royal state). The first 'k' thus represents Franz Joseph's role as the emperor of the aforementioned non-Hungarian lands; the other, his role as the king of Hungary. Robert Musil explains this in more detail in the following passage.

KAKANIA

There, in Kakania, that state since vanished that no one understood, in many ways an exemplary state, though unappreciated, there was a tempo too, but not too much tempo. Whenever one thought of that country from someplace abroad, the memory that hovered before one's eyes was white, wide, prosperous-looking roads dating from the era of foot marches and mail coaches, roads that criss-crossed the country in every direction like rivers of order, like ribbons of bright military twill, the paper-white arm of the administration holding all the provinces in its embrace. And what provinces they were! Glaciers and sea, Karst limestone and Bohemian fields of grain, nights on the Adriatic chirping with restless cicadas, and Slovakian villages where the smoke rose from chimneys as from upturned nostrils while the village cowered between two small hills as if the earth had parted its lips to warm its child

---

[1] Pieter M. Judson, *The Habsburg Empire. A New History*, Cambridge 2016.

between them. Of course cars rolled on these roads too, but not too many! The conquest of the air was being prepared here too, but not too intensively. A ship would now and then be sent off to South America or East Asia, but not too often. There was no ambition for world markets or world power. Here at the very centre of Europe, where the world's old axes crossed, words such as 'colony' and 'overseas' sounded like something quite untried and remote. There was some show of luxury, but by no means as in such overrefined ways as the French. People went in for sports, but not as fanatically as the English. Ruinous sums of money were spent on the army, but only just enough to secure its position as the second-weakest among the great powers. The capital, too, was somewhat smaller than all the other biggest cities of the world, but considerably bigger than a mere big city. And the country's administration was conducted in an enlightened, unobtrusive manner, with all sharp edges cautiously smoothed over, by the best bureaucracy in Europe, which could be faulted only in that it regarded genius, and any brilliant private initiative not backed by noble birth or official status, as insolent and presumptuous. But then who welcomes interference from unqualified outsiders? And in Kakania, at least, it would only happen that a genius would be regarded as a lout, but never was a mere lout taken – as happens elsewhere – for a genius.

All in all, how many amazing things might be said about this vanished Kakania! Everything and every person in it, for instance, bore the label of *kaiserlich-königlich* (Imperial-Royal) or *kaiserlich* und *königlich* (Imperial *and* Royal), abbreviated as 'k. k.' or 'k.&k.', but to be sure which institutions and persons were to be designated by 'k.k.' and which by 'k.&k.' required the mastery of a secret science. On paper it was called the Austro-Hungarian Monarchy, but in conversation it was called Austria, a name solemnly abjured officially while stubbornly retained emotionally, just to show that feelings are quite as important as constitutional law and that regulations are one thing but real life is something else entirely. Liberal in its constitution, it was administered clerically. The government was clerical, but everyday life was liberal. All citizens were equal before the law, but not everyone was a citizen. There was a Parliament, which asserted its freedom so forcefully that it was usually kept shut; there was also an Emergency Powers Act that enabled the government to get along without Parliament, but then, when everyone had happily settled for absolutism, the Crown decreed that it was time to go back to parliamentary rule. The country was full of such goings-on, among them the sort of nationalist movements that rightly attracted so much attention in Europe and are so thoroughly misunderstood today. They were so violent that they jammed the machinery of government and brought it to a dead stop several times a year, but in the intervals and during the deadlocks people got along perfectly well and acted as if nothing had happened. And in fact, nothing really *had* happened. It was only that everyone's natural resentment of everyone else's efforts to get ahead, a resentment we all feel nowadays, had crystallized earlier in Kakania, where it can be said to have assumed the form of a sublimated ceremonial rite, which could have had a great future had its development not been cut prematurely short by a catastrophe.

For it was not only the resentment of one's fellow-citizens that had become intensified there into a strong sense of community; even the lack of faith in oneself and one's own fate took on the character of a deep self-certainty. In this country one acted – sometimes to the highest degree of passion and its consequences – differently from the way one thought, or one thought differently from the way one acted. Uninformed observers have mistaken this for charm, or even for a weakness in what they thought to be the Austrian character. But they were wrong; it is always wrong to explain what happens in a country by the character of its inhabitants. For the inhabitant of a country has at least nine characters: a professional, a national, a civic, a class, a geographical, a sexual, a conscious, an unconscious, and possibly even a private character to boot. He unites them in himself, but they dissolve him, so that he is really nothing more than a small basin hollowed out by these many streamlets that trickle into it and drain out of it again, to join other such rills in filling some other basin. Which is why every inhabitant of the earth also has a tenth character that is nothing else than the passive fantasy of spaces yet unfilled. This permits a person all but one thing: to take seriously what his at least nine other characters do and what happens to them; in other words, it prevents precisely what should be his true fulfilment. This interior space – admittedly hard to describe – is of a different shade and shape in Italy from what it is in England, because everything that stands out in relief against it is of a different shade and shape; and yet it is in both places the same: an empty, invisible space, with reality standing inside it like a child's toy town deserted by the imagination.

Insofar as this can become visible to all eyes it had happened in Kakania, making Kakania, unbeknownst to the world, the most progressive state of all; a state just barely able to go along with itself. One enjoyed a negative freedom there, always with a sense of insufficient grounds for one's own existence, and lapped around by the great fantasy of all that had not happened or at least not yet happened irrevocably as by the breath of those oceans from which mankind had once emerged.

Events that might be regarded as momentous elsewhere were here introduced with a casual '*Es ist passiert* ... ' – a peculiar form of 'it happened' unknown elsewhere in German or any other language, whose breath could transform facts and blows of fate into something as light as thistledown or thought. Perhaps, despite so much that can be said against it, Kakania was, after all, a country for geniuses; which is probably what brought it to its ruin.[2]

The various lands of the Austro-Hungarian Empire were developing at an uneven pace. Both capitals were among the most modern European cities. Budapest acquired its first metro line in 1896; Vienna followed two years later. Bohemia and Moravia could easily rival the highly developed regions of Western Europe, while Galicia and Bukovina were closer to their eastern and south-eastern neighbours than they were to modernity.

---

[2] Robert Musil, *The Man without Qualities*, vol. 1, translated by Sophie Wilkins and Burton Pike, New York, NY, 1995, pp. 28–31.

Yet sentiment, loyalty to the monarchy, and national consciousness had little to do with this asynchronous development. Austria-Hungary was a country in which everyone was more or less dissatisfied; its citizens increasingly began to think in national terms – they did not wish to live in a community with people who spoke a different language. Hannah Arendt would later write that 'tribal nationalism always insists that its own people is surrounded by "a world of enemies", "one against all", that a fundamental difference exists between this people and all others',[3] but for now the ethnicization of relations within the monarchy was generally not based on violence, and thus the state persisted. Its symbol was the Emperor, who from 1867 was also King of Hungary. Virtually no one remembered a monarch other than Franz Joseph, who had ruled since 1848. The belief in a just ruler – one who rules from afar, high above the quarrels and disputes of politicians and students – gave people hope: the monarchy had for decades ensured peace and a tranquillity of sorts, so would it not survive the latest turmoil engulfing European politics in the early twentieth century?

The empires would not be empires were they not seeking to gain advantage over others. In this race Russia had the lowest chances of success, for despite enormous progress it remained the weakest of the imperial powers. It had suffered defeat in the Far East, and in Central Asia it no longer presented a threat to Great Britain. Russia's weakest opponent was the Ottoman Empire. Petersburg actively supported the decomposition of the Ottoman Empire's European foothold and entered into alliances with the Balkan states. Of greatest importance were its close ties with Bulgaria and Serbia, the latter having switched from the Austro-Hungarian to the Russian camp in 1903. Serbia became the mainstay of Russia's Balkan policy, according to which Russia was the protector of the South Slavs and the Orthodox Church.

Petersburg's alliance with Belgrade was a huge irritation for the Habsburg monarchy. First, Serbia's role as an advocate of South Slav unification threatened the southern borders of Austria-Hungary, inhabited mainly by Croats, Slovenes, Bosnians, and Serbs. Second, Belgrade's alliance with Petersburg had its extension in the Entente, in other words, in Russia's diplomatic agreements with both France and Britain. The Austrian military saw Russia's relationship with Serbia as an existential threat to the Habsburg monarchy and pushed for a quick resolution to the problem: from 1906, the influential Chief of the General Staff, Franz Conrad von Hötzendorf, argued for a preventive war against Serbia. Historians estimate that in 1913 alone, von Hötzendorf proposed to attack Belgrade on twenty-five separate occasions. In May 1914 he reiterated his proposal, which – for now – the Emperor and the politicians once again ignored.

---

[3] Hannah Arendt, *The Origins of Totalitarianism*, Houghton Mifflin Harcourt, Orlando, FL 2008, p. 227.

THE FRIEDJUNG AFFAIR

When in 1908 Austria-Hungary decided to annex Bosnia-Herzegovina, Europe stood on the brink of war. Although the region had been occupied by the Habsburg Monarchy since 1878, once Serbia had entered the Russian sphere of influence the decision to formally incorporate the province took on a political meaning. Russia regarded the annexation as a hostile act that violated its interests in the Balkans; it eventually stood down, but the two monarchies would never again be on friendly terms. Russia's influence in Belgrade increased, however, and within a few years this led to the creation of an anti-Ottoman coalition.

Given that the Austro-Hungarian Ministry of Finance had for decades pursued a sovereign policy in Bosnia-Herzegovina, the formal annexation of the province need not have taken place in such dramatic circumstances. Yet a deterioration in the situation lay very much in the interests of the Imperial Foreign Minister, Count Alois Lexa von Aehrenthal, the main instigator of the so-called Bosnian crisis. Aehrenthal was strongly in favour of an aggressive policy that befitted a superpower. To his surprise, Western public opinion did not respond at all well to the annexation, which prompted Aehrenthal to try to justify the action retrospectively.

His idea seemed perfect, but ultimately it embarrassed the Austro-Hungarian authorities. In 1909, dozens of Serb politicians from Croatia stood before a court on charges of treason. They were accused of being Serbian agents who were conspiring to harm the monarchy. The purpose of the trial was not merely to justify Aehrenthal's aggressive policy; it was also in the interests of the Hungarians, who wanted to put an end to Croatian autonomy within the Kingdom of Hungary. The problem was that the charge of treason rested on very flimsy evidence. Robert W. Seton-Watson, a British specialist on Central and Eastern Europe and the Balkans, observed the trial in Zagreb from the public gallery. In his report for the *Morning Post*, Seton-Watson wrote: 'The whole trial is a travesty of justice, inspired and controlled by what to English ideas is a despotic government.'[4] In a private letter to Henry Wickham Steed, another British expert and future editor of *The Times*, Seton-Watson added that the judges appointed to conduct the show trial looked as though they themselves had just been released from a penal colony. Since this impression was shared by many of the others present, Aehrenthal decided that it was time for a new batch of incriminating evidence.

It was precisely at this moment that Heinrich Friedjung entered the political arena. Born in Moravia to Jewish parents, Friedjung was a historian, one of the pioneers of modern political history, as well as a German nationalist. His ambitions went further, however: he wanted to become the leader of the Austrian Germans. He had worked with Aehrenthal for several years and shared his political views. In the autumn of 1909, Friedjung published an article in the *Neue Freie Presse*, a liberal daily, in which he cited documents allegedly given to him by the Austro-Hungarian Embassy in Belgrade. The documents ostensibly proved that Serbia was preparing

[4] Quoted in Hugh Seton-Watson and Christopher Seton-Watson, *The Making of a New Europe. R. W. Seton-Watson and the Last Years of Austria-Hungary*, Seattle, WA 1981, p. 69.

an armed attack on the Habsburg monarchy and that it was financing politicians in the Serbo-Croat coalition. It soon transpired, however, that the documents were forgeries, and at the end of the year a group of Croatian politicians sued Friedjung for libel. Tomáš Garrigue Masaryk spoke about the affair in the Viennese parliament (the *Reichsrat*), denouncing the Foreign Minister for his dirty tricks.

The whole affair was a humiliation both for Friedjung and for the Austro-Hungarian authorities, but its psychological effects proved far more serious. First, the rule of law, with which Austria-Hungary was rightly associated, had been undermined by the personal imperial ambitions of a handful of politicians. Second, the hysterical reaction of the authorities towards Serbian, Croatian, and Slovenian politicians who had hitherto been completely loyal to the monarchy did in fact push them into the arms of Serbia. Third, the Friedjung affair called into question the ability of Austria-Hungary to soothe relations between the feuding peoples of Central and Eastern Europe and the Balkans.

The permanent conflict between Vienna and Petersburg over Serbia had its counterpart in the north. Galicia was governed by the Poles. The vast majority of them felt attached to the monarchy, but they were also building national institutions, lending assistance to émigrés from the Kingdom of Poland, and encouraging young people to join paramilitary organizations. Somewhat different was the situation of the Ukrainians, who at that time were generally referred to as 'Ruthenians' by Poles and as 'Little Russians' by Russians. Both the Poles and the Russians consistently denied Ukrainians the right to call themselves a nation, but they, too, were creating their own associations and institutions, and were mostly pro-Habsburg, with an active pro-Russian minority (the 'Russophiles'). The difference between the politically active Poles and Ukrainians was that the former had power, elites, and a clear sense of national identity, whereas the latter organized themselves at the grassroots level and had few elites to speak of; some Ukrainian intellectuals believed in the creation of a Ukrainian nation allied with the monarchy, while others treated the Ruthenians as part of a greater Russia. Petersburg accused Vienna of supporting the Poles and the 'national' Ukrainians; Vienna accused Petersburg of inciting 'Russophilia'. There was seemingly no end to political trials, not to mention bitter polemics in the press.

Serbia was incomparably more important than Galicia. From 1903, the European press wrote about the situation on Austria-Hungary's southern border almost constantly; it was not only Conrad von Hötzendorf who perceived the seeds of a future war there. What was clear was that a localized conflict between Vienna and Belgrade was just one of many possible scenarios – and by far the least dangerous one. Austria-Hungary had been in an alliance with Germany since 1879, and after Italy joined in 1882 it was known as the Triple Alliance. But Italy was an uncertain partner and could not be relied upon. France and Great Britain resolved their colonial disputes in 1904 with the signing of the Entente Cordiale. In 1907, the nascent alliance was joined by Russia – Serbia's protector – which had hitherto been allied with France alone. Following its defeat in the Far East in 1904–1905, there was one thing Russia certainly could not afford: humiliation in the eyes of Europe.

Each of the powers prepared for war in different ways. Russia, aware of its limitations, invested proportionally the most in its armed forces (30 per cent of the national budget) in the years leading up to 1914. Over six years, Russia's military spending increased by 40 per cent and its naval budget tripled, surpassing Germany's; by 1917, Russia's army will be three times bigger than that of its western neighbour.

But none of this was enough: the army did not teach the peasants how to write, nor did it build an efficient arms industry or eliminate the structural backwardness of the Czarist state.

It had long been known that railways were crucial to modern warfare. In October 1850, during the Austro-Prussian crisis, the Habsburg monarchy was able to transport 75,000 soldiers and 8,000 horses to its northern border in less than four weeks. Prussia backed down. Sixteen years later, Prussia needed only three weeks to move almost 200,000 soldiers and 55,000 horses to the front. This time Austria was the loser. And four years after that, the French were unable to make proper use of their otherwise modern railway network: on the twenty-third day of mobilization they had 270,000 battle-ready soldiers, whereas Prussia mobilized 460,000 in the same amount of time. All the general staffs studied the wars of 1866 and 1870 and they all reached the same conclusion: that a future war could not be won without a dense and efficient railway network.

In subsequent decades the Reich built railways to enhance its power. Prussia became the largest employer in Germany; on the eve of war, it employed approximately 700,000 railway workers. Russia had the lowest-density rail network. This difference was most stark on Russia's border with its two neighbours, Austria-Hungary and Germany: whereas in the Kingdom of Poland there were 25 metres of track *per capita*, in Galicia the figure was twice as high, and in the eastern provinces of the Reich it was six times higher.[5]

Austria-Hungary's military preparedness was likewise far below the level that its generals had for years been demanding. While the monarchy believed that the railway network on the borders with Serbia and Russia was probably sufficient, it was definitely not prepared for one thing: a rapid campaign with maximum effort on two fronts simultaneously. Nevertheless, the monarchy knew that this would be the worst-case scenario if Russia came to Serbia's

---

[5] Andrzej Chwalba, *Historia Polski 1795–1918*, Cracow 2000, p. 65.

defence. In that event, Vienna would be forced into close cooperation with Berlin as soon as military operations began, for it could not wage a war on two fronts simultaneously if Germany did not engage some of the Russian forces from the outset. And it was only the Reich that was properly prepared for war in the East. However, the head of the Supreme Army Command (Oberste Heeresleitung, OHL), Helmuth von Moltke, feared that these were the last moments when Germany still had the advantage. A preventive war had to be fought now or never, insisted Moltke to the Foreign Minister in May 1914. 'Later' might simply mean 'too late'. Since the Russian armaments programme had already begun, argued Moltke, by 1917 Germany would lose its trump cards in the East; the very trump cards that currently allowed it to treat Russia as a second-rate opponent.

To this day, the decision-makers in uniform are adjudged to have completely failed. Indeed, many of them promised politicians and public opinion a short and victorious war. Whether this was due more to a lack of imagination than to a lack of competence is hard to determine. In the military academies, future officers of the general staffs were taught war planning using nineteenth-century models; it was thus difficult to blame them for thinking in terms of the Crimean War and the Franco-Prussian war of 1870. Fortresses, bristling ever more densely with artillery, were constantly being upgraded and in 1914 would prove as useless in the East as in the West. On the future northern section of the Eastern Front, the Russians built huge complexes of fortifications in Osowiec, Modlin (Novogeorgievsk), Dęblin (Ivangorod), and Kaunas. The Germans massively fortified the fields on the outskirts of Königsberg, while the Austrians built an impregnable fortress in Przemyśl (Premissel) and protected Cracow with a ring of forts and bunkers.

Many a general was troubled not just by the millions of tons of cement and steel needed to build the fortresses. The army now possessed fantastic means of killing the enemy, the latest innovation being the heavy machine gun. But enemies had exactly the same equipment. The continental powers could draw upon vast numbers of reservists, but each state introduced compulsory military service; in other words, millions were set against millions. Finally, everyone had powerful allies, and indeed that was the problem: everyone.

Their doubts notwithstanding, the generals devised plans for a future war. They all knew that rail transportation would play a key role, but they had limited influence over investment in the railways. To mitigate this, they demanded more money for everything and the extension of compulsory military service. In the most recent major conflict, the Russo-Japanese war of 1904–1905, the Russians had run out of artillery ammunition (besides everything else) and had been forced to import it, since local factories had been unable to increase production in line with demand. General staffs thus assumed that artillery ammunition would be used on an unprecedented scale and accordingly built huge warehouses to store it. Austria-Hungary and Russia kept much of their munitions in their fortresses. When, in the summer of 1915, the Germans captured Kaunas and Novogeorgievsk with relative ease, 3,000 artillery pieces and 2 million shells fell into their hands. In the previous year, the Russian armaments industry manufactured only 285 artillery guns and 660,000 shells.[6]

In Germany, despite opposition from the SPD (the largest parliamentary party), the government managed to force through a bill in the summer of 1913 that increased the size of the peacetime army from 754,000 to 890,000 men, or 1.3 per cent of the population. This confirmed foreign observers in their belief that the threat of 'Prussian militarism' was indeed hanging over Europe. In fact, in France, the proportion of men under arms was 2.3 per cent (in Russia and Austria-Hungary it hovered around 0.8–0.85 per cent). France and Russia spent roughly 5 per cent of GDP on the military, whereas Germany spent less than 4 per cent and Austria-Hungary just over 3 per cent.

None of the plans laid by the imperial general staffs survived the first weeks of fighting in August 1914. This was also because no general or field marshal would publicly admit that he shared the misgivings of the leading light of the profession, Helmuth von Moltke. The legendary architect of Prussia's fast, victorious wars with Austria and France appeared in the Reichstag for the last time in May 1890. His words astounded the deputies:

> The age of cabinet war is behind us – all we have now is people's war, and any prudent government will hesitate to bring about a war of this nature, with all its incalculable consequences. [...] Gentlemen, if the war which has been hanging over our heads like the Sword of Damocles for more than a decade – if this war were to break out, then no one will be able to foresee how long it will last or how it will end. The greatest powers in Europe, armed as never before, will confront each other in battle. [...] Gentlemen, it may be a seven years' war or a thirty years' war – and woe to him who sets Europe alight, who puts the first fuse to the powder keg.[7]

The ninety-year-old elder statesman was gladly forgiven this flight of fancy as it was so clearly not part of the *Zeitgeist*. Age takes its toll – it was said – and von Moltke's time had passed. Others would not have got away with such overt defeatism. Von Moltke's nephew and namesake, the aforementioned head of the Supreme Army Command in 1914, who was younger by two generations, privately harboured similar concerns. But in that summer, neither he nor his colleagues in other European capitals would dare to challenge the widespread view that the war would be short and victorious.

---

[6] Peter Gatrell, 'Poor Russia, Poor Show: Mobilising a Backward Economy for War, 1914–1917', in *The Economics of World War I*, ed. Stephen Broadberry and Mark Harrison, Cambridge 2005, pp. 235–275, here p. 242.

[7] *Stenographische Berichte über die Verhandlungen des Deutschen Reichstags, 1890/91*, vol. 114, p. 76 n, 14 May 1890.

It was only minorities who challenged this view. The biggest among them were the socialist parties united in the Second International, and this now forgotten tradition is worthy of some attention. The socialists were afraid of war: millions of mobilized workers, killing their comrades in enemy uniform just so that the capitalists sitting in their offices could make a handsome profit, was a nightmarish vision. At their congresses they often debated the issue. Radicals proposed a preventive, international general strike in the armaments industries; the majority believed that this was impractical and pointless because an international general strike would surely break out across the world as soon as the spectre of war had begun to materialize.

In July 1914, all the Western socialist deputies joined the parliamentary majorities in their own countries and voted for war. Not for the first or last time, the Marxist dream of international proletarian solidarity would be crushed by nationalism.

An altogether different kind of pacifism was represented by Baroness Bertha von Suttner, née Countess Kinsky, a well-known and widely read writer on the human condition and winner of the 1905 Nobel Prize. Her most important work, *Die Waffen Nieder* (*Lay Down Your Arms!*), was published in 1889 and became a bestseller in the German-speaking world. Suttner's book was translated into many languages. The novel's protagonist is a woman who loses her loved ones during the endless conflicts between the European powers (beginning with the war of 1859 between Austria, Piedmont, and France, and ending with the Franco-Prussian War of 1870–1871). Suttner's commitment to the struggle for peace saw her participate in various international peace conferences, including the First Hague Peace Conference of 1899. She certainly contributed more to the pacifist cause than the initiator of the Hague Conference, Czar Nicholas II of Russia.

The Warsaw banker Jan (Ivan, Jean de, Johann von) Gotlib Bloch arrived at the Hague by a different route. In 1893 he began to publish a series of articles in Polish entitled *Future War and Its Economic Consequences*. Over the next five years these essays evolved into a five-volume work called *The War of the Future in Its Technical, Economic and Political Relations*, published in 1898–1900 in Polish, Russian, French, German, and Dutch, and in an abridged version in English as *Is War Now Impossible?*[8] Bloch was a kind of pseudo-scientist who can more accurately be described as a hobbyist; unlike his rivals, he was wealthy enough to have a team of researchers work on his amateur project. He treated war from the standpoint of an enlightened European who was concerned about the fate of the Old Continent. For Bloch, the return of

---

[8] Jan G. Bloch, *Przyszła wojna pod względem technicznym, politycznym i ekonomicznym*, Warsaw 1900. A new edition of extensive sections of the work, compiled by Grzegorz P. Bąbiak, was published by the Polish Institute of International Affairs in 2005. The translations are generally restricted to the most important sections.

violence to international relations was an absolute evil – the most fundamental threat to civilization in the *fin de siècle*. His rather dull disquisition, overburdened with statistics and numbering 3,000 pages, showed that the European powers had already accumulated enough firepower to annihilate the entire continent. In support of his argument Bloch offered a comprehensive analysis of the unprecedented growth in the means of destruction. From this perspective the fact that a future war would quickly ruin the European economy seemed rather trivial, although for Bloch's fellow bankers it would soon become of paramount importance. In the month of disgrace, July 1914, their warnings about the impending apocalypse would fall on deaf ears.

Bloch viewed the world from a Warsaw perspective. He lived in a vibrant city that was fast approaching one million inhabitants. Its early modern fortifications had long since been demolished, although, as in many other cities in the region, new ones had been erected. However, such fortifications became obsolete the moment they were completed and hampered urban development. Indeed, it was hard to find a better illustration of the futility of the arms race.[9] At the same time, Bloch lived in a country where, as in most parts of Europe, military service had been mandatory for decades. He was one of very few to draw the logical conclusion that a war between the empires would not only cause the death of hundreds of thousands of young men but would also present a challenge that no society or economy can meet. A future war would end in defeat for all its participants: advances in technology would turn battlefields into slaughterhouses from which no modern state could emerge victorious. Each state could commit an unimaginable number of people and resources to a supposedly final battle. The war would ruin both the winners and the losers in equal measure – materially, physically, morally. Hence, the categories of 'winner' and 'loser' were a thing of the past.

At the turn of the century, Bloch became the leading advocate of a small minority among the *haute bourgeoisie* (we should not hesitate to use this term as he was one of the richest men in Russia) which recognized that a future war between the great powers would signal catastrophe for all its participants: the probability of victory was vanishingly small and the costs utterly disproportionate. The military planners of the day rejected the theories of this Varsovian amateur in disgust. They knew better. What riled them most about Bloch was that *The War of the Future* was not just about war: lurking in the background of this weighty tome was the fundamental question of whether a civilized society should entrust its fate to military men. And it is precisely this question that generals, of whatever time, place, and uniform, cannot bear.

---

[9] The Warsaw Fortress was abandoned in 1909, yet reconstruction commenced in 1913. In the 1890s Bloch believed that the city was part of the Russian system of fortifications on the Vistula and was profoundly troubled by that thought.

THE OFFENSIVE DOCTRINE

In the first months of the Great War, quite unexpectedly, one of the most frequently quoted German writers on both sides of the front was Friedrich von Bernhardi. Although this cavalry general and military theorist was not the most elegant of writers, he responded perfectly to the exigencies of the moment. Germany and its allies drew from Bernhardi's works the comforting belief that they were certain to emerge victorious from the unfolding conflict. Their opponents regarded Bernhardi as a symbol of German chauvinism and militarism, and not without reason. Here, for example, is what the author believed to be the impact of the arms race on the society of the pre-war Reich: 'We have accustomed ourselves to looking upon our armaments as a heavy burden, forgetting thereby that the army is the well from which our people constantly draws new strength, self-sacrificing spirit, and patriotism.'[10] Despite the severe reprimands he meted out to German public opinion, which he believed was overly pacifist, Bernhardi was optimistic about the outcome of what he regarded as an inevitable future European conflict. His hopes for victory rested on an unshakeable belief in the superior war morale of the Germans. The most important factor in this victory would be initiative (or, as he put it, 'the principle of action').

A reader who takes the trouble to distil Bernhardi's views from the poetic efflorescence of Greater-German chauvinism will have to concede that he expressed not just the views of German strategists but also the beliefs prevalent in all the general staffs of Europe. In very simple terms these can be summarized as the superiority of spirit over matter and the superiority of attack over defence. Bernhardi's optimism about Germany's chances of victory was based on the otherwise sound observation that, hitherto, these principles had been most effectively implemented during the Prussian campaign against France in 1870–1871. In addition, the period leading up to the Great War seemed to provide new arguments to the advocates of the offensive doctrine. In the years 1904–1905, European military officers had their eyes fixed on the Russo-Japanese war. The Russian commander in Manchuria, General Alexei Kuropatkin, was a proponent of the defensive doctrine. In contrast, the Japanese – trained by German instructors – embraced the idea of a permanent offensive. Although the Russian defeat had many different causes, observers focused precisely on the difference in strategy. Indeed, Kuropatkin, looking to excuse his own incompetence, also invoked one of these magical formulas:

> In the late war [...] our moral strength was less than that of the Japanese; and it was this inferiority, rather than mistakes in generalship, that caused our defeats. [...] The lack of martial spirit, of moral exaltation, and of heroic impulse, affected particularly our stubbornness in battle. In many cases we did not have sufficient resolution to conquer such antagonists as the Japanese.[11]

---

[10] Friedrich von Bernhardi, *On War of To-Day* [*Vom heutigen Kriege*], authorized translation by Karl von Donat, New York, NY 1914, vol. 1, p. 12.

[11] A[lexei] Kuropatkin, *The Russian Army and the Japanese War*, vol. 2, London 1909, p. 80.

28 THE FRONTS

> Military analysts completely ignored the cost of the Japanese victory. In fact, the Japanese losses were much higher than those of the defeated Russians. Both sides already had modern artillery and machine guns. A mass of Japanese infantry perished in relentless attacks using bayonets, especially during the assault on Port Arthur. Their fanaticism aroused the admiration of European general staffs, who were not too troubled by the Japanese losses. After all, the future war was going to be swift anyway. Impressed by Manchuria, the French adopted the so-called Grandmaison doctrine in 1911, which assumed *l'attaque à outrance* (attack to excess).The preferred tactic was to push forces as close as possible to enemy lines and then launch a massive assault using bayonets. Even heavy losses were less important than the supposedly beneficial effect such an attack would have on troop morale.
>
> In 1914, almost without exception, the armies that faced each other were focused on attack at the level of both strategy and tactics. The only lesson drawn from the war of 1904–1905 was that, for an attack to be effective, it had to be massive. The cost of this doctrine proved appallingly high.

Our final note before we turn to the Great War in the East will become clearer in this context.

The 1912–1916 period witnessed manoeuvre warfare no less bloody than in the trenches of Verdun or the Somme. Official dispatches often mentioned the Habsburg archdukes, the nearest relatives of Nicholas II of Russia, and the members of ruling dynasties from various parts of the Reich. Meanwhile, generals on both sides of the Russian front were typical members of the *noblesse de robe*, whom the aristocracy viewed as nobodies, and who owed their careers not to noble birth, but to individual talents. August von Mackensen (1849–1945) received a noble rank only in 1889; in the Great War, he proved to be the finest German commander in the East, with a combat trail beginning in East Prussia in 1914 (where he lost a battle, but gave the German units time to regroup), through the Gorlice offensive of 1915, the capture of Belgrade in December of that year, and culminating in the defeat of Romania in 1916. Alexei Brusilov (1853–1926), the only Russian general who managed to shake up the Southwest Front, was one of the few generals to be respected, perhaps even supported, by Russian public opinion. Still, he could not take up a seat either in the Duma or in the State Council as, under Russian law (which was quite consistent on this point), serving officers were forbidden from doing so. Brusilov's political career ended before it had even started. Conrad von Hötzendorf (1852–1925) may have been born a nobleman, but earned the title of count only in July 1918, as a palliative following his dismissal as commander of the Italian Front (where he had just suffered another defeat).[12] We might also add to this cohort Marshal Paul von

---

[12] Wolfram Dornik, *Des Kaisers Falke. Wirken und Nach-Wirken von Franz Conrad von Hötzendorf*, Innsbruck 2013, p. 175.

Hindenburg (1847–1934), the Poznań-born legend of the German army, retired due to advanced age, but returned to active duty in the summer of 1914.[13] The resulting image is of a group of old men (with an average age in 1915 of 65 years); professional soldiers, probably ailing, locked in a world of map pennants, and removed from the reality faced by soldiers who could be their grandsons, but whom they were now about to send out to die.

July 1914

The empires' month of disgrace began with the assassination of Franz Ferdinand. For four weeks, cabinets deliberated and foreign ministries churned out memos at the same rate as the general staffs. In the monarchies, meetings were held with the Emperor. Here and there, influential bankers, industrialists, editors-in-chief, and occasionally the chairmen of parliamentary clubs appeared in the background. But they all played a lesser role in this game, because it was not about money but about prestige and Great Power status. Politicians outside the government and the publishers of mass-circulation newspapers likewise had little to say, but they did count because they could mobilize public opinion. And without public support, neither a monarchy nor a republic would venture into war.

In each country, all the major decisions were taken by a group of a dozen or perhaps several dozen men, who were predominantly middle-aged (although elderly men quite often made an appearance too). This group was greatly depleted on account of the season: July was the month when gentlemen would take their annual leave, usually with their wives. Wilhelm II spent these crucial weeks on a yacht. His Minister of War, General Erich von Falkenhayn, was relaxing on an island in the North Sea. Helmuth von Moltke the Younger arrived in the spa town of Carlsbad for his annual holiday on the day Franz Ferdinand was assassinated. The death of the Archduke apparently made little impression on him. He cut short his holiday only after learning of the Austro-Hungarian ultimatum to Serbia and returned to Berlin on 25 July. Germany was no exception: the Serbian Chief of the General Staff, Radomir Putnik, almost missed the war entirely. He spent the summer of 1914 in a sanatorium in Bad Gleichenberg in the enemy state of Austria. On his way home he was arrested in Budapest by the Hungarian gendarmerie, before being released at the personal request of Franz Joseph; it appears that the Emperor could not countenance the arrest of an enemy who had come to the monarchy as a fellow bather.

---

[13] Wolfram Pyta, *Hindenburg. Herrschaft zwischen Hohenzollern und Hitler*, Munich 2007.

The experiences of other decision-makers were not as thrilling as Putnik's. Slowly they returned to their offices at the end of the month. Few of them cared that share prices on the stock exchanges were beginning to nose-dive. Bloch was dead, and the economic catastrophe he predicted was beginning to be felt by his fellow financiers; soon it would spread to petty savers. Although the newspapers were agitated about the threat of war, military men were not especially in evidence. Politicians believed in their promise that the war could be won quickly, and public opinion believed it all the more. On the whole, decision-makers were badly informed. Their principal sources of information were press dispatches and diplomatic reports, in other words, sources that usually described yesterday's news. The French delegation, which was headed by the President and Prime Minister, returned from its trip to Russia by boat. The journey took six days. Germany was adept at jamming communications; the exchange of messages in the crucial days of the crisis took even longer than normal. The telephone still played a secondary role and was mainly used for local calls. Secure communications were unknown at the beginning of the twentieth century, but in all probability they would not have changed much.

Few players in this game felt they had anything to win. All Great Britain could do was to protect its global position, the foundations of which lay outside of Europe anyway. London would only be forced to intervene when provoked by Germany, which for a good twenty years had been questioning Britain's unique position. The construction by the Reich of a powerful navy had long been a bone of contention – nothing did more to undermine relations between the two countries than Wilhelm's idiotic plan to rival Britain on the seas. During the war the German fleet waged one major battle against the British, which it half-won, yet it was still unable to break out of its ports on the North Sea and the Baltic. The German revolution of 1918 began in the country's naval bases.

The Reich was indeed the only power that questioned the European order. Historians have written many thousands of pages on this subject and have tried to reconcile two contradictory points of view: on the one hand, the Reich had for years been developing at a much faster pace than Great Britain. In 1913 there was no doubt that, if peace held, Germany's position as the most economically powerful country would strengthen with each passing year. Germany did not have the possibility to expand its territory, but it didn't want to anyway: in the west this could be done only at the expense of Belgium, the Netherlands, or France, which was unthinkable; in the east, only at the expense of Russia, which in practice would mean incorporating millions of Poles into the Reich. This was not an especially appealing prospect. 'What could we possibly want from Russia?', asked the liberal Prince Heinrich zu Schoenaich-Carolath during a parliamentary debate in May 1914: 'Perhaps Warsaw and the Poles? I thought we'd had enough of them.'[14]

On the other hand, regardless of the Emperor's pugnacious personality, it was the Reich that engaged most often and most willingly in sabre rattling. Various attempts have been made to explain this behaviour: Germany as a 'belated nation', which did not experience unification until 1871; the tradition of Prussian militarism; the interests of big business (a particularly nonsensical claim given that industrialists and bankers, even if they were unfamiliar with the works of Bloch, knew full well that peace served their interests much better than war did); the desire to resolve apparently growing internal tensions at a single stroke; and nationalism. All these factors were important but they do not explain why, in July 1914, Germany heightened its belligerent and aggressive stance much more than the other European powers. Public opinion – excluding the social democrats, who were reluctant to endorse pro-war sentiment – believed that Germany was surrounded by a hostile coalition of states. Besieged-fortress syndrome is a tremendously destructive force: German students, who volunteered for the army even more eagerly than their British counterparts, clearly believed that they would be fighting to defend their fatherland against the barbarous East and materialistic West, that they were the defenders of the only true European culture.

The British and French, and the Russians, likewise believed in their own moral superiority: the former were defending Europe as a whole; the latter were protecting their brother-Slavs against Prussian militarism and German arrogance. The French were also hoping to avenge the defeat of 1870. They felt wellprepared. Without the joyful excitement of people on the streets, before editorial offices, and in churches, and without the support of socialist parties urging their constituents to stand shoulder to shoulder with the defenders of the fatherland, it is hard to imagine the disgraceful month of July 1914. At the same time, we know that, although millions of peasants – who accounted for the vast majority of the population of Central and South-Eastern Europe – allowed themselves to be conscripted into the army and obediently marched to the front, their faces revealed very little enthusiasm. In parts of Russia mobilization was accompanied by disturbances and unrest, often associated with the mass consumption of alcohol. Binge drinking was a ritual practised by every new conscript, but on this occasion the young men were being sent not to the barracks but to the front. For the time being all this seemed unimportant, as did the fact that the only parties of the Socialist International to remain faithful to the principles proclaimed by European socialists and to openly oppose the war were the Russian Bolsheviks and Mensheviks and their comrades in the Serbian parliament.

The image of feverish crowds on the streets demanding war remained in the memory of West European societies. This created a feedback loop: the masses

---

[14] Quoted in Włodzimierz Borodziej, *Geschichte Polens im 20. Jahrhundert*, Munich 2010, p. 77.

were easy to incite, while the politicians and journalists, who were calling for a reckoning with the enemy, saw the result of their efforts as further evidence that they reflected the views and interests of the people. The unity of the nation in the face of danger, moral superiority over the enemy, the defence of a just cause, and faith in a rapid victory – all this conspired to make the summer of 1914 seem beautiful and sublime.

Yet the decisions were taken in offices, and not at rallies. The story still evokes astonishment today – rarely in history have the European elites been so lacking in reason. On 28 June, a young Serb citizen of the Austro-Hungarian Empire managed, somewhat fortuitously, to shoot the heir to the throne, the Archduke Franz Ferdinand and his wife.

FRANZ FERDINAND D'ESTE

Franz Ferdinand had long been the most controversial successor to the Habsburg throne in Vienna. A nephew of Franz Joseph, he was known for his arrogance and dogmatism and had a talent for alienating people. He became the heir-presumptive in 1896 after the death of his father, the Emperor's younger brother. Franz Ferdinand underwent a decent military education and had experience as an army officer. He appreciated modern military technology and lent his support to like-minded staff officers. From his many travels to exotic places he brought back hunting trophies in bulk quantities. At the family's seat in Konopiště, Bohemia, one can still see the remnants of his vast collection of game kills, which is said to have numbered at least a quarter of a million. Against the will of the Viennese court, Franz Ferdinand married the beautiful countess Sophie Chotek. As a person of lower rank (everything is relative ...), she was not invited to official ceremonies. The couple's children were excluded from the succession and thus could not inherit the throne. Franz Ferdinand loathed the court and most of the political establishment.

But appearances were deceptive, at least in part. Franz Ferdinand was more than just an arrogant archduke typical of every ruling family. He believed that the state was in a critical condition and required radical change. The enemies of the monarchy were 'Jews, freemasons, socialists, and Hungarians'.[15] He felt that the Hungarians, in particular, were an utter disgrace to the Habsburg Empire as they were ruthless and adept in taking advantage of their (theoretically weaker) position in the system of dual power – a system in which neither member could exist without the other. Franz Ferdinand also had an original solution to the problem of the South Slavs, that is, Serbia (an enemy since 1903), Bosnia-Herzegovina (annexed in 1908), the Kingdom of Croatia (which belonged to Hungary), and the Slovenes (who inhabited Cisleithania). Serbia had proclaimed the unification of fraternal nations under its own leadership. But Franz Ferdinand pushed for a different solution: the creation of a kingdom of South Slavs as the third element of the Habsburg monarchy. Hungarians dismissed the idea outright, Austrian Germans were

---

[15] Quoted in Dornik, *Des Kaisers Falke*, p. 67.

ambivalent, and Poles and Czechs also rejected this version of trialism because they aspired to a different kind of tripartite monarchy: one in which they were the third pillar. The heir-presumptive concocted his plan in the beautiful Belvedere Palace in Vienna, ignoring the angry murmurings within the monarchy's political class. In Europe, Franz Ferdinand was seen as the leader of the Viennese 'hawks', but this was a mistaken view because he opposed the idea of a preventive war. Although he generally supported the dashing Conrad von Hötzendorf – the two men were united in their belief that the army was the mainstay of the monarchy – he argued constantly with the Chief of the General Staff: for the heir to the throne, military conflict seemed altogether too risky.

Franz Ferdinand ignored all the warnings about his planned visit to Sarajevo. We shall never know whether the person who died on 28 June 1914 was a political visionary or a charlatan.

Europe was outraged. People were aware that, without the long-standing conflict between Austria and Serbia, the assassination would not have happened. In the view of many, the conspiracy trail led to Belgrade. There was no hard evidence for this, but who needed evidence when Vienna had received European sympathy, solidarity, and compassion on a plate, and now had the perfect excuse to finally settle scores with the 'swineherds' south of the border?

The Austrian military urged war. It easily secured the unconditional support of Berlin, where von Hötzendorf's colleague, the head of the Supreme Army Command von Moltke, had also been waiting patiently for the opportunity to strike. Who cared that the war plans of Germany and Austria-Hungary were contradictory? Berlin wanted to throw seven-eighths of its army against the French and along the way violate the neutrality of Luxembourg and Belgium. Only after defeating its western neighbour did it intend to shift the bulk of its ground forces to the Russian front. The Habsburg monarchy planned to punish Serbia in spectacular fashion, through humiliation and international disgrace. War with Russia did not seem particularly enticing given weak German support in the initial phase, but von Hötzendorf was a risk-taker and regarded the Russians (not to mention the Serbs) with disdain. During the Berlin talks one week after the assassination in Sarajevo, Germany pledged its full support to Austria-Hungary in the event of an attack on Serbia.

In Vienna a complicated decision-making process was under way. The Hungarian Prime Minister, Count István Tisza, feared attacking Serbia. His arguments were similar to those advanced by Prince Heinrich zu Schoenaich-Carolath, only that the Serbs took the place of the Poles: why did the monarchy need yet more Slavs? But after a week of discussions he came around to the idea. History can be cruel: the only Central European politician to successfully oppose the impending catastrophe for several days was gunned down in October 1918 by assassins who held him responsible for starting the war.

After Tisza's capitulation, Vienna waited. The President and Prime Minister of France visited Russia. Vienna felt it would be a mistake to do anything so long as potential adversaries could confer on the spot rather than by telegraph or through diplomatic channels. On 23 July the French delegation left St Petersburg. That same day Vienna handed Belgrade an ultimatum. It was carefully constructed in such a way that no sovereign state could possibly accept it. One of the demands was that the monarchy's officials should participate in the investigations of the Serbian authorities into the Sarajevo assassination and into the suppression of movements that sought to undermine the territorial integrity of Austria-Hungary; in both cases this meant allowing foreign officials to act against Serb citizens within the territory of Serbia. Vienna intended to wait no longer than forty-eight hours for an answer.

On 25 July Belgrade acceded to almost all of the Austrians' demands with the exception of the two mentioned above, as these were clearly contrary to the principle of sovereignty. Serbia's deft response, which promised to cease anti-Habsburg propaganda and punish the assassins, astonished even Wilhelm II. Somewhat crestfallen, the Emperor wrote that, since Belgrade had allowed itself to be publicly humiliated, there was no reason to start a war. Vienna seized the opportunity regardless – after all, the Serbs had failed to meet two of their demands – and on 28 July declared war.

Berlin and Vienna had received numerous warnings during the month: that Russia would not countenance another loss of face and would spring to Serbia's defence; that the Franco-Russian Alliance would trigger an automatic response; that Italy could not be counted on; and that Great Britain would in all likelihood not remain passive. But it was all for nothing. On 30 July Russia announced general mobilization, followed a day later by Austria-Hungary and Belgium. On 1 August Germany and France followed suit. Germany declared war on Russia and on the following day occupied Luxembourg and presented an ultimatum to Belgium. On 3 August the Reich declared war on France and received an ultimatum from Great Britain. A day later Germany attacked Belgium, prompting Britain to declare war on Germany. On 6 August Austria-Hungary declared war on Russia. On the following day the first troops of the British Expeditionary Force disembarked in France. Austro-Hungarian troops attacked Serbia on 12 August, and three days later the Russians entered East Prussia. Montenegro had already allied itself with Serbia; the Ottoman Empire joined the war in October as an ally of the Central Powers – the war thus engulfed all of Central and Eastern Europe. In the Balkans, three states – Bulgaria, Romania, and Greece – for now remained neutral.

***

The central and eastern parts of the continent were sucked into the war by megalomaniac empires. This applies least of all to Germany and the Germans – the Reich, uniquely, was at once an empire and a modern nation-state, and its politicians and military were used to thinking in both imperial and national terms. Yet, despite this, they were no less megalomaniac than the other empires, for they convinced themselves and their fellow countrymen that Germany was surrounded by enemies, and that only a massive pre-emptive strike to the east and to the west could destroy the thickening cordon before it was too late. Austria-Hungary essentially wanted just to punish Serbia, and later, as war fever intensified, to annihilate it. Russia went to war for the sole purpose of recovering its tarnished Great Power status. The empires sent their citizens to the front, although none harboured the traditional war aim of securing regional hegemony, annexing a disputed province, or installing a puppet on a foreign throne. Christopher Clark, the author of one of the most prominent recent books about the summer of 1914, quite reasonably refers to the imperial policy-makers as 'sleepwalkers'.[16]

A few weeks after the July domino effect, which had already managed to destroy the European order, the Russian Prime Minister Sergei Witte complained that the war was pure madness: what could Russia expect to gain from it? More territory, perhaps? Surely the lands of His Imperial Highness were already sufficiently large ...[17]

If, in the summer of 1914, any imperial politician had known what lay in store for his country, he would certainly not have done his bit to seal the fate of nineteenth-century Europe, that is, the world of empires.

[16] Christopher Clark, *The Sleepwalkers. How Europe Went to War in 1914*, London 2012.
[17] Alexander V. Prusin, *Nationalizing a Borderland. War, Ethnicity and Anti-Jewish Violence in East Galicia, 1914–1920*, Tuscaloosa, AL 2005, p. 13.

2

Prelude: The Balkans 1912–1913

In the summer of 1914 it had been more than forty years since the last major European war. That period had witnessed unprecedented economic growth and the flourishing of culture. Lasting peace was conducive to prosperity, technological progress, and social change. Between the Franco-Prussian war of 1871 and the outbreak of the Great War in 1914 trams appeared on the streets of European cities, and the bigger capitals – London, Paris, Berlin, Budapest – acquired underground metro lines. New factories were built and the urban proletariat grew so rapidly that politicians began to vie for its support. Although the European powers pursued overseas campaigns, the latter's impact on the daily life of Europeans was limited to articles in the morning press. Nor were peace and development the sole preserve of the West. In Central and Eastern Europe, too, war was not within living memory for the vast majority of citizens. The experience of war was essentially remote in time and space. Manchuria, where Russia had suffered defeat at the hands of the Japanese in early 1905, was over 8,000 kilometres from Warsaw.

For the countries south of the Danube this period (1871–1914) was marked by a succession of wars, uprisings, rebellions, and revolutions. Even if we ignore the 'ordinary' *coups d'état* and royal assassinations, the incidence of violent change was remarkable. In 1876 a Bulgarian uprising broke out against the Turks, which the Serbs and Montenegrins also joined. It transformed into a two-year war when Russia, eager to avenge the merciless treatment being meted out to its 'Slavic brothers', entered the fray; its campaign ended at the gates of Istanbul. The Congress of Berlin did not calm the situation for long. In 1883 Serbian peasants turned against their own state. They had had enough of oppressive taxation, but what triggered the uprising was the attempt to confiscate the weapons they kept in their homes. This was only the beginning of a whole series of peasant revolts in the Balkan countries. The biggest of these took place in 1907 in Romanian Moldavia, where approximately 10,000 people died in clashes with the army, i.e. proportionally more than in the Russian Revolution of 1905–1907. In 1885 Bulgaria annexed Ottoman Eastern Rumelia, to which the Serbs reacted with unexpected aggression. The Bulgarians repelled the Serb attack at the Battle of Slivnitsa. In 1893 the Internal Macedonian Revolutionary Organization (IMRO) was formed. Its

PRELUDE: THE BALKANS 1912–1913

aim was to gain autonomy for the Macedonian *vilayets* (provinces) of the Ottoman Empire, initially by political means and later by means of terror. Three years later Greece declared war on Turkey with the aim of occupying Crete. The campaign ended in defeat for Greece, but the Great Powers forced the Sultan to grant autonomy to the island anyway, which came under the control of Western troops.

Non-stop conflict was one of the reasons why modernization was delayed in the Balkans. Wars cost money, and the region suffered from a chronic lack of funds. Only the Romanian oil industry managed to attract a reasonable amount of foreign investment prior to 1914. In any case, Romania, just like every other country, took out loans in France, Germany, and Austria-Hungary in order to finance its investments. Without this injection of capital there was no chance of creating a modern state complete with railways, schools, hospitals, and especially an army. The Balkans were made up of conservative, predominantly peasant societies. Greece was the only country where urban inhabitants accounted for more than 20 per cent of the national population. The biggest city of the region, Bucharest (the 'Paris of the East'), had just over 300,000 residents in 1910 – slightly more than half the population of Łódź in Russian Poland. The capital of Serbia had fewer than 100,000 inhabitants and was five times smaller than Riga.

Despite the fact that the fledgling Balkan countries could not keep up with Europe economically, their brief history was a series of civilizational and territorial successes. Nevertheless, these successes always came at the expense of the Ottoman Empire. Constantly humiliated by neighbouring countries and by the Great Powers that sprang to their defence, the Ottoman army revolted, giving rise to the Young Turk revolution. This was not a movement with stable structures, and its political programme was short on detail aside from a general consensus about the need for reform. First, the liberal constitution of 1876 was restored (or, rather, it was introduced, having never entered into force) and finally in 1909 the arch-conservative Sultan Abdul Hamid II was deposed. Initially, the young officers who formed the backbone of the revolution enjoyed the support of national minorities, particularly the Albanians. It soon turned out, however, that the weakening empire was to be held together by authoritarian means. Newly formed political parties and organizations were banned. The outrage was greatest in Albania, where the revolution had done most to energize society. Soon Albanian resistance was transformed into an uprising against extortionate taxes and the policy of centralization. The Ottoman army was unable to suppress it, largely on account of the mountainous terrain, hostile local population, and secret supply of weapons to the insurgents by the Montenegrins. But the greatest threat to the Ottoman government lay elsewhere. Hitherto, it was precisely the Muslim Albanians who had traditionally supplied the Ottoman army with its biggest contingent of men (after the ethnic Turks and Kurds), and many Albanians had pursued brilliant military careers. Even during the Balkan Wars several commanders in the Ottoman army were of Albanian origin. The upsurge in Albanian nationalism called all this into question. Meanwhile, the position of the Ottoman Porte was weakening with each passing month. And, as if internal problems were not enough, in September 1911 Italy finally joined the colonial race. Desperate for an overseas presence, the Italians set their sights on Ottoman Tripolitania (Libya) and attacked Tripoli. Cut off from the centre of the country, the Turkish garrisons fought bravely and their surrender was hardly a foregone conclusion. However, the situation of the Ottoman Empire quickly deteriorated due to Italy's actions outside the main theatre of war. The Italian fleet blocked the Dardanelles, thus disrupting maritime trade, and shelled Beirut. To make matters worse, it supplied weapons and money to the rebellious Albanians.

The Macedonian Question

The 'Balkan cauldron' was bubbling and the highest temperatures were recorded in four *vilayets*: Manastir, Salonika, Kosovo, and Edirne, which made up the provinces of Macedonia and Thrace. Macedonia was the Balkans in miniature; its residents included Christians and Muslims, people who identified as Bulgarians, Serbs, Albanians, or Greeks, as well as Gypsies, and the biggest city of the region, Salonika, had the largest community of Sephardic Jews in the empire. There were ethnic groups in the region whose existence would, not for the first time, leave European diplomats in a quandary: the Kutso-Vlachs (a pastoral people speaking a language similar to Romanian), for instance, or the Pomaks (Bulgarian-speaking Muslims). There were also the Ottoman Turks: peasants, landowners, and a large group of military men. It was precisely here, in the Salonika garrison, that the organization of Ottoman reformers which would eventually lead to the Young Turk revolution was born.

The elites – both the imperial Turkish-Ottoman and the local Slavic, Albanian, and Greek elites – were feverishly active, concocting fantastical plans and drafting dramatic manifestos. A Young Turk officer, Albanian journalist, or Bulgarian teacher all had reason to be excited: each felt isolated and each had a sense of the ghastly uphill struggle – not just against the enemy but also against the inertia of potential allies and compatriots, who for some reason were not signing up *en masse* to the movements led by reformers, rousers, and revivers. Most inhabitants of the provinces were illiterate peasants without a sense of national identity, yet it was over those people that the struggle, which would ultimately engulf the entire Balkans, was fought.

The aim of the elites was to fundamentally transform the amorphous masses into a nation. Local identity was to be replaced by a sense of belonging to a community defined by language, history, culture, and – in the best-case scenario – by new national borders that would soon come into being. At each turn, however, the rousers realized that few people were excited by this prospect. When one member of the Greek elite began to interrogate Macedonian peasants about whether they felt more Greek or more Bulgarian, they crossed themselves and replied: 'Well, we're Christians. Are you asking if we are from the *Romaioi* [Greeks] or the *Voulgaroi* [Bulgarians]?' The rousers would begin with entreaties, soon followed by threats; often the most effective argument was the gun. When soldiers or local warlords (sometimes hired by a neighbouring state) encountered their Orthodox brethren, they would generally not have to execute recalcitrant local leaders; threats were enough. Peasants declared their allegiance to any nationality indicated to them at the point of a gun (Muslims were not so fortunate).[1]

IMRO, established in 1893, operated in a similar vein. It never fully defined its programme. The obvious aim was to destroy the authority of the Sultan, but what was to replace it was based on a mixture of socialist, anarchist, and federalist ideas. The Macedonian revolutionaries were closest to Bulgaria, to which they were related linguistically and culturally. Bulgaria was the main source of money and weapons and the place where activists would hide to escape arrest. Indeed, they were only a small part of the large and influential Macedonian émigré community, which was particularly in evidence in Sofia. In 1900 nearly a quarter of Sofia's 70,000 inhabitants came from one of the three Macedonian *vilayets*. It was thanks to Bulgarian influence in IMRO that the decision was taken to abandon guerrilla warfare in favour of an uprising proper. In 1903, first in Macedonia and then in neighbouring Thrace, the insurgents (who, depending on their self-declared nationality, were referred to as *komiti, komitacı,* or *komitaji*) carried out ill-prepared operations that yielded only Turkish repression and the weakening of Bulgaria's position in the region.

As far as taking control of the province was concerned, however, IMRO was not the only contender. In early-twentieth-century Macedonia political and armed groups of at least five different factions clashed with one another. The Serbs and Greeks maintained their own guerrilla forces (known as *chets*) in the region. The Turkish authorities likewise armed the local Muslim population and turned a blind eye to its acts of terror against Orthodox neighbours. The rule was that such units were led by former military commanders or officers on leave from the regular army. This further inflamed the already fierce conflict. Army officers deployed to Macedonia went there in the belief that they would be defending their compatriots against Ottoman oppression and Christian

---

[1] Dimitris Livanios, '"Conquering the Souls": Nationalism and Greek Guerrilla Warfare in Ottoman Macedonia, 1904–1908', *Byzantine and Modern Greek Studies* 23 (1999), pp. 195–221, here pp. 204–205. For more, see Mark Biondich, *The Balkans. Revolution, War and Political Violence since 1878*, Oxford 2011.

violence or at least against hostile neighbours. When the reality proved different and no one greeted the officers with open arms, their logical (albeit erroneous) conclusion was that their opponents' 'propaganda' was wholly to blame. The guerrillas, unused to political argument, would normally resort to the gun and the knife in order to resolve such conflicts. As a result, the victims of terror were very often diverse members of the local intelligentsia, who were accused of 'proselytism', in other words, of 'converting' locals to their particular national faith. In the end, even within IMRO, a group of activists became tired of this situation. The failure of the 1903 uprisings and the wave of violence they had caused prompted the creation of a programme for Macedonian autonomy. A few months after the fighting had ended, one of the intellectuals associated with IMRO, Krste Petkov Misirkov, wrote the following words (NB: in a book published in Sofia):

> I have no intention of politicizing in the Bulgarian fashion. I am a Macedonian and this is how I see the position of my country: it is not Russia or Austria-Hungary that are the enemies of Macedonia, but Bulgaria, Greece and Serbia. Our country can be saved from ruin only by struggling fiercely against these states.[2]

Bulgaria, weakened by the defeat of the uprising it had sponsored, began to look for other ways to take possession of the Ottoman Empire's European provinces. An alternative to independent action was an alliance with other Balkan rivals. Such an alliance was neither self-evident nor easy to secure. The only thing that united Serbia, Bulgaria, and Greece was a desire for territorial gains at the expense of the Turks. What divided them was the memory of recent conflicts and, naturally, the Macedonian question. Indeed, even countries as close as Serbia and Montenegro engaged in disputes over territory and prestige (the Serbian Karađorđević and the Montenegrin Njegoš dynasties believed themselves to be the rightful leaders of both countries). On the other hand, what favoured cooperation was the growing crisis of the Ottoman state, the chaos in the Albanian *vilayets*, and – from the point of view of Serbia in particular – the increasing threat of Austria-Hungary, which in 1908 formally annexed Bosnia and Herzegovina.

A deal was not struck until the spring of 1912, and not without the input of Russian diplomacy. The interests of the Balkan allies diverged so much that the ultimate division of Macedonian spheres of interest between Bulgaria and Serbia was left to the future decisions of Russia, while the agreement between Bulgaria and Greece did not even touch on territorial issues. The outbreak of the First

---

[2] Krste Petkov Misirkov, 'On Macedonian Matters', translated and edited by Nikola Iordanovski, in *Discourses of Collective Identity in Central and Southeast Europe (1770–1945). Texts and Commentaries*, vol. 3, part 2. *Modernism: Representations of National Culture*, ed. Ahmet Ersoy, Maciej Górny, and Vangelis Kechriotis, Budapest and New York, NY 2010, pp. 351–356, here p. 355.

Fig. 1 A demonstration in Sofia in support of the war with Turkey (1912). Courtesy of Mr Peyo Kolev, lostbulgaria.com.

Balkan War was precipitated by the fear that further delay would wreck the annexation plans. In the Albanian *vilayets* it looked increasingly as though some form of Albanian statehood would be achieved under the auspices of Austria-Hungary, while Italy shifted its military action against the Turks to the Aegean Sea. In accordance with the norms of nineteenth-century diplomacy, another intervention by the Great Powers was to be expected. Although the Balkan states felt confident enough to occasionally ignore the suggestions of the Great Powers, they were too weak to risk open opposition. They needed to extract as much as possible in the shortest possible time and only later to defend their gains. The final date of the attack was determined by yet another factor, important for rural economies: mobilization could take place only after the harvest. Bulgaria, Serbia, Montenegro, and Greece coordinated their assault, which occurred almost simultaneously. The first clashes took place in October on the Turkish–Montenegrin border.

The First Balkan War

This conflict was fought between armies that were in various stages of reorganization. Least advanced in the process was Montenegro, which was gradually transforming its modest armed forces from a tribal militia into something more

42   THE FRONTS

akin to a regular army. The Ottoman Empire was already in the next phase of a root-and-branch reform of its military, the first effect of which was disorganization and the near-collapse of the existing system. Indeed, on the eve of war, the German General and Turkish Field Marshal Wilhelm Colmar von der Goltz, a man equally distinguished for his services to German arms exports and for his contributions to Turkish army reform, accurately diagnosed the latter's ills:

> The jewel of the Turkish army is the rank-and-file soldier. There is no other soldier in the world who can match him for strength, proficiency, and endurance. I have witnessed battalions which, despite a lack of provisions and after an exceptionally long march, have reached their designated positions in a timely manner. Yet it seems that the modest needs of the Turkish soldier are taken for granted, for the greatest weakness of the Turkish army is stewardship and the supply of food and ammunition. In that regard – so vital in the reality of war – nothing works as it should.[3]

Despite having German instructors and despite its officers being educated at German military academies, the Turkish army was slow to modernize. At the outbreak of the war the regular soldiers (*nizam*) had a passable level of training, but this new type of conflict demanded the introduction of a mass of conscripts into battle. The Turkish reserve units (*redif*) were significantly less well-armed (and had rifles of different calibres, which greatly complicated the supply of ammunition), while the officers were local officials who were often devoid of military knowledge. It soon turned out that even if the *redif* had been equipped with modern guns they would not have been transformed into an efficient army. During the fighting with the Bulgarians it became apparent that some reservists were familiar only with the old types of weapons and were unable to open the cartridge chamber of a newly issued Mauser. No less important was the fact that, whereas most of the *nizam* were ethnically Turkish and Muslim, the *redif* included Jews and Christians. Many members of the Turkish military openly questioned the loyalty of the *redif*, which hardly improved morale. Distrust, bordering on espionage psychosis, as usual did far more damage than the potential conspiracies of foreign agents. It was manifested in different ways. Already during the Thracian campaign Turkish telegraph operators were ordered to transmit messages in German, which meant that the messages were incomprehensible not only to the operators themselves but also to a section of the Turkish officer corps. The fear that sensitive information could be leaked thus made it necessary for certain orders to be received only by officers educated in Germany, who were not so great in number. Another manifestation of distrust with even more serious implications was the sacking of all Christian railway workers in the theatre of

---

[3] Alfred Meyer, *Der Balkankrieg 1912/13 unter Benutzung zuverlässiger Quellen kulturgeschichtlich und militärisch dargestellt*, part I, Berlin 1913, pp. 27–28.

operations. This foolish decision, combined with the autumn rains, virtually paralysed rail transport. And if that wasn't enough, part of the Ottoman Empire's regular armed forces were stranded in North Africa, where the war with Italy was only just ending, while the rudimentary rail network meant that Asian reserve units could not be drafted in quickly. Sea crossings, in turn, were greatly hindered by the operations of the Greek Navy.

Turkey's strongest and most well-organized opponent was Bulgaria. It was the only country to educate its top cadres not just abroad but also in its own military academy in Sofia, and the only country to take a serious approach to the training of conscripts. Virtually no one could avoid Bulgarian military service, which was two years for infantry and three years for cavalry; no one, that is, except the Muslims, who could buy their way out of it. Nor was any leniency shown when it came to the training of reservists. Universal education had a considerable impact on the quality of the Bulgarian troops. The country prided itself on being the most successful in relative terms at combating illiteracy. At the turn of the century 72 per cent of the population was unable to read or write (compared with 78 per cent in Romania and 80 per cent in Serbia), but the Bulgarians invested the most in education: Serbia had three teachers per 1,000 children, whereas Bulgaria had ten, and 80 per cent of all Bulgarian children attended school – an unachievable figure for the other Balkan states.

Other societies in the Balkans were neither as educated nor as militarized. Military service in Greece and Serbia was much shorter than in Bulgaria. Constantly on the brink of bankruptcy, Greece trained only a portion of its conscripts each year, while Serbia cut short the period of training semi-officially. As a result, Bulgaria was able not only to muster the best and largest army but also to mobilize the greatest number of reservists; it sent soldiers even older than forty to Thrace and Macedonia, whereas most of the Serbs and Greeks who fought there were under thirty.

The allies did not differ much in terms of their ordnance. The armies that marched off to the First Balkan War were equipped with modern weapons – Mannlicher or Mauser rifles and cavalry carbines, Maxim machine guns, and French and German artillery made by Schneider-Creusot and Krupp. Competition among Europe's largest armaments companies captured the attention of the international press. For journalists in Germany and France the burning question was whether the French-made guns used by the Bulgarians and Serbs were more efficient than the German ones used by the Turks. All the equipment used by regular troops on both sides of the Balkan conflict was no different from that used by the armies of Western Europe, and two years later that equipment would be tested once again on the battlefronts of the Great War. Deep reserve units had weaponry that was greatly inferior. Some were still equipped with single-shot black powder cartridge rifles (which

44 THE FRONTS

immediately betrayed the shooter's position as soon as a shot was fired), but their participation in offensives on enemy territory was relatively low.

The belligerent mood began to intensify in the spring of 1912. In Bulgaria, Serbia, and Greece the press suddenly stopped criticizing its country's allies and instead began to emphasize religious unity, and, in the case of Serbia and Bulgaria, Slavic unity too. The conflict in Macedonia was now attributed to Turkish intrigue and Albanian barbarism. At the news that war had broken out with the 'eternal enemy', Sofia, Belgrade, and Athens reacted with enthusiasm. George I, the Greek monarch, declared that the conflict would be fought in defence of civilization. Even in Istanbul, where it was difficult to be optimistic about the prospect of another war, the mood was positive:

> One still sees long columns of men, hand in hand, being led through the streets accompanied by singing towards the barracks on Taksim Square, where they receive their uniforms. In Istanbul a military camp has been set up on the great square in front of the War Ministry; from there, units head off to the station before being loaded onto carriages bound for the front.[4]

The Turkish Minister of War, Nizam Pasha, was not a great strategist. In common with most experts of the day he accepted as self-evident the notion that in virtually all circumstances the attacking side had the advantage. Thus, although the Ottoman Empire had essentially been attacked, it decided to go on the offensive wherever possible. In Europe, however, its forces were less than half as numerous as those of its opponents, mainly due to transportation problems, organizational chaos, and the distances involved. To make matters worse, half the population of the European *vilayets* (provinces) were Christians, whom the Turks distrusted and did not treat as fellow citizens. The fate of a weak army fighting a dogged and more powerful opponent in hostile territory would prove tragic.

The war was settled in Thrace – practically within ten days. Having repelled the Turkish assault, between 22 October and 2 November the Bulgarians pushed on towards Istanbul, defeating the Ottoman army in two major battles at Kirkkilise and Bunarhisar (Luleburgas). In the prevailing weather conditions – rain turning into snow, with night-time temperatures falling below zero – von der Goltz's warnings proved frighteningly prescient. The Turks put up a determined resistance from the outset, especially in Bunarhisar, where the losses on both sides amounted to around 20,000 wounded, killed, or captured. Yet all the engagements followed a similar pattern. At night, after a day of bloody fighting, the Turkish *redif* would rest, paying little heed to their safety. But the darkness did not deter the Bulgarians, who would carry out armed

---

[4] G[ustav] von Hochwächter, *Mit den Türken in der Front im Stabe Mahmud Michtar Paschas. Mein Kriegstagebuch über die Kämpfe bei Kirk Kilisse, Lüle Burgas und Cataldza*, Berlin 1913, p. 3.

raids, prompting panic among the *redif* and causing them to flee *en masse* from the battlefield. In line with the preferred strategy of Russian military officers, with whom several of the Bulgarian commanders maintained personal contacts, the Bulgarians often attacked with bayonets. Against a better-trained and well-dug-in enemy this would have been a risky strategy at best, but here, beyond the barbed wire, sat exhausted and demoralized reservists. The fanaticism of the Bulgarian attacks made a huge impression on them. Gustav von Hochwächter – a German officer on the staff of the Turkish III Corps under Mahmoud Mukhtar Pasha – fought at Kirkkilise and Bunarhisar and witnessed both those embarrassing defeats. His account paints a picture of an army that was the architect of its own misfortune. The III Corps lacked competent officers and NCOs bold enough to take decisions. The closer they got to the enemy the less initiative they showed, and they also committed a series of simple but costly errors. Observers were amazed at how stubbornly the Turks would place their artillery in advanced positions. As a result, any successful attack by the Bulgarian infantry meant the loss not only of men and territory but also of valuable equipment. The reservists had no boots, had not been taught how to dig trenches, and even included invalids in their ranks; Hochwächter encountered blind soldiers who were in the army due to family tradition, having followed their fathers into the profession. Each outbreak of group panic was accompanied by wild and uncoordinated heavy gunfire. In this way the Turkish soldiers wasted ammunition by firing into the air and then could not replenish it on the following day. Morale was low. The Turkish soldiers were clearly unwilling to risk their necks for their homeland, and this is evidenced by the injury they suffered most often: a gunshot to the hand (which they had deliberately raised above the trench). As the baggage trains sank in the mud their terror-stricken drivers would unhitch the horses and flee in the direction of Istanbul. Units marching to the front line would pass piles of discarded equipment, boxes of ammunition, and heavy guns. No thought was given to the fate of the wounded: 'The sight of drenched and freezing men is demoralizing. There are no ambulances. No dressing stations. There is not even any water to wash wounds.' The retreat turned into yet another disaster: 'Troops everywhere. The roads are blocked by ammunition carts and artillery, and the locals (Christian peasants) shoot at the officers from the windows of their huts. The noise and mayhem is indescribable.'[5] During the retreat the Turkish artillery often shelled its own troops by mistake. The commander of the III Corps tried to control the chaos by personally chasing fleeing soldiers back into the trenches, but without success. In his memoirs he bitterly remarked:

[5] Ibid., pp. 25 and 28.

Fig. 2 Bulgarian soldiers and volunteers guarding the remains of a bridge over the Arda River blown up by the retreating Turks. Courtesy of Mr Peyo Kolev, lostbulgaria.com.

> Military history gives no other such example of a similar rout beginning without cause. Without fighting the Bulgarians had achieved a great victory. Without having been pressured by the enemy, beaten only by the bad weather and the conditions of the roads, the Turks fled as if they had suffered an irreparable disaster, and lost one third of their war materials.[6]

Soon the Turks faced a new enemy: cholera, which had probably been brought over by reservists from Anatolia. The humidity and lack of clean drinking water accelerated the epidemic. As Hochwächter noted, by the middle of November only the frontline units looked reasonably healthy. The rear areas were full of diseased men, who had no one to look after them:

> At the train station [in Hadımköy] it was a struggle to get through the crowds. Thousands of emaciated people with burning eyes, their gazes fixed, shuffled in the direction of the two trains, attempting to get into the carriages or onto the roof. Corpses were already lying there – people whom death had caught unawares at that very spot, their arms and legs

---

[6] Mahmoud Moukhtar Pasha (Mahmut Muhtar Pasha), *Mon commandement au cours de la campagne des Balkans de 1912*, Paris 1913, p. 43, cited in Richard C. Hall, *The Balkan Wars 1912–1913. Prelude to the First World War*, London 2000, p. 27.

PRELUDE: THE BALKANS 1912–1913

dangling from the carriage platforms; some even lay between the carriages. Whoever was not already ill would certainly have become infected there. No officers or doctors were to be seen. They, too, had probably fallen victim to the plague.[7]

Together with the sick and healthy soldiers fled Muslim civilians. Everyone wanted to reach Istanbul. Halidé Edib, a Turkish writer and political activist, watched in horror as the cadaverous multitudes arrived:

> When the Turkish refugees flocked in panic to Constantinople to escape from massacre, when cholera broke out among the immigrants and in the army, when one saw an entire population dying in the mosque yards under the icy grip of winter, the sight of the misery in Constantinople seemed too grim to be true.[8]

Meanwhile, the Bulgarian offensive began to seriously threaten the capital. Re-establishment of the Byzantine Empire under the Bulgarian Czar Ferdinand I suddenly became a tantalizing possibility. On 6 November the Grand Vizier Kâmil Pasha made a desperate plea for the Great Powers to send a fleet to defend Istanbul against the Bulgarians, who were purposefully marching 'on Czargrad' to fulfil the centuries-old dream of restoring the Byzantine Empire. The last line of defence where the Bulgarians could be stopped was the fortifications at Çatalca, which occupied a narrow isthmus between the Black Sea and the Sea of Marmara. The fortifications had been strengthened according to the instructions of German experts, and, although some of the artillery had been moved to Edirne just prior to the war, Çatalca nevertheless remained an excellent defensive position. On this occasion fortune favoured the Turks. As the Bulgarians ventured deeper and deeper into Ottoman territory they became cut off from their supply base. Transport into the country was difficult for the same reasons that had paralysed the Turks: bad roads, terrible weather, mud. Feeding several hundred thousand men on the spot was completely unrealistic. Indeed, from the beginning of the Thracian campaign the Bulgarians halted their offensive after each successive victory. Rather than pursue the fleeing Turks they rested and waited for supplies to arrive. After each defeat, therefore, the Turks had time to reassemble their scattered forces. Initially, the Bulgarians had made use of a fairly efficient system of field hospitals and had transported their wounded to nearby towns. Of great assistance in this regard were volunteer doctors from Bohemia who had answered the call of their trade union, published in *Národní Politika*, urging them to help their 'Slavic brothers'. However, after a month of fighting

---

[7] Von Hochwächter, *Mit den Türken in der Front*, p. 103.
[8] Halidé Edib, *Memoirs of Halidé Edib*, London 1926, p. 334, cited in Syed Tanvir Wasti, 'The 1912–13 Balkan Wars and the Siege of Edirne', *Middle Eastern Studies*, 40, 4 (2004), pp. 59–78, here p. 60.

Fig. 3 A Bulgarian hospital unit next to the station in Stara Zagora, shortly before heading to the front. Courtesy of Mr Peyo Kolev, lostbulgaria.com.

and the rapid progress of the Thracian campaign, the Bulgarian health system also began to buckle. The absence of prompt medical attention was all the more dangerous as the Bulgarian soldiers had no personal dressings. This reduced the chance of survival of the wounded until they could get to a field hospital. But the final blow to the Bulgarian offensive was dealt by *Vibrio cholerae*, the bacterium that causes cholera. And it was precisely at Çatalca that an epidemic took hold within the Bulgarian ranks.

Paradoxically, the unexpected success of the Bulgarian offensive also benefited the Turks. Because the victories had been so easy, the Bulgarian generals were bolstered in their belief that any battle could be won with a decisive attack using bayonets. Radko Dimitriev, the Bulgarian commander at Çatalca, egged on by the impatient Czar Ferdinand, simply underestimated the resolve and preparedness of the Turks. A French-government observer at the Bulgarian army headquarters, the Polish engineer Józef Lipkowski, mercilessly denounced the mistakes of the Bulgarians:

> In the rush to storm the positions as quickly as possible, no initial artillery attacks were planned. The Bulgarian gunners shelled the entire Turkish front uniformly, from Lake Durusu to Çekmece Bay; at no time did they

PRELUDE: THE BALKANS 1912–1913   49

focus their fire on predetermined targets. The best regiments were sent in to battle [. . .] The result was that those regiments, shelled from both sides, had to retreat having lost half their men, since neither the artillery nor any other unit had covered them [. . .] In addition, as the survivors returned to their own side, the Bulgarian gunners mistook them for the enemy and massacred the lot of them. From the entire regiment only a few dozen soldiers made it back. The fighting at Çatalca was generally dispersed across the entire front, and not one serious attempt was made to break through the Turkish lines at any point.[9]

Dimitriev's tactics were disastrous. More than 10,000 men, including a high proportion of the young, educated officers, were either killed or wounded in the frontal attacks. That was the price the Bulgarians paid for capturing the Turkish positions a few times and only briefly. In the absence of a quick victory, even such an attack-minded commander as Dimitriev had to admit defeat. Soon the number of cholera victims was double the number of dead and wounded. Ultimately, the threat of a mass epidemic within the ranks forced the Bulgarians to accept the truce that the Turks offered as early as on 12 November. The fighting in Thrace ended in early December.

While the Battle of Kirkkilise was still raging, in Macedonia the campaign reached its climax. Here, too, the weaker Turkish forces tried to seize the initiative by attacking the advancing and much stronger Serbs. The clash took place at Kumanovo, and the course of events was similar to what happened in Thrace. After a day of fierce fighting in the rain the Serbs launched a counterattack just before dawn on 24 October, surprising the Turks and forcing them to retreat. Once again the Ottoman forces were saved from humiliating defeat largely because the Serb artillery was unable to advance quickly enough along the appalling roads. After Kumanovo the attackers gradually occupied the northern part of Macedonia. They also entered areas inhabited by Albanians, occupying Pristina, Durrës, and Lezhë, and assisted the Montenegrins stranded at the fortified town of Shkodër. In the territories they seized, the Serbs immediately closed mosques and forced local Muslims to convert to Orthodoxy. Not surprisingly, therefore, they soon found themselves fighting not just the Ottoman army but also an ever-growing legion of Albanian volunteers. The Great War would add a tragic epilogue to the Serb atrocities in Albania. In the winter of 1915–1916, when the defeated Serbs undertook their nightmarish long march to the Adriatic, the Albanians showed them no mercy.

While the Turkish army was repelling Serb and Montenegrin attacks in Macedonia, the Greek army appeared from the rear. Western observers were

---

[9] Józef Lipkowski, *Wojna na Bałkanach przez naocznego świadka i uczestnika wojny*, Warsaw, no date, pp. 130–131, cited in Andrzej Malinowski, *Kwestia macedońska w Bułgarii w latach 1878–1918*, Toruń 2006, pp. 138–139.

full of praise for the offensive strategy of the Greeks, which they claimed was free of the blunders committed by the Serbs and Bulgarians alike. The Greeks did not disperse their forces and were consistent in implementing their predetermined plan. The aim of the campaign was to seize two cities: Salonika (Thessaloniki), the largest in the region, and Ioannina, which the Greeks quickly surrounded but for a long time could not capture. In the former case, in particular, speed was of the essence. Greece had not signed any agreements regarding the division of spoils; it was thus keen to acquire the greatest amount of territory in the shortest possible time in order to strengthen its negotiating position after the war. A race began among the allies. Luckily for the Greeks, the Serb commander Radomir Putnik resisted calls from some of his country's politicians to send Serb forces to Salonika as well, but he could not stop the Bulgarians from doing so. The Serb army in Macedonia included one Bulgarian division, which was ordered to immediately march on Salonika. The Greeks were the first to arrive, however. On 26 October Tahsin Pasha surrendered to Crown Prince Constantine, the successor to the Greek throne. A Greek officer, Filippos Dragoumis, recounted the events of that day:

> The capitulation of Tahsin Pasha and his 35,000 soldiers [in fact, there were approximately 10,000 fewer] brings me no comfort whatsoever. My heart is filled with deep anxiety and I am pessimistic about the future. The Bulgarians are probably not far away and I fear there will be complications with our 'beloved allies'.[10]

The 'beloved allies' were determined. They did not recognize the Turkish surrender to the Greeks and pushed on towards Salonika. Having reached the city they demanded that Tahsin Pasha surrender the Turkish garrison, to which the commander is said to have replied that, with regret, he had only one Salonika at his disposal and had already surrendered it to the Greeks.

With winter approaching, the hostilities became focused on three areas. The Greeks encircled Ioannina, the Montenegrins and Serbs Shkodër, and the Bulgarians besieged Edirne, the largest Turkish fortress and one of the greatest fortifications on the continent. For the Turks, retaining control over Edirne was especially important as it effectively prevented their enemies from using the railway line to Istanbul (the same line used by the famous Orient Express). The siege lasted until the spring of 1913, interrupted by a ceasefire and fruitless negotiations between the Turks and the Serbs and between the Turks and the Bulgarians, in December and January, respectively. Despite the mass exodus of people, a great many civilians, including the consuls of the European powers, remained in the city. Transport paralysis and the speed of the Bulgarian

---

[10] Kyriaki Doukelli, *Geschichte Makedoniens und Thrakiens von den Balkankriegen bis zum Ersten Weltkrieg. Außenpolitische Ereignisse und ihre innenpolitischen Rückwirkungen*, PhD dissertation, Universität Mannheim 2008, p. 254.

PRELUDE: THE BALKANS 1912–1913

offensive prevented evacuation. This badly affected the defenders' prospects, for they had to feed not just an army but also a civilian population. First there was a shortage of salt. For a while chemists were able to produce a salt substitute locally, which tasted the same despite its yellowish tint, but the ingredients needed to make it soon ran out. By February 1913 soldiers' rations had been reduced to 450 grams of poor-quality bread. The black market thrived. A diary of the siege kept by Hafiz Rakim Ertür, a Turkish officer, captured the hopelessness felt by the defenders of Edirne on the eve of surrender:

> The poor soldiers were terribly emaciated. They literally did not have the strength to walk and sat in small groups, covered with snow. I doubt any other nation could endure such adversity. Of course, the besieging forces were not living in luxury either, but most of their troops had warm shelter and decent food. As a result of the glacial cold and paroxysms of hunger, the skin of our soldiers took on an unhealthy dark hue. At night, some would knock on doors asking for a piece of bread – in vain. In those houses the people also went to bed hungry.[11]

Did the besieging forces really have it any better? They were certainly not cut off from the outside world, but the area around Edirne was treeless and the villages had been razed. All the provisions had to be brought in from Bulgaria and Serbia. Snowstorms raged in February, there was a lack of drinking water, and cholera and typhus quickly spread among the troops. The determined Bulgarians, although cold and hungry, shelled the former imperial capital continuously and effectively. Help came in the form of the Serbs, who supported their allies with several batteries of heavy artillery. Thanks to Christian deserters from the Turkish army and civilian refugees, the besieging forces had a good understanding of how the defences were organized. They also had aerial reconnaissance and even carried out raids on the city. The bombs were dropped by the pilots manually and did not cause much damage. Of greater significance was the psychological impact. The modernity of the Bulgarian army must have been all the more impressive as the bombing of Edirne was the first bombing raid in the history of Europe. In February one of the Bulgarian aircraft had to make an emergency landing in the city. The population greeted it with enthusiasm, thinking it was a Turkish machine. Once the misunderstanding had been clarified, the incident must have badly affected the defenders' morale.

For the mercilessly pummelled Turks the heroic defence of Edirne acquired a huge psychological significance. In January the Young Turks carried out another successful coup, the sole purpose of which was to resist the Bulgarians' territorial demands, in other words, the ceding of Edirne. The ceasefire was

[11] Wasti, 'The 1912–13 Balkan Wars', p. 68.

Fig. 4 The triumphant entry of the Bulgarian cavalry into Edirne. Courtesy of Mr Peyo Kolev, lostbulgaria.com.

broken and an attempt was made to rescue the city. On this occasion, too, the Turks attacked frontally. During the storming of the Bulgarian trenches at Çatalca they suffered huge losses without making any noteworthy gains. In parallel the Bulgarians launched an attack on Edirne, losing more than 10,000 men but eventually occupying the city. Edirne fell on 26 March after the exhaustion of food supplies and the loss of ammunition following a fire at the arsenal, which had taken a direct hit. Ioannina surrendered a little earlier, and a month later Shkodër capitulated.

The Second Balkan War

Under pressure from the great powers, all sides in the conflict returned to peace negotiations, which took place in London. A treaty was signed at the end of May, but it satisfied no one. The Turks forfeited almost all of the Sultan's European possessions – four-fifths of the territory and over two-thirds of the population. The new state of Albania, established by the Great Powers, took control of territory to which Montenegro, Serbia, and Greece had claims, yet it did not receive all the lands inhabited by Albanians. Serbia and Greece decided that in return for the land ceded to Albania they deserved the equivalent amount of territory in Macedonia, which they *de facto* occupied. This, in

PRELUDE: THE BALKANS 1912–1913

turn, was unacceptable to Bulgaria. Ultimately, it was Macedonia that would be the cause of the Second Balkan War. Bulgaria demanded territorial gains that were proportional to the losses it had suffered and to its role in the fighting.

Meanwhile, a new participant joined the dispute taking place among the allies. Romania demanded an amount of territory in Dobruja (Dobrogea) equivalent to Bulgaria's territorial gains from the Turks. Although it had not taken part in the war against the Ottoman Empire, Romania felt that the excessive expansion of Bulgaria would disturb the balance of power in the Balkans. The prominent liberal economist Ştefan Zeletin published a bitter satire entitled 'Caracterul naţional al măgarilor' ('The National Character of Donkeys') in which he mercilessly ridiculed the stance taken by his fellow Romanians. One of the characters in the donkey parliament sings a song that mocks and insults the Bulgarians before demanding a 'tip'[12] from them for the territorial gains. It appears that the song reflected not only Zeletin's own views on the matter but also the position of the Bulgarian government, which was outraged at the insolence of its neighbour.

The multilateral negotiations stalled not just because of Romania. The Bulgarians did not want to offer any concessions, and their allies were reluctant to vacate areas that Sofia considered to be its part of Macedonia. Greece and Serbia treated Macedonia as their inviolable property. The policy of national 'proselytism' went full steam ahead. Bulgarian teachers in Macedonia faced a choice: they could begin to teach in Serbian or Greek, they could clear off to Bulgaria (the preferred option), or they would end up in one of the over-crowded prisons in Skopje and Salonika. There were cases of local activists and priests 'vanishing without a trace'. Most often, however, locals were simply forced to 'voluntarily' accede to the dominant nationality. After the fighting had ended, experts from the Carnegie Endowment for International Peace conducted an investigation into war crimes committed by all sides in the conflict. In their report they cited the following account from the Greek part of Macedonia:

> The first care of the Greek officers and soldiers arriving here is to discover if the population of the said village and its environs is Bulgarian or Greek. If the population is pure Bulgarian, the officers order the peasants to 'become Greeks again, that being the condition of a peaceful life'.[13]

---

[12] Ştefan Zeletin, 'The National Character of Donkeys', translated and edited by Marius Turda, in *Discourses of Collective Identity in Central and Southeast Europe (1770–1945). Texts and Commentaries*, vol. 3, part 2. *Modernism: Representations of National Culture*, ed. Ahmet Ersoy, Maciej Górny, and Vangelis Kechriotis, Budapest and New York, NY 2010, pp. 198–205, here pp. 203–204.

[13] George F. Kennan (ed.), *The Other Balkan Wars. A 1913 Carnegie Endowment Inquiry in Retrospect*, Washington, DC 1993, p. 56.

54   THE FRONTS

The Bulgarian press was full of indignation at the real or imagined brutality of
the country's former allies. There were reports of Macedonian children having
been murdered by Greek and Serbian soldiers simply because, in answer to the
question: 'What are you?', they had responded: 'I am Bulgarian.' By the middle
of the year the whole country was completely obsessed with Macedonia. In
June, *Mir*, a Sofia daily, felt impelled to write:

> To get into alliance with your brother with the single thought of swindling
> him, robbing him, taking away from him what had formed the very
> subject of the alliance itself ... after he had suffered the heaviest losses
> and won the bloodiest battles – this is a crime unheard of among nations,
> this is the crime committed by Serbia.[14]

Another war, as yet undeclared, was hanging in the air. It broke out in rather
strange circumstances. In May Greece and Serbia signed a secret agreement
aimed at Sofia. Yet it was Bulgaria that struck first, attacking Serbian and Greek
units in Macedonia on the night of 29 June 1913. The order was issued by the
Czar himself, although some of his military commanders and government
ministers were unaware of it. The chaos in decision-making meant that despite
initial successes the offensive was halted, which inadvertently gave Bulgaria's
opponents time to regroup and counter-attack. Now the Bulgarian government tried to avert conflict with its former allies. The Serbs and Greeks,
however, were not going to wait for the outcome of the power struggle taking
place within the Bulgarian authorities. The war had come at a convenient
moment: they were prepared for it, and the fact that the Bulgarians had dealt
the first blow absolved the Serbs and Greeks of responsibility for breaking the
alliance. The Serbian King, Peter I, could announce the declaration of war with
a clear conscience:

> The Bulgarians, our brothers in blood and faith, our allies, have murdered
> the wounded in a barbarous manner, trampled upon treaties, and broken
> the bonds of friendship and fraternity. They have forgotten the assistance
> lent to them by Serbia and have thus exemplified ingratitude and greed to
> the Slavic peoples and to the whole world. This tragic war has been forced
> upon us.[15]

The retreating Bulgarians were shelled by artillery fire and pursued by the well-
equipped forces of their enemy. Soon the war shifted from Macedonia to the
country's former territory prior to the border changes of the previous year. The
threat of Serbian occupation hung over Sofia.

---

[14] *Mir*, 19 June 1913, cited by Diana Mishkova, 'Friends Turned Foes: Bulgarian National
Attitudes to Neighbours', in *Pride and Prejudice. National Stereotypes in 19th and 20th
Century Europe East to West*, ed. László Kontler, Budapest 1995, p. 176.
[15] Cited in [Friedrich] Immanuel, *Der Balkankrieg 1912/13*, vol. 5, Berlin 1914, pp. 38–39.

After its initial slip-up, the Bulgarian army showed that observers of the First Balkan War had not been wrong to regard it as the most effective army in the region. At the beginning of July IMRO *chetas* controlled by Sofia attacked the Serbian army from the rear. Two weeks later one of the most brilliant commanders of the previous war, General Mikhail Savov, halted the Serbian offensive at Kalimanci before redirecting his forces southwards; at the end of the month he managed to almost completely encircle the Greek army at Kresna Gorge. The Greeks' commander-in-chief, King Constantine, who had succeeded his murdered father a few months earlier, also found himself in danger, but diplomacy saved the Greeks from total disaster. The new Bulgarian government, convinced that war was not winnable, called for a truce.

Two events prompted the Bulgarians to give up the fight. On 10 July Romania decided to collect the 'tip' that it was due. Several hundred thousand men crossed the border and, unperturbed by the weak Bulgarian forces, marched in the direction of Sofia. There was hardly any fighting, and the several thousand Romanians who perished died not from bullet wounds but from disease. The Romanians proved to be relatively civilized occupiers, especially when compared with the other participants of the Balkan Wars. True, Romanian aircraft did carry out raids on Sofia, but only to drop leaflets. Despite the risk of the capital falling to the enemy, the fighting continued in Macedonia and ended only when the Ottoman Empire entered the war. The leader of the Young Turk government, Enver Pasha, with an army of more than 200,000 men at his disposal, captured the Bulgarian positions at Çatalca and then Edirne almost without resistance. This was the first Turkish success after a long sequence of military humiliations and diplomatic failures.

Although it lasted only a month, the Second Balkan War was more bloody than the first. The Bulgarian losses were especially high – on this occasion it was Bulgaria's opponents who had had the numerical advantage. The circumstances under which peace was negotiated were also different. Delegates from all the Balkan states sat down to negotiate in Bucharest, and the participation of the Great Powers was kept to a minimum. Bulgaria had to give up many of the gains it had made a few months earlier as well as cede part of Dobruja (Dobrogea), together with the Tutrakan (Turtucaia) fortress, to Romania. The Turko-Bulgarian negotiations took place not in Bucharest but in Istanbul. In September the Ottoman Empire regained Edirne and much of eastern Thrace, including the fields where the bloodiest battles of the First Balkan War had taken place. Peace in the Balkans would last for one more year.

***

Richard C. Hall, the author of a classic monograph on the Balkan Wars, gave his book the subtitle 'Prelude to the First World War'. In retrospect it is hard to disagree with him. The wars of 1912 and 1913 were indeed conflicts of the same type as the Great War. Similar weapons were used (the Balkan countries did not manufacture weapons and thus had to import them from the same sources as the Great Powers). Commanders in 1914, both in the East and in the West, used the same tactics that had failed in 1912 and 1913. The Turks were the victims of a doctrine that demanded attack at any price and under any conditions, and it was only when they were forced into a desperate defence of Istanbul that their run of defeats finally ended. For the Turkish attackers the attempt to 'regain the initiative' in February 1913 ended in bloody slaughter and brought no benefit whatsoever. The campaign in Thrace, waged on fairly flat terrain with huge numbers of infantry, foreshadowed what was soon to happen in Flanders. When, at Çatalca, waves of Bulgarian infantry attacked with bayonets in the 'Japanese style' (i.e. not in isolation but as a compact mass), they quickly perished in the fire of Turkish machine guns and artillery. Medical units on all sides proved hopelessly inadequate, and in the case of the Ottoman army this was not surprising as they hardly existed at all. Even the Bulgarian field hospitals, which were lauded in the European press and used the services of volunteer doctors from abroad, were unable to help such large numbers of wounded. Observers of the fighting in the Balkans could also draw attention to the questionable value of great fortresses such as Edirne. These proved too massive and too difficult to maintain, not least because they housed a civilian population alongside thousands of soldiers. In the decisive battles of the campaign the Turks ran out of men and artillery, which had been stranded in places such as Edirne, Ioannina, and Shkodër. And yet, ultimately, none of the fortresses was able to withstand a siege.

The Balkan Wars were also 'modern' when it came to the fate of civilians. All sides in the conflict were guilty of war crimes and all, to a varying degree, encountered the problem of civilian refugees who had to be housed, fed, and clothed; medical care was virtually non-existent. None of the participants in the Balkan Wars was prepared for such a challenge: by 1914 the number of Muslim refugees in Anatolia had increased to over 400,000. A total of 170,000 Greeks fled Asia Minor and Bulgaria, while Bulgaria itself had to deal with 150,000 new arrivals, all of them homeless and destitute. The total number of displaced persons is estimated at nearly 900,000.[16] To understand the political, social, and economic drama caused by this mass forced migration – the first in the history of twentieth-century Europe – the figure of 900,000 must be set against other data: approximately 750,000 men in uniform actively participated in both Balkan Wars. After two victories Greece had fewer than 5 million inhabitants, Bulgaria had 4.7 million, and Serbia 4.5 million. No country was able to finance and organize the integration of hundreds of thousands of refugees and provide them with homes and jobs. It is no wonder, then, that

---

[16] Philipp Ther, *The Dark Side of Nation-States. Ethnic Cleansing in Modern Europe*, New York, NY 2014, pp. 113–128, here pp. 117–118. Similarly, Dan Diner, *Das Jahrhundert verstehen. Eine universalhistorische Deutung*, Munich 1999.

PRELUDE: THE BALKANS 1912–1913

people often took justice into their own hands, attacking the 'foreigners' in their new temporary abodes – Orthodox believers instigated pogroms against Muslims in Greece, while Muslims butchered Orthodox believers in Eastern Thrace. Sometimes they were assisted by the local police, at other times by long-standing residents for whom this was a cheap way of eliminating their traditional competitors in commerce or crafts.

Barely two years after the conclusion of peace in Bucharest, an even greater mass of Poles, Jews, Germans, Belarusians, Latvians, Lithuanians, Ukrainians, and Russians would be on the move, fleeing the German and Austro-Hungarian offensives or being forcibly evacuated. The presence of millions of homeless, hungry, unemployed, and helpless people is rightly considered to have been one of the factors behind the Russian revolutions of 1917.

Let us return, however, to Rumelia in the years 1912 and 1913. Although the two Balkan Wars were widely reported in the European press, neither politicians nor military commanders drew any conclusions from them. They did not understand that infectious disease could be almost as dangerous to their armies as enemy bullets. Nor did they understand that there was no point in forcing massed ranks of infantry to attack under machine gun fire. Strategists clung stubbornly to the notion that what counted was 'initiative' and 'morale' and that these flourished most beautifully when attacking with bayonets. Mighty fortresses were constructed and equipped with weaponry and huge numbers of men. Future losses and the need for medical assistance were grossly underestimated. Little was done to relieve civilian populations in areas where the war was taking place.

What was the root of this terrifying short-sightedness? Not everyone ignored the lessons of the Balkan Wars. The problem, however, was that those who drew the right conclusions had no influence over the military. Experts from the Carnegie Endowment for International Peace managed to stir the conscience of a portion of Western public opinion, but – just like Bloch a decade earlier – they could not get through to the generals. Following in Bloch's footsteps, the eminent Polish linguist Jan Baudouin de Courtenay was in no doubt that modern warfare had turned into wild carnage and that a repetition of the Balkan scenario was looming on the horizon, only on a much bigger scale. By comparing the population of each country that had taken part in the Balkan conflict with the number of its dead and wounded, de Courtenay even predicted the losses the European powers would suffer in the coming war. He wasn't far wrong.[17] The response of military experts to prophecies of this kind was straightforward:

> One hears of the horrific atrocities of the Balkan Wars and of the destruction and decline that are sure to follow if another war is waged by such means. This is a huge and dangerous exaggeration. [...] The atrocities of which the parties to the conflict are accused may be explained by the ferocity of the national disputes, the long-standing animosities, and the (at best) semi-

[17] Jan Baudouin de Courtenay, 'Bracia Słowianie', *Krytyka* IX–X 1913, pp. 94–103 and 147–160.

civilized state in which the tribes of the Balkan Peninsula still find themselves. There is no evidence to suggest that a future war will be more bloody and destructive than the one which has just ended. It is therefore wicked to argue on that basis that a future war will be a war of attrition for all its participants. With the greatest of respect to those who seek peace, it is precisely the Balkan Wars which reveal the unassailable truth that only a nation which cherishes its belligerence has the right to exist.[18]

The majority of military experts dismissed the experience of the Balkan Wars simply because those conflicts had taken place in the Balkans.[19] For such disregard the armies of the great powers would pay a heavy price. Barely a year later the 'semi-civilized' Serbs inflicted an embarrassing defeat on the far better equipped Austro-Hungarian army. Shortly thereafter the Turks, humiliated in 1912 and 1913, would force the British to abort their Gallipoli campaign. The Bulgarians, in turn, would almost single-handedly repel the Allied offensives on the Salonika Front.

The Balkan Wars were important for Europe for yet another reason, which we have so far omitted from the narrative because it played virtually no role during the Great War (this issue returned to the Balkans after 1918 and entered European policy in 1939). The main actors in the Balkan conflicts were convinced that the new national borders required the resettlement of people who had suddenly become minorities. Religious, ethnic, and religious-and-ethnic minorities had lived side by side in various places for centuries; the Ottoman Empire had developed numerous ways of co-existing with them and had never entertained the idea of expelling people who had been subjects of the Ottoman Porte ever since the conquest of Constantinople and the Balkans. The Young Turks saw the situation rather differently, as did their Bulgarian, Serbian, and Greek counterparts. This shift of opinion was already evident in the early interpretations of the Balkan Wars, including that of Mahmoud Mukhtar Pasha himself. For this brave and competent Ottoman officer, Christians ceased to belong to the nation. No longer compatriots, they were now seen as potential traitors whose presence endangered the unity of the state.[20]

---

[18] Immanuel, *Der Balkankrieg*, vol. 4, p. 79.

[19] On the French and German conclusions from the Balkan Wars, see Adrian Wettstein, 'The French Military Mind and the Wars before the War', in *The Wars before the Great War. Conflict and International Politics before the Outbreak of the First World War*, ed. Dominik Geppert, William Mulligan, and Andreas Rose, Cambridge 2015, pp. 176–188; and Markus Pöhlmann, 'Between Manchuria and the Marne: The German Army and Its Perception of the Military Conflicts of 1911–1914', in *The Wars before the Great War. Conflict and International Politics before the Outbreak of the First World War*, ed. Dominik Geppert, William Mulligan, and Andreas Rose, Cambridge 2015, pp. 204–229.

[20] Eyal Ginio, 'Paving the Way for Ethnic Cleansing: Eastern Thrace during the Balkan Wars (1912–1913) and Their Aftermath', in *Shatterzone of Empires: Coexistence and Violence in the German, Habsburg, Russian, and Ottoman Borderlands*, ed. Omer Bartov and Eric D. Weitz, Bloomington, IN and Indianapolis, IN 2013, pp. 283–297, here pp. 287–288.

PRELUDE: THE BALKANS 1912–1913

Twentieth-century, i.e. modern, nationalism treated the minorities that arose due to border changes as an onerous obstacle to the construction of a 'normal' state – one such as Germany or Great Britain, where no one was overly concerned about the fortunes of the Poles or Irish. In the Balkans, however, there was a disproportionately high number of 'others' – people who did not conform to the idealized vision of the nation-state. Even if states had managed to rid themselves of large number of such people during the Balkan Wars, the 'problem' was still present and demanded a modern approach. This involved brushing aside tradition, deeply ingrained common law, and nascent international law, none of which countenanced the idea of cross-border displacement. Bulgaria and the Ottoman Empire began to negotiate an 'exchange of populations' in 1913. In September of that year the relevant agreement was signed in Istanbul. It was a thoroughly modern arrangement, for it envisaged the transfer of populations along a 15-kilometre-wide border zone, in other words, it *de facto* sanctioned the flight of tens of thousands of people over the previous two years. It likewise envisaged – six years before the first of the Minority Treaties was signed at Versailles – full protection of the rights of minorities that remained within the territory of the other country. Six months later Greek and Turkish diplomats sat down to negotiate and came up with another treaty; its importance is aptly described by Philipp Ther, who shows that for the Greek and Ottoman leaderships the exchange of populations was a technical, rather than a human or moral, problem:

> In general terms, the negotiations of 1914 were held in a strikingly rational manner. Certainly, diplomats still today must maintain sangfroid, but these negotiations were so coolly conducted that, combined with the population utopias informing them, they launched a remarkable dynamic toward abandoning scruples. Some months after the Greek and Turkish negotiators initially met to discuss Thrace and medium-sized population groups, they were considering about half of Greece and the entire western portion of Asia Minor. The talks concerned the fate of far more than a million people. These were not refugees, but for the most part native citizens. It was not, then, a matter of confirming the status quo resulting from war, but of forward-looking measures.[21]

For now, this fundamentally new approach to the rules of group co-existence and individual human rights did not elicit much interest in 'civilized Europe'. But for the peoples and countries of the Balkan Peninsula the resolution of the conflict and widespread acceptance of the idea of population exchanges set the policy trajectory for the coming years. The ease with which population exchanges had been agreed in 1913 and 1914 raised the hope that after another victorious war it would be relatively easy to cleanse acquired territories. Serbia, which was refused access to the Adriatic in Albania, would increasingly focus

---

[21] Ther, *The Dark Side of Nation-States*, pp. 63–64.

60 THE FRONTS

its expansion in the direction of Austria-Hungary. Greece, whose territorial appetite was satisfied with interest in Macedonia, would now turn towards Asia Minor, where the Greeks would attempt to realize the *Megali Idea* – the reconstruction of a Hellenic empire. And Bulgaria, 'crucified' and 'betrayed' by all of its neighbours, would grab every opportunity to change the status quo. Yet it was the Ottoman Empire that experienced the most profound changes as a result of the Balkan conflict. When it began, the Ottoman Empire was a sprawling multinational state that needed an idea that could unite its diverse provinces, which stretched from present-day Albania to present-day Israel, Palestine, Jordan, and Iraq. When the conflict ended, the Turkish nation-state was already beginning to take shape. Three 'questions' remained to be resolved: the Arab, Armenian, and Greek (the fourth – the Kurdish question – had not yet gained significance). A story by Ömer Seyfeddin entitled 'Primo, Türk Çocuğu' ('Primo, the Turkish Child') provides a fascinating insight into the mental transformation that Turkey underwent during this period. Part one, written during the Italian invasion of Libya, describes the breakdown of a marriage between an enlightened Turkish engineer and an Italian woman who live together in Salonika. Their son, Primo, refuses to go to Italy with his mother and discovers his Turkish identity. In 1914 Seyfeddin published the next chapter of Primo's story. After the occupation of Salonika by the Greeks, the devastated boy, unable to bear the humiliation of his homeland, decides to commit suicide. In the night before the act he has a dream that expresses the hopes of Turkish nationalism:

> [He] walked in broad valleys filled with warm red blood, teeming with millions of enemy corpses [...]. [Then] from the east, from the land of Turan, a crescent rose in the azure sky ... There was a tiny star inside it ... Primo watched in awe ... His feet were wet ... he bent forward and saw that he was immersed in blood up to his knees ... This was it, the blood of the Turk's enemies ... The blood turned into a huge lake ... An endless crimson lake ... reflecting the image of the crescent and the star in the sky ... Ah, our flag comes to life; our real flag, the physical embodiment of our holy flag.[22]

When Seyfeddin published his nationalist parable, 'valleys of blood' in the Balkans were no longer the stuff of fantasy. And, soon, similar images would become a reality for the whole of Europe at war.

---

[22] Ömer Seyfeddin, 'Primo, the Turkish Child', translated and edited by Ahmet Ersoy, in *Discourses of Collective Identity in Central and Southeast Europe (1770–1945). Texts and Commentaries*, vol. 3, part 2. *Modernism: Representations of National Culture*, ed. Ahmet Ersoy, Maciej Górny, and Vangelis Kechriotis, Budapest and New York, NY 2010, pp. 190–197, here p. 197.

3

Before the Leaves Fall from the Trees . . .

Combat Reconnaissance

In the summer of 1914 the armies that went to war in the East were formed according to similar rules and used similar tactics; all were based on conscription and all boasted vast numbers of men. It was believed that the biggest reservoir of human beings offered the best chance of victory. In this respect the statistics were unequivocal: no state could rival Russia. Moreover, even on a peace footing, the Russian army was three times the size of the German army and ten times that of the Austro-Hungarian army. One could attempt to redress this imbalance through training and equipment, and indeed that is what the Central Powers started to do on a large scale, once war had begun. In July 1914 all sides in the conflict – Russia, Germany, Austria-Hungary, and Serbia – had comparable ordnance which did not differ much from the arsenals tested recently on the battlefields of Thrace and Macedonia. Every army had repeating rifles and cavalry carbines, detachments with machine guns, various types of artillery, and standardized uniforms for their infantry – the manufacturers and models may have been different, but the equipment was essentially the same. The cavalry of every army that entered the war retained its colourful, somewhat archaic uniforms; each rode into battle sporting more or less extravagant caps or shakos. When describing the numerical strength of their troops, staff officers would still refer to the number of 'sabres' or 'bayonets'. Of course, certain national specializations were in evidence. Russia, for instance, traditionally had slightly more artillery, although this advantage was negated by the fact that much of it was trapped inside fortresses. In the Czarist army lighter artillery was dominant. Austria-Hungary, in turn, led the way in terms of the number and quality of its super-heavy howitzers. Soon this weapon would prove to be of great service to the Central Powers. In particular, the 305 mm calibre howitzer manufactured in the Škoda factory would prove so effective that it would be 'borrowed' by both Germany and the Ottoman Empire for use on the Western and Mesopotamian fronts, respectively.

These essentially minor differences in the countries' armaments programmes were rarely noticed, and if they were, no one concluded that they had any far-reaching implications. Instead, military commanders put their faith in the power of massed ranks of infantry and cavalry, and this faith inclined them to bet on a Russian victory, especially if the Central Powers had to fight on two or three fronts (as indeed happened). For this reason the Austro-Hungarian and German generals assumed that only together could they keep Russia at bay while in the meantime turning their attention to France. They believed that so long as the main German forces were engaged in the West they could only slow down, but not stop, the Russian 'steam-roller'. What this clearly implied was that, in the first weeks of the war, time would play a decisive role. The calculation made sense, but only if the war in the West ended quickly (a view widely held, and not just by the Central Powers). Kaiser Wilhelm II promised his soldiers that they would return home before the leaves fell from the trees; the war in the West would be resolved before Russia could mobilize, leaving Germany able to negotiate from a position of strength.

This whole scenario proved entirely fanciful, however. First, the Russian mobilization proceeded much faster than the German and Austro-Hungarian general staffs had imagined. Although in several dozen(!) provinces there were incidents involving rebellious conscripts, and across the country hundreds died as the authorities quelled unrest, the numbers were trivial given that mobilization involved millions of people. Besides, as a result of French pressure, the Russians decided to launch a rapid offensive even before they had put all their units together. They changed their plan of attack for the same reason. Initially, the Russians had believed that their main enemy was the Habsburg monarchy. Yet now they wanted to carry out two attacks simultaneously – on both Austria-Hungary and Germany. Russian ordnance maps denoted these attacks with the letters 'A' (Avstriya) and 'G' (Gyermaniya). Then, after securing a line of departure for their next offensive, the Russian troops were to head straight for Berlin.

For the moment, however, it was assumed that Austria-Hungary would shoulder the main burden of engaging the Russians while Germany dealt with France. Russia's numerical advantage compared with the forces of the Habsburg monarchy was considerable. Nevertheless, in keeping with the tenets of the offensive doctrine, the Chief of the General Staff, Conrad von Hötzendorf, intended to attack. His intention was to push into the Kingdom of Poland and he hoped that Germany would engage some of the enemy forces. A few years before the war von Hötzendorf had exacted a promise from the German Chief of the General Staff, Helmuth von Moltke, that, if the Russians did not deploy some of their forces in East Prussia, Germany would enter the Kingdom of Poland and attack in the direction of the Narew River. This rather dubious pledge – the two men had not even discussed the size of the promised relief offensive – allowed von Hötzendorf to indulge in his favourite activity: devising plans for military operations for which he lacked sufficient resources.

Austro-Hungarian strategic thought was both rigid and full of fantasy; it was a faithful reflection of von Hötzendorf's complex personality. The Chief of the General Staff was an outstanding theorist, a mentor to a whole generation of army officers, and an authority of international repute. His limited practical experience left an indelible mark on the strategy of the Habsburg monarchy. He combined a passion for great and brilliant military campaigns with an urge to humiliate the 'regicidal' Serbs. For this reason von Hötzendorf stubbornly and irrespective of the circumstances pressed for an attack on Serbia, denoted in the operational plans with the letter 'B' (for 'Balkans'). He did not alter his position even when it became obvious that Russia would also enter the war, forcing the monarchy to launch plan 'R'. The likelihood of a Serb offensive on Austro-Hungarian territory was negligible, but a Russian attack was certain. Despite this, the decision was taken to divide the Austro-Hungarian forces: against the Serbs the monarchy would put up an army slightly stronger than that of its opponent; against the Russians it would put up a much weaker one. On the other hand, von Hötzendorf rejected the idea of immediately retreating to the Carpathians, temporarily sacrificing Galicia to the Russians in order to buy time. He did not wish to cede the initiative on any front. In the event of an emergency, von Hötzendorf had a very complicated and ambitious plan that involved transferring strategic reserve units by train to the south, and, if need be, to Galicia in the north. The problem was that such a huge transport operation required appropriate logistics and meant that the decision could not be quickly reversed. Every procedure had to be followed to the letter, according to an extremely detailed timetable.[1] In other words, reserve units sent to the border with Serbia had to arrive there first before they could be loaded back onto trains and returned north – to where the Russians had crossed the border. In the event these units reached neither front on time; instead, they languished on trains somewhere between Belgrade and Stanisławów (today Ivano-Frankivsk).

Despite the weakness of its forces, Austria-Hungary intended to go on the offensive on every front. Since the Russians had the same intention, a very interesting situation developed. All the participants of the war in the East, except for Serbia, launched an offensive or – like the Germans in East Prussia – were about to do so when they themselves were attacked. They all had a rough idea of their opponent's operational plans, but little information about its current activities. At the beginning of the war, aerial reconnaissance was still fairly unreliable and the more conservative commanders treated aircraft with a high degree of distrust. What remained was the traditional approach, that is, cavalry reconnaissance.

---

[1] Alexander Watson, *Ring of Steel. Germany and Austria-Hungary in World War I*, New York, NY 2014, pp. 112–118.

64 THE FRONTS

This first phase of the conflict largely corresponded to the way in which the war had been imagined by commanders and soldiers alike – somewhat akin to an adventure novel. A young Pole by the name of Franciszek Bratek-Kozłowski accidentally witnessed one of the first clashes on the German–Russian border:

> Suddenly we saw Germans on great bay horses, sabres drawn, charging into a large orchard by the road to the Szczytniki estate [in the Kalisz district], pursued by Cossacks on their small horses. A fight began; two of the Germans were hacked to death, six were wounded, and the rest fled.[2]

Both sides simultaneously sent dozens of squadrons, even entire cavalry divisions, on reconnaissance. The clashes that ensued were everywhere similar, but their scale and the number of victims was often much greater than in the German–Cossack skirmish described above. For example, on the Zbruch River there occurred fierce clashes between the Cossacks and sizeable detachments of the Royal Hungarian Hussars. After crossing the river, the Hungarians encountered a strong unit of Russian cavalry, which had evidently also been sent on reconnaissance. They dispersed it and gave chase to the edge of a forest in which Russian machine gunners had taken up concealed positions. Under fire, the Hungarians retreated to the Galician side and reported to their HQ that 'the Russian border troops have already concentrated their forces and remain in a state of combat readiness from the Vistula to the Dniester rivers'.[3] They had not seen any other units apart from those border troops. The Hungarian reconnaissance force suffered considerable losses, especially when compared with the gains: it merely learned that the Russian army was combat-ready nearly two weeks after Austria-Hungary had declared war on the Romanov empire. This hardly warranted sending troops across the border.

Generally, the results of reconnaissance were hugely disappointing. In the summer of 1914 everyone lacked reliable information about the preparations of the enemy. What is interesting is that the Habsburg monarchy's armed forces were slow to learn, if at all. In the spring of 1915 Austrian generals complained that the reconnaissance offered by the Russian cavalry was 'excellent – they know everything, down to the very last detail', whereas the Austrians' own intelligence efforts produced 'zero' results. The Habsburg troops were saved by the Russians' astonishing weakness when it came to cryptography: radio correspondence within the Czar's army was decoded by the Austrian military command without any difficulty.[4]

---

[2] Franciszek Bratek-Kozłowski, *Życie z bagnetem i lancetem. Wspomnienia—refleksje*, Toronto 1989, p. 14.

[3] Hermann Stegemann, *Geschichte des Krieges*, vol. 1, Stuttgart and Berlin 1917, p. 272.

[4] Martin Schmitz, 'Tapfer, zäh und schlecht geführt. Kriegserfahrungen österreichisch-ungarischer Offiziere mit den russischen Gegnern 1914–1917', in *Jenseits des Schützengrabens. Der Erste Weltkrieg im Osten: Erfahrung – Wahrnehmung – Kontext*, ed. Bernhard Bachinger and Wolfram Dornik, Innsbruck 2013, pp. 45–63, here p. 54.

Under such circumstances a wait-and-see attitude might have been in order, but this is not what was taught in the military academies. Instead, officers were instructed to take the initiative and to impose their own war plan on the enemy, especially as every strategist advocated offensive action as the surest way to success. Thus, the first weeks of the war witnessed four huge offensives, each involving hundreds of thousands of men on each side. The Austrians attacked Serbia from the north-west in the direction of Kragujevac, where the Serbian military headquarters and supply base were located. They also entered the Kingdom of Poland and advanced on Lublin. At the same time, two Russian armies attacked East Prussia. A few days later several hundred thousand Russians crossed the Zbruch River and entered Galicia. Clearly, the information that the heroic Hungarian Hussars had managed to gather, at great cost to themselves, was worth very little.

The First Offensives

As mentioned earlier, the Serbian Chief of the General Staff, Radomir Putnik, who was soon to earn a well-deserved reputation, almost missed the war entirely. When, following his adventures with the Hungarian gendarmerie, he finally returned home, the Serbian army was already mobilized and had moved north from Macedonia, where it had been guarding its recent gains. On 12 August, as the Austro-Hungarian 5th and 6th Armies crossed the Drina River into Serbia, Putnik regrouped his forces and prepared to face the enemy at the Čer plateau. The Serbs used a manoeuvre they had rehearsed two years previously in the war against Turkey: attack by night. The effect was spectacular. Chaos broke out in the ranks of the invaders. The Serbs attacked again, not giving the enemy time to rest and regroup. Stepa Stepanović, the Serb commander at Čer, skilfully urged his subordinates into the fray. Before the battle his soldiers were read the following order:

> Heroes, I have come to say this to you. I know that you are exhausted by two wars, and I know your wounds have not yet healed. That is why I release from his oath any man who wishes to go home. But any man who wishes to fight, let him stay with me in the trenches to defend the honour of our fatherland.[5]

The emptiness of this promise must have been plain to everyone, but it fulfilled its purpose. Although the Serbs had to endure the same level of fatigue and lack of provisions as their opponent, they were more battle-hardened and willing to fight. The Austro-Hungarian commander, General Oskar Potiorek, also made

---

[5] Cited in Daniela Schanes, *Serbien im Ersten Weltkrieg. Feind- und Kriegdarstellungen in österreichisch-ungarischen, deutschen und serbischen Selbstzeugnissen*, Frankfurt am Main 2011, p. 121.

the mistake of spreading his forces too thinly. At the decisive moment the 6th Army was unable to come to the aid of the fighting 5th Army. On 16 August the invaders failed to repel the Serbs south of Šabac, a town that would soon earn a grim reputation. Panic took hold among the Austro-Hungarian troops fighting there. Barely a week later Serbia was free.

As the first victory of the Entente Powers was reaching its conclusion in Serbia, in distant East Prussia an almost identical operation was taking place, albeit on a much larger scale. Two Russian armies commanded by two generals, Pavel Rennenkampf and Alexander Samsonov, who had hated each other ever since the war with Japan, attacked from the north-east and south. Communication between them was hindered not only by the Germans but also by the natural obstacle of the Masurian Lakes. Good organization and modern technology might have helped, yet both were lacking. Soon after marching out, Samsonov stopped receiving telegrams from the General Staff. It was only a few days later that a Russian officer, who happened to be visiting Warsaw on another matter, discovered an entire file of unsent messages in the local telegraph office. The staff at the office explained to the officer that there was no direct connection to Samsonov's headquarters and that all the other lines were overloaded. In East Prussia the situation was hardly any better. Although the Russian divisions used modern radio communications, their messages were not encrypted and thus easily fell into the hands of the Germans. The latter, meanwhile, moved around using interior lines, which were naturally shorter and operated by railwaymen with many years of experience. East Prussia was poor and agricultural, but one element of its infrastructure was state of the art: the railway network. Six railway lines came out of Allenstein (today Olsztyn), a town lying deep in the provinces. Warsaw, with nearly one million inhabitants, had only three lines going north, one of which ended in Ostrołęka, which was still 50 kilometres short of the border. But, in any case, Samsonov's troops alighted dozens of kilometres before the border and many were not even transported by train.

The first major clashes involving General Rennenkampf's 1st Army took place at Gumbinnen and Stallupöhnen on 17 August. In both battles the weaker German forces managed to inflict significant losses on the Russians. Despite this, the German commander in East Prussia, Maximilian von Prittwitz, decided that the enemy had too great an advantage and ordered his troops to retreat across the Vistula. This step was contrary to German plans and also broke the promise given to the Austro-Hungarians, since the German relief offensive in the Kingdom of Poland would now be impossible to execute. The evacuation of East Prussia would mean that Austria-Hungary received no German support. In the event, however, this is not what happened. Barely four days after the Supreme Army Command had received news of his intentions, Prittwitz was summarily dismissed. He was replaced by General Paul von Hindenburg, who became the new German commander in East Prussia, with General Erich Ludendorff as his chief of staff. The retreat was halted. Since

Fig. 5 A Bulgarian widow with a child. Thrace. Courtesy of Mr Peyo Kolev, lostbulgaria.com.

Fig. 6 The town of Lyck (today Ełk) destroyed during the fighting between Germany and Russia in 1914. Courtesy of the Herder-Institut, Marburg, Bildarchiv.

Rennenkampf's army was moving westwards at a snail's pace, Hindenburg and Ludendorff decided to launch a concentrated attack against Samsonov's 2nd Army with all the troops they could muster. Samsonov, having encountered little resistance, pushed north, even occupying Allenstein for a brief period. The Russians did not ponder the sudden weakness of the German defences and also neglected their reconnaissance activities. Soon Samsonov's army was almost completely surrounded. The Russian commander belatedly realized that he had fallen into a trap set by Hindenburg and Ludendorff. The fighting lasted a week and ended on 31 August. Nearly 100,000 Russians were captured, while the numbers of dead, wounded, and missing were similar to the losses suffered by the Austro-Hungarians in Serbia – more than 30,000 men. Samsonov and some of his officers tried to break through the cordon on their own. During his escape through the Masurian forests the hapless commander decided to commit suicide. One of his fellow fugitives recalled: 'None of the staff officers felt compelled to kneel by the corpse of General Samsonov and bid him farewell with the words: You are not to blame, only we are!'[6]

In actual fact Samsonov was not the only person responsible for the defeat. Also culpable was his great rival, who at the decisive moment did not come to Samsonov's aid. General Rennenkampf displayed such indolence in the subsequent stages of the East Prussian campaign that many observers considered his behaviour to be tantamount to sabotage (an absurdity seemingly corroborated by his German heritage). When the fate of the 2nd Army was being sealed in the vicinity of Allenstein, Rennenkampf was quietly waiting for the Germans to arrive. Although he managed to avoid being encircled during the week-long battle on the Masurian Lakes, he suffered huge losses during the retreat. By the middle of September East Prussia was almost entirely free of Russian troops. Hindenburg's victory was blown out of all proportion and completely severed from its original context, becoming in subsequent decades a universal source of pride for German nationalists. It was Erich Ludendorff who came up with the idea of naming the first of the victorious clashes the 'Battle of Tannenberg'. Justifying his proposal after the war, he asked rhetorically: 'Is any German, as then, ever going to allow the Lithuanian, and more especially the Pole, to take advantage of our misfortune and to do us violence? Are centuries of old German culture to be lost?'[7]

The wily general faithfully – though perhaps unconsciously – repeated the rhetorical device used by, among others, Polish deputies in the Russian Duma when they pledged undying loyalty to the Czar following the outbreak of the war, which was seen as a part of the continuous Slavo-German struggle. The difference lay in the fact that the German chauvinist coined the phrase 'Battle of Tannenberg' after the victory in the environs of Allenstein. That the 'revenge for the first battle

---

[6] Rudolf von Wehrt, *Tannenberg. Wie Hindenburg die Russen schlug*, Berlin 1934, p. 272.

[7] Erich Ludendorff, *Ludendorff's Own Story, August 1914–November 1918*, New York, NY 1919, vol. 1. p. 68.

† Генералъ-отъ-кавалеріи
Алекоандръ Васильевичъ
САМСОНОВЪ.

Во время упорнаго сраженія съ нѣмцами въ Восточной Пруссіи погибъ генералъ-отъ-кавалеріи Самсоновъ. Покойный родился въ 1859 году, получилъ образованіе въ Кіевской военной гимназіи, Николаевскомъ кавалерійскомъ училищѣ и Николаевской академіи генеральнаго штаба.

Fig. 7 Obituary of General Alexander Samsonov, published at the end of August 1914 in the journal *Razvedchik*. The Russian press did not delve into the circumstances of his death, merely stating that he was killed in action in East Prussia. Courtesy of Mariusz Kulik.

of Tannenberg' (fought between Poland–Lithuania and the Teutonic Knights in the fifteenth century) was exacted on a completely different opponent did not bother the general at all, and rightly so. Ludendorff had an excellent nose for modern propaganda, and the press immediately bought his ridiculous historical parallel; it was perfectly in tune with popular notions about the Middle Ages as the cradle of modern nationalism.

At the same time as the offensives in Serbia and East Prussia, the Austro-Hungarian army attacked Lublin. Just prior to this, a smaller German force had captured the town of Kalisz and set it ablaze, while a Polish rifle unit of the Austrian army led Józef Piłsudski had entered Kielce. On 21 August General Viktor Dankl's 1st Army crossed the Tanew River, which marked the border, and then repelled the Russian 4th Army at Kraśnik in a bloody three-day battle. To the east of Dankl's forces the 4th Army of General Moritz Auffenberg entered the territory of Russia, winning the Battle of Komarów on 26 August–2 September. Yet these victories brought Austria-Hungary no benefit whatsoever. Even before the Battle of Komarów was over the Russian offensive in Eastern Galicia had

Fig. 8 A patriotic postcard from Neidenburg (today Nidzica) reflecting both the enormity of the devastation caused by the Russian invasion and the magnitude of the German success, measured by the number of prisoners of war. Above all, however, it pays tribute to the victors of the East Prussian campaign. Courtesy of the Herder-Institut, Marburg, Bildarchiv.

reached the provincial capital. On the night of 2 September Lwów (L'viv, Lemberg) was evacuated.

The failure in Galicia turned the hitherto successful Austro-Hungarian advance on Lublin into a ghastly experience. One of its participants was Stanisław Kawczak, a soldier of the 20th Infantry Regiment, I Corps (Cracow) of General Dankl's 1st Army, who described how the offensive became a nightmarish rout:

> We pick ourselves up and run [...]. The Russians are pursuing us. I run like a hare, seemingly flying in the air because I do not feel the ground under my feet. Onwards another hundred yards before I fall over, half-alive, into a ditch. It's full of soldiers from our regiment, all crouching down. [...] We move from place to place. All sense of time and space is lost. At night we march; during the day – guns and grenades. [...] On a hillock dozens of people throw themselves at each other; a 'Slovak' strips naked and with terrifying laugh that makes my hair stand on end beckons me towards him, shouting: 'Come here, comrade!' I see a captain of the 100th Regiment shoot himself in the head with a revolver.[8]

---

[8] Stanisław Kawczak, *Milknące echa. Wspomnienia z wojny 1914–1920*, Warsaw 1991, pp. 33, 35, and 40.

In the rearguard of the retreating Austro-Hungarian army fought Józef Piłsudski's Legionnaires. They were mostly young men from the intelligentsia who would leave an exceptionally rich legacy of memoirs and reminiscences. Many of them went to war not so much in search of glory as of adventure, which was all the more colourful and literary because in the first weeks of the conflict their principal opponents were the Cossacks. When the Legionnaires entered the Kingdom of Poland at the beginning of August they encountered little resistance from the Russians. Their retreat under pressure from the powerful Russian armies was the first time they experienced truly modern warfare, such as the effects of machine gun fire:

> Several bodies were thrashing about on the ground in convulsions. Faces twisted, deathly green . . . Eyes becoming web-like . . . Heads with detached skulls, throats slashed as if with a razor . . . The corpses tumbled down one after another. Every now and then one of the soldiers would slip from the mound, arms outstretched, and fall to the ground in spasms. Whoever stuck his head above the parapet would perish. The moans of the wounded and the death rattle of the dying rang out in an instant. Blood streamed over the earth, turning the bottom of the trench into rust-coloured mud, while the machine guns carried on. The gunfire lasted a good five minutes and the result was seven corpses, horrible and cold.[9]

Finally, at the end of September, the Legionnaires also found themselves on the Galician side of the border. Here they encountered fresh Austro-Hungarian divisions readying themselves for another attack. The war, which only a few days earlier they had witnessed for the first time in all its cruelty, now revealed its true scale:

> At 6.00 a.m. we all set off, but where we are going we do not know. Only now do we realize the potency of war – on the parallel expanses of ground, as far as the eye can see, stand armies: infantry, cavalry, artillery. At around 10.00 a.m. we rest in the field – there are thousands of us.[10]

The retreat from the Kingdom of Poland would not have been so chaotic were it not for the Russian invasion of Eastern Galicia. This was the only successful summer offensive on the Eastern Front. Austro-Hungarian cavalry reconnaissance had failed to establish that sizeable Russian forces were stationed on the Zbruch River, ready to march on Lwów. But even if Conrad von Hötzendorf had been privy to this information it is by no means certain that it would have affected his plans. The proponents of von Hötzendorf's military talent often emphasized the boldness of his manoeuvres and the courage with which he led his perennially outnumbered forces. On the outskirts of Lwów the

---

[9] Cited in Urszula Oettingen, *Czarkowy – na drodze do niepodległości*, part 1. *Bój 16–24 września 1914 r.*, Kielce 2002, p. 100.

[10] From the diary of Dr Ryszard Łączyński, cited in Oettingen, *Czarkowy*, p. 148.

Russians held an overwhelming advantage and the only hope left for the defenders was the immediate arrival of the 2nd Army from the Serbian front, a hope that was to be in vain. Meanwhile, the holes were patched up in whichever way possible. Already at the beginning of September von Hötzendorf transferred some of the forces being withdrawn from the Kingdom of Poland to Eastern Galicia, launching an immediate counter-offensive. Once again the monarchy's forces were significantly weaker than those of the Russians and once again they were defeated. On 11 September von Hötzendorf ordered his exhausted troops to disengage from the enemy and swiftly retreat across the San River. Another quick march soon turned into a chaotic escape. In panic, some of the retreating Austro-Hungarian forces passed the designated positions and stopped a few kilometres further west. Finally, in the middle of September, the Austrian–Russian front established itself along a line that went from Radom in the north-west, through Tarnów in Galicia, to the north-eastern part of Máramaros County (nowadays the vicinity of Sighetu Marmației on the Romanian–Ukrainian border). Cracow was threatened with siege. The historian Jan Dąbrowski, a native of the city, noted on 21 September: 'There is a growing sense of pessimism. People are already entertaining the possibility of Russian rule. Tension is reaching its peak, for we shall see some sort of resolution in the coming days.'[11] In the area controlled by the Russians there remained the modern and well-defended fortress of Przemyśl. Over the next few months the fortress would become the main source of hope and main focus for public opinion in the Habsburg monarchy.

The balance-sheet of the four summer offensives was frightening. The Russian and Austrian losses, in particular, surpassed people's expectations of what the coming war would be like. The 400,000 killed, injured, and captured equated to approximately one-fifth of the losses suffered by the Habsburg monarchy in the war overall. The Russian losses were similar, and their scale is worth putting into context: the number of Russian soldiers captured at the Battle of Tannenberg was comparable to the number of Germans captured at Stalingrad in the winter of 1943. Both sides lost huge amounts of equipment – the Russians as a result of defeat in East Prussia, and the Austrians during the retreat from Galicia and Serbia. Even professional military men had not been prepared for such slaughter. Stanisław Kawczak described a review of the remnants of the 20th Infantry Regiment after it had returned from its abortive mission to the Kingdom of Poland:

> He counted us. All together, including the auxiliary staff, doctors and clerks, there were 108 of us, quite clearly one hundred and eight. Out of three thousand soldiers after less than one month of war [. . .]. I saw how

[11] Jan Dąbrowski, *Dziennik 1914–1918*, ed. Jerzy Zdrada and Elżbieta Dąbrowska, Cracow 1977, p. 39.

Colonel Puchalski went aside and ... wiped his eyes thoroughly with a handkerchief.[12]

Staff officers, convinced that the war would be short, had thrown their best men and equipment into the summer offensives. Their miscalculation meant that they now had to quickly rebuild their decimated armies and corps. The human losses could be redressed, provided that the conscription and recruiting authorities were working smoothly. At the same time, training became less thorough and the social profile of armies changed (before the war, armies usually recruited farmers and peasants, whereas workers and members of the intelligentsia often received deferrals). However, it was not possible to quickly train new officers. As a result, by the autumn of 1914 the lack of professional military personnel had already become apparent. A review of the 28th Prague Infantry Regiment at the beginning of September revealed there to be only nineteen active officers ready for duty. In the first autumn of the war, reservists (civilians) were already beginning to replace professional officers.

For the armies of the Habsburg monarchy this gave rise to a particular problem that was unknown in other armed forces. In general the language of command was German, while in a minority of units – i.e. the Royal Hungarian Honvéd (Magyar Királyi Honvédség) – Hungarian was used. Since lower-level recruits spoke a multitude of different languages, additional regulations were introduced: in the infantry the language of command (*Kommandosprache*) included around eighty words which officers and NCOs needed to know in order to give orders to their subordinates. Then there was the regiment language (*Regimentssprache*), which included around 400 words in a language other than German, which officers and NCOs needed to know if that language was spoken by at least 20 per cent of soldiers in the regiment. In practice the situation was rather different. Commanders' attempts to speak the languages of their subordinates were invariably appalling. 'For their part non-German soldiers rarely succeeded in mastering *Kommandosprache*, which in their utterances took on a life of its own, unexpectedly acquiring the sound and form of slang – as useless as the *Regimentssprache* of most officers.'[13] The death of huge numbers of officers and NCOs – their replacements had long since forgotten *Kommandosprache* and *Regimentssprache*, even if they had vaguely learnt them years ago when training as reservists – reduced communication within the armed forces to gestures and shouts. Many anecdotes arose on this subject. An Austrian NCO commanding a four-person communications unit explained to a German colleague the specific nature of his mission, which was to command three soldiers of the monarchy: 'One is a Bosnian, the other a Czech, and the third is a Hungarian. Not one of them understands German. They are even unable to communicate with each other. I can only issue orders by

---

[12] Kawczak, *Milknące echa*, p. 42.

[13] Jan Rydel, *W służbie cesarza i króla. Generałowie i admirałowie narodowości polskiej w siłach zbrojnych Austro-Węgier w latach 1868–1918*, Cracow 2001, pp. 81–85, here p. 85.

74   THE FRONTS

gesticulating. Sometimes I would like to hang all three of them from a telegraph pole.'[14]

In Russia the situation was tense for other reasons. Students were exempted from military service. Thus, in order to tap this well of potential reserve officers, it was necessary to wait until they had undergone training. Meanwhile, this led to a sharp decline in the quality of command, but not only that. Both monarchies rightly considered their officer corps to be the mainstay of royal power. The increasing use of reservists of uncertain political leanings meant that this situation gradually began to change.

The Second Wave

Unperturbed by losses, Russia, Germany, and Austria-Hungary prepared themselves for further offensives. Conrad von Hötzendorf's main goal was now to rescue the besieged Przemyśl and to regain Lwów. The Central Powers intended to achieve this goal by attacking on two fronts: in the Kingdom of Poland the German and Austro-Hungarian armies marched in the direction of Warsaw and Dęblin (Ivangorod); in Eastern Galicia the Austro-Hungarian offensive reached the San River, briefly liberating Przemyśl. The Germans, under the command of General August von Mackensen, took the city of Łódź in the Kingdom of Poland on 6 December, but this marked the end of the Central Powers' successes. The Russian forces, which were twice as strong, repelled the attackers on both fronts, causing heavy losses. By now it had become patently obvious that the war was turning into mindless unmitigated slaughter. The most shocking of all the clashes was the Austro-Hungarian 4th Army's completely unnecessary attempt, repeated over several days, to force its way across the San River. This offensive 'at any cost' soon transformed into another 'disengagement from the enemy'. Once again the retreat was hardly one of the best organized:

> On the baggage trains the artillery and ammunition parks began to press violently, shouting and cursing in every possible language as they struggled, cutting themselves a road by sheer weight and unscrupulousness. The infantry and machine guns began to come in amongst the baggage trains and artillery. In a word, with the army fallen on top of its own baggage trains, the retreat began to take on a character of a disorderly flight in which each man tried to be the first in order to be further from the enemy.[15]

The campaign took place almost exactly two years after the Bulgarian offensive in Eastern Thrace, under similar weather conditions and with only slightly better medical care. To make matters worse, there was an outbreak of cholera and typhus in the Austro-Hungarian ranks. Caring for the sick and wounded

---

[14] Gerhard Velburg, *Rumänische Etappe. Der Weltkrieg, wie ich ihn sah*, Minden 1930, p. 126.
[15] Joseph Pilsudski [Józef Piłsudski], *The Memories of a Polish Revolutionary and Soldier*, translated by Darsie Rutherford Gillie, New York, NY 1931, p. 232.

during constant marches was especially difficult. Sławoj Felicjan Składkowski, a doctor assigned to the Legionnaires who would later become Prime Minister of the Second Polish Republic, described the second retreat from the Kingdom of Poland as one of the most tragic experiences of the first year of the war:

> As we passed one of the barns we noticed a Red Cross flag that had been left there by the Austrians. We decided to put it onto our cart. Just as we began to roll up the flag we heard groans and muffled voices coming from the barn. We ran in to look. Janek shone his torch . . . we froze. The whole barn, laid out with straw, was filled with the most terribly wounded soldiers whom the Austrians had abandoned. Suddenly, in various languages: Polish, German, Czech, Hungarian, they began to cry out to us. 'Help! Water! Save us!' were the words that came from this grave of still-alive victims. Some moved from their places and started crawling towards us through the straw. There were around a hundred wounded, if not more. There was no question of taking them with us.[16]

A similar scene was described by a Hungarian soldier. Fighting on the front line, he and his unit passed over heaps of dead and wounded:

> I cannot forgive my lack of heart as I made my way through the narrow trenches, trampling on the wounded. We ran – I remember – over silent corpses, honouring their heroic death regardless of nationality or uniform. With our boots we trod on their warm, soft, massacred, bleeding bodies. The wounded, both the Russians and our own, lying between the corpses or sitting among them, busy tending to their own wounds, looked at us with horror: a band of rampaging barbarians. They begged us not to trample on their defenceless bodies. But we had to push on, ruthlessly, risking that we would trample on them, because we had not yet reached our goal.[17]

We spare the reader the rest of the description.

In November and December unrelenting clashes took place along the Galician front and in the Polish Kingdom. The Russians drew near to Cracow on several occasions. By 5 December they were 12 kilometres from the Market Square. The city readied its defences:

> Villages within a few kilometres of the city have been set on fire so as not to give shelter to the enemy; their inhabitants have been evacuated. The whole area is protected by a ring of new forts, earthworks, etc. Anyone who does not have a three-month supply of food is being expelled from the city. All the grocery shops have been closed for a few days now. This is to force

---

[16] Sławoj Felicjan Składkowski, *Moja służba w Brygadzie. Pamiętnik polowy*, Warsaw 1990, pp. 33–34.

[17] Ferenc Pollmann, 'Die Ostfront des "Großen Krieges" – aus ungarischer Perspektive', in *Jenseits des Schützengrabens. Der Erste Weltkrieg im Osten: Erfahrung – Wahrnehmung – Kontext*, ed. Bernhard Bachinger and Wolfram Dornik, Innsbruck 2013, pp. 87–104, here p. 103 n.

76   THE FRONTS

people without provisions to leave the city and also to protect the supplies from being bought out by the thousands of troops passing through Cracow. Cafés and restaurants are open for only a couple of hours and close at 9 p.m. Soldiers are being billeted in people's homes.[18]

Just as on the Marne a few months earlier, so in Western Galicia hotel carriages ferried the heavily wounded from the front to the rear and delivered reinforcements and ammunition in the opposite direction. The Russians still had the numerical advantage, particularly as Conrad von Hötzendorf's ambitious operations had decimated his troops. However, the terrain was on the side of the defenders. Behind them they had a large fortified city with a good transport infrastructure. Supply problems had ended, which was not just thanks to the work of the army intendants. The army enjoyed the support of the civilian population. In the Małopolska and Podkarpacie regions soldiers were welcomed. In December the Austro-Hungarian counter-offensive was launched from Cracow. The fighting lasted until Christmas. It was only in the final week of 1914 that the war in Galicia became briefly similar to the battles on the Western Front. Both sides dug in along a front that bulged slightly to the west, stretching from Przasnysz in the north to Vatra Dornei in Bukovina in the south-east.

CHEMICAL WARFARE

At the outbreak of the war both the Germans and the French possessed chemical weapons. Despite such weapons having been prohibited under the Second Hague Declaration of 1899, neither side had any particular qualms about using them. The problem was rather that these weapons were not very effective. The chemical substances that were used on the fronts from as early as 1914 were derivatives of tear gas. The French employed them in August 1914, the Germans slightly later. In both cases the advocates of chemical warfare were disappointed: the new weapons were not as potent as had been hoped. The first German gas attack on the Western Front was such a failure that the enemy learned of it only after the war had ended. Yet, despite these setbacks, gas shell trials continued. The Germans used them on the Eastern Front at Bolimów in the Skierniewice district towards the end of January 1915. They attacked the Russian positions with shells containing benzyl and xylyl bromide, a powerful tear gas. Ludendorff's plan was unsuccessful, however, as the low temperatures prevented the gas from spreading, as a result of which the Russian artillery was unaffected. Instead of easily capturing enemy trenches manned by temporarily blinded soldiers, the Germans suffered heavy losses and had to retreat after the Russian counterattack. The *New York Times* correspondent reported that the wounded Russian soldiers in the hospital in Żyrardów were so infused with chemicals that the doctors had to interrupt their work to get some fresh air.[19]

---

[18] Dąbrowski, *Dziennik 1914–1918*, p. 46.
[19] Perceval Gibbon, 'Hurricane of Fire in Bolimow Battle', *New York Times*, 12 February 1915, p. 3.

Fig. 9   Bulgarian soldiers on the Salonika Front in 1917 already had German gas masks. Courtesy of Mr Peyo Kolev, lostbulgaria.com.

Although the first trials were rather inauspicious, work on the new weapon proceeded apace. In Germany, which had the most advanced chemical industry, the work was led by the eminent scientist Fritz Haber, a subsequent winner of the Nobel Prize, who headed the Chemistry Section at the Ministry of War. Together with his team of chemists, Haber looked at ways of producing new poisonous substances and of protecting German soldiers in the event of such attacks by the enemy – the first gas masks were not introduced in the German army until September 1915, but this was still much earlier than in other countries at war. Between 1914 and 1918 more than twenty different chemical substances, and an even greater number of mixtures obtained from those substances, were used in over 400 chemical attacks. The development trajectory of the new weapon was clear: from irritants, which could in some way or another temporarily neutralize the enemy, to strong and lethal poisons. Haber himself was a fervent advocate of poisonous and suffocating gases. Both he and the German command hoped that such gases could be used to break the stalemate at the front. Indeed, this hope was almost fulfilled at Ypres in April 1915. Haber personally supervised the use of liquid chlorine cylinders which, wind conditions permitting, were emptied in the direction of the enemy positions. Yet, despite heavy losses and panic in the French trenches, the Germans did not manage to break through. Battles in the vicinity of Ypres, of varying intensity, continued until the end of the war.

In late April the German command sent Haber to the Eastern Front together with a team of engineers trained in the use of chlorine. Once again the experiment was to be conducted in the area around Żyrardów and Sochaczew. Chlorine attacks were carried out there in late May, June, and early July. The battles of the Bzura and Rawka Rivers demonstrated to the German commanders, even more emphatically than in winter time, that the effectiveness of the new weapon depended greatly on the weather. One of the first attacks failed when a gust of wind blew the cloud of poisonous gas over and beyond the first line of Russian trenches. The Russians could therefore put up strong resistance to the advancing Germans. In July one of the attacks ended in disaster. The wind suddenly changed direction and the poisonous cloud enveloped the German positions, killing many unsuspecting German soldiers who were not sufficiently protected.

The clashes in the vicinity of Żyrardów and Sochaczew were the biggest tests of chemical weapons on the Eastern Front. These weapons were also used, albeit on a smaller scale, during the fighting in Romania, in Volhynia, and on the Salonika Front. From 1916 chemical units became part of the Austro-Hungarian army. Opinions were divided about these new weapons. Many military men, particularly of the older generation, considered them to be immoral and indecent. General Karl von Einem, the former Prussian Minister of War, wrote in a letter to his wife:

> I am furious about this new gas and the use of it. I have always found it to be repugnant. The introduction of such an indecent, unscrupulous, and criminal weapon of war is naturally the work of that scoundrel Falkenhayn, who believed it would allow us to win the war in a jiffy. Now our enemies have it too.[20]

How effective were poison gases in combat? Measured by the number of killed, sick, and wounded, they were certainly less effective than conventional weapons. This is shown by a straightforward comparison of the data: at the end of the war every third German shell contained a chemical charge, yet the number of soldiers killed or wounded by such shells accounted for less than 4 per cent of all victims on the Western Front. The technology allowed poison gases to be used only in particular weather conditions and on certain types of terrain. Winds, which in Europe usually blow from west to east, made it easier for the Central Powers to use the new weapons in Poland and Ukraine, but more difficult on the Western Front. Protective clothing against chemical weapons developed in parallel, hence the effectiveness of gases decreased over time. However, from the point of view of the general staffs, chemical weapons had one advantage that was not to be ignored. Clouds of poisonous gas caused panic among enemy troops, especially where chemical defence measures were inadequate. This was especially true of the Russian army, which was very late in joining the chemical arms race. Alfred Knox, the British Military Attaché in Russia, recalled that during the

---

[20] Adolf Wild von Hohenborn, *Briefe und Tagebuchaufzeichnungen des preußischen Generals als Kriegsminister und Truppenführer im Ersten Weltkrieg*, ed. Helmut Reichold, Boppard am Rhein 1986, p. 167.

June attack on the Rawka River the Russians were not equipped with prototype gas masks, despite the fact that the military warehouses already had plenty of them:

> The Press, in describing the attack, stated that the Russians 'had time to take the necessary measures'. It transpired later that the 'necessary measures' consisted of urinating on handkerchiefs and tying them round the face, for the respirators sent from Petrograd were still lying at Warsaw and had not been distributed to the troops. Over one thousand men died from gas-poisoning.[21]

The precise extent of Russian losses due to German and Austro-Hungarian chemical attacks is not known. Not all the wounded and killed were included in the military data; during the retreat from the Kingdom of Poland in the spring and summer of 1915 in particular, there was such chaos that few bothered to keep records. Historians more or less agree, however, about the scale of Russian losses compared with the number of killed and wounded on the Western Front. According to various post-war estimates, those losses could account for one-half, or possibly two-thirds, of all those wounded or killed by poison gas during the First

Fig. 10   Russian gunners in makeshift gas masks during the Brusilov Offensive. Courtesy of Mariusz Kulik.

World War.[22] If one adds to this the German and Austro-Hungarian losses in Central and Eastern Europe, it becomes clear on which front the chemical war was waged on a truly massive scale. The fact that it was Ypres, and not Bolimów, that came to symbolize chemical warfare says less about the true nature of the Great War and much more about the dominance of the Western Front in European cultural memory.

---

[21] Alfred Knox, *With the Russian Army 1914–1917*, vol. 1, London 1921, p. 276.
[22] Harry L. Gilchrist, *A Comparative Study of World War Casualties from Gas and Other Weapons*, Edgewood, MA 1928, pp. 6–7.

80 THE FRONTS

Winter

While the turn of the year was relatively calm in the north after the Germans had occupied Łódź, on the Carpathian section of the front a bloody positional war was just beginning. Neither side was prepared for it nor could they have been: the railway network was sparse and there was a lack of food and fuel; meanwhile, a severe continental winter was fast approaching. The Austro-Hungarian army, aided by modest reinforcements from Germany, tried to force its way through to the besieged town of Przemyśl. Just as had occurred two months earlier, the attack once again collided with the Russian offensive, which was aiming to break through into Hungary. The fighting lasted all winter and was conducted in unimaginably difficult conditions: high up in mountains with temperatures falling to −30 °C and snow up to the waist or even neck. Against a white backdrop of snow, attackers were an excellent target. Soldiers on both sides had not been given helmets, which meant that splinters from shattered rock increased the already high losses. The hand grenades used by the Russians were a novelty, however. A participant of the fighting in the Bieszczady Mountains recalled:

> On the first day of March there was a blizzard and fog. Orientation was impossible. Entire regiments wandered about aimlessly, resulting in huge losses; on 6 March the weather changed again: a cloudless sky, thaw during the day, and at night −20 °C. This turned the mountain slopes into sheets of ice, such that any attack, even in the absence of an enemy counter-attack, became a feat of dexterity. When all these obstacles had been overcome the sun would set, having warmed the combatants a little during the day, and a cold north-westerly wind would drain any remnants of heat from them. There was not a single place to take shelter throughout the territory where the fighting took place. Soldiers would not remove their clothes for days or weeks and their uniforms would turn into hard-ened ice armour that stuck to their bodies. Because the earth was frozen solid it was impossible for the attackers to dig in and protect themselves against enemy fire. Losses vastly increased; the wounded, whom it was extremely difficult to evacuate, died *en masse*. Exhausted by weeks of fighting and lack of food, people could not even hope to sleep at night, since this meant instant death from exposure. On 10 March a snowstorm arrived: the attack broke down and the advancing lines became forever enveloped in a shroud of snow.[23]

---

[23] Cited in Juliusz Bator, *Wojna galicyjska. Działania armii austro-węgierskiej na froncie północnym (galicyjskim) w latach 1914–1915*, Cracow 2005, pp. 165–166.

The conditions described above are borne out by meteorological data: on 4 February the temperature in the Carpathian mountain passes was −25 °C, with strong winds and snowfall. Three days later the thermometers recorded a temperature of 0 °C, rising to +6 °C on 12 February. Avalanches of melting snow covered the roads, trenches, and dugouts. On 7 March the temperature was −13 °C and everything turned to ice.

A similar impression was made on a German aristocrat in uniform: 'Throughout the day, amidst clouds of snow, picturesque columns trudged past our cottage', wrote Count Harry Kessler on 1 February 1915. 'Animals laden with heavy, snow-covered packs, carts pulled by oxen (between fifty and a hundred, one after the other), sledges carrying food and ammunition, and Austrian infantrymen wearily dragging themselves forwards; or, heading in the opposite direction, Russian prisoners of war with vacant expressions, upon whom the snow falls like fate itself. One sits here as in a cinema and watches the crossing of the Carpathians' – this is how the German officer summed up his day from the comfort of a warm cottage.[24] Such luxuries were afforded to very few on either side of the front. Both armies were tired, badly provisioned, and unprepared for winter in the mountain wilderness. The colder it got, the scarcer became the supplies needed for basic survival. Time and again the Austro-Hungarian troops tried to attack, only to discover that their guns had frozen.

In the Carpathian mountain passes hurricane fire was not necessary in order to decimate the enemy; weeks of toil, hunger, and cold were just as effective. On 14 March 1915 the 2nd Austro-Hungarian Army reported the loss of 40,000 of its 95,000 soldiers – 6,000 killed or injured in combat, the remainder falling victim to illness and frost. Every week hundreds of soldiers froze to death and hundreds of wounded died due to the lack of medical assistance in the trenches. As the thaw began, avalanches of melted snow descended from the mountains, carrying with them the buried bodies of Russian and Austrian soldiers.[25] Statistically speaking, during that winter a soldier of the Austro-Hungarian monarchy could avoid injury or death in the Carpathian Mountains for around six weeks; on the Russian side the chances were probably similar. It is estimated that Austro-Hungarian losses in anonymous battles on the mountain passes amounted to a staggering 600,000 sick, injured, missing, or killed. Neither side managed to achieve its goals. No help reached Przemyśl and the Russians crossed the mountains for only a brief period.

---

[24] Cited in Jens Flemming, Klaus Saul, and Peter-Christian Witt (eds.), *Lebenswelten im Ausnahmezustand. Die Deutschen, der Alltag und der Krieg, 1914–1918*, Frankfurt am Main 2011, p. 59.

[25] Harry Graf Kessler, *Das Tagebuch*, vol. 5 (1914–1916), ed. Günter Riederer, Ulrich Ott, Christoph Hilse, and Janna Brechmacher, Stuttgart 2008, p. 238.

At the beginning of November Austria-Hungary also renewed its general attack on Serbia. The fighting on this front had been going on since August almost without interruption, but now the time had come for another massive strike. The Serbs had begun to run out of reservists. Radomir Putnik asked Prime Minister Pašić to enter into peace negotiations, but the Serbian government decided that resistance had to continue. In any case, bad weather, poor conditions in the field, and supply problems were starting to be felt by both sides. Despite the snowy conditions, both Austro-Hungarian armies lacked warm clothing and many soldiers did not even have boots. Morale was at its lowest ebb since the beginning of the war. The enemy was hardly in better shape. In November desertion became such a serious problem in the Serbian army that it was punished not just by execution but also by the requisition of property and the repression of deserters' families. No one spoke any more – even in theory – about releasing soldiers from their oath. Those who did not desert often had no weapons with which to fight. After the enemy had entered Valjevo and Obrenovac, the Serbs turned to their allies with a dramatic plea for an immediate consignment of ammunition.

At the beginning of December it seemed that General Potiorek had finally managed to achieve the success for which Vienna had been yearning. On Emperor Franz Joseph's name day the 5th Austro-Hungarian

Fig. 11   Austro-Hungarian soldiers in the Carpathians.

BEFORE THE LEAVES FALL FROM THE TREES ...

Army captured Belgrade. The defenders left the city voluntarily, as the Austrians had done three months earlier in Lwów. It was not a triumphant victory parade:

> As we entered Belgrade we saw not a single soul on any of the streets we walked along or passed. There was a deathly silence throughout the city; it seemed completely deserted, having been badly scarred by artillery fire.[26]

Despite the seizure of the enemy's capital the offensive was losing momentum. The Austrian advance got bogged down in the narrow dirt roads; the baggage trains and artillery struggled along them, while the infantry had to make its own way through the countryside. Moreover, the attackers fell victim to their own brutality. During the August invasion Serb civilians had reacted to the arrival of Austro-Hungarian troops with equanimity. However, the repression and gratuitous violence they suffered over the subsequent days and weeks left a lasting imprint on the Serbian collective memory. When the Austrians returned in the autumn, many peasants preferred to load their families onto carts and follow their own retreating army rather than risk being left to the tender mercies of the Austrians. The already clogged roads became flooded with refugees. An outbreak of cholera and typhus exacerbated the situation. Serbia had been tormented by these diseases since 1912 and now they were taking their toll on the Austrians.

Although the occupation of Belgrade provoked euphoria in both Vienna and Berlin, time was on the side of the Serbs. Retreating eastwards, they drew ever closer to their supply base in Kragujevac. The Austrians pursued them, but in doing so moved further away from their own resources, while the narrow-gauge railway was not robust enough to bring in supplies. Meanwhile, the ammunition that the Serbian government had requested from France finally arrived in Salonika, from where it was transported to the front. Now it was the turn of the Austro-Hungarian artillery to suffer from a shortage of shells; the Serbs had plenty of them. At the beginning of December the Serbs began a counter-offensive, which in the course of ten days pushed the remnants of the two Austro-Hungarian armies out of the country. The speed of this operation was the reason for the Habsburg monarchy's spectacular defeat. Once again General Potiorek lost control of the situation. Instead of issuing sensible orders, his staff attempted to rouse the troops with combative slogans: 'Persevere at all costs. The enemy's plight is equally arduous. The hardiest shall prevail.'[27] The chaos that ensued among the 5th and 6th Armies was even greater than that experienced

---

[26] Account of Eduard Zanantoni, cited in Daniela Schanes, *Serbien im Ersten Weltkrieg*, pp. 163–164.

[27] Ibid., p. 117.

84 THE FRONTS

during the two Austro-Hungarian retreats in the north. Jaroslav Hašek described the events with starting realism; in six months time he was due to be posted to the Eastern Front:

> It is enough for me to remember how at Belgrade the Hungarians shot at our second march battalion, who didn't know that it was the Hungarians who were shooting at them and began to fire at the Deutschmeisters on the right wing. Then the Deutschmeisters got muddled as well and opened fire on the Bosnian regiment which stood alongside them. That was a nice situation! [...] The Serbs probably thought that a mutiny had broken out on our side and so they began to fire at us from all sides and to cross the river towards us. [...] Brigade telephone exchange reported that it couldn't get any connection anywhere but that the staff of the 75th Regiment was reporting that it had received from the next division the order 'stand firm',[28] that it was not possible to communicate with our division, that the Serbs had occupied points 212, 226 and 327, that a battalion was required to act as liaison and provide telephone communication with our division. We transferred the call to the division but the connection was already broken, because in the meantime the Serbs had got behind us on both flanks and cut up our centre into a triangle. Inside that everything stayed, regiments, artillery and baggage train with the whole column of cars, the stores and the field-hospital. I was two days in the saddle and the divisional commander was captured together with our brigade commander.[29]

In the middle of December the remnants of the two Austro-Hungarian armies left Serbian territory. The attack, whose purpose had been to enhance the prestige of the monarchy in the Balkans, and perhaps even to persuade Bulgaria to join the Central Powers, ended in abject failure. Nearly half a million soldiers had fought against the Serbs, and their absence had been felt most keenly in Eastern Galicia. The number of killed and wounded exceeded 150,000, and more than 80,000 prisoners of war remained in Serbia; only a few survived to return home. The Serb losses, although much smaller, were more difficult to redress. Typhus, cholera, and dysentery raged across the country and the Serbian health service was unable to contain the epidemic. The war had barely started for Austria-Hungary, but for the Serbs it was already the third year of fighting.

---

[28] German: *ausharren*.
[29] Jaroslav Hašek, *The Good Soldier Švejk*, translated by Cecil Parrott, Harmondsworth 1973, pp. 376–377.

Life at the Front

Those few months between the outbreak of the war and the easing of tensions at the end of the year proved a harsh lesson for all sides in the conflict. This was not just because of the constant threat of attack. As Wolfram Dornik explains, nature also made her presence known:

> Atmospheric conditions on all the fronts were a direct physical threat to the combatants. Though difficult to estimate, some of the losses were caused by the challenges linked to the weather and season. At the front on the Soča River these consisted in the explosive qualities of Karst rock (especially during periods of drought and frost); in the Alps, avalanches; in the Carpathians, cold storms and snowdrifts; and in Eastern Galicia and Volhynia, marshes and mud in the autumn and floods in the spring (when the trenches filled with water); dehydration, frostbite, colds, constantly damp bodies, and the illnesses these caused, were often more dangerous to the soldiers than the threat posed by the enemy.[30]

Those who survived long enough to gain experience worked out myriad ways to avoid death and facilitate life at the front. On long marches one of the imperatives was to discard unnecessary kit. Every foot soldier carried a pack weighing approximately 30 kilograms. Austro-Hungarian soldiers had the most equipment, Russians slightly less. It is no wonder, then, that after a 50-kilometre march the route was usually littered with spare magazines that had been thrown into ditches. The huge shields mounted on machine guns were likewise a heavy load that soldiers were reluctant to bear. Despite the excess of equipment, certain essential items such as helmets were lacking. A year would elapse before helmets became standard issue in the German army; the Russians would have to wait even longer to receive their French helmets, and the Austrians German ones. In the meantime, soldiers wore caps, shakos, calpacs, leather *Pickelhauben*, or fur caps – all rather picturesque, but completely useless against shrapnel and rock splinters. Sometimes the best protection for a prone soldier was to shield his head with his overloaded pack. Already in the second week of fighting Stanisław Kawczak collected seven fragments of shrapnel lodged in his standard issue blanket and spare underwear. Soldiers soon appreciated the benefits of camouflage. In the first phase of the war, during the reconnaissance missions undertaken by all sides, it was noted that extravagantly dressed cavalrymen on white horses were an excellent target. The long-term solution was to make cavalry uniforms resemble those used by

---

[30] Wolfram Dornik, "'Ganz in den Rahmen dieses Bildes hinein passt auch die Bevölkerung." Raumerfahrung und Raumwahrnehmung von österreichisch-ungarischen Soldaten an der Ostfront des Ersten Weltkriegs', in *Jenseits des Schützengrabens. Der Erste Weltkrieg im Osten: Erfahrung – Wahrnehmung – Kontext*, ed. Bernhard Bachinger and Wolfram Dornik, Innsbruck 2013, pp. 27–43, here p. 33.

86   THE FRONTS

the infantry. In the short term the problem was dealt with in various ways. Rennenkampf's army, for instance, as some civilians reported, took the dramatic decision to paint its horses green.[31]

Soldiers often complained about excess equipment; the reverse was true of food. In general only the German army supplied its soldiers adequately, thus confirming the popular stereotype. Among the Russian and Austrian troops, soldiers would often steal food and sometimes even equipment from each other. At times this almost led to fratricidal fighting. Particularly strong tensions prevailed in the multinational Austro-Hungarian army. At the start of the war the elite units of Polish Legionnaires and Ukrainian Sich Riflemen (although 'elite' was an adjective only they used in relation to themselves) were dramatically under-funded. Formally, they were part of the Austro-Hungarian Landsturm, which comprised reservists who had the lowest level of training and poorest weapons. These units, armed with old Werndl rifles, had no machine guns and often incomplete uniforms. For example, in September 1914 in the Polish Legion, the 1st Battalion's 1st Company, which numbered 118 soldiers, lacked the following kit: 110 overcoats, 107 jackets, 108 pairs of trousers, 96 pairs of boots, and 85 warm shirts. These numbers meant that worn apparel could not be replaced. Consequently, by the end of September, most of the soldiers had no boots. Knapsacks, torches, raincoats, and blankets were also in short supply. The memoirs of soldiers from these units recount numerous anecdotes about stealing horses, equipment, and even weapons from neighbouring Austro-Hungarian units.

However, theft on a truly grand scale occurred elsewhere. The problem with manoeuvre warfare was that provisioning would usually begin to fail as the army moved further away from its rear. This was in stark contrast to the heady atmosphere when troops setting off for the front would be showered with gifts. In August, as the armies moved out, everything remained civilized. Eugeniusz Romer, a Lithuanian landowner, was almost surprised by the attitude of the Russians *en route* to East Prussia:

> The officers came to us for breakfast or for milk and the soldiers bought up all our supplies of lard, butter, bread, and apples. Everything was exceptionally orderly and pleasant. One regiment, which passed by as we stood on the bridge in Gryzów, even struck up the *Cracovienne* especially for us; there was no theft, nor any excesses.[32]

Initially, the purchases made by the army intendants likewise caused no major conflicts between the military and civilians. Payments were made in cash. However, it soon transpired that when one party was armed a mutually beneficial transaction could be problematic. A few months later Romer complained:

---

[31] Cezary Jellenta, *Wielki zmierzch. Pamiętnik*, Warsaw 1985, p. 30.
[32] Eugeniusz Romer, *Dziennik 1914–1918*, vol. 1, Warsaw 1995, p. 49.

BEFORE THE LEAVES FALL FROM THE TREES . . .

> Since the departure of the Germans our troops have become anxious again. They demand everything: oats, barley, cows. Although they pay, the price is often arbitrary and does not reflect the real price; they often underpay.[33]

The Russian practice of requisitioning invited abuse, and indeed army intendants worked hand in hand with enterprising landowners in this regard. An especially lucrative operation was to seek compensation for destroyed crops and for the grazing of military cattle, for which pasture owners were paid by the Treasury. Peasants, who were forced to sell their produce and livestock for a pittance, had it worse: 'The peasant values his pig at 50 crowns, the requisitioner offers him 5, and he buys it for 15', recalled one Austrian-Hungarian soldier.[34] By no means were all the purchased goods intended for soldiers. Many were sold on immediately and the profits kept by the army intendants. This practice later gained in popularity when the army, instead of paying cash, began to issue peasants with requisition receipts. In theory these receipts were to be exchanged for remuneration immediately after the end of hostilities in a given area (and – as we shall later see – this is indeed what sometimes happened). However, in places through which the front passed three or four times in as many months there was no longer anything left to requisition. When asking for food, Austro-Hungarian soldiers so often heard the phrase 'the Moskale (Muscovites) took it' that one of them used the phrase in the chorus of a song he composed.[35] Even if such assurances were not strictly true, peasants became increasingly unwilling to share their food, even in Galicia:

> Then there was this peasant family, who were like cranes minding their eggs. The father kept an eye on the horse and cows, the mother – the pigsty, one child – the poultry, another child – the potatoes, a third child – the rye or the cabbage in the barrel, while the grandfather remained in the place with all the belongings. Naturally, there was nothing to eat in that place. Time and again we heard the same phrase: 'The Moskale took the lot', but they had never been there.[36]

---

[33] Ibid., p. 142.

[34] Kawczak, *Milknące echa*, p. 61.

[35] 'The Moskale plundered Poland / In hell I hope they rot / For everywhere I hear the phrase: / The Moskale took the lot! / Once I wished good morning / To a woman on a plot / Nothing here, she quickly said / The Moskale took the lot! / When I ask the farmers / To sell me what they've got / They interrupt my sentence with: / The Moskale took the lot! / Once we asked a group of girls / Which one the wreath had caught / We have no wreaths, the girls replied / The Moskale took the lot! / Unhappy is our Poland / For no one cares a jot / Everything we had is gone / The Moskale took the lot!', Legionnaire Filipowicz, *Wiersz z wojny 1915–16 roku. Moskale zabrali*, Cracow 1916, unpaginated.

[36] Kawczak, *Milknące echa*, p. 45.

88 THE FRONTS

No wonder the army became increasingly hungry. Składkowski recalled his stay in the Świętokrzyskie Mountains:

> We were so hungry that we took some tiny potatoes from a peasant woman who was putting them in the trough for her pigs. The woman was utterly speechless and didn't even try to stop us. All she could do was shout: 'God help me! I've never seen a squaddie pinch spuds from a pig!'[37]

The above encounter passed without conflict, but this was not the rule during the war. Soldiers and civilians often communicated with each other with great difficulty. Indeed, they did not always want to reach agreement, as is evidenced by the requisition receipts, which were a mix of honesty and soldierly humour. Quite often there were silly poems or pious maxims written on them; in some cases goods were simply plundered and no receipt given. Soldiers who arrived subsequently would be surprised by the behaviour of the peasants, who on seeing them would flee into the forest or, if they remained, would look completely terrified. When reading soldiers' memoirs it is worth taking a critical look at such relationships. Take, for instance, the memoirs of Fritz Nagel, a German NCO in the anti-aircraft artillery, which appeared in English after he had emigrated to the United States. Nagel was undoubtedly not alone in believing that the farmers with whom he lodged were essentially still serfs. He was also convinced that he was dealing with Russians, yet the place he mentions suggests that they were more likely to be Belarusian or Polish peasants. In any case, they behaved just as he imagined a 'Russian *muzhik*', tied to the land, would behave. He rationalized taking their food (as well as a samovar, which he wanted as a souvenir) in the following manner: he was not taking their property, but rather things that belonged to a local Polish nobleman for whom he had little sympathy. The fact that no one was able to sign the receipt he had written out for the samovar convinced him that the village was a hotbed of backwardness. It is easy to be taken in by this story, one of many similar such accounts. Perhaps Nagel was not mistaken, and it was true that apart from himself and his comrades there was no one in the village who could read or write. But the villagers' reluctance to sign receipts can just as easily be explained by their previous unpleasant experiences. During the war both sides were guilty of sometimes hanging suspicious individuals on whom they had found documents belonging to the enemy – 'just in case'. Alleged collusion and secret dealings with the enemy could also be reported by ill-disposed neighbours. Thus, in addition to genuine illiterates, there were also 'occasional illiterates' – people whose reluctance to flaunt their language skills was dictated by common sense.

Soldiers did not always get away with their wilful behaviour towards civilians. The first months of the war witnessed a huge number of violations of

---

[37] Składkowski, *Moja służba w Brygadzie*, p. 35.

Fig. 12 Polish peasants in the Congress Kingdom bowing before their temporary new masters – the Hungarian Honvéd (1915).

army regulations (desertion, ordinary criminal offences, and offences against civilians) as well as many executions. A further increase in military crime occurred in Russia in the second half of 1915 and in Germany and Austria-Hungary at the end of 1916. During these periods, interestingly, army doctors noted a higher incidence of hand and leg injuries. Clearly, soldiers had found a way of cutting short their stay on the front, just as the Turkish reserve units had done a few years earlier. A relatively common form of self-inflicted injury, which usually resulted in hospitalization rather than court martial, was to shoot one's own leg – through a loaf of bread to make it look as if the bullet had been fired from a distance rather than from a weapon held in one's own hands. The causes of this second wave of desertion and self-mutilation are understandable – defeat at the front, war weariness, general disorder. However, the first wave is more difficult to explain. The mood was still positive in the autumn of 1914, hence widespread unrest was not to blame. It seems that the reasons should be sought in the psychology of the combatants. For many soldiers the reality of modern warfare was too far removed from how they had imagined it. Their response was shock and sometimes a refusal to participate. In addition, their superiors generally lacked experience.

For soldiers the measure of correct behaviour was the army manual and barrack life during peacetime. The more the memory of peace and barrack life receded, the more the behaviour of soldiers changed and adapted itself to the new conditions. Deviations from army regulations became the norm. As a result, in the chaos of constant offensives and counter-offensives, officers began to turn a blind eye to misdemeanours that in August 1914 would have been punished by immediate execution. A good example of this change in attitude was found in the 2nd Brigade of the Polish Legion. In the first few weeks of the war several executions were carried out. Yet, in October 1914, an unusual event occurred during the Battle of Mołotków (Molotkiv) in which the Legionnaires participated. The captain of the gendarmerie (military police) shot a Legionnaire on the spot for refusing to return to the battlefield. A few days later, one of the other Legionnaires killed the captain. From that moment until the beginning of 1915 no further executions were carried out, although ten deserters and seventeen soldiers accused of refusing to obey orders were put up for court martial.[38] Moreover, the brigade took on deserters from other Austro-Hungarian units, registering them under different names.

Of the armies that fought in the East, Russia undoubtedly stood out in terms of its approach to the problem of maintaining discipline. It is hard to say whether this was related to Russia's experiences in the war with Japan or whether it was for other reasons. In any case, the Russian leadership reacted calmly to over 100,000 or so desertions in the first year of the war alone. Captured deserters were simply sent back to their parent units. Russian soldiers got away with many of the offences for which German or Austrian soldiers would have been court-martialled. This was particularly true of crimes against civilians in occupied territories. Sometimes there was simply tacit consent to violence. Nobody even pretended that any punishment would be meted out to the instigators of and participants in anti-Jewish pogroms, which occurred almost everywhere the Russian military came into contact with Jews. Paradoxically, for soldiers from Central Asia or Siberia, it was military service and the invasion of Galicia that gave them their first practical training in anti-Semitism.

Pogroms and other forms of violence against civilians were an inseparable element of the war in the East. No one was blameless, but the populations of territories visited by successive armies soon established a view about each of those armies. Most feared were the Russians, and not only in Galicia, where they were the aggressor, but also in the Kingdom of Poland, which after all belonged to Russia. The prelate of the Sandomierz chapter, Father Józef Rokoszny, recorded in his war diary many of the conversations he had with the inhabitants of Radom and its environs, that is, Russian Poland. The following 'ranking' of misfortunes emerges from those conversations: in first place were the Russians, whose behaviour was only to some extent predictable, but because it was known that they would beat the Jews, Christians were advised to put a cross above their doors or display sacred images in their windows in order to protect themselves and their property; next were the

[38] Stanisław Czerep, *II Brygada Legionów Polskich*, Warsaw 1991, p. 50.

BEFORE THE LEAVES FALL FROM THE TREES ... 91

Hungarians, who were accused of mindless destruction, cruelty, and rape; then the Germans, who were brutal in their enforcement of strict rules and who engaged in ruthless requisitions; and finally the Austrians, towards whom the population had the least objection but also the least respect. At times, however, any attempt to rationalize the behaviour of the occupiers failed. Encounters between the army and civilians were so common, and the nervous tension so great, that violence erupted even in situations that seemed quite banal. A young cavalryman recalled an 'amusing' adventure from November 1914. In search of bread for himself and his comrades he went to a bakery in the town of Wolbrom, newly occupied by the Austrians. The shop owners, a Jewish family, told him that all the bread had been taken by the infantry some time earlier. The vigilant soldier was not to be duped, however:

> The smell of fresh bread prevents me from believing the Jew and it turns out that I am right: on top of the broad baking oven is a whole stack of loaves and a few trays of wheat pancakes. Having admonished the Jew I place two loaves in my bag and two pancakes under my arm. I then return to the horses while taking bites of the pancakes sticking out from under my arm.[39]

In Składkowski's memoirs the same anecdote has a slightly more serious tone:

> That night, while on patrol, our cavalry entered Wolbrom and took away some very fresh and delicious sourdough bread. The Cossacks had ordered the inhabitants to bake several hundred loaves of white bread at an appointed time, after which they had departed, solemnly announcing they would return. Terrified, the inhabitants got to work, and just as the bakers had finished making the bread, our uhlans entered and took their war booty ... That is how we got the bread. After our uhlans had gone, the poor inhabitants of Wolbrom had to start making those 'war reparations' in the form of fresh bread all over again, for the Cossacks undoubtedly came back.[40]

Even such a trivial episode could have triggered a wave of uncontrolled violence against the civilian population, not just because the Cossacks were reluctant to pass up any opportunity to beat the Jews but also because of fear, which was felt on all sides.

The Spy Craze

Despite being armed to the teeth, never before in history had armies been so fearful of civilians. Betrayal was expected at every step. The belief that troop movements were under constant surveillance by hundreds of enemy spies was

[39] Wincenty Solek, *Pamiętnik legionisty*, ed. Wiesław Budzyński, Warsaw 1988, p. 58.
[40] Składkowski, *Moja służba w Brygadzie*, p. 35.

nurtured on both sides of the front. Russian generals of German origin were accused of treason, especially when their actions were as incompetent as Rennenkampf's in East Prussia. At the front and immediately behind it, however, it was not the Livonian barons but the Jews who were most at risk from the Russians. The aforementioned pogroms were accompanied by a campaign of slander against the Jews – the Czar's subjects. Already in August 1914 the army ordered the evacuation of Jewish residents from the provinces of Radom, Łomża, Lublin, and later Warsaw. The reason given was 'security considerations'. After the Russian army had crossed the border into Galicia, reports from the front became awash with conspiracy theories so bizarre that they cannot be solely attributed to the deep anti-Semitism within the Russian army.

Some commanders reported to the Stavka (the imperial high command) about secret Jewish organizations that were digging tunnels several kilometres long to reach the Austrian positions; others warned of Jewish agents who were orchestrating enemy fire from balloons, passing confidential information to the Austrians, luring Russian units into traps, burning their own homes before escaping west, and cutting telephone lines.[41]

Even if some of these claims sound ridiculous, they were treated with complete seriousness. In the words of Alexander Victor Prusin, each of them 'acquired momentum on its own, whereby the Russian army, counterintelligence, and the police were alarmed by the very rumours they had helped to generate'.[42] In the early months of the war the military still believed that the cavalry could carry out reconnaissance at the front and that a broad spy network would be able to provide most of the information needed for a victorious campaign. By August it had become abundantly clear that both these assumptions were incorrect, but it took a long time for each side to process this fact. One Austrian officer was convinced that betrayal was everywhere to be found:

> They must have set up schools, even colleges, to teach the people of Galicia and the Russian borderlands how to send signals using every conceivable system [...]. Everyone sent signals – children, the elderly, women. They used all possible means: secret signals, underground telephone lines, windmill blades, drying linen, grazing cattle, and open and closed window shutters.

While the author of the above text could be deemed a pathological fantasist – though this would imply that his illness was astonishingly contagious – it

---

[41] Alexander Victor Prusin, *Nationalizing a Borderland. War, Ethnicity, and Anti-Jewish Violence in East Galicia, 1914–1920*, Tuscaloosa, AL 2005, p. 27.

[42] Alexander Victor Prusin, 'The Russian Military and the Jews in Galicia, 1914–15', in *The Military and Society in Russia 1450–1917*, ed. Eric Lohr and Marshall Poe, Leiden, Boston, MA, and Cologne 2002, pp. 525–544, here p. 544.

BEFORE THE LEAVES FALL FROM THE TREES . . .

would be difficult to regard as mentally ill the Austro-Hungarian officers who conducted a study on Russian intelligence. They, too, believed in the ubiquitousness of Czarist spies; the youngest among them – claimed the experts with deadly seriousness – were 'child-spies', 'morally depraved boys and girls (eleven year-old prostitutes!), mostly orphans, always poorly dressed', who went around 'begging and attempting to infiltrate military transports'.[43] The head of Austro-Hungarian military intelligence, Max Ronge, ostensibly a professional, wrote in his post-war memoirs with the authority of a retired spymaster that an effective and commonly used method of informing the enemy about troop movements was to sound church bells in an agreed manner and that Ukrainian spies in Eastern Galicia relayed secret information to the Russians using a hidden telephone line (despite the fact that the Russian army had enormous problems communicating with even its biggest units):

> Signals were transmitted using window shutters – a simple method that raised no suspicion. Each of the three windows represented one section of our front. [...] It is understandable, therefore, that when the blades of a windmill turned or the hands of a church clock moved and a shell then hit its target, our soldiers felt deceived and betrayed.[44]

Ronge was no exception. The Austro-Hungarian command assumed that a great many of the monarchy's subjects were prone to treason. Most untrustworthy were the Serbs, the Czechs, and the Galician Ruthenians. Political and cultural activists, priests, and local government officials were preventively interned. By the end of 1914 nearly 1,000 people had been arrested on suspicion of espionage. Every tenth person to be tried was found guilty, and three-quarters of those were sentenced to death. Not all the judgements were enforced, and some were later overturned. Ultimately, in legal terms, the offence of high treason was committed by no more than 1 per cent of those arrested on that charge. It is very likely that a similar result would have been achieved by arresting 1,000 random walkers in Vienna's Prater Park.

The belief in the omnipresence of spies and traitors, despite having no basis in fact, stubbornly persisted. Indeed, people arrested by the gendarmerie and incarcerated far from the battlefields could have considered themselves lucky, for it was far more dangerous to be accused of espionage anywhere near the front. In the latter case the outcome might be court martial or execution without trial, and the army used both methods willingly. It is not known how many people fell victim to terror in the hinterland. When, in May 1917, the Austrian Parliament was convened after a three-year hiatus, Polish, Ukrainian, and South Slavic deputies tried to outdo each other in accusing

---

[43] Cited in Martin Schmitz, 'Tapfer, zäh und schlecht geführt', p. 49.
[44] Max Ronge, *Kriegs- und Industriespionage. Zwölf Jahre Kundschaftsdienst*, Vienna 1930, p. 112.

94 THE FRONTS

the dissolute *soldatesca* of murdering Slavs in the east and south. For unknown reasons the accusers eagerly cited the round (and to this day magical) figure of 30,000 deaths in Galicia (the Polish socialist politician Ignacy Daszyński added: 'Others say that it's twice as many') and in Serbia.[45] While most of the crimes were indeed committed in those areas, it is difficult to obtain accurate and reliable data. In Serbia the Austrians had not been prepared for such dogged resistance, hence they automatically sought additional justification for their failures. 'Betrayal' by Serb civilians was the perfect explanation. The accusations were also strengthened by the fact that the Serbian army, which had been forced to rely on its deepest reserve units, did not have enough uniforms for all the conscripts: the so-called second-line units were partially uniformed, while men in the third-line units wore civilian clothing. This gave credence to the myth that the whole Serb nation, including women and children, had fought deceitfully and unlawfully against the Austro-Hungarian monarchy. 'In response' the armies of the monarchy had murdered all the suspects. Jonathan Gumz and Mark Biondich estimate the number of victims of repression by the retreating Austro-Hungarian army in December 1914 to be between 3,500 and 4,000 people.[46]

The situation in Eastern Galicia in 1914 and 1915 was quite similar. Already during their retreat in the first months of the war the monarchy's troops took revenge on the Ukrainian 'Russophiles' – whether real or imagined.[47] The largest group to suffer repression comprised 10,000 Ukrainians, who were deported to the soon-to-be-infamous internment camp at Thalerhof near Graz as well as to other lesser-known places of incarceration.[48] There were also cases of execution without trial and sham trials – in this way, helpless in the face of the enemy, the armies of the monarchy tried to justify their successive defeats. As the commanders of the Przemyśl fortress explained at the end of September 1914, correct

---

[45] Christoph Mick, 'Krieg und Ethnizität: Lemberg im Zeitalter der Weltkriege', in *Stadt und Krieg im 20. Jahrhundert. Neue Perspektiven auf Deutschland und Ostmitteleuropa*, ed. Christoph Cornelißen, Václav Petrbok, and Martin Pekár, Essen 2019, pp. 173–189, here p. 176.

[46] Jonathan E. Gumz, *The Resurrection and Collapse of Empire in Habsburg Serbia, 1914–1918*, Cambridge 2009, pp. 53–58, here p. 58; Mark Biondich, *The Balkans. Revolution, War and Political Violence since 1878*, Oxford 2011, p. 86.

[47] Iryna Orlevych, 'The Thalehof Tragedy in the Intellectual Thought of Galician Russophiles in the Interwar Period', in *Intellectuals and World War I. A Central European Perspective*, ed. Tomasz Pudłocki and Kamil Ruszała, Cracow 2018, pp. 321–347.

[48] Although the figure may be slightly overstated, it is known that at least 6,000 prisoners passed through Thalerhof. It is also certain that the mortality rate was 1 in 3, mainly due to the epidemic of 1914–1915. See Katharina Wesener, 'Internment in WWI: The Case of Thalerhof', in *The Great War and Memory in Central and South-Eastern Europe*, ed. Oto Luthar, Leiden 2016, pp. 111–122.

Fig. 13 The title above the illustration reads: 'The Arrest of Spies Dressed as Nuns', *Ilustrowany Kuryer Codzienny*, a Cracow daily, 10 January 1915.

application of the right to self-defence in wartime entailed the execution of every suspect, not merely his arrest.

The repression in Western Galicia was on a slightly smaller scale, but here, too, civilians were not treated leniently. There was no time to determine whether alleged traitors actually served the enemy or whether they had simply annoyed their neighbours. Sławoj Felicjan Składkowski participated in the

96   THE FRONTS

execution of one such unfortunate. His role as a physician was to officially declare the death:

> Today, beyond the village, we executed a highlander whom the villagers had brought to us of their own accord. They claimed that he had received money to guide the Muscovites along the mountain paths to our rear, as a result of which we had been forced to retreat. The court martial sentenced him to death. [...] A fresh pit had already been dug. On the way to it the highlander asked for a light. The hands of the soldier who gave him the light were shaking as if with fever. Finally, we reached the pit. The officer ordered a blindfold be put on the condemned man. The highlander responded: 'Let me pray before I die.' He knelt down and placed the blindfold next to him. The officer nodded to the soldiers, who pulled out their rifles and took aim. The officer waved his handkerchief and a volley of gunshots rang out. The highlander rolled over on the grass and let out a cry: 'Oh Jesus!' and began to twitch, screaming and wheezing. The officer ran over to him, but his Browning revolver jammed. The highlander was still alive. Seconds passed, which seemed like an eternity. I grabbed my own revolver, put it against his head, and fired. He fell silent and died instantly.[49]

When writing about war crimes, however, it is easy to exaggerate. The number of confirmed fatalities resulting from military execution in Galicia – in 1914 and in the following year – was 620.[50] Even assuming that the army concealed its crimes where possible, that in 1917 the members of the Reichsrat did not have the capacity to carry out rigorous research, and that over the next 100 years historians did not add much that was new, then even if the number of unknown victims was much more than 620 we would still arrive at a figure of a few thousand people (not tens of thousands) killed by the monarchy's army. It is also true that within a few weeks of the start of the war both the Emperor and the Austrian General Staff were warning against overly repressive measures. In September 1914 the Imperial–Royal Ministry of the Interior intervened to avert similar acts being perpetrated against the Slovenes. In April of the following year, before the reconquest of Galicia and Bukovina had begun, the Ministry of the Interior warned the army not to exact revenge on civilians: draconian judgements handed down by a flawed judiciary were incompatible both with civil rights and with the interests of the state on whose behalf they were pronounced.

It is not known how many people were shot and hanged by other armies. What is certain, however, is that the fear of civilians that led to crimes being

---

[49] Składkowski, *Moja służba w Brygadzie*, p. 51.
[50] Hannes Leidinger, Verena Moritz, Karin Moser, and Wolfram Dornik, *Habsburgs schmutziger Krieg. Ermittlungen zur österreichisch-ungarischen Kriegsführung 1914–1918*, St Pölten 2014, p. 86.

committed was – paradoxically – felt by all sides in the conflict. It also made itself felt in the German army. At the beginning of August, when the Germans entered Kalisz, several shots were fired in unclear circumstances. In all likelihood soldiers from one of the German units had accidentally shot at their comrades. However, the blame was placed on the citizens of Kalisz and as punishment the city was shelled, set ablaze, and some of its population murdered. A similar pattern – the chaos of manoeuvre warfare, especially during night-time marches, friendly fire, the blaming of civilians for 'shots in the back', and repressive measures – was repeated in Belgium and northern France. The only difference between the Eastern and the Western Front was the extent to which such events were publicized. The world was much less interested in the provincial backwaters of Galicia, Serbia, and the Kingdom of Poland.

ŠABAC AND KALISZ

One of the best known and most poignant symbols of the horror of war is Leuven (Louvain). This Belgian university town was occupied by the German army in the second half of August 1914. Although the Germans took hostages from among the urban elites, this was not because the latter presented any particular threat. From the very first weeks of the war the taking of hostages had almost become a ritual. A few days later, on 25 August in the evening, panic broke out among the German soldiers stationed in Leuven. As is usual in such cases, it is hard to determine precisely who fired the first shot and who started shouting that the British were attacking. In addition, a rumour quickly spread among the Germans that the inhabitants of Leuven were shooting at the occupiers from the windows and rooftops. This was absurd: even if such desperate people did exist, they would have had no weapons to fight with; a few days earlier the Germans had disarmed the entire population. Still, the soldiers dragged hundreds of civilians out of their homes, shot some of them on the spot, arrested others, and burned down all the apartment buildings. Next they vandalized the historic university library with its valuable collections. On the following day the Germans continued their orgy of destruction. They wrecked houses and public offices, killing more than 200 civilians, and brutally abused the now homeless inhabitants of Leuven. Over 1,000 people were deported to Germany. On the third day the artillery completed the job by shelling the town centre. Almost immediately, the events in Leuven became headline news in neutral states and a motive for anti-German propaganda. The newspapers launched a massive campaign, accusing the German 'Huns' of 'raping Belgium'.

Yet German war crimes in Belgium were neither exceptional nor especially bloody. As the artillery shells fell on Leuven, in several towns in Serbia and in the town of Kalisz located near the western border of the Congress Kingdom, the fires were petering out and the most recent victims of military repression were being buried. The Austro-Hungarian forces that took part in the first invasion of Serbia proceeded with the utmost brutality. By the middle of August Serb civilians had been executed in

Krupanj, Loznica, and Lešnica. But the local symbol of Habsburg savagery was the town of Šabac. In the middle of August the Austrians occupied and thoroughly pillaged the town. Around 100 people were taken to the Orthodox church, where they were tortured and beaten and the women raped. On 17 August the soldiers led the detainees onto the square in front of the church. It is not known who gave the order to fire, but it is certain that there were women and children among the 100 or so victims.

Two weeks before the massacre in Šabac the German army occupied Kalisz, a town of 25,000 inhabitants. The scenes that took place there would be repeated in Leuven in almost the minutest detail. Initially, although hostages were taken, there was nothing to suggest that a tragedy was about to unfold. On 2 August chaotic shooting began in circumstances that remain unexplained to this day. German soldiers, convinced that they were being attacked by civilians, started to drag people from their homes and shoot random individuals. Then the centre of Kalisz was shelled. The commander of the German unit, Major Hans Preusker (who died of wounds on the Western Front in 1918), accused the townspeople of attacking the army. He imposed reparations on the town and tightened the ban on assembly. A few days later there was a second massacre. This time the victims were people attending the weekly market. Once again it began with unexplained gunfire. Preusker responded by ordering mass arrests and shelling the town. Several hundred residents were deported to Germany, while others fled.[51]

Fig. 14 The stamp reads: 'Warszawska Street in the town of Kalisz'. Courtesy of the Herder-Institut, Marburg, Bildarchiv.

---

[51] The most recent, extensive, and nuanced description of the events in Kalisz is by Laura Engelstein, '"A Belgium of Our Own": The Sack of Russian Kalisz, August 1914', *Kritika: Explorations in Russian and Eurasian History* 10, 3 (2009), pp. 441–473.

Fig. 15 Kalisz town centre in ruins. Courtesy of the Herder-Institut, Marburg, Bildarchiv.

Šabac and Kalisz, although never as well known as Leuven, also served the propaganda of the Entente Powers. Russian newspapers in particular used the events in Šabac and Kalisz to counter German claims of alleged atrocities committed during the invasion of East Prussia.

In the opinion of historians the mechanism behind all such events was similar. It was based on a psychosis that deemed the civilian population to be a threat. The Germans feared a repeat of 1871, when they had faced not just the regular French army but also the *francs-tireurs* (non-uniformed partisans). The Austro-Hungarian army, in turn, mistrusted the Serb minority in its own country and feared the Serb civilian population, whom it accused of fighting alongside the regular troops. It seems that civilians also fell victim to the overwhelming need to maintain the prestige of the armed forces. The repression that Preusker ordered in Kalisz after the massacres was an attempt, conscious or not, to absolve the German army of responsibility for the chaos, panic, and accidental shooting of its own soldiers. The Austrians were more willing to murder Serb civilians the less successful they were in fighting the enemy's regular forces.

Many of these crimes, repressions, and atrocities defy rational explanation. It is hard to find a real justification for them: repressive measures were either disproportionate or completely unjustified. They attest not so much to the pervasiveness of espionage and treason as to the psychological state of the soldiers and the stress they were under. A little more needs to be said about this last phenomenon.

Fig. 16 The stamp reads: 'Wrocławska Street in the town of Kalisz'. Courtesy of the Herder-Institut, Marburg, Bildarchiv.

The Sick and Wounded

For the vast majority of soldiers the Great War was the only war they had experienced at first hand. Artillery fire, machine guns, the sight of comrades dying – all this was to shock them deeply. For some, the shock was definitely too much to bear. A field doctor recalled the behaviour of young soldiers who had spent long periods under fire: 'The mentally ill either sat at the bottom of a trench utterly despondent or were eager to avenge the death of their comrades and jump out over the top.'[52] During one of the retreats the doctor had been unable to take a 'madman' with him, since the man had been throwing himself about in the cart and attacking other wounded soldiers: 'What could we do with him? [...] Aided by two orderlies I pushed the madman into a windowless barrack, padlocked the door, and with a piece of chalk wrote on it in Russian: 'умопомешанний' (madman). Perhaps this would protect him from the inevitable fury of the Muscovites.'[53]

The background to many of the psychoses experienced at the front was a fear of injury to one's own body. Austrian and Hungarian psychoanalysts had much to say on this subject and after 1914 focused on helping patients in uniform. One of Freud's most eminent disciples, Sándor Ferenczi, treated the survivors of the Royal Hungarian Hussars who, at the very start of the war, had carried out reconnaissance on the Zbruch River at great cost to themselves. In a letter to Freud he wrote:

[52] Składkowski, *Moja służba w Brygadzie*, p. 33.
[53] Ibid., pp. 362–363.

BEFORE THE LEAVES FALL FROM THE TREES ...

Forty-one officers and approximately 1,000 men were killed or taken prisoner. [...] The Cherkessians [or Circassians] [...] cut off a young cadet's penis and put it in his mouth. I think to myself: this strange and very widespread act of vengeance can be traced back to ambivalence. Consciousness is only filled with hate, but repressed sympathy expresses itself through punishment (as in the curse: fuck your mother, etc.).[54]

Similar anxieties were widespread, although not every observer was as sensitive to their sexual connotations as the psychoanalysts were. Most often these anxieties took the form of a story about gouging out the eyes or cutting off the hands of prisoners of war. The German pacifist Helmut von Gerlach noted (wrongly) that particular types of accusations were specific to particular regions:

The Russians are mainly accused of cutting off the hands and feet of men and the breasts of women. The French and Belgians are accused of gouging out eyes. There are different variants and combinations, but the leitmotif is always the same: chopping and cutting in the East, gouging in the West.[55]

Składkowski evaluated such stories in a similar tone: 'Apparently, somewhere in the vicinity a peasant woman found a wounded Austrian soldier lying in a field and put an end to his misery using a pitchfork (you'd have to be an Austrian to allow yourself to be finished off by a woman!).'[56] However, what appeared absurd to outside observers was of existential importance to civilians and prisoners accused of similar deeds. The fear and anxiety felt by soldiers put not just themselves but also others, at risk of death.

At the start of the war only Russia had experience in providing psychiatric care at the front. The war in Manchuria had exposed the vulnerability of the human psyche to physical trauma and shock. Thus, in the years 1905–1907, the Czarist empire finally abandoned the idea that war provided the best schooling for young men. Fear was identified as a medical problem. The other countries participating in the Great War had no such experiences. Both in Germany and in Austria-Hungary there were two competing and contradictory positions within the psychiatric profession. The first held that events at the front were analogous to railway disasters or accidents in the workplace. Physical injury causes not just the body but also the mind to suffer. Trauma is therefore the direct cause of the illness requiring treatment, and in cases where treatment is not possible the victim should be granted a disability pension. The second position was similar to the earlier Russian idea that war invigorates the mind. If so, then the psychiatric disorders revealed at the front are not caused by the experience of war but instead

[54] Letter of 8 July 1915, cited in Ferenc Erős, 'Gender, Hysteria, and War Neurosis', in *Gender and Modernity in Central Europe: The Austro-Hungarian Monarchy and Its Legacy*, ed. Agatha Schwartz, Ottawa 2010, pp. 185–201, here p. 189.
[55] Helmut von Gerlach, *Die große Zeit der Lüge. Der Erste Weltkrieg und die deutsche Mentalität (1871–1921)*, ed. H. Donat and A. Wild, Bremen 1994, pp. 73–74.
[56] Składkowski, *Moja służba w Brygadzie*, p. 154.

102   THE FRONTS

signal the development of primitive, hysterical tendencies. What follows is that the war is not responsible for the illness and hence the state is not obliged to grant anyone a disability pension or to pay compensation. The advantages that the second solution seemed to offer both to the military authorities and to the overburdened state budget ensured that it gained the upper hand. This had dramatic consequences for thousands of soldiers – the victims of what was to become known on the Western Front as shell shock.

FARADIZATION

One of the Good Soldier Švejk's more colourful adventures was his sojourn in a 'hospital for malingerers'. Hašek describes this sanctuary as follows:

> In these great times the army doctors took unusual pains to drive the devil of sabotage out of the malingerers and restore them to the bosom of the army. Various degrees of torture had been introduced for malingerers and suspected malingerers, such as consumptives, rheumatics, people with hernia, kidney disease, typhus, diabetes, pneumonia and other illnesses. The tortures to which the malingerers were subjected were systematized and the grades were as follows:
>
> 1. Strict diet, a cup of tea each morning and evening for three days, during which, irrespective, of course, of their complaints, aspirin to be given to induce sweating.
> 2. To ensure they did not think that war was all beer and skittles, quinine in
>   powder to be served in generous portions, or so-called 'quinine licking'.
> 3. The stomach to be pumped out twice a day with a litre of warm water.
> 4. Enemas with soapy water and glycerine to be applied.
> 5. Wrapping up in a sheet soaked in cold water.
>
> There were stalwart men who endured all five degrees of torture and let themselves be carried off to the military cemetery in a simple coffin. But there were also pusillanimous souls who, when they reached the stage of the enema, declared that they were now well and desired nothing better than to march off to the trenches with the next march battalion.[57]

Literature lives by its own rules and need not be concerned with historical accuracy. Furthermore, the light and ironic tone of Hašek's novel suggests that what he is offering is an embellished version of reality. Yet it is precisely this fragment of the novel that is one of the most realistic. The scene depicted by Hašek is not just supported by the post-war accounts of patients who spent

---

[57] Hašek, *The Good Soldier Švejk*, p. 62.

BEFORE THE LEAVES FALL FROM THE TREES ...   103

time in military hospitals, but also by professional publications and doctors' memories. In Hašek's novel Dr Grünstein's patients are 'treated' in almost exactly the same way as thousands of German and Austro-Hungarian soldiers, and soldiers of every other nationality, who wanted to avoid frontline duty by complaining about ailments more difficult to diagnose than losing their limbs. The chicanery they were typically subjected to included compulsory isolation, starvation, a ban on smoking, and the administration of unpalatable medicines (not quinine, which was useful on the Balkan Front in the prevention of malaria, but asafoetida – a foul-tasting resin extracted from the Ferula plant, also known as Devil's Dung). Sometimes the 'treatment' was cut short simply by threatening the 'malingerers' with denunciation if they did not return to the front voluntarily. The list of 'treatments' and psychological tricks was endless. Ingenious physicians would add their own cures in order to 'drive the devil of sabotage out of the malingerers'.

In 1916 a young Hungarian doctor published an article whose impact on the fate of patients in military hospitals cannot be overestimated. Viktor Gonda from the hospital in Rózsahegy (now Ružomberok in Slovakia) found that a combination of suggestion and electric shocks produced excellent results in the treatment of neurological disorders in soldiers.[58] The Austro-Hungarian military authorities were delighted and soon a procedure euphemistically called 'faradization' came to be used in all the monarchy's hospitals. In the Reich an almost identical therapy based on the clinical experience of the Hamburg psychiatrist Max Nonne was developed. These two doctors used similar methods. Usually, electrodes were attached to the most sensitive areas of the body: the underarms, the area between the fingers and between the toes, the genitals, and the nipples. For this therapy was all about causing the greatest amount of pain. As the future Nobel laureate Julius Wagner-Jauregg, one of the doctors who administered faradization, recalled, it was sometimes enough just to show a new patient what lay in store for him: he would soon give up his efforts to be discharged from military service.[59]

Although faradization was used on patients of all nationalities, a kind of regional differentiation emerged. Max Nonne and many other psychiatrists put the emphasis on combining two elements of the therapy: electric shocks and suggestion. In their view the patient was not only to be tortured but also to be convinced that his health had actually improved. He had at once to fear the therapy and believe that it would cure him. However, the reality of the war in the East meant that adherence to these guidelines was nigh on impossible. As Wagner-Jauregg noted, 'hypnosis and hypnotic suggestion cannot be conducted through an interpreter. And yet, due to the ethnic composition of our army, our psychogenic cases have mainly been soldiers whose mother tongue is

[58] Viktor Gonda, 'A háború okozta "traumás neurosis" tüneteinek gyors gyógyítása', *Orvosi Hetilap* 33 (1916), pp. 445–446; also in German as 'Rasche Heilung der Symptome der im Kriege entstandenen "traumatischen Neurose"', *Wiener Klinische Wochenschrift* 29 (1916), pp. 960–961.

[59] Julius Wagner von Jauregg, *Erfahrungen über Kriegsneurosen*, Vienna 1917, p. 16 (reprinted from a series of articles in the *Wiener Medizinische Wochenschrift*).

not German.'[60] Consequently, physicians in Austro-Hungarian hospitals restricted themselves to faradization and regarded talking to the patient as secondary.

It soon became apparent that the new method of instilling discipline in the troops at times produced undesirable results. The effect of electricity on the human organism was not yet well known. In their zeal, some physicians, led by Gonda himself, used current with a voltage that was too high. Increasing numbers of 'unbreakable patients' left hospital in a coffin. In 1916 and 1917 a wave of suicides among hospitalized 'malingerers' was also noted. Eventually, open protest ensued. Patients objected to the arrival in their hospital of 'physician-electricians', as the proponents of the new method were nicknamed. The military authorities received an avalanche of complaints. Meanwhile, there was a parallel struggle going on within the psychiatric community between the supporters of faradization and the psychoanalysts who fought it tooth and nail. What this meant was that from the beginning of 1917, first in Germany and a few months later in Austria-Hungary, electric shock therapy was less frequently used.

The postscript to the faradization story is to be found in the tempestuous period that followed the surrender of the Central Powers. In Germany, revolutionary soldiers tried to lynch Nonne. He managed to escape at the last minute, so the attackers unleashed their rage by demolishing his office. Meanwhile, in Austria, Wagner-Jauregg had to defend himself against public accusations made by one of his former patients, although this incident did not interrupt his glittering medical career. Only Gonda managed to avoid any unpleasantness. Immediately after the war he practised in Romania, before emigrating to the United States. Gonda's wartime experiences proved invaluable, and he became one of the pioneers of electroconvulsive therapy in the United States.

Most victims at the front did not suffer from psychosis, however. They mostly suffered on account of wounds and diseases. During the war, officers and physicians alike doggedly insisted that the losses due to venereal disease, typhus, dysentery, cholera, and influenza were possibly twenty times higher than the losses on the battlefield. In fact, in the German army deaths due to disease accounted for around 10 per cent of total losses, while in the Austro-Hungarian army the figure was slightly higher.[61] The Great War was the first conflict in which these figures remained lower than the sum of those killed or wounded in battle.

Diseased patients were relatively privileged on account of the time that was left to treat them. Neither typhus nor cholera killed as quickly as blood loss. In terms of hygiene, the condition of Russian soldiers was the worst, and it was probably they who contributed to the spread of certain diseases, especially cholera. On the Austro-Hungarian and German side, epidemics were dealt

[60] Ibid., p. 18.
[61] Elisabeth Dietrich, 'Der andere Tod. Seuchen, Volkskrankheiten und Gesundheitswesen im Ersten Weltkrieg', in *Tirol und der Erste Weltkrieg*, ed. Klaus Eisterer and Rolf Steiniger, Innsbruck and Vienna 1995, pp. 255–275.

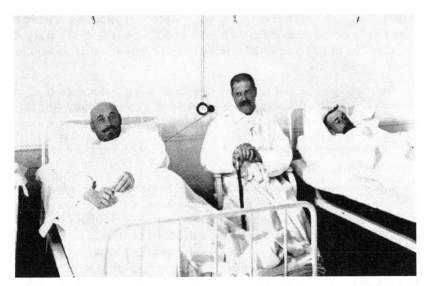

Fig. 17 Military hierarchy was maintained even behind the lines. Wounded officers could expect better care than rank-and-file soldiers. The photograph shows wounded Russian officers in a military hospital in the depths of the empire. Courtesy of Mariusz Kulik.

with determinedly; infirmaries for patients with typhus and cholera were set up in separate barracks. Work in infirmaries was extremely stressful for army doctors due to the danger of infection, and for this reason duty hours were strictly limited. As for helping the wounded when battles were ongoing, it was not always possible to bring them back behind the lines quickly. Infections were also quite frequent. It is worth recalling that no antibiotics or blood transfusions were used at the time. Despite this, medical assistance was unquestionably better than during the Balkan Wars and subsequent conflicts in Central and Eastern Europe. The real catastrophe came in 1918 with the arrival of the great Spanish flu epidemic, and then in 1919 and 1920 during the Polish–Bolshevik and Polish–Ukrainian wars, when an outbreak of typhus fever extinguished Ukrainian aspirations for independence.

In the first months of the war, sick and wounded Serbs and the Austro-Hungarian soldiers they captured found themselves in the worst situation. This was for several reasons. Since 1912 Serbia had been almost constantly at war. The population was impoverished and the 1914 summer campaign impacted negatively on the harvest. There was widespread hunger, which encouraged the spread of diseases imported by the army. Cholera and typhus arrived along with the victors of the First Balkan War. Worse still, in the territories gained by the Serbs during the Second Balkan War, cholera and

106 THE FRONTS

malaria were endemic. Devastated and poor, the country lacked the resources to effectively fight disease and care for its wounded. Robert W. Seton-Watson described one of the improvised Serbian hospitals, which was more akin to a home for the dying:

> The need here is terrible. One hospital we visited in Skopje is characteristic. It is a tobacco factory, merely improved as a hospital. Each floor contains a huge room running the whole length of the building, and in each of these there are 250 wounded men, lying in their clothes on beds and mattresses without sheets or blankets, with no lighting, without nurses or proper attendance.[62]

But the biggest problem was the lack of doctors. Prime Minister Pašić's government made no secret of this, and the Serbs officially asked for international help. Dozens of brave doctors and nurses came to the rescue. Some of them not only aided Serbia but also made great careers for themselves. One example is Ludwik Hirszfeld, who together with his wife Hanna conducted serological and bacteriological research while working in a Serbian field hospital. Most quantifiable, however, was the assistance given by British NGOs. The Serbian Relief Foundation and private donors set up their own hospitals. British (mainly Scottish) physicians and nurses were also employed in Serbian field hospitals, and some of them paid for it with their lives. Yet, despite the assistance, epidemics took a terrible toll on the ravaged country: the number of civilian deaths in the spring of 1915 was estimated at around 100,000; over 30,000 of the 70,000 prisoners of war, and 30,000 of the 250,000 soldiers, also perished.[63]

The ordeal suffered by the Serbs was not typical – other countries were affected more by the war than by epidemics, while the number of victims remained at a proportionally much lower level, and not just in the first half of the year. Nevertheless, Serbia encapsulated the lethal nature of the First World War, hitherto unimaginable.

Positional Warfare

At the same time as cholera and typhus were raging among soldiers and civilians in Serbia, in the Carpathians a positional war was under way. It was interrupted by operations conducted across a limited area and with limited goals. For the soldiers who had been chased from place to place over the course of a few months this was a completely new situation. The process of adaptation was similar to that on the Western Front and involved working out a number of small, daily compromises with the enemy, who was dug in just a few hundred metres away. Składkowski

---

[62] Hugh Seton-Watson and Christopher Seton-Watson, *The Making of a New Europe. R. W. Seton-Watson and the Last Years of Austria-Hungary*, Seattle, WA 1981, p. 113.
[63] Mira Radojević and Ljubodrag Dimić, *Serbia in the Great War 1914–1918. A Short History*, translated by Mirjana Jovanović, Belgrade 2014, pp. 171–173.

described the arrival of the Polish Legionnaires to the Austro-Hungarian line of defence on the Nida River. The soldiers already stationed there had reached an agreement with the Russians that neither side would shoot at the water-carriers. The Poles either learned of this too late or deliberately ignored the arrangement and shot several Russians who were returning to their trenches with full buckets of water. In response the enemy shelled the Legionnaires' positions, injuring several men. Then, on 'no-man's land', Russian envoys bearing white flags appeared. They had a simple message for the Poles: 'Why did you shoot at us yesterday? It'd be better if you didn't!' The agreement was approved once again and probably lasted until the next change of personnel.[64]

In the winter and spring spectacular acts of fraternization between Russian and Austro-Hungarian soldiers took place on some sections of the Eastern Front. The first attempts during the Catholic Christmas of 1914 were somewhat timid – in places where the enemy trenches were only a short distance away, Poles on both sides sang carols together. Easter on the Nida River was much more impressive:

> 'The Muscovites are standing on the bank of the Nida – look!' Not really understanding what this meant, we went out and saw that there, on the far bank of the Nida [...], the Muscovites were standing in a line, with our boys facing them on the other side, unarmed. The two groups were talking to each other and we could hear them from where we were standing. Baffled by this extraordinary phenomenon, soldiers began to run out from the Russian trenches and from ours and head across the sun-lit no-man's land and water meadows [...] to the river bank. [...] Along the entire battle line not a single shot from a machine gun or cannon was to be heard. A festive mood had descended – it was Easter![65]

Temporary agreements between the middle and lower ranks of enemy armies were also a daily occurrence. Składkowski, for instance, mentioned seeing a searchlight in the battalion HQ which, rather than being used to illuminate enemy positions, served as a 'tabouret': 'Let's not switch it on in the trenches, because the Muscovites will only switch on their one that is stationed on the hill beyond Pińczów; it will completely drown out the light from ours and they'll be laughing at us from the other side of the Nida. Why embarrass ourselves?'[66] Sometimes arrangements with the enemy needed to be more precise, especially when it came to the exchange of food. Goods for barter would be left by patrols at the agreed spot. Although the Russians were generally better fed, they had a low opinion of the bread they were given. At times they also lacked tobacco, which the Central Powers had in abundance thanks to imports from Bulgaria and Albania. However, the scarcest commodity in the Russian trenches was

---

[64] Składkowski, *Moja służba w Brygadzie*, p. 84.
[65] Solek, *Pamiętnik legionisty*, p. 103.
[66] Składkowski, *Moja służba w Brygadzie*, p. 88.

Fig. 18 Red wine being dispensed on the first day of Orthodox Christmas, 1915. Courtesy of Mariusz Kulik.

alcohol. The wartime prohibition introduced in Russia often had a devastating effect. At the front and behind the lines hard-drinking officers and soldiers quaffed methylated spirit and wood alcohol; deaths also occurred after the consumption of spirit-laden cubes intended for portable cooking stoves. For some, a much safer method of acquiring of alcohol was barter with the Austrians: sausage and bread in exchange for rum, biscuits, and tobacco.

Commanders resisted every attempt to mitigate the hardship of life at the front. They tried, albeit not very successfully, to ban all trade and contact with the enemy. Quite simply, the longer soldiers remained in a situation of relative calm, the less they viewed their neighbours in the opposite trenches as enemies. In the long run the most effective means of maintaining discipline and motivation was to go on the offensive, and this gave the advocates of aggressive tactics another argument: keeping the army moving was necessary not just to seize the initiative but also to maintain discipline in the ranks. As an Austrian lieutenant explains in *The Last Days of Mankind*: when soldiers start complaining about food it's best to order them to attack, just so they don't get out of practice. Even in hopeless situations attack has many advantages. The lieutenant colonel is hopping mad when too many of his subordinates survive after a retreat. Colloquially, continues the lieutenant colonel, 'they call it the Pflanzer-Baltin system' (after the commander of one of the armies on the

Fig. 19 Attempts were made on all the fronts to come to terms with the reality of war. The photograph shows the Christmas celebrations of the 1st (Sofia) Infantry Regiment in 1916. Courtesy of Mr Peyo Kolev, lostbulgaria.com.

Russian Front, General Karl von Pflanzer-Baltin). It was this strategist who coined the phrase 'I will teach my men how to die.'[67]

Pflanzer-Baltin would have no doubt subscribed to the view that an army that does not fight might as well disband. Daily life in the trenches was indeed filled with many apparently mundane activities. Because of the cold, only a small number of soldiers remained in the advanced trenches; the rest sat in dugouts, which were heated after a fashion. The medical units took advantage of the breaks in fighting to carry out vaccinations and delousing. Combating lice was an important element of the daily schedule in the trenches:

> Lice breed abundantly in the seams of clothing. The bigger specimens can be caught with one's fingers, but the smaller ones are not worth the effort; the eggs can be scratched off onto paper using a pen knife and then burnt in the chimney. Clean underwear must also be examined, as here too one often finds well-fed specimens. Dirty underwear must be taken outside and thrown away – washing it is out of the question.[68]

---

[67] Karl Kraus, *The Last Days of Mankind: A Tragedy in Five Acts*, translated by Patrick Healy, Amsterdam 2016, pp. 97, 528.
[68] Solek, *Pamiętnik legionisty*, p. 100.

Fig. 20 A 'domesticated' shelter for Bulgarian telephone operators on the Salonika Front. Courtesy of Mr Peyo Kolev, lostbulgaria.com.

One of the most original methods of combating lice, which was observed on the Galician Front, was to leave clothes on an anthill for a period of time.

With the arrival of the spring thaw in late March and early April, the trenches filled with mud and water leached into the latrines. Soldiers would accordingly move to huts that had been spared by the artillery. Some were still inhabited, as not all civilians complied with evacuation orders. As the temperatures rose, the local population would become more visible and the most stubborn villagers would begin working in the fields. Despite the dangers, life moved outside: 'A strange scene: playing in the sand atop the trenches are small children who live in the huts beyond the trenches that people have not yet abandoned.'[69]

---

[69] Skladkowski, *Moja służba w Brygadzie*, p. 113.

Fig. 21 An Austrian trench in a village in the Stryj (today Stryi) district. Sometimes the separation of the front from civilian areas was entirely arbitrary. Courtesy of Mariusz Kulik.

The Przemyśl Fortress

In March 1915 there were no such 'strange scenes' in the largest besieged fortress on the Eastern Front. The Russians tried to take Przemyśl by storm, and when they failed they embarked on a long siege. It was the defenders who then seized the initiative, organizing a total of six sorties from the fortress, all of which were unsuccessful despite the great cost in men. The fortifications at Przemyśl covered an area 45 kilometres in circumference; there were two rings of entrenchments with artillery emplacements and several dozen forts. Located within the fortifications was the town of Przemyśl itself as well as neighbouring villages that had been razed in the autumn of 1914 so as not to impede artillery fire. By the middle of September, as a result of the first Russian offensive in Eastern Galicia, Przemyśl was already under siege. In the reasonably well-stocked fortress the main problem was civilian refugees from local villages. There were scores of them, and the pace of the Russian offensive had prevented planned civilian evacuations from being carried out. News of the pogroms perpetrated by the Russians prompted many Jews to take refuge in Przemyśl. Some inhabitants of the villages razed by the army also remained within the fortress. Without a roof over their head, they camped in fields or in dugouts, relying on help from the authorities and subsisting on the last remaining potatoes they had carefully buried. The forefield of the fortress was a sorry sight:

112   THE FRONTS

The deserted villages are inhabited by cats that have run wild. Officers often bring in lost children wrapped in coats. Sitting there amidst a rain of shrapnel was a three year-old boy, all alone, laughing and playing in a field. The soldiers who found him could not get anything out of him, except for the words: 'Granny, America!'[70]

The first assault launched by Radko Dimitriev (the same commander who had led the Bulgarians at Çatalca) did not succeed nor could it have done. The Russians had no heavy artillery, and their attempt to quickly capture the well-defended fortress, which housed a personnel of over 100,000, owed much to the reckless ambition of the Bulgarian general in the service of the Czar. The operation was extremely bloody and completely ineffective; it lasted for a week, ending on 9 October after the arrival of a relief force in the form of the 3rd Austro-Hungarian Army. The fortress commander, General Hermann Kusmanek, also ordered his troops to attack; the Russians, assailed from two sides, had to abandon the siege. A Hungarian officer defending the fortress described the harrowing impression that the battle made on him:

> As dawn broke we saw the battlefield, the length and breadth of which was covered in Russian corpses. Not a single shot was to be heard from the Russian side. [. . .] There were hundreds of Russians dug in along a single line – all dead. Those that were still moving were being taken away by stretcher-bearers. Here and there we saw individual soldiers armed with wire cutters. A dead officer in a fire trench was holding in his hands a precise plan of the fort I/3 and a map of the Byków resistance point. Behind him was a thin line of dug-in gunners. All had perished! It was a terrible sight. In front of the barbed wire itself lay hundreds of bodies, and further back thousands. We had been diligent in our work. I shall never forget that scene.[71]

One of the Czech defenders of Przemyśl, Jan Vit, remembered a different image from that day. His attention was focused on the living rather than the dead. The Russian survivors still sitting in the trenches and furrows would sometimes throw their arms around the necks of the Hungarian stretcher-bearers combing the battlefield. The latter, in turn, divided their time between helping the wounded and robbing the dead.[72]

---

[70] Ilka Künigl-Ehrenburg, *W oblężonym Przemyślu. Kartki z dziennika z czasów Wielkiej Wojny (1914–1915)*, translated by Edward Pietraszek and Anna Szczak, ed. Stanisław Stępień, Przemyśl 2010, p. 104 (originally published pseudonymously as Ilka von Michaelsburg, *Im belagerten Przemysl. Tagebuchblätter aus großer Zeit*, Leipzig 1915).

[71] Cited in Bator, *Wojna galicyjska*, p. 197.

[72] Jan Vit, *Wspomnienia z mojego pobytu w Przemyślu podczas rosyjskiego oblężenia 1914–1915*, translated by Ladislav Hofbauer and Jerzy Husar, ed. Stanisław Stępień, Przemyśl 1995, p. 53.

Fig. 22 Children greeting soldiers of the 3rd Austro-Hungarian Army with flowers. The joy of liberation did not last long.

Although it was a success for the defenders, the first siege of Przemyśl contained the seeds of future defeat. The relief force was tired and hungry, with many sick and wounded soldiers. It is hard to say whether cholera was brought to the fortress by the Austro-Hungarian soldiers or by the Russian prisoners of war; in any case, at the beginning of October it became necessary to set up isolation barracks for the afflicted. This was not the only problem to emerge after the arrival of the relief force, however. The army also had to be fed, and the only well-stocked food stores within easy reach were precisely in Przemyśl. Since the fortress was temporarily out of danger, and to the east of it fighting was still raging, it was decided that some of the personnel and equipment, mainly heavy artillery, would be merged with the 3rd Army. The shortages of food, men, and equipment could have been made good were it not for the rapid failure of the Austro-Hungarian offensive and the chaotic retreat across the San River. At the beginning of November Przemyśl once again found itself under siege, this time for a longer period.

The Russians had learned the lessons of their first unsuccessful assault. This time they restricted themselves to blockading the fortress and shelling it with artillery. Russian planes flew over Przemyśl in an attempt to bomb the food stores. But even without this, provisioning soon became the most pressing problem for personnel and civilians within the fortress. The prices of goods

114   THE FRONTS

began to rise exponentially. In November a loaf of bread cost twice as much as before the war, salt was five times more expensive, and some goods (such as butter) had completely run out. In January the landlady of a tenement house, Helena Jabłońska née Seifert, noted: 'The hunger is unprecedented; the masses that have come here, by what means one does not know, are principally Jews from the vicinity of Lwów [. . .]. The faces on the streets are completely foreign. Some suffer from terrible hunger; they have become blackened and dehydrated.'[73] By February the problem was not so much high prices as simply a shortage of goods. Hungry soldiers and civilians fought over horse bones thrown out of soup kitchens. The price of an egg surpassed 1 crown, that is, twenty times the pre-war price.

The food rations issued to personnel, and from the end of January to early March also to starving civilians, got ever smaller. Beginning in December, one day in the week was designated as a no-bread day. People started to capture cats and crows for food, and in the military posts around the town officers used their patrols to hunt for deer and hare. Finally, General Kusmanek took the decision to slaughter many of the horses, which had numbered around 20,000 at the beginning of the siege. This was a desperate measure, for it significantly reduced the chances of being able to break out of the fortress into friendly territory. Without horses it was impossible to transport food, artillery, and sick and wounded people. The provisioning improved, but only for a brief period.

It was not just food that was in short supply. The bitterly cold winter of 1914/1915 presented a huge challenge for soldiers in the field, especially as the personnel were not prepared for it. Most soldiers had received their uniforms when mobilizing for the August offensive; the warm overcoats they had been promised never reached them. People remedied the shortages by whatever means possible:

> The uniforms one sees on the streets today are so lax. Gone are the days when every half hour a soldier would be reprimanded by a superior for having his cap or collar askew or for marching too slowly. [. . .] All the warm underwear in the fortress has long since been bought up. [. . .] The officers return to the forts sitting on peasant carts wrapped in chequered shawls. Others [. . .] are dressed in mottled black-and-white oilcloths of the kind that are used to cover tables – they buy them and convert them into raincoats.[74]

The military headquarters organized workshops where products in shortest supply were manufactured from what was still available. Collections of secondary raw materials and scrap were enthusiastically promoted. The knapsacks of Landsturm soldiers were used to produce warm vests; wood was

---

[73] Helena z Seifertów Jabłońska, *Dziennik z oblężonego Przemyśla 1914–1915*, ed. Hanna Imbs, Przemyśl 1994, p. 112.

[74] Künigl-Ehrenburg, *W oblężonym Przemyślu*, pp. 123–124.

combined with prepared rags to create the soles of shoes; and completely non-regulation straw slippers appeared. Throughout the siege, soap factories and distilleries worked around the clock. Rum and vodka never ran out. The military commanders tried to infect the personnel with enthusiasm. They triumphantly announced, for instance, that it would be possible to feed the surviving horses with specially prepared shavings, which were also added to bread. In a similar tone they proclaimed that one portion of vegetables would be replaced with sugar beet. Both these orders had to be quietly withdrawn; their only (relatively) positive effect was to increase the supply of meat from slaughtered horses, since the latter could not stomach the new diet.

The hardships of the siege were not the same for everyone. A very rigid social hierarchy held sway within the fortress. At the bottom of it were civilians – Ruthenian peasants from villages near Przemyśl. As well as suffering from hunger, they also fell victim to the spy craze. Already during the first siege several lynchings of alleged 'Russophiles', including a number of women, took place on the streets of the town. Later, members of this social group would often be brought before a court martial, which would sentence them to death for alleged espionage or, in some cases, even for 'defeatism'. The failure of every poorly prepared sortie from the fortress was attributed to treason. Rumours about maps of the Przemyśl fortifications having been found on the corpses of Russian officers only reinforced these suspicions, yet no one asked themselves how a Ukrainian peasant could have come into possession of such documents. After all, emaciated and starving civilians had no information of any great military significance; otherwise, they would have in all likelihood happily sold it for food and shelter. Some starving refugees did indeed shuttle between the Russian and Austrian positions, offering to one or the other side information about the enemy, some of it imaginary, and demanding food in return. The value of these 'confidants' was, we may assume, directly proportional to the remuneration they received.

The situation of Jewish refugees was hardly better than the plight of the Ruthenians. That their numbers were great is shown by the fact that, according to witness accounts, they constituted the majority of the victims of Russian aerial bombardment. The problem, which for many religious Jews took on an existential meaning, concerned food. Horsemeat, which was not considered kosher, in time became the mainstay of the fortress diet. The choice between death by starvation and failure to observe religious rules was a dramatic one. Uniquely, however, Jews did not raise any suspicions among the Austro-Hungarian military authorities, who saw them as loyal subjects. On the other hand, the prospects for Jews in the event of the fortress capitulating were especially bleak. Their fears were confirmed shortly after the Russians occupied Przemyśl:

116 THE FRONTS

> The pogrom of the Jews started today, or rather last night. They waited until the Jews had gone to pray at the synagogue. There the Cossacks attacked them with whips. With no questions asked, and irrespective of age, they drove them from their synagogues and communities, from the streets and from the thresholds of their homes, towards the huge barracks in Bakończyce. [...] The old and weak who could not keep up were whipped. [...] Such wailing, such despair! Some have hidden in cellars, but there the Cossacks will seek them out too.[75]

Meanwhile, the siege was still in progress. The situation of soldiers was hardly better than that of the Jewish refugees. Although they received food rations throughout the siege, these were starvation rations. 'Evaders' and the sick and wounded were fed so poorly that they were forced to beg. The troops that remained in their posts were fed slightly better, but nonetheless inadequately. Weak and malnourished, soldiers died of exposure, lost their hands and feet to frostbite, and fainted on duty. The Ruthenians in the Landsturm, who found it easiest to communicate with the besiegers, deserted *en masse* due to hunger. The civilians who remained in the fortress coped in different ways. Their situation depended on what valuables and supplies they had and on their arrangements with the army. As supplies ran out, the number of prostitutes in the fortress rapidly increased. A good way of ensuring modest but regular meals was to work in the military hospital as a nurse. Memoirists recall that in certain hospitals in Przemyśl there was such an excess of nurses that, with the best will in the world, some of them had nothing to do.

It was characteristic of the Austro-Hungarian army that the command hierarchy was maintained even in the most dramatic circumstances. This was also true in Przemyśl. Whereas rank-and-file soldiers froze while standing guard and patrols were led by sergeants, the officers had their own canteens; it was they who formed the 'middle class' in the besieged fortress. Although they complained about the increasingly meagre portions and especially about the monotony of the cuisine, which alternated between horse sirloin, horse tongue, and horse roast, they did not starve. Yet even they were indignant at the behaviour of Commander Kusmanek. One officer in the Royal Hungarian Honvéd, whose memoirs were discovered in the 1960s during the renovation of a Przemyśl tenement house, grumbled:

> Kusmanek's behaviour towards the army is completely inappropriate. Instead of looking after the unit he strolls around checking how the men salute. Not once has he visited a hospital and he would certainly have much to see there. We have huge numbers of fatalities due to botched operations and the careless dressing of wounds. Hygiene standards are inadequate and consequently every third patient that goes under the knife dies of blood infection. [...] We have received news that only thirty horses

---

[75] Jabłońska, *Dziennik z oblężonego Przemyśla*, p. 162.

BEFORE THE LEAVES FALL FROM THE TREES ...   117

will remain in the division. His excellency will keep all of them, naturally, and indeed purchase a further two so that his whore can go on excursions in a carriage. Meanwhile, our own horses will be slaughtered for food.[76]

The criticism of Kusmanek might have been milder had he not been so eager to organize sorties from the fortress that were as pointless as they were bloody. Only one of these had aimed to break the siege and link up with the relief force that was headed for Przemyśl. The other sorties had sought to improve the strategic situation, tie up Russian forces that would otherwise be sent to another section of the front, and ultimately keep the defenders' 'fighting spirit' alive, if nothing else. The final sortie took place on 19 March. Kusmanek decided to advance not to the west or south, but to the east, towards the Russian food stores in Mościska. His hungry soldiers were given several days' worth of rations. The plan was to attack with bayonets under the cover of the night, hence all cartridges were confiscated to ensure that the enemy would not be forewarned. The effect was pitiful. Those who managed to reach the Russian positions were discovered in time and decimated, but many soldiers did not even get that far. The more disciplined men fainted from hunger, since they had obeyed the order not to touch the canned food they had been given for the journey. Those who had disobeyed the order likewise floundered because eating a large portion of canned horsemeat had caused diarrhoea. The return to the fortress was all the more melancholic when it transpired that the men's quarters had been thoroughly looted. As the Czech officer Jan Vit recalled: 'The civilians, thinking we would never return, robbed us of everything. They took whatever could be removed – bedding, straw mattresses, stoves – and looted the stores.'[77] Even in Kusmanek's eyes, further resistance made no sense. On the first day of spring he took the decision to destroy the forts, cannons, and magazines. It was probably the biggest pyrotechnic display in the history of Galicia:

> At 3.00 a.m. the police were sent to all areas of the town to wake up the inhabitants and warn them of the noise and commotion that was about to begin. Both powder magazines, three bridges, and the railway workshops were to be blown up at 5.00 a.m. We stood in front of the gate. Crowds of people carrying trunks, bundles, and children were running in panic along our street and along Słowackiego, their eyes wide with fear. [...] Shivering with cold we waited until 5.00 a.m. [...] Then, suddenly, with a terrifying bang, the first powder magazine was detonated; the earth shook and many windows were blown out. Soot and ash spewed from the chimneys, dust cascaded from the walls, and bits of plaster fell from the ceilings; doors flew open. A moment

---

[76] Cited in Antoni Kroh, *O Szwejku i o nas*, Nowy Sącz 1992, p. 91.
[77] Vit, *Wspomnienia z mojego pobytu w Przemyślu*, p. 84.

Fig. 23 The shell-blasted Siedliska fort after the recapture of Przemyśl by the German and Austro-Hungarian armies.

> later there was a second bang, with the same effect. [...] Soldiers knelt on the balconies in prayer.[78]

Przemyśl capitulated on 22 March 1915. More than 100,000 defenders ended up in Russian captivity. The Russians gained 900 guns – including the heaviest guns, which they had never possessed – and plenty of other equipment. Austria-Hungary had to bid farewell to its largest fortress on the Russian border. Russia, in turn, could redirect its 11th Army to the bloody battlefields of the Carpathian Mountains. The defeat of the monarchy now seemed certain.

THE 28TH INFANTRY REGIMENT AT ESZTEBNEKHUTA (STEBNÍCKA HUTA)

The excellent essayist and ethnographer Antoni Kroh recounts the following anecdote in one of his books:

> A teacher raises his hand with his thumb and fingers extended and asks Jasio the following question: 'How many?' 'Five', answers Jasio. 'And how many now?', asks the teacher, raising his other hand. 'Twenty-eight', replies Jasio with conviction.[79]

---

[78] Jabłońska, *Dziennik z oblężonego Przemyśla*, p. 139.
[79] Kroh, *O Szwejku i o nas*, pp. 38–39.

BEFORE THE LEAVES FALL FROM THE TREES ...

This joke, which has long since ceased to be funny, came into being after the winter campaign in the Carpathians. At the end of March 1915 the Austro-Hungarian line of defence was broken in the vicinity of Stebnícka Huta (now in northern Slovakia, near the Polish border). In early April some members of the 28th Infantry Regiment, most of whom had been recruited in Prague, were captured by the Russians. In the preceding weeks there had already been cases of desertion and insubordination by Czech soldiers. In the middle of February František Boubelík, a foot soldier from the 102nd Infantry Regiment, had been caught in a trench holding a white flag in his hand; an officer shot him on the spot. In March several platoons from the 11th and 91st Infantry Regiments had gone unaccounted for, and just before the Battle of Stebnícka Huta the 8th Regiment (21st Division) of the Landsturm lost two-thirds of its men in combat. The fact that there were many Czechs among them did not escape the notice of the military commanders, who were likewise aware of the supposedly cowardly attitude of the 20th Brigade (10th Infantry Division). When, in the chaos of the fighting that took place in the still snow-covered Carpathians, 1,500 members of the 28th Infantry Regiment 'disappeared', military men and civilian observers alike drew far-reaching conclusions. A rumour quickly spread that part of the regiment, in full order and led by an orchestra, had gone over to the Russians. The fact that it was the Prague regiment sat perfectly with this conspiracy theory: instead of fighting for the Emperor, these men from the Czech capital (the 'Prague children', as the regiment was unofficially called) had shamefully betrayed him and in so doing had manifested their Pan-Slavic sympathies.

The military authorities reacted nervously. Almost immediately, without even waiting for witness reports, they decided to punish the regiment for 'dishonouring the flag'. Emperor Franz Joseph did not hesitate to sign the relevant order. Although the decision was made known to the army, it was important to keep it from the public. The censors were not up to the task, though. Rumours about the fate of the 28th Regiment soon began to circulate throughout the monarchy; the joke quoted by Kroh is just one example of their destructive power. Different versions of the story were told and with a different emotional tinge. For German nationalists it was yet more proof of Czech treason. Other nationalities within the monarchy likewise showed little goodwill to the Czech soldiers. Upon seeing them, civilians would sometimes raise their hands demonstratively, while comrades on the battlefield were mistrustful. Further mass desertions from the Czech regiments were widely expected; some even claimed to have 'seen' such acts, accompanied by the ritual allegedly born at Stebnícka Huta. One of the Polish Legionnaires declared, for instance, that in May he had witnessed a similar occurrence on the Nida River:

> Suddenly, to our right, we heard a distant cry, one so piercing that we could hear every word: 'Nicht schießen! Nicht schießen! (Don't shoot!)', shortly followed by the sound of an orchestra, which gradually got further away and then fell silent. [...] After a long and anxious moment the following message did the rounds: 'The 8th

> Regiment has gone over to the Muscovites.' [...] strong words were said in relation to our Czech brethren.[80]

From the point of view of the authorities the rumours that appeared in Bohemia and Moravia about the events at Stebnícka Huta were worrying. In May 1915 the military authorities in Prague reported on the popular mood:

> The dissolution of the 28th Infantry Regiment is commented upon in various ways, but generally with an antipathy towards the army. According to the most popular version the 28th Infantry Regiment was left for dead by our other units and, driven forward under German machine gun fire, had no choice but to surrender.[81]

What really happened? The exact course of events will probably never be known. Recent research suggests that the Czechs fought no worse than other Austro-Hungarian forces. Poorly led and deprived of support from neighbouring units, the 'Prague Children's' Regiment was taken by surprise – just like many other Czech and non-Czech formations. The investigation into the 28th Infantry Regiment lasted until the fall of the monarchy, when the whole affair lost significance.

The fighting in the Carpathians came to an end in late April. It was a moment that was especially difficult for the Central Powers. On the Western Front they were on the defensive, and the enemy had meanwhile landed in the Dardanelles. Through constant offensives, regardless of the losses, Austria-Hungary had lost its most experienced troops. Between January and the end of March 1915, 600,000 men had been killed, wounded, taken ill, or captured; it was a deficit that could no longer be remedied. Neither Austria-Hungary's allies nor its civilian population had any respect for the soldiers who remained in the empire's armed forces. In the occupied part of the Kingdom of Poland Austrians earned the unflattering epithet of 'beggars', a term also used by the Polish Legionnaires. The prestige of the monarchy had fallen so low that a German battalion had to be brought to the Banat in order to guard against potential Serb attacks; its only purpose was to make the Serbs believe that they were facing not just the Austrians, whom they had twice beaten, but also a more serious opponent. The monarchy would never recover from this collapse. Henceforth in major operations the initiative would always be down to the German generals, and German soldiers would fight as the nucleus ('backbone') of the Habsburg units. When, in April,

---

[80] Solek, *Pamiętnik legionisty*, p. 114.

[81] Cited in Richard Lein, *Pflichterfüllung oder Hochverrat? Die tschechischen Soldaten Österreich-Ungarns im Ersten Weltkrieg*, Vienna 2011, p. 159. The author convincingly shows that there is no evidence either for the alleged treason of the 28th Regiment or for the more famous 'desertion' of the Czechs at Zboriv two years later.

the German commander Georg von der Marwitz demanded that the incompetent commander of the Austro-Hungarian X Corps be replaced, Conrad von Hötzendorf fulfilled his wish within 24 hours. No one had the slightest doubt who called the shots in the alliance.

The fighting in Galicia and East Prussia exhausted the Russians, too. Despite having a much larger population and a larger contingent of reservists, Russia also recruited into its ranks many who lacked the necessary training. The Russian army faced another problem that was not so acute in the Central Powers: it lacked weapons and ammunition. The latter was largely manufactured on the spot, also thanks to ready-made production lines imported from Britain and France. Still, Russia had to rely on its allies for a large proportion of its artillery and infantry rifles. This was due not only to the weakness of the Russian armaments industry but also to the enormous number of Russian prisoners of war, whose weapons had to be written off.

The battles of 1914 and 1915 had a bad effect on morale in the army. Alfred Knox, the British military attaché in Russia, observed that Russian officers (not to mention rank-and-file soldiers) spoke in glowing terms about the capabilities of the German commanders and the initiative of the German soldiers. In their opinion, 'the German is capable of anything'.[82] With that attitude, it was hard to expect any great victories in future.

Gorlice

The 'German' was indeed getting ready for something big. In the spring a mixed German–Austro-Hungarian army was assembled under the command of the old cavalry officer August von Mackensen to face the Russians in Galicia. The choice of von Mackensen was dictated not just by his professionalism but also by his temperament. Compared with the boorish and pompous Prussian generals, he had a reputation for tact, which made it considerably easier to liaise with Germany's allies. The operation was prepared in a manner that exhibited none of the chaos of previous actions on the Eastern Front. German aerial reconnaissance provided accurate and – crucially – reliable information on the size of the enemy's forces and their location. Radio interception was effective. Although the Russians did eventually begin to encrypt their messages, Austro-Hungarian intelligence successfully broke the codes. There were also improvements in the way the German armed forces were organized. In February 1915 the imperial army underwent restructuring, the main purpose of which was to increase firepower and prevent the unnecessary loss of experienced personnel. The divisions were reduced in size from four to three infantry regiments, and the strength of the artillery and number of machine guns were increased. In each regiment 'old' soldiers were mixed with 'new'

---

[82] Knox, *With the Russian Army 1914–1917*, vol. 1, p. 349.

ones. Mackensen received additional artillery, which he deployed in particular corps. He also had at his disposal large and, more importantly, mobile reserves of ammunition. Austria-Hungary, Germany's ally, provided excellent ordnance maps (the same ones that until recently had been used by tourists in the Eastern and Romanian Carpathians). The German army also switched to the means of transport used by the Austro-Hungarians: light trucks and peasant wagons, which were better adapted to the poor-quality Galician roads. The railway system worked perfectly. Towards the end of April around 100 trains filled with troops, guns, and ammunition were sent in the direction of Tarnów and Gorlice. Such was the attention to detail that the military authorities organized extra fitness training for the infantry to prepare them for long marches in difficult terrain.

The Russians prepared themselves reasonably well. They were used to digging in properly and defending bravely, even if their artillery invariably lacked ammunition. This time, however, they were confronted with a completely new type of combat. The Gorlice Offensive was the first time during the Great War that frontal attack was used to effectively breach enemy lines; it was preceded by many hours of artillery fire – so heavy that some of the Russian positions simply ceased to exist. The commander of an Austro-Hungarian artillery battery noted that, unlike previously, he no longer feared running out of ammunition. 'The orders I received that morning from my superiors were very straightforward. They alternated between "rapid fire" and "extra rapid fire".' That day the Russian artillery had five or at most ten shells per gun.[83]

The town of Gorlice itself was also a target for the bombardment. Hundreds of civilians took refuge in the cellars and perished. The terrified town mayor first miraculously escaped death in his own apartment and then took more than a quarter of an hour to walk the 100 steps from his home to the town hall under a hail of shells ('only those who experienced the bombing could have the faintest idea about the sheer number of shells that fell on Gorlice that day'). Before his eyes the town was laid to ruin: in the market square, 'except for two tenements and the town hall, all the houses were in flames'; hundreds of people remained in the town hall praying to be rescued. 'Extreme panic' and 'a hell worthy of Dante' were the phrases that the mayor (a priest, intellectual, and eccentric all in one) used to describe the events of that day; fortunately, not a single shell hit the town hall and, thanks to the presence of mind of a certain police sergeant, it was possible to extinguish the fire caused by 'sparks carried on the wind' from adjacent burning houses. Father Bronisław Świeykowski concluded his account of 2 May 1915 thus: 'It was difficult to breathe. We were choking on the smoke and it was stinging our eyes. It was hard to see anything on the market square that was more than a couple of steps from the town hall [. . .]. These were surely the most testing moments of my life that Providence

---

[83] Martin Schmitz, 'Tapfer, zäh und schlecht geführt', p. 57.

BEFORE THE LEAVES FALL FROM THE TREES ...

had given me.' In the afternoon the first German cavalry patrol arrived in Gorlice; the inhabitants of the burning town greeted the Bavarians as liberators.[84]

By the evening of the first day, Mackensen was already about 8 kilometres behind the Russian lines. At night the first-line units were given fresh ammunition and the artillery moved forward. Equally important was the fact that the field kitchens arrived on time. Instead of appeals to patriotism and soldierly honour, the exhausted men were given a hot meal. Those who had participated in recent battles in the Carpathians certainly appreciated the change.

The Germans cut through the Russian defensive line like a knife through butter. In places where the defenders continued to resist, the attack was halted and artillery fire resumed. Reconnaissance aircraft detected the Russian counterattacks before they even reached the battlefield, as a result of which they were stopped with massive and precise artillery fire. In the following days Mackensen implemented a plan based on the idea that breaking through the front line made sense only if the enemy was given no time to recover from the initial shock. On 5 May his 11th Army was already 25 kilometres behind the first line of Russian trenches. The imperial Russian high command had to hastily withdraw its troops from the mountains; one of its delayed divisions was captured at Dukla. Meanwhile, the Germans did not let up. It was only after reaching the San River that they stopped for a few days to replenish their losses and regroup. From there they headed towards Przemyśl, which – to the dissatisfaction of Vienna – the Bavarians, not the Austrians, entered first. After quickly capturing the fortress, Mackensen set off for Lwów, entering the city on 22 June. A month later the aforementioned landlady of the Przemyśl tenement house, Helena Jabłońska née Seifert, went on a trip to Sanok. From the windows of the train she saw fresh evidence of the broken enemy front:

> The town of Ustrzyki is the most terrible scene of destruction. The church has survived and only a few of the apartment buildings have roofs. The petroleum tanks, all the lumbermills, the refineries, and the factories in general have been obliterated. The hills around the town are a curious sight. It was there that the fiercest fighting took place. Fire trenches are visible on the summits, and carved into the bare slopes are huge cavities caused by high-calibre shells. The valleys and gorges are fenced off by barbed wire a few metres wide on which tin cans, probably once containing food, have been suspended. [...] It was on this barbed wire that human bodies were meant to quiver, sometimes for several days, in the most unbearable torment and then die. The corpses in the valleys lie several metres high. In the distance one can already see swarms of black birds. As the train approaches we see a long, very long mound, flat on both sides, with a few Catholic and schismatic crosses on top of it. It is a single

[84] Bronisław Świeykowski, *Z dni grozy w Gorlicach. Od 25 IX 1914 do 2 V 1915*, Cracow 1919, pp. 123–126.

tomb containing thousands of bodies; the earth covering it is so thin that, here and there, arms and legs or skulls pecked out by rooks and ravens stick out. The earth has subsided, washed out by the rain! [...] The gusts of wind carry an awful smell.[85]

The catastrophe in Galicia had a huge impact on the situation of the Russians in the Kingdom of Poland. Almost overnight they risked being outflanked from the south. Retreat became necessary, and initially it occurred in a fairly orderly fashion. The Russians put up resistance against German and Austrian attacks despite a chronic lack of ammunition for their artillery and soon for their rifles as well. There were also local successes for the defenders. On 23 July the Germans tried to force their way across the Narew River. Lieutenant Hans Tröbst witnessed their retreat to the trenches:

> After half an hour the companies began to withdraw from their positions. Detachments and individual soldiers returned, tired and broken, like a passive human flock [...]. Kramme ordered the losses to be counted. Three officers and 261 NCOs and soldiers were dead, wounded or missing. To put it plainly: half the battalion had gone to hell.[86]

Increasingly often, however, the Russian gunners had to watch helplessly as their infantry was massacred by enemy shells. Their own ammunition stocks were limited to emergency reserves or were completely exhausted. The imperial high command sent reinforcements to the front without weapons or with sticks instead of rifles. Soldiers were supposed to use the rifles of their killed comrades, but many died before they even got their hands on a weapon.

It is no wonder, then, that morale deteriorated. At the beginning of August Warsaw was evacuated. The historian Aleksander Kraushar recounted the scene:

> The panic among the Russians escaping to the Praga district was so great that the wagons on which they fled could not accommodate all the fugitives. Sitting next to the often bareheaded court dignitaries were their ushers, unarmed soldiers, and the wives of civil servants with their children. Sometimes on these wagons one saw pigs, stacks of wholemeal bread, home appliances, and paintings of saints carried by Orthodox priests. All this created a grotesque image of an anxious, cowardly throng seeking to abscond before a dangerous, vindictive enemy greedy for spoils.[87]

---

[85] Jabłońska, *Dziennik z oblężonego Przemyśla*, p. 222.

[86] Cited in Gerhard P. Groß, 'Im Schatten des Westens', in *Die vergessene Front. Der Osten 1914/15. Ereignis, Wirkung, Nachwirkung*, ed. Gerhard P. Groß, Paderborn 2006, p. 61.

[87] Aleksander Kraushar, *Warszawa podczas okupacji niemieckiej 1915–1918*, Lwów 1921, p. 7.

Fig. 24 Russian prisoners of war marching along Piotrkowska Street in Łódź. Courtesy of the Herder-Institut, Marburg, Bildarchiv.

In the second half of August the fortress of Modlin (Novogeorgievsk) fell. Russian resistance was weakening. Alfred Knox noted a conversation he had conducted at that time with a young Russian pilot. According to his interlocutor, Russia would never again return to the Polish Kingdom because its army had lost all willingness to fight. There were so few regular officers that it would be possible to fill only the posts of battalion commanders. Companies were already being led by reserve officers, who were quite unfit to command them. They could not even read maps.[88]

The impression of total catastrophe was deepened by the crowds of refugees and villages ablaze. The retreating Russians were ordered to leave scorched earth behind them. They did not always follow this order, of course, but there had to be at least some material damage. Józef Dominik Kłoczowski, a resident of the Mława district, recalled several visits by Russian officers who wanted to set fire to his village. On each occasion the matter was resolved with a bribe. In the end, 'an officer was passing by and said that the stacks of hay had to be burned, if nothing else, but luckily no action was taken'.[89] In the summer of 1915 a paradoxical situation arose in the Kingdom of Poland. The army was pursuing a policy of ruthless violence against its own people. For the inhabitants of the Kingdom, therefore, the soldiers of the Central Powers were now

---

[88] Alfred Knox, *With the Russian Army 1914–1917*, vol. 1, p. 67.
[89] Memoirs of Józef Dominik Kłoczowski, in *Teraz będzie Polska. Wybór z pamiętników z okresu I wojny światowej*, ed. Andrzej Rosner, Warsaw 1988, pp. 208–228, here p. 209.

Fig. 25 Germans before the fortress of Dęblin (Ivangorod). Courtesy of the Herder-Institut, Marburg, Bildarchiv.

allies. The Austro-Hungarian and German gendarmerie executed captured arsonists. Sometimes the locals defended themselves too:

> Yesterday morning the town residents killed a Muscovite who had crept in at dawn to set fire to a house. Our soldiers say that the residents have Austrian rifles from the Austrian soldiers who were killed a few days ago by the Muscovites and that now they are using those rifles to defend their homes against the arsonists sent by the Russians. The rifles are carefully hidden from both the Muscovites and the Austrians. [...] A man in a Russian soldier's jacket, riding a horse and cart, was captured a few days ago and hanged from a willow on the outskirts of Urzędów.[90]

Although the Russians were not able to evacuate the entire civilian population, circumstances often left people with no choice but to flee. Those who remained simply had their property confiscated. On the way to Bielsk Podlaski a British attaché witnessed an uninterrupted, 20-mile-long procession of wagons loaded with families and property. In his diary, the Polish economist Stanisław Dzierzbicki expressed his irritation with the Russian authorities that had caused this catastrophe:

> The situation is terrible – tens of thousands of people expelled from their burnt towns and villages are thronging the roads and obstructing the movement of troops. Yesterday the Governor of Warsaw received news that 30,000 or so fleeing civilians had gathered in the vicinity of Jabłonna.

[90] Składkowski, *Moja służba w Brygadzie*, p. 183.

Fig. 26   The route of the Russian retreat was marked by villages in flames.

The authorities do not want to let them enter Warsaw, but they have no food and nowhere to go.[91]

Some of these refugees would soon return, but others would remain in the depths of Russia for longer.

In less than four months the offensive launched by the Central Powers had pushed the Russians over 500 kilometres to the east. The route taken by some of the German and Austro-Hungarian units was even twice that long. Perfect organization and continuous attack by the allied armies proved to be the keys to success. In contrast to earlier operations, the enemy was not allowed to rest even for a moment; the offensive was continued until the attacker had no more strength. Berlin and Vienna not only recovered everything they had previously lost to the enemy but also occupied the Polish lands. For the Polish Legionnaires, who were fighting in the ranks of the victorious armies, it was a struggle in defence of their homeland. This changed only at the end of August, when the offensive left the territories inhabited by Poles. One resident of the Polish Kingdom, who wore an Austrian uniform, wrote in his diary: 'The sightseeing tour is over. Now the war begins again. We are standing in an Orthodox village, where the local peasants treat us with a submissive and silent hostility.'[92]

[91] Stanisław Dzierzbicki, *Pamiętnik z lat wojny 1915–1918*, ed. Janusz Pajewski and Danuta Płygawko, Warsaw 1983, p. 55.
[92] Solek, *Pamiętnik legionisty*, p. 140.

Fig. 27   The Russian evacuation affected a large part of the rural population. In the towns and cities the authorities restricted themselves to removing the property of the inhabitants. Courtesy of Mariusz Kulik.

Replay in the Balkans

Mackensen's offensive was a great success; so great, in fact, that it would have been a mistake not to use the tactical and technical experience gained at Gorlice on other fronts. The Austro-Hungarian General Staff had never abandoned its plan for a final showdown with Serbia. What the two disastrous campaigns had revealed, however, was that an attack had to be both well prepared and executed with clearly superior forces. From May 1915, when Italy joined the war on the side of the Entente, an independent Austro-Hungarian offensive was practically impossible. Most of the meagre Austro-Hungarian forces, which from the end of 1914 had been guarding the southern border, were moved to the new front on the Isonzo (Soča) River. Finding new allies was essential but time-consuming. As early as in the autumn of 1914 Vienna remembered that, according to the custom of European monarchs, the Bulgarian Czar Ferdinand I was formally an Austro-Hungarian officer; it accordingly began to send him regular reports from the fronts. But what really mattered were concrete proposals. A bidding war lasted until September 1915: who could offer Bulgaria the best deal and whose offer would Sofia consider the most reliable. Great Britain and France were in a weaker position from the outset, because to satisfy Bulgaria's territorial claims would have meant ceding part of Serbian Macedonia. Austria-Hungary's offer was naturally more generous, especially as it promised Bulgaria territory that belonged to its enemy.

The negotiations disrupted Serbia's defensive preparations. Radomir Putnik, the Serbian Chief of the General Staff, initially planned to launch a pre-emptive strike against the weakest opponent, which to his mind was Bulgaria. This plan was never realized, primarily due to vehement opposition from Serbia's allies, who still hoped to bring the Bulgarians on side. Consequently, the Serbs assembled the majority of their forces on the Danube and Sava and deployed their smaller and weaker units on the Drina and along the border with Bulgaria. Mackensen actually attacked to the north in what was one of the biggest landing operations ever attempted. On 7 October, under cover of night, hundreds of boats and pontoons sailed along the Sava towards Belgrade, protected by the Austro-Hungarian Danube Flotilla and heavy artillery on the north bank. The Serbs, initially taken by surprise, quickly grasped the seriousness of the situation. They shone searchlights on the river to pick out targets for their artillery. The attackers suffered major losses, but they managed to secure a bridgehead in Belgrade. For the whole of the next day the Germans and Austrians repelled the Serbian counterattacks; with no other means of shielding themselves, they took cover behind the bodies of fallen comrades and enemy combatants. That night reinforcements arrived from the northern bank, and on the following day the offensive began to force the defenders southwards. The Serbian capital fell to the Austrians, but, according to the plan devised in Galicia a few months earlier, there were no victory parades this time; instead, the attack continued. The Serbs retreated in the direction of their supply base and armaments centre in Kragujevac. There they could get weapons, ammunition, and food sent by the British and French through the port at Salonika. During the previous winter campaign the Serbs had succeeded in repelling the attackers largely thanks to this supply line. On this occasion, however, the entry of the Bulgarians thwarted their plans. The supply line to Salonika was severed. On 20 October the Bulgarians entered Skopje and gradually occupied the entire Serbian part of Macedonia. It was only decisive intervention by Berlin that prevented the Bulgarians from settling accounts with their other enemies from the Second Balkan War and attacking Greece, which was formally still neutral.

One of the most tragic episodes in the history of the war in the Balkans had begun. The two previous Austro-Hungarian invasions had been a traumatic experience for Serb civilians. This time anyone who could avoid remaining under Austro-Hungarian occupation did so. Accordingly, a mass of Serb civilians began to follow the army. Successive towns and cities experienced an invasion of cold and hungry people as well as growing numbers of diseased unfortunates. The Serbian socialist politician Dragiša Lapčević met some of them in Jagodina:

Fig. 28 A cartoon comparing the military strengths of the Balkan states on the eve of the autumn campaign of 1915, *Ilustrowany Kuryer Codzienny*, a Cracow daily, 1 October 1915.

> Since the beginning of the war Jagodina has been full of refugees, especially from Belgrade. Now, when the enemy has started to infiltrate from all sides, refugees have been arriving constantly, night and day, in trains, carts and on foot, and then going on [...]. Many are homeless and without food, and the poor, barefoot and in tatters, are unable to withstand the cold October weather.[93]

---

[93] Dragiša Lapčević, *Okupacija*, Belgrade 1926, pp. 32, 35; cited in Andrej Mitrović, *Serbia's Great War 1914–1918*, London 2007, p. 146.

Fig. 29   Austro-Hungarian soldiers after the capture of Belgrade.

The first frosts arrived in October. In November the retreating Serbs crossed the Morava River and entered increasingly mountainous terrain. The chance of victory was declining with each passing day. Austrian intelligence intercepted a message sent by Danilo, the Crown Prince of Montenegro, which said everything the Austrians needed to know about the mood in the enemy camp: 'Save yourselves, whoever can!'[94] At the end of the month, after heated discussions between the politicians and generals, the decision was taken to leave the country and head for the Adriatic coast via Montenegro and Albania. There the Serbs would receive help from their allies and launch a counterattack.

The decision was a dramatic one for at least three reasons. First of all, the army and those refugees who decided to remain with it had experienced several years of almost constant fighting; they were weakened and without supplies. Secondly, winter was just beginning in the mountains and the overwhelming majority of the escapees had to travel on foot. Thirdly, two years earlier the Serbs and Montenegrins had occupied northern Albania, which the local inhabitants remembered with bitterness. The Serbs had to assume that not only would they not be helped in the villages through which they passed but also they would encounter active resistance, all the more so because Vienna had a great deal of influence in Albania. Under these circumstances, some of the participants of the march decided to take their chances with the occupier and return to Serbia. In

[94] Ronge, *Kriegs- und Industriespionage*, p. 119.

Fig. 30   The autumn and winter offensive in Serbia was a completely new experience for the Austro-Hungarian soldiers. For the first time the Serbs gave up without a fight and in large numbers.

November whole units of Serbian soldiers began to desert. There were even clashes between deserters and army units that blocked their way. Small groups wandered north in the hope of ending up in German or Austrian rather than Bulgarian captivity. A mass of refugees headed off in the same direction. In Kruševac they were met by the *Berliner Tageblatt* correspondent, Wilhelm Hegeler, who was horrified by the chaos and misery he witnessed:

> I have seen thousands of refugees camped in an open field. Bags containing their belongings serve as pillows and their beds are bundles of straw. The lucky ones have managed to find shelter, crammed into small huts, ten or twenty of them in each. During the day they throng the roads, standing on the verges exhausted. They disperse in panic at the first silly rumour and besiege the local military HQ, pestering the officers with questions, pleas, and hysterical sobbing. With the best will in the world they cannot be allowed home just yet, for they would block the way for the army columns headed in the opposite direction. What a wretched nation, severed from its homeland! It is only the countless Gypsies who are in their element here. They skulk around with their big bags, reaping a rich harvest, and view the nomads with condescension, as an artist would a dilettante imitator.[95]

---

[95] Wilhelm Hegeler, *Der Siegeszug durch Serbien*, Berlin 1916, pp. 72–73.

The King, the government, much of the army, and thousands of civilians, however, decided to march through the mountains. Their journey earned the only partly deserved epithet of the 'Albanian Golgotha' of the Serbs; partly deserved not because the facts did not measure up to the gruesome legend – the losses, i.e. the number of deaths due to cold, hunger, and disease, as well as desertions, amounted to at least 70,000 and according to some estimates to well over 100,000 – but because non-Serbs participated in these tragic events too. Along with the retreating army, albeit against their will, travelled around 40,000 Austro-Hungarian prisoners of war: the infantry on foot, the officers initially on carts. At the moment of departure the prisoners, whose job it was to clear a route for the marchers, were in the most abject state of health. The provisions they received were even worse than those given to the Serbs. Two weeks of marching cost the lives of around 15,000 of them. The condition of the remaining 24,000 prisoners, who, against all the odds, reached the Albanian coast in the middle of December, plumbed the depths of misery, squalor, and exhaustion.

The Italians who took on the task of evacuating the Serbs and prisoners of war had no love for their Slavic ally or for the Habsburg monarchy. Their accounts of the condition of those who survived the 'Golgotha' are thus all the more reliable. The first to arrive were the captured Austro-Hungarian officers, whom the Serbs treated much better than the rank-and-file troops: 'Hardly any of them had shoes and some had wrapped their naked, swollen feet in muddy, blood-stained rags. What was once probably a uniform now looked like an assortment of dirty tatters that barely covered the genitalia.'

Fig. 31   Serbian peasants on their way back to an abandoned village (autumn 1915).

134   THE FRONTS

The appearance of the second wave of prisoners was not especially different: 'barefoot, starved, half-naked, wounded, and sick', 'a silent procession of living skeletons [...] a parade of shadows, touching the earth in a monotonous rhythm, in deathly silence, without sound'. Next came the Serbs, who did not look much better than their captives. One of the marchers recalled: 'Spectres; emaciated, pale, burnt-out, with sunken eyes, long hair, beards, and torn and dirty clothes, barefoot. Spectres; begging for bread; [...] Chaos: women in army overcoats; despairing, helpless mothers.'[96] The Italian general had a scale of comparison, as he had previously seen the prisoners of war. He considered the 'spectacle' of the Serbs' arrival to be on a par with that of the captives: 'They were almost all without shoes, which they had replaced with bundles made from blankets. In their ragged clothes, infested with insects, diseased, they moved with great difficulty.' Hundreds more of the marchers would later die while waiting to embark on ships in the Albanian ports.[97]

The supplies sent by Great Britain and France to Brindisi left Italy very late. When the Italian convoys set off for Albania, it turned out that the route to the northernmost port of Shkodër (only a few kilometres from the Greek island of Corfu) was too dangerous due to attacks by Austro-Hungarian submarines. In the end these essential supplies were delivered not to Shkodër, but to Durrës, more than 100 kilometres to the south, and to Vlorë, a further 100 kilometres along the coast. Even reaching the Albanian ports, where food and medicines supplied by the Entente were waiting, did not necessarily signal the end of the 'Golgotha', for the fugitives were at risk of being pursued. The combined German and Austro-Hungarian army marched through the same mountains, struggling with supply shortages and the winter frost. In parallel, part of Mackensen's group attacked Montenegro. If the Montenegrin resistance was broken too quickly, the Serbs would be hunted down on the Albanian coast and destroyed. The defenders held out until 25 January. Most of the Serbian refugees embarked by 19 February, before the Austrians arrived. As agreed by the allies, the Serbs were to be transported to Corfu, where the French mission had begun to organize camps for them (without asking permission from Greece, to which the island belonged). Ultimately, according to French data – the Italian figures vary considerably – over 170,000 Serbs, the vast majority of them soldiers, and more than 20,000 prisoners of war were evacuated. They were in a terrible condition. Every twelfth prisoner died aboard the ship. Another 5,000 deaths

---

[96] Milorad Marković, 'Povlačenije kroz Albaniju', in *Golgota i vaskrs Srbije 1915–1918*, ed. Silvija Đurić and Vidoslav Stevanović, Belgrade 1989, p. 327; cited in Schanes, *Serbien im Ersten Weltkrieg*, p. 206.

[97] Luca Gorgolini, *Kriegsgefangenschaft auf Asinara. Österreichisch-ungarische Soldaten des Ersten Weltkriegs in italienischem Gewahrsam*, translated by Günther Gerlach, Innsbruck 2012, p. 72 n. 77 (originally published as *I dannati dell'Asinara. L'odissea dei prigionieri austro-ungarici nella Prima guerra mondiale*, Turin 2011).

were registered after the prisoners landed on the island of Asinara, where they would remain for the rest of the war. The Serbs, too, continued to die in their thousands. From the island of Vido near Corfu, where the sick were quarantined, more than 5,000 people never returned;[98] the time needed to restore them to health proved longer than the optimists had hoped.

In military terms the effect of the Serbian campaign was the humiliation of the Habsburg monarchy, the entry of Bulgaria into the war, and the occupation of all of Serbia and Montenegro. The front persisted in Albania, where the Austro-Hungarians together with Albanian volunteers fought the Italians, and then also the French, who were aided by a small Serbian contingent that managed to break through to its allies. In time the moral dimension of the Serbian campaign gained in importance. Serbia became the hero of Allied public opinion, yet the epos did not need another hero; the fate of the captives did not sit well with it, and nor did the lament of the ageing King Peter: 'Even if Serbia survives, I fear there will soon be no more Serbs.'[99] No country suffered comparable losses in the First World War. In 1918 the 'Albanian Golgotha' provided an irrefutable argument for the construction of a 'state of the South Slavs', centred on Serbia, with its capital in Belgrade.

Fig. 32   The Serbian retreat demanded a superhuman effort from the exhausted soldiers. The photograph shows the passage of troops across a river in Albania.

[98] Ibid., p. 78.
[99] Mitrović, *Serbia's Great War 1914–1918*, p. 154.

136 THE FRONTS

DISEASE AMONG THE FRENCH IN THE BALKANS

Even the best-prepared armies suffered from disease and epidemics, sometimes to the same extent as they did from warfare. Approximately 378,000 soldiers were recruited to the French Army of the East that was stationed in Greece between 1915 and 1918. As many as 357,000 of them, i.e. almost 95 per cent, fell ill with various diseases. A total of 102,000 French personnel had to be evacuated from the Peloponnese. It is not known how many of them were sick, but illness was certainly not an unlikely reason for evacuation.

After decades of colonial experience, the French army was undoubtedly one of the best prepared when it came to surviving difficult climates and poor hygiene. It was helpless in the face of Spanish flu, of course, which decimated the Army of the East in 1918. Of the 242,000 soldiers who fought in the final year of the war, 124,000 fell ill, most of them having contracted Spanish flu. Nearly 6,000 people died – more than half were diagnosed with this infection.

What is astonishing, however, is that in 1916 and 1917, of the 120,000 French who were hospitalized, as many as 96,000 contracted malaria, a disease well known in the colonies. 'My army is immobilized in hospital,' noted General Maurice Sarrail, the commander-in-chief on the Salonika Front during the sanitary disaster of 1916.[100] Quinine worked wonders, and the mortality rate even at the worst of times was never above 3 per cent and usually much lower. However, in the end, for an army that did not really enter the fighting until September 1918, the losses due to disease were only slightly lower than the losses on the battlefield. Around 13,000 soldiers died in combat (including wounded soldiers who could not be saved), while over 9,000 died from disease, including more than 1,125 from malaria and 3,224 from Spanish flu.

For the time being, in February 1916, it might have seemed that the war in the East was nearing its conclusion. The great success of the Gorlice operation came just in time to bolster the worsening morale of the Austro-Hungarian generals. A German liaison officer on Conrad von Hötzendorf's staff fully appreciated its psychological significance:

> Only somebody who has lived through the profound depression following the Carpathian campaign can really understand what Gorlice meant: liberation from an almost unbearable pressure, relief from the greatest worries, renewed confidence, and a sudden hope of victory.[101]

Germany, Austria-Hungary, and their new ally in the region, Bulgaria, controlled the situation on all fronts. Turkey was victorious in the Dardanelles campaign, defeating a hostile landing force in the vicinity

---

[100] Patrick Facon, 'Le soldat français d'Orient face à la maladie', in *The Salonica Theatre of Operations and the Outcome of the Great War*, ed. National Research Foundation 'Eleftherios K. Venizelos', Thessaloniki 2005, pp. 223–235, here p. 228.

[101] August von Cramon, *Unser österreichisch-ungarischer Bundesgenosse im Weltkriege. Erinnerungen aus meiner vierjährigen Tätigkeit als bevollmächtigter deutscher General beim k.u.k. Armeeoberkommando*, Berlin 1920, p. 15, cited in József Galántai, *Hungary in the First World War*, translated by Éva Grusz and Judit Pokoly, Budapest 1989, p. 139.

of its capital and effectively blocking the best maritime route between Russia and her western allies. The failure of the British in the Dardanelles meant that the delivery of arms and raw materials to Russia would have to continue via Murmansk, a more dangerous and less convenient route. Despite heavy losses, the mood in Germany was excellent. One of the most renowned propagandists of the Central Powers, the Swedish geographer Sven Hedin, gave expression to this mood in his description of the first-anniversary celebrations of the victorious Battle of Tannenberg:

> Against a background of flaming torches appeared the massive silhouette of Hindenburg. There he stood, the incarnation of German will and German power, the embodiment of all of Germany at war. His greatcoat undone, his arms folded behind him, he observed the rippling stream of youth as it marched forwards into the night to thunderous cheers. Like a sturdy oak he rose above the young forest. Before him he saw the future and hope of Germany; his countenance expressed seriousness, pride, and certainty, yet a tear came to his eye.[102]

There was just one minor flaw in this joyous image of the victorious Central Powers: the parade of strong and serried Germanic heroes before their great leader took place not on the Champs-Elysées but on the market square of provincial Ostrołęka in north-eastern Poland . . .

---

[102] Sven Hedin, *Nach Osten!*, Leipzig 1916, p. 510.

4

Breakthrough

In March 1916 General Aleksei Alekseevich Brusilov was appointed commander of the Russian Southwest Front. He had been one of the most effective Russian commanders in the summer of 1914, and it was his army that had occupied Lwów in September. During the 'great retreat' in the spring of 1915 Brusilov once again proved himself to be able and level-headed. A year later he was seen as the man who was to change the course of the war on the Eastern Front.

In the first years of the war the Russian generals understood that without a huge increase in munitions production Czarism was doomed to fail. The army lacked everything. Only 10 per cent of the new recruits in the spring of 1915 received rifles. In March of that year, as the fighting ended in the Carpathians, Brusilov reported that his regiments were at between 25 and 50 per cent of their original strength. Meanwhile, the reinforcements he was being given had no weapons and there was a shortage of weapons in his own army's stores. Brusilov warned that the small-arms ammunition would run out after one or two days of intense combat. In May 1915 Germany and Austria-Hungary had destroyed the Russian positions with hurricane artillery fire, while Russia's own artillery had been constantly short of ammunition.

By the spring of the following year the Russian munitions programme had begun to produce results. Experts believed that, in order to break through a triple line of German defence 50 metres wide, 400 rounds of heavy ammunition and 2,500 rounds of light ammunition would be needed. For the first time since the outbreak of the war Russian industry was able to meet the requirements of the army. While in Austria-Hungary the production of artillery ammunition increased seven-fold over two years (from 300,000 to 2 million shells per month), in Russia the increase was fifty-fold over the same period (from 660,000 to over 33 million shells per year). At the same time, supplies of arms and ammunition arrived from the West. At last there was no longer a shortage of rifles. Between the summer of 1915 and March 1916 two million men were conscripted into the army and each soldier received a weapon.

Fighting desperately at Verdun, the French demanded that Russia relieve the Western Front. In the middle of March the Russians attacked at Lake Narach in Belarus. Despite their clear numerical advantage over the defending

Germans, the Russians suffered another defeat. Falkenhayn noted, almost with a degree of sympathy, that the Russians' efforts more resembled gory acts of sacrifice than attacks as such. The easy victory tempted the Central Powers to be less vigilant. Austria-Hungary moved its better units and officers from the Eastern Front to Italy. The Eastern Front, and especially its southern section, appeared safe; the numbers of men and guns on the opposing sides were similar.

Meanwhile, Brusilov prepared for the offensive conscientiously and innovatively. The aim was not to gain an advantage on a narrow section of the front (this was precisely the tactic that had once again failed at Lake Narach) but to launch well-prepared attacks along a section of the Southwest Front at least several dozen or, ideally, 450 kilometres long. The idea was that, after losing its main line of entrenchments, the enemy would not be able to concentrate its reserve forces on a single narrow section in order to plug the hole, but would instead have to disperse them across a much larger area. This new strategy was accompanied by new tactics learned from the French. Russian soldiers now dug their trenches as close as possible to enemy lines: the closer they got, the shorter the distance they would have to cover on the day of the attack. A distance of 400 steps was considered the maximum. The attack was to take place after a brief period of artillery fire. Brusilov's orders to his artillery emphasized that there was no need for hurricane fire. Instead, the shelling had to be accurate, corrected during the fight, and, most importantly, had to move forward together with the advancing infantry. Finally, for the first time Russian planes appeared in the sky in numbers.

The Brusilov Offensive began on 4 June. It did indeed encompass the entire Southwest Front, from Pinsk in the north to Czernowitz (Chernivtsi) in the south. Memoirists agree that never before had they come up against such a vast mass of enemy forces:

> I witnessed a huge and unforgettable scene, one worthy of Wojciech Kossak's brush.[1] One after another the Russian squadrons galloped forward in a deployed formation, their sabres and lances gleaming among the densely bursting shrapnel from our artillery, whose commander, Major Brzoza, directed the shelling himself from a position behind our firing line. Our advanced lines unleashed their fury; mad with rage, our soldiers fired fanatically, only to be restrained by the commanders. At the village of Vovcheck – a swarm of people and horses. Across the entire battlefield rushed horses without riders and riders without horses. They won't pass! They're faltering! They're withdrawing! They're driving forward again![2]

---

[1] Wojciech Kossak (1856–1942) was a Polish artist known for his historical paintings on themes from Polish and Prussian military history.

[2] Account of Marian Kukiel, cited in Stanisław Czerep, *II Brygada Legionów Polskich*, Warsaw 1991, p. 145.

The Russians 'drove forward' mostly on foot and very effectively. Within five days they had crushed two Austro-Hungarian armies: the 4th Army lost more than two-thirds of its men (from 118,000 soldiers down to 36,000); the 7th Army suffered 40 per cent losses during the first few days (76,000 out of 194,000 soldiers), but this rose to 57 per cent by 16 June. Within a month the Russians had reached the environs of Kovel, one of the few towns in the region and a junction of two railway lines. They occupied a large part of Volhynia and Bukovina as well as Stanisławów (today Ivano-Frankivsk) in Eastern Galicia, among other towns. In June and July the losses of the Habsburg monarchy stood at 400,000 men captured, wounded, or killed, with another 70,000 unable to fight due to disease. However, the Russians never gained an advantage on any section of the front where they encountered the Germans. In the north, where they attacked von Woyrsch's forces with a five-fold numerical advantage, the Russians lost 7,000 men, the Germans only 150. It was no secret who was the star on the Eastern Front and who was the extra. Rumours persisted among the Austro-Hungarian officers about the severe dressing-down that the Archduke Joseph Ferdinand Habsburg had received from Alexander von Linsingen, a German general. After the loss of Lutsk, Linsingen is said to have told the archduke: 'That was not a mistake, it was a crime,' and when the archduke asked rhetorically whether Linsingen knew who he was talking to, the latter replied: 'To an Austrian general, who is my subordinate.'[3] Even insults as egregious as these had to be swallowed, for without German assistance the monarchy faced total catastrophe. The archduke was dismissed – this was neither the first nor the last time that the incompetence of a member of the ruling dynasty had cost the lives of thousands of men. As early as on 12 June four German divisions were deployed to Galicia to rescue their Habsburg ally.

The defeat of Austria-Hungary in the summer of 1916 sealed the fate of the alliance.[4] After April 1915 the German Supreme Army Command (Oberste Heeresleitung, OHL) had been headquartered in Pless (today Pszczyna) in Upper Silesia, and between February and August 1916 in France. In the months leading up to January 1917 it returned once again to the Hochberg Palace in Pless. The Austrian Army Command (Armeeoberkommando, AOK) was located in the town of Teschen (Cieszyn) until the end of November 1916. The distance between Pless and Teschen was almost exactly 50 kilometres, in other words, a one-hour journey by car. There was no shortage of taverns on either side of the road; the beer network was probably more dense than it is nowadays and no different from that in Lower Austria or Württemberg.

---

[3] Cited in August Krasicki, *Dziennik z kampanii rosyjskiej 1914–1916*, Cracow 1988, p. 462.

[4] Rudolf Jeřábek, 'Taktische Voraussetzungen der Brusilowschlacht Juni 1916', in *Schlachtfeld Galizien*, ed. Claudia Reichl-Ham, Irmgard Nöbauer, and Werner Fröhlich, Vienna 2016, pp. 157–185.

Meanwhile, both general staffs behaved as if one was located in Hamburg and the other in Zagreb: there was no social interaction whatsoever. The Austrians were afraid of the Germans, and the Germans despised the Austrians. The urbane von Falkenhayn would appear occasionally in Teschen by car, wearing sports glasses and an equally unconventional shawl and smoking a cigar. From the outset he dominated Conrad von Hötzendorf, who was ten years his senior. Falkenhayn always knew more and always knew better. Thus, for quite some time there had been few subjects that the two allies could discuss over a beer, and after the Brusilov Offensive there were fewer still.

As the Austro-Hungarian army retreated under Russian pressure, the Polish Legions fought in the rearguard. The heaviest fighting took place at the beginning of July in Kostyukhnivka (Kostiuchnówka). During a surge in the fighting towards the end of June the losses of the 2nd Brigade amounted to nearly 360 killed, wounded, or missing. The nightmare began for the Poles on 4 July. From sunrise until six o'clock in the evening the Russians systematically bombarded the otherwise well-prepared positions of the 5th Regiment. When they attacked from the flank, where the defence mounted by a neighbouring Hungarian regiment gave way, soldiers began to flee. Sergeant Roman Starzyński remembered that moment of despair:

> The place had emptied out and there was no one to be seen. I wanted to organize the defence myself. There were ten, perhaps fifteen soldiers with me. Summoning my reserves of strength, I shouted: 'Halt!' No one listened, they simply ran on. They were fleeing in panic, not even knowing where to go. I called after them, but I was spent. They ran as far as the regiment HQ. There they were stopped by the commander, Lieutenant Colonel Berbecki, brandishing a pistol. He ordered them to return to their positions immediately. Those very same soldiers who a few moments earlier had ignored me when I called on them to stop suddenly came to their senses when confronted with Berbecki's Steyr [a pistol]. They turned around and I led them to the trenches at the edge of the forest [...]. Of the 109 soldiers who were with us in the morning, 13 remained.[5]

The fate of the Polish Legionnaires did not differ much from that of other Habsburg units in Volhynia. Starzyński's regiment probably lost around 50 per cent of its men, but it did not fall into disarray. The defeat of the Habsburg army had two aspects: although after a month of fighting the front moved westwards, the enemy had not been defeated, despite the Russians having lost more than half a million soldiers. The pride of the Russian Empire, the elite Imperial Guard, had practically ceased to exist – its losses amounted to 54,000 soldiers and 500 officers. The reason was disastrous

---

[5] Roman Starzyński, *Cztery lata w służbie Komendanta. Przeżycia wojenne 1914–1919*, Warsaw 2012, p. 305 n.

142   THE FRONTS

leadership, over which Brusilov had no influence; the commanders of the
Imperial Guard units were appointed solely by the Czar.

Most Russian officers had not learned the lessons of the first year of the war.
Whereas Brusilov tried to achieve his goals through good reconnaissance and
precise attack, Russian officers tried to do the same using massed ranks of men,
regardless of the losses. Not even the Austrians fought in this way, despite
previously being so profligate with the lives of their troops. To Sławoj Felicjan
Składkowski the Russian offensive at times bordered on the absurd:

> Our boys were pounding the Muscovites, standing 30 feet from them, just
> as in *November Night*[6] at the theatre. The brown swarm advanced, or
> rather pretended to advance, towards the thin blue strip that was our
> company. Their faces looked puzzled and weary rather than fierce. They
> marched on the spot, clearly not wanting to charge forward, and let out
> a languorous cry: 'Hurrah! Hurrah!' [. . .]. Our boys laughed and carried
> on pummelling the swarm. [. . .] But behind the barbed wire the
> Muscovites kept coming. [. . .] Multitudes began to throw themselves
> clumsily at the wire, pressed from the back by a new mass of mottled
> grey cannon fodder. One ginger-haired peasant took off his coat, laid it on
> the wire, and then slid his comrade over it. Half-serious, half-joking, he
> called out: 'Don't shoot, Sir!' Our boys ignored these pleas and mowed
> them down like ducks.[7]

By the summer the greatest Russian victory in the First World War had lost its
sparkle. Although the Austro-Hungarian army had barely survived the
Brusilov Offensive – two million of its soldiers lost in 1916 and attacks on
the Italian Front had to be discontinued – it did not fall apart. Germany
survived the defeat of its ally without too many losses of its own. Russia lost
two million soldiers – the price of moving the fronts in the north and south by
approximately 50 kilometres and 125 kilometres, respectively. The Russian
losses were particularly acute among the officer corps: in 1914 it had numbered
80,000 men, including reserve officers. In the campaigns of 1914 and 1915
around 66,000 commanders died; in 1916, mainly as a result of the Brusilov
Offensive, the losses amounted to approximately 26,500 officers. Only the
colonels and generals survived intact. The new commanders of battalions
and companies, whose wartime military training had been fast-tracked, did
not belong to the old officer corps. For the time being they remained loyal, but
the attitude of the conscripts was very different: the number of deserters from
the Czar's army was estimated at half a million in the summer of 1915, and
later only grew. Russian censors, who monitored letters home from the front,
noticed an interesting and recurrent theme: the Russian soldier was rather

---

[6] *Noc listopadowa* (1904) – a symbolic drama by Stanisław Wyspiański (1869–1907).
[7] Sławoj Felicjan Składkowski, *Moja służba w Brygadzie. Pamiętnik połowy*, Warsaw 1990, p.
357.

neutral towards the enemy. He fought for the Czar without much enthusiasm, and did not particularly believe in the Teutonic threat to his homeland. The people who really hated the Germans were those who knew them: the Poles and the Latvians.

Czarism paid a high price for meeting its obligations to its allies. In the autumn of 1916 the new conscripts brought in to ameliorate the losses of the previous summer came from a country that was hungry, exhausted, and undermined. Their belief in the Czar increasingly wavered. Towards the end of the year insubordination was rife; in December revolts broke out in twelve regiments. Even soldiers of the Special Army, that is, the rump of the Imperial Guard, exhibited a lack of faith in victory.

The most recent victory of the Czarist army had proved ineffective: it had not brought peace any closer. As for the war which had been going on for a year in Courland, Lithuania, Belarus, and Ukraine, no one even dreamed that it would end favourably.

The Romanian Campaign

The Brusilov Offensive also contributed to radical changes in the south-east of Europe. In order to understand the drama that would play out in the summer of 1916, we need to go back in time.

After the Bulgarian attack on Serbia in October 1915 and the seizure by the coalition forces of Serbia, Montenegro, and Albania, the only two countries to remain neutral in the Balkans were Greece and Romania. The situation in Athens and Bucharest was similar: both had a monarch from a German dynasty and a deeply divided political class around the throne. Some politicians promised victory after an alliance with the Central Powers, others favoured the Entente. The advice of sensible people was to avoid being drawn into the war on either side, to continue trading with all concerned, and ... to wait. This seemed to be the safe option, rather like a high rate of interest at a reliable bank, but it did not satisfy the ambition of politicians. The politicians' recipe for success was based more on a gamble than a safe investment: everything had to be put on one horse.

In Greece the conflict centred on the Germanophile monarch, Constantine I, and the pro-Western Prime Minister, Eleftherios Venizelos. The latter wanted a 'Greater Greece' (a programme known as *Megali Idea*) at the expense of the Ottoman Empire. Quite rightly, as hindsight tells us, Venizelos believed that this greatness could be achieved only through an alliance with the Western powers. In his view the war in the Balkans presented an opportunity to complete the 'unification project' that had resumed in 1912. To ignore this opportunity could have disastrous consequences for the country. From the parliamentary tribune he warned Constantine's supporters that

144   THE FRONTS

> [...] you are leading Greece, unwittingly, but surely, to disaster, for you
> will make the country go to war out of necessity, under the harshest terms
> and under the most adverse conditions, and you will lose this opportunity
> to create a greater and powerful Greece, an opportunity which is only
> given to a nation once every millennium.[8]

On 7 October 1915 the King dismissed the ambitious Prime Minister for the second time in six months (Venizelos had returned to office following the Liberal Party's victory in the May 1915 election). However, Constantine had got rid of his popular head of government too late: on 5 October the British–French Expeditionary Force began to disembark in Salonika. It seemed that Venizelos's prediction had come true: since Greece had not wanted to join the war, the war had come to Greece instead. In fact, it was simply a scandal. France and Britain had violated the sovereignty of a neutral country. From then on, Greece – including the King and the supporters of the Central Powers – found itself in the situation of a half-occupied country. In November 1916 a brief civil war broke out between the royalists and the followers of Venizelos; an Allied fleet bombarded Athens. In June 1917 the Allies finally forced Constantine to abdicate and Venizelos returned to the post of Prime Minister; Athens declared war on the Central Powers.

Greece had no choice. Its elites were divided, but the Allies forced it into the war. In Romania the elites were similarly at odds with each other, but the Allies could not land an expeditionary force in Constanța. Decisions were taken by the King, the politicians, and the army. Ferdinand I (von Hohenzollern-Sigmaringen), like Constantine in Greece (a descendant of the dukes of Schleswig and Holstein), came from the German aristocracy. Just like the Greek monarch, he found himself in constant conflict with his pro-Western Prime Minister, although for the first eighteen months the position of the liberal Ion Brătianu was stronger than that of Venizelos. Both the Central Powers and the Allies made generous promises to Romania, as they had done to Greece. The difference lay in the biggest potential prize: the *Megali Idea* could be realized only in the event of the Ottoman Empire's defeat, whereas the corresponding idea of *România Mare* (Greater Romania) could be achieved only at the cost of Russia (Bessarabia) or the Habsburg monarchy (Transylvania). From the point of view of the Greeks, a war in Anatolia, in other words, on the western coast of present-day Turkey, could not succeed if the British navy opposed Greece. The Romanians could be aided by the Central Powers in a war with Russia. In an attack on Transylvania assistance could be provided only by Russia, which could bolster the new front with land forces,

---

[8] Eleftherios Venizelos, 'The Program of His Foreign Policy', ed. Vangelis Kechriotis, translated by Mary Kitroeff, in *Modernism. The Creation of Nation-States*, ed. Ahmet Ersoy, Maciej Górny, and Vangelis Kechriotis, Budapest and New York, NY 2010, pp. 258–266, here p. 266.

although it was far from certain whether it would do so. Nevertheless, following the Second Balkan War, Romania felt almost like a major player.

The discussions in Bucharest lasted a full two years, from 1914 to 1916. Brusilov's successes in June and July suggested the imminent collapse of the Austro-Hungarian army. At the same time, the Allies made a more generous offer. On 17 August 1916 they promised to recognize Romania's right to Transylvania and to Bukovina, Austro-Hungarian provinces on its northern border, if Romania entered the war on the side of the Entente. Ten days later the Romanian Crown Council acceded to the King's request to begin hostilities against Austria-Hungary. Brătianu later explained that this was a historic moment, that the country was to be more fully unified, and that a better opportunity had not presented itself for centuries. In his proclamation Ferdinand I encouraged his subjects to take up arms and promised to unite 'Romanians on both sides of the Carpathians'. The King and the intellectuals gave speeches and wrote passionate articles in which they invoked Michael I the Brave, the legendary Hospodar of Wallachia from the days of Stephen Báthory, who did in fact briefly unite Wallachia, Moldavia, and Transylvania. He died in 1601, murdered by a rival, and his subjects hated his brutish *soldatesca*, but none of this mattered in the national mythology: Ferdinand I had set his eyes on finally completing the work of his illustrious predecessor.

On 27 August 1916 Bucharest celebrated; it resembled Berlin or Petersburg from two years previously. The conservative politician Constantin Argetoianu remembered the mood in Karlovy Vary and Prague in the summer of 1914 – there, too, the first days of the war had been marvellous. In both cases he found the widespread enthusiasm to be somewhat childish, but on this occasion, as a Romanian, he had reason to give in to the national fervour. According to Argetoianu it was the Prime Minister who misread the situation. As he admitted in his memoirs: 'Brătianu managed to convince almost everyone that thanks to his diplomacy we were waiting for the war to enter its final phase and that our intervention in 1916, as in 1913, would be more a demonstration of strength than a proper war. [...] I was as blinded by this as the rest of us were.'[9]

The Romanian army numbered well over half a million soldiers. Although two years of neutrality had given the General Staff ample time to prepare for a new war, it was not a modern army. The leadership was only partly responsible for this, however. Quite simply, from the moment Romania's neighbours found themselves in a state of war, they stopped allowing any arms shipments across the border. Between 1914 and 1916 the only source of arms supplies was Russia, a country struggling with huge problems of its own. Romania's

---

[9] Ioan Scurtu, 'August 1916: Starea de spirit a românilor', *Dosarele Istoriei* 11, 8 (2006), pp. 13–19, here p. 18.

146 THE FRONTS

strength, therefore, had more to do with its strategic position than with its military might. Hindenburg believed that Romania was completely unique:

> It is certain that never before in the history of the world had a relatively small country such as Romania played so significant and decisive a role. Never before had two major powers, such as Germany and Austria, been so dependent on the favour and armed strength of a country whose population was at least twenty times smaller than that of both monarchies. Judging from the situation on the fronts, it would have sufficed for Romania to enter the territories to which it laid claim in order to settle the world war in favour of the powers which for years had fought against us in vain. Everything seemed to depend on whether Romania would be ready to take advantage of the opportunity that had arisen.[10]

To facilitate the Romanian attack the Entente launched an offensive on all fronts, even in Macedonia. Finally, Romania also struck. The bulk of Romania's forces set off west, entering Transylvania and reaching Brassó (Brașov, Kronstadt) and Nagyszeben (Sibiu, Hermannstadt); the weak Hungarian units stationed there could not mount an effective resistance. Austria-Hungary waited for reinforcements. Following the attack on its ally, Germany declared war on Romania and mobilized its forces for a counterattack, which was to be led in Transylvania by Erich von Falkenhayn – who had recently been ousted from the post of head of the Supreme Army Command – as commander of the nascent 9th Army.

The Romanian operational plans predicted that the attack on Hungary would provoke a declaration of war by Bulgaria, which occurred on 1 September. It seemed to the Romanians that they could defend their southern border effectively and for a long time. On the southern bank of the Danube, at the northwestern tip of Southern Dobruja, they held the fortress of Turtucaia (Tutrakan), which was eagerly compared to Przemyśl or Modlin (Novogeorgievsk). The commander of the Bulgarian armies that were gathering in the region (there were very few German or Turkish troops) was Field Marshal August von Mackensen, the victor of the Serbian and Polish campaigns. In a thoroughly modern fashion, von Mackensen directed operations from a saloon carriage, which ensured that the staff of 'my mixed coterie' (as he would refer to his troops) were quite mobile. There was not a huge number of railway lines in the area, but just about enough. By comparison, the commander-in-chief of the southern Romanian front did not stick his nose outside Bucharest for the first week of war, nor did he encounter another problem that cost von Mackensen much time and nerves. The 'mixed coterie' required determined and continuous work. The problem was not that many of the German liaison officers could not converse in French, but rather that they displayed a profound contempt for their Balkan allies. 'Essentially, the Bulgarian soldier belongs to the world's

[10] Generalfeldmarschall von Hindenburg, *Aus meinem Leben*, Leipzig 1920, p. 181.

elite', wrote von Mackensen in December 1915. 'The Bulgarians are rightly referred to as the "Prussians of the Balkans" in this regard.' His subordinates, however, were generally of a different opinion and were quick to let their allies know about it: cruelty, unpredictability, unreliability, lack of discipline, and a propensity for theft made up the German image of the Bulgarian savage, who – regrettably – was now a comrade-in-arms. 'Stolen cattle are as valuable to the Bulgarian regiment as the flag is to us'[11] – this view was not at all uncommon. The Balkan allies had their own axe to grind: describing a particular 'German mindset', the Chief of the General Staff of the Bulgarian Army emphasized 'a strong tendency to indulge in stereotypes, to act in accordance with conventions that are divorced from reality, and a lack of mental flexibility'.[12] In a situation of constant emotional tension, much depended on the diplomatic skills of the commander of the southern front.

The Bulgarians attacked Tutrakan on 2 September and already on the first day captured the outer line of defence. On 5 September they drove the Romanians out from their main line of defence, and a day later victory was certain: of the 40,000 or so defenders of the fortress around 4,000 crossed to the north bank of the Danube, more than 28,000 were taken prisoner, and the rest were either killed or wounded. General Basarabescu's troops were crushed, and their commander drowned while retreating across the river. The Bulgarian losses amounted to nearly 10,000 men killed, wounded, or missing, but this was very little compared with the psychological effect of the victory: in less than a week after the commencement of von Mackensen's attack the largest fortress in the region had fallen. The Romanian southern front had become a large gaping hole. For the moment the road to Bucharest was blocked by the Danube, but the Black Sea coast, i.e. Dobruja, had no natural obstacle to protect it. The Romanians had to quickly withdraw their troops from Transylvania, yet the combined Bulgarian–Turkish–German units forced them north. Panic broke out in Dobruja. The locals were afraid of the Bulgarians. Over the following weeks two-thirds of the population fled; around 82,000 of the 235,000 inhabitants stayed behind. Constanța, the largest city of the region, became deserted; barely one in five inhabitants decided to remain.

For the time being no one fled Bucharest, but the shock was huge. Witnesses recalled that, for two weeks, neither the King nor Brătianu could collect themselves: their intricate plans, discussed over two years, had failed within a mere ten days! Instead of a victory parade, German

---

[11] Citations in Oliver Stein, '"Wer das nicht mitgemacht hat, glaubt es nicht." Erfahrungen deutscher Offiziere mit den bulgarischen Verbündeten 1915–1918', in *Der Erste Weltkrieg auf dem Balkan. Perspektiven der Forschung*, ed. Jürgen Angelow, Berlin 2011, pp. 271–287, here pp. 276, 278.

[12] Stefan Minkov, 'Der Status der Nord-Dobrudscha im Kontext des deutsch-bulgarischen Verhältnisses im Ersten Weltkrieg', in *Der Erste Weltkrieg auf dem Balkan. Perspektiven der Forschung*, ed. Jürgen Angelow, Berlin 2011, pp. 241–255, here p. 249.

Fig. 33 The progress of the combined German and Austro-Hungarian offensive was hampered by extremely poor roads. The photograph shows a track in the Polesie region during the spring thaw of 1916.

Fig. 34 Weapons and war materials captured by the Bulgarians in the Tutrakan fortress. Courtesy of Mr Peyo Kolev, lostbulgaria.com.

BREAKTHROUGH

zeppelins appeared over the city. The British nurse Dorothy Kennard witnessed the unfolding catastrophe:

> All the church bells rang wildly when the signal came through, and the guns were infernal, popping like mad. I counted twelve searchlights and tried to believe in the actuality of the happening, but honestly, if I had not hurt myself by bumping into a tin trunk in the dark, I should feel today as if I had dreamt the whole thing. One thing, however, struck me forcibly, and will remain as a humorous recollection until I die: in this quiet town, lying peacefully under a starlit heaven with no sound of traffic to spoil the silence, the sound that deafened us was not the shooting, but the dogs!! Thousands of them barked, every age and size of yap imaginable, and I pictured them all with surprised, stiff noses, furious and impotent. [...] Only five bombs were dropped last night, and I feel somehow as if they were reserving themselves for something really nasty.[13]

Sister Kennard soon came to the conclusion that the real problem facing the city was not the German bombardment but the dramatically rising number of wounded, who filled the hospitals and improvised dressing stations:

> I had been under the impression that our own hospital was primitive, but, alas! it is luxurious and well stocked compared to the others that I saw. The two best and grandest were overcrowded in treble proportion to their powers of accommodation, but they had, at least, an atmosphere of antiseptics [...]; all the others were pathetic. The men lay on the ground, which was covered with wooden boards. Some shared a mattress with four or five others, the rest lay without even a pillow to their heads. It was obvious that they had not been attended to for hours; this was not from neglect, but for the reason that the doctors are working night and day to keep belated pace with the wounded who arrive in batches of several hundreds at a time. [...] I am told on all sides that the chloroform will shortly give out, even though it is most sparingly used. As for the ordinary hospital requisites, they are simply non-existent. From the point of view of the unfortunate wounded [...], it would be a godsend to them if the Germans captured the town. Therein lies their only hope of obtaining supplies.[14]

Wounded soldiers arrived in the capital from both the northern and southern fronts, but the biggest clouds were gathering over Transylvania. So far, the Romanians had been able to advance because the Hungarian reserve units they faced had been significantly weaker in numbers. Thanks to the efficient Hungarian railway network, von Falkenhayn amassed his 9th Army within a few weeks and launched a counterattack. The Romanians suffered their first defeat at the end of September in fighting around Sibiu that lasted a few days; in the middle of October the Germans pushed their enemy to the Hungarian–

---

[13] Dorothy Kennard, *A Roumanian Diary 1915, 1916, 1917*, New York, NY 1918, pp. 54–55.
[14] Ibid., pp. 93–94.

Romanian border (in other words, back to the starting point) before crossing the Carpathians and continuing the offensive. Aleksander Majkowski, who worked as an army doctor during the Romanian campaign, likened it to an exhausting experience of wading through mud. He saw the corpses of Romanian and Russian soldiers along the way, as well as severely wounded men, who delayed the retreat:

> In the adjacent room I saw a dead Russian soldier and next to him one still alive who had been wounded in the leg. In the spacious third room two men were lying on a thin bed of straw; next to one of them was a large pool of congealed blood. Nearby, a couple of steps from the dead men, stood a sheep, looking at them fixedly; it was dressed in a damask girl's gown, which hung down on both sides and behind. The sheep was so motionless that at first I thought it was a wooden figure, until I went over to it. Even though I had become accustomed to various scenes of war, this sheep in its comical clothing juxtaposed with the horror of death [...] made such an impression that the image has never left me.[15]

On 17 October it began to snow, which made the ground slippery and brought a chill to the air. The draught-horses and other beasts of burden ceased to be useful on the Carpathian passes. They were replaced by people – soldiers and local villagers – commandeered to perform transportation duties. Despite this setback, the German and Austrian Alpine riflemen pressed forward. On 14 November they took control of the passes – the way to the Romanian capital was now open.

It was still easier to reach Bucharest from the south, however. On 23 November von Mackensen's army forced its way across the Danube, taking the enemy by surprise, and began its march towards the capital.

Two years earlier the Field Marshal had entered Łódź on his sixty-fifth birthday. On 6 December 1916, for his sixty-seventh birthday, he arranged a truly cinematic scene. He got into a car with three officers, overtook his troops that were approaching Bucharest, and drove into the capital of the defeated enemy. Before the Royal Palace he was greeted by a patrol of the 9th Army, which had entered the city from the west on the same day.

All this happened against a bizarre backdrop. Like many other East European cities, in the 1880s and 1890s Bucharest had been encircled with a vast network of forts, which by 1916 had become obsolete, just like all the others. The Romanian army drew the logical conclusion from this: before heading off to Transylvania it dismantled the fortress artillery. The capital was declared an open city and there was indeed no one to defend it. Moreover, a proclamation by the local prefect of police ordered the inhabitants to welcome the occupiers in a friendly manner: shops were to remain open and

---

[15] Aleksander Majkowski, *Pamiętnik z wojny europejskiej roku 1914*, ed. Tadeusz Linkner, Wejherowo and Pelplin 2000, pp. 296–297.

Fig. 35 A fallen Romanian soldier near the Tutrakan fortress. Courtesy of Mr Peyo Kolev, lostbulgaria.com.

the curfew was not to begin until 10.00 p.m. The bemused Germans entered a city in which the trams were running normally, the cafés and taverns were crowded with people, the shops were open, and the streets were full of pedestrians. Interestingly, a great many residents welcomed the Germans as effusively as they had bid farewell to their own troops heading off to the front at the end of August. Von Mackensen was indignant: 'All this enthusiasm is truly scandalous, for those cheering us are precisely the same rabble who wanted to go to war with us previously [...]. I could understand it in a friendly country, but in a hostile country I find it simply abhorrent.'[16] The Field Marshal was convinced that the Romanians were traitors, typical Balkan types: riff-raff. He rightly sensed that the inhabitants of Bucharest would have been just as enthusiastic welcoming a victorious King Ferdinand, who at that moment was withdrawing north-east to Moldavia with the remnants of his army. What von Mackensen did not understand, however, was that the inhabitants of Bucharest had no particular reason to mourn the demise of the King and the political class, who, after two years of debate – with all options on the table – had chosen the worst possible one, consigning their country to defeat and occupation.

From the perspective of Vienna and Berlin the balance-sheet of the Romanian campaign was more than impressive. The Central Powers – *de*

---

[16] Cited in Raymund Netzhammer, *Bischof in Rumänien. Im Spannungsfeld zwischen Staat und Vatikan*, vol. 1, Munich 1995, p. 698, note from 16 December 1916.

Fig. 36 Mass being said for fallen Bulgarian soldiers. Courtesy of Mr Peyo Kolev, lostbulgaria.com.

facto the Germans – had in less than four months scored an important victory, and had done so in precisely the style in which, back in 1914, they had imagined the whole war would proceed. This time everything had gone seamlessly: from the coordination of multinational troops and the efficiency of the railways, through the skills of the commanders, to the discipline of soldiers who, in difficult weather conditions, had managed to force a way across the Danube and across the snow-covered Carpathian passes. Indeed, the average distance covered when marching on level ground (20 kilometres) meant that the best units in the Romanian campaign covered, in full gear, up to 40 kilometres within a single day. The losses proved to be incomparably smaller than on the eastern fronts hitherto.

As a result of the victory over Romania, in December 1916 the Central Powers controlled all of the Balkans except for Greece, forcing Russia to open another front in Moldavia, where the remnants of the Romanian army had found refuge: of the 560,000 soldiers mobilized in 1916, 73,000 had been killed or wounded, 147,000 had been captured, and 90,000 were missing. On the other hand, the Russians had finally come to the aid of their ally; the kingdom had not capitulated and wanted to continue the fight.

The Central Powers had captured one of the breadbaskets of Europe. The oil industry – Romania's other great asset – had suffered heavily during the campaign (British engineers, in the face of their ally's defeat, had tried to

BREAKTHROUGH 153

blow up as many wells and refineries as possible), but the damage could be repaired relatively fast. German euphoria was therefore justified, and seldom did anyone dare question it. One of the few who did was Bogislav Tilka, a lawyer from Jena, who wrote under the pen name of Gerhard Velburg. Tilka's health was clearly not as robust as that of his peers, and thus he did not undergo military training. Unlike his university friends, he did not become an officer, and in 1916 he found himself in the Landsturm, i.e. the reserve units. Private Tilka arrived in Bucharest in December and immediately noticed that food was in abundance; in Germany, after two years of war, the situation was completely different. Delighted, he and his comrades immediately paid a visit to a well-known Bucharest patisserie: 'Our group of friends also tucked in because we knew that soon, with German precision, regulations would be put up on the walls of the shop ordering people to limit their consumption of fat and sugar.'[17] In Romania, in the early months of the occupation, Tilka and his comrades gorged themselves like never before – until, that is, they began to rule the country; it was then, with 'German precision', that they turned the country into a huge black market where only the occupiers, peasants, and wealthier city dwellers could eat their fill.

***

On the eastern fronts the regular war practically ended in December 1916 due to exhaustion. Neither Russia nor Austria-Hungary was able to launch any further big offensives. In the west Russia had lost provinces the size of France. Austria-Hungary had suffered minimal territorial losses – Bukovina and parts of Eastern Galicia – but its army had been decimated in the east, just as the Russian army had. The great victor – Germany – had no intention of continuing the offensive to Petrograd or Moscow; it now looked west for a resolution to the war. And it was only the Germans who still believed that the war could end in victory.

Prisoners of War

In the late summer of 1914 everyone still thought that the war could be quickly settled: a victory parade would be organized in the defeated enemy's capital and the troops would be home before winter. After two years of slaughter on an unprecedented scale even the die-hard optimists had to tame their enthusiasm. The war was no longer a kind of holiday, a short break from everyday life, a transient state; it had become the daily grind. One had to learn how to live with it and to find solutions to problems that had initially been thought to be merely temporary.

---

[17] Cited in Lisa Mayerhofer, *Zwischen Freund und Feind – Deutsche Besatzung in Rumänien 1916–1918*, Munich 2010, p. 227.

Fig. 37 Austro-Hungarian prisoners of war eating dinner in Galicia. In 1915 the provision of food was better on the Russian side than in the monarchy. Courtesy of Mariusz Kulik.

One such problem was prisoners of war. Every country that participated in the war was unprepared when it came to dealing with masses of prisoners, who had to be isolated but also fed. The total number of POWs in all the combatant states is hard to determine precisely, but it was roughly between 8.5 and 9 million, of whom the vast majority – slightly less than 7 million – were being held in Germany, Russia, and Austria-Hungary. In the first six months of the conflict there were nearly 1.5 million POWs. Most soldiers taken captive throughout the war fought on the Eastern and Balkan fronts, and almost 3.5 million were Russian soldiers. Camps consisting of huts surrounded by barbed wire began to appear in the autumn of 1914; the first prisoners were housed in army barracks and other military buildings, which soon led to catastrophic overcrowding. Under such conditions the outbreak of epidemics was only a matter of time.

The death rate among prisoners of war depended on several factors. It was important whether a prisoner received help from his home country. All POWs on the Western Front received assistance in the form of parcels and as a result, in relative terms, Belgian, British, and French prisoners were less likely to die in German camps than Italian soldiers, who did not receive parcels for a long time. Another determinant of survival was the goodwill of the camp staff; in its absence mass deaths occurred, as was the case in the German camp in Heiderode (today Czersk) in Pomerania. Although the death rates in other Pomeranian POW camps were not high, in Heiderode the prisoners were beaten and starved and sometimes dozens of people died in a single day. Under normal circumstances outbreaks of typhus, cholera, and dysentery in German and Austro-Hungarian prisoner-of-war camps were quickly brought under control thanks to the dedication of medical staff. This was not the case either in Heiderode or in Mauthausen in Austria, where a typhus epidemic in early 1915 led to the death of at least several thousand Serbs. The Austrian lawyer, intellectual, and politician Josef Redlich believed, not without reason, that Serbian prisoners had become subject to 'a policy of systematic extermination'.[18] The situation of Entente soldiers captured by the Central Powers began to improve significantly in the spring of 1915, when they were sent to work in the fields. Such work generally prevented starvation and also relieved overcrowding in the camps. The importance of this factor is once again revealed by the history of the German camps in Pomerania. After the successful Romanian campaign the death rate in those camps rapidly increased; the victims were no longer Russians, however, but Romanians. The cause was mundane: there was no work in the vicinity for Romanian POWs, which meant that they were forced to stay within the camp and subsist on basic rations. The high death rate among Romanians (approximately 9 per cent per year for those in German captivity) was also compounded by other factors.[19] Some were sent to camps in occupied Romania, where conditions were even worse than in the Reich: the level of hunger was similar, but there was a shortage of accommodation and the lack of hygiene and medical care took a terrible toll. Romanian POWs fell ill and died in large numbers from typhus and typhoid fever. Faced with this situation, the Germans released more than 20,000 prisoners (who were given 'leave' to work on the land in their native villages).

ANTHROPOLOGY

The military and civilian authorities were not expecting such a large number of prisoners of war, and dealing with them was a major challenge. But there were also those who saw the situation as an opportunity. Perhaps the most unconventional beneficiaries of the First World War were physical anthropologists. Hitherto, in order to gather research material (photographs, measurements, and casts of body

---

[18] Matthew Stibbe, 'Civilian Internment and Civilian Internees in Europe, 1914–1920', *Immigrants & Minorities* 26, 1–2 (2008), pp. 49–81, here p. 63.

[19] For an estimate of the number of prisoners of war in German camps, see Mark Spoerer, 'The Mortality of Allied Prisoners of War and Belgian Civilian Deportees in German Custody during the First World War: A Reappraisal of the Effects of Forced Labour', *Population Studies* 60, 2 (2006), pp. 121–136, especially p. 129.

156   THE FRONTS

parts of people from different 'races'), they had been forced to go on expensive trips to faraway places. Quite unexpectedly, prisoner-of-war camps made all this unnecessary. Now the 'research material' came to the researchers, and in large volumes to boot; it was concentrated in a small number of well-guarded sites and was subject to military discipline. All the researchers had to do was to obtain the necessary permits. Within a few months the prominent Austrian anthropologist Rudolf Pöch asked the Viennese Academy of Sciences to fund a project that involved carrying out extensive measurements of Russian prisoners of war. He wrote:

> Since the beginning of the war hundreds of thousands of Russian prisoners have been interned in Austrian prisoner-of-war camps, and thus various nationalities, some from the furthest reaches of the vast Russian Empire, have been concentrated in several places within the monarchy. These exceptional circumstances, which the war has brought about, present the scientific community with an unprecedented and in all likelihood never-to-be-repeated opportunity to further our anthropological knowledge about those peoples. The task is all the more rewarding since our familiarity with many of the peoples of Russia is still rather scant. This is because studying them under ordinary circumstances is difficult, time-consuming, and costly.[20]

The research eventually undertaken by Pöch analysed more than 10,000 people. However, the example set by the Austro-Hungarian anthropologists proved contagious, and their German colleagues soon joined in. The two groups exchanged data and allowed each other access to the more exotic prisoners (in Austria-Hungary Russian prisoners predominated, while in the German camps there was no shortage of African and Asian soldiers serving in the French and British armies). The research proceeded as follows. First, the anthropologists conducted a brief interview with the prisoner and recorded his personal details, particularly his ethnicity and religion (the questions and answers were translated). Then the subject had to undress and stand on a low platform surrounded by several people, who carried out measurements and took photographs. The main instrument used by the anthropologists was an anthropometer (similar to the ones used today in doctors' surgeries). They also used a set of sample-cards to help determine the colour of the eyes, hair, and skin. In the case of some prisoners facial plaster casts were made (during this process the subject would breathe through straws placed in his nostrils). In the case of particularly 'exotic' nationalities, linguistics experts from Budapest, who were also employed on the project, would record short stories and folk songs. The researchers also made films that showed prisoners sculpting in wood, performing folk dances, and engaging in Islamic prayer.

---

[20] Archiv der Österreichischen Akademie der Wissenschaften, Subventionen der math.-nat. Klasse 1914–1919 – Karton 6, 411/1915, Ansuchen um eine Subvention von K 4000 für anthropologische Untersuchungen in den russischen Gefangenenlagern, 24 June 1915.

It was mainly people from Central and Eastern Europe and the Balkans who took part in the research, either passively (as the objects of measurement) or actively (as the anthropologists carrying out the measurements). The Entente countries did not undertake similar research, while scientists from the Reich and Austria-Hungary were not especially interested in British and French research subjects. The pursuit of the exotic meant that the anthropological measurement programme mainly concerned people from non-European nations serving in the British and French armies. In time, other places also came to be seen as exotic, which broadened the group of individuals to be researched. After the Czar's Asian subjects – Turkmen, Buryats, Tatars, Georgians, and Armenians – came the turn of the Russians, Ukrainians, Serbs, and Poles. Already during the war there were Ukrainians, Poles, Serbs, and Hungarians among the researchers, and measurements were also carried out in prisoner-of-war camps located in Poland, Serbia, and Romania. After 1918 these experiences proved crucial to the development of physical anthropology in the newly formed states of the region. The new national schools of anthropology were based on the know-how acquired in wartime, with one major difference: the object of their interest was no longer that which Pöch had set out in his grant application. The new times demanded that, instead of pursuing the exotic, researchers should set the racial boundaries of their own nation. Thanks to the Great War, physical anthropology became yet another tool for constructing national identities.

The fate of prisoners in Russia was highly dependent on how their labour was used. Up to 1918 there were approximately 2.5 million Habsburg, nearly 200,000 German, and over 50,000 Ottoman POWs in Russia. Those who were sent to improvised camps were exposed to epidemics. The situation of some deteriorated in 1915, when the Russian authorities began to utilize huge numbers of Austro-Hungarian prisoners in the construction of railways, primarily the strategic line to the port in Murmansk. Disease, malnutrition, and work under harsh conditions caused the death of tens of thousands of people. At the other extreme were the many prisoners sent to work on the land. Their social status was relatively high – they had expertise or other skills that were lacking at the local level. One of these 'privileged' prisoners was Roman Dyboski, who had been held in Russian captivity from December 1914. In civilian life he had been a professor of English Literature at the Jagiellonian University in Cracow. He recalled:

> Those soldiers who, at the beginning of their captivity, were fortunate enough to be sent to do farm labour for rich peasants in various parts of Russia and Siberia experienced the kind of material prosperity about which our own peasants would not even dare to dream.[21]

[21] Roman Dyboski, *Siedem lat w Rosji i na Syberii (1915–1921). Przygody i wrażenia*, ed. Tomasz Bohun, Warsaw 2007, p. 81.

Fig. 38 The return of prisoners often took a long time. The photograph shows French (colonial) soldiers in a camp accompanied by their former Bulgarian guards (1919). Courtesy of Mr Peyo Kolev, lostbulgaria.com.

Bread, a warm stove, and medicine in the event of illness were of course the basic things that prisoners needed. But, at the latest from the winter of 1916/1917, many of them were asking themselves and their neighbours questions that were of little interest to the guards: Why am I here? What is the point of this war? What do I have in common with the officers, who even in this place are much better off?

The news from the front did not answer any of these questions.

PART II

The Rear

5

The Hinterland

A visitor wandering the streets of Vienna, Belgrade, Berlin, or Bucharest in the penultimate year of the Great War would have witnessed more or less the same scene in each of those cities: men in oversized suits or uniforms and women in dresses that had fitted them perfectly a few years earlier. The same visitor would have also noticed a proliferation of fruit and vegetable gardens, even in front of the Schwarzenberg Palace in Vienna. The difference between the hinterland and occupied territories was simple: in the former these miniature garden-plots were owned by local residents, whereas on the boulevards of Belgrade or Bucharest they were owned partly by the residents and partly by the occupier's military units stationed nearby. Life during wartime was hardly better in one's 'own' hinterland than it was in occupied territories.

Most civilians in areas behind the Eastern Front never realized that they had spent the war in the hinterland. This term is now accepted in historiography: it means one's own territory, unoccupied by the enemy, that extends from areas adjacent to the front all the way to the national border at the opposite end of the country. The hinterland included East Prussia and Dalmatia as well as Salonika, Cracow, Iași, Prague, and until 1918, also Kiev and Tallinn.

The first days of the war were similar everywhere: crowds outside newspaper offices, mobilization notices, manifestos and solemn religious services, pledges of loyalty to the emperor, gatherings, speeches, assemblies, resolutions. Occasionally, there were spontaneous or organized outbursts of hatred for the enemy:

> Hordes demanding the removal of foreign signs marched through Berlin. The establishment known as 'The Continental Bodega' dropped the definite article from its name and was now considered sufficiently Germanized. Without much fuss the 'Café Windsor' became 'Kaffee Winzer'. [...] Englische Straße in Charlottenburg was renamed Deutsche Straße.[1]

In other places patriots lacked not only the seriousness but also the ardour that had consumed many Berliners. Initially, the Russian authorities were unable to

---

[1] Hellmut von Gerlach, *Die große Zeit der Lüge. Der Erste Weltkrieg und die deutsche Mentalität (1871–1921)*, ed. H. Donat and A. Wild, Bremen 1994, p. 38.

162   THE REAR

muster any enthusiasm among the inhabitants of Warsaw. At the end of
July 1914 the journalist Czesław Jankowski noted:

> So when, on the evening of 30 July, the sound of a procession could be
> heard on Aleje Jerozolimskie and some sort of choral singing cut through
> the rattle of trams and street noise, people went to their windows and
> balconies and stopped on the pavements in curiosity: what the hell was
> going on? It was a procession of 200 predominantly Russian students
> going off to demonstrate before the Austrian consulate. [...] The pro-
> testers, whose number eventually grew to 1,000 or so (*Varšaskij Dnevnik*
> reported 5,000), pulled up in front of the Regional Military Command,
> where they were given a portrait of the monarch, and then headed down
> ul. Wierzbowa and ul. Senatorska to the Serbian consulate. [...]
> Generally, the demonstration did not make a good impression and was
> altogether frivolous; its only purpose was to allow the Petersburg Agency
> to notify the rest of Russia that Warsaw, too, had witnessed a patriotic
> demonstration.[2]

While all this was going on, the railway stations were beginning to burst at
the seams, and not just because of the troop trains: holidaymakers suddenly
returned home, foreigners and citizens of enemy states abandoned their homes
in panic, and the first refugees appeared in the border towns. The streets were
busy: soldiers bade farewell to their loved ones, flowers were everywhere to be
seen, and conscripts were handed cigarettes and confectionery. A local orchestra would often play as the troops boarded the trains, but there was much more
to be heard at the stations than hymns and marches: 'The train left at 2:15',
wrote the twenty-year-old conscript André Kertész, a future photographer of
world repute, 'the crying, the last words of farewell almost drowned out the
band that was supposed to fire us up with enthusiasm ... I saw a desperate,
shrieking mother who could hardly be stopped from running after the train.
One of the sergeants jumped off the already moving train to go to his wife ...
and gave one last goodbye kiss to this unhappy woman who did not want to let
him go.'[3] Faith in a swift, victorious war and the rapid return of the soldiers
was mixed with fear and uncertainty. Feelings exploded like fireworks, leaving
behind a smoke of ambiguous and at times conflicting emotions and memories. On the Vienna–Budapest train a teenage boy recalled a lively discussion
among the passengers, prompted by the sight of numerous military transports
on their way to the front: 'Some of [our] fellow passengers ... remarked to my
parents that it was heartening to see all this enthusiasm; and I remember my
comment was that I could not see as much enthusiasm as drunkenness.'[4]

---

[2] Czesław Jankowski, *Z dnia na dzień. Warszawa 1914–1915 Wilno*, Wilno (Vilnius) 1923, p. 29.

[3] Cited in Kati Marton, *The Great Escape. Nine Jews Who Fled Hitler and Changed the World*, New York, NY 2006, p. 53.

[4] Recollection of Leo Szilard, cited in Marton, *The Great Escape*, p. 60.

THE HINTERLAND   163

BLACK CARS FULL OF GOLD

The German pacifist Hellmut von Gerlach kept a war diary in which he recorded particularly interesting events as well as the most absurd propagandist slogans and rumours. One of the stories he recounted concerned a fleet of mysterious cars that was allegedly circulating around Europe in August 1914. The cars were said to be filled with French gold that was being sent to Russia. It turned out that this rumour was to have a dazzling career. All over Germany, the local press reported on the mysterious cars, and as it did so their number inexorably grew. Initially there were supposed to be twelve cars, but this soon rose to twenty-four and finally thirty-six. Enhanced patrols conducted by the police and by civilian volunteers began to appear on the roads. Gerlach claimed that the story about the French cars had been invented by the mayor of the Düsseldorf district, Francis Kruse (other evidence points to the area of Geldern near the border with the Netherlands).[5] Even if there was a grain of truth to this, the rumour quickly got out of control. People were detained for no reason and cars were even fired upon if a driver failed to stop when summoned to do so. According to Gerlach the government denied the rumour only when over-zealous civilians began to flag down officers and aristocrats who were travelling around the country.[6]

The problem, however, was that it was much easier to spread the rumour than to stop it. Indeed, the story about the French cars managed to go beyond the borders of the Reich. In a hurry to get to his unit in Przemyśl (Premissel), the Austrian reserve officer August Krasicki recorded the following observation in his diary:

> Just as I began heading in the direction of Jarosław, I noticed soldiers guarding the road and bridge. I was told that the reason for this was that a secret message had been intercepted: the French were about to send large amounts of money in gold, several million in fact, to Russia. Automobiles carrying these riches were going to be crossing Europe, hence the order had come to guard all roads heading east in order to catch them. It seemed like an April Fool's joke, but orders are orders, and the soldiers had their bayonets at the ready![7]

It was definitely not a joke, as Helena Jabłońska discovered to her cost on 4 August when travelling to Przemyśl with her mother. They were stopped for the first time in Olszanica:

> They were screaming at the driver for having attempted to escape across the fields and fences. He tried to explain, but they were having none of it and threatened to shoot. I myself tried. 'Quiet or I'll jab you!,' shouted the soldier, holding the bayonet two inches under my ribs. My mother was crying, terrified. [. . .] There we stood for an hour and ten minutes. [. . .] Our permits meant nothing in light of the

---

[5] Alexander Watson, *Ring of Steel. Germany and Austria-Hungary in World War I*, New York, NY 2014, pp. 77–78.

[6] Gerlach, *Die große Zeit der Lüge*, p. 54.

[7] August Krasicki, *Dziennik z kampanii rosyjskiej*, Cracow 1988, p. 38.

164   THE REAR

telegram that had ordered them to stop all cars, as apparently two women were smuggling millions in gold from France to Russia.[8]

At another forced stop in Krościenko several cars were already waiting, also suspected of carrying gold and silver. Among the passengers were officers, who were treated more gently than the two women:

> Finally, they let the officers go. They stopped us and even confiscated a few of our bonbons that were suspected of containing the cholera bacillus. 'Any heavy silver?,' asked one of them in French. I answered. They were almost certain that I was smuggling millions. My mother could barely stand, crying like a baby, urging me to go back. Going back was not allowed. Then they began to interrogate me about my friends and acquaintances in Sanok. [...] I mentioned Dr Jaremkiewicz. That night – Thank God! – they let us through.[9]

On the other side of the Carpathians the Hungarian gendarmes were put on high alert. In Trenčín (Trencsén) they even stopped a car carrying a message from Emperor Franz Joseph to the Poles. After a search, the driver was released, but he did not get very far. A patrol stopped him a few kilometres further on:

> The gendarmes would not allow themselves to be persuaded. The driver was already sitting at the train station under escort, waiting to be taken to the nearest court, when, by a stroke of luck, a military transport arrived. There were several officers in it. They took one look at the alleged spy and gold smuggler and immediately recognized their comrade from the reserves.[10]

In Styria a patrol accidentally shot a Red Cross nurse whose car had braked too slowly. 'The slave has been empowered' – commented the appalled Viennese intellectual Karl Kraus – 'His nature will hardly be able to stand it.'[11] In the end, also the Austro-Hungarian authorities denied the rumour about the mysterious transport. In any case, shortly thereafter the French gold ceased to be of interest to anyone. With the onset of proper warfare the focus of espionage and collective hysteria shifted elsewhere.

The history of the rumour about the French cars perfectly illustrates how infectious gossip could be and how quickly it could spread. An entirely fabricated report required barely a few hours, not days, to travel from the Franco-German border to

---

[8] Helena z Seifertów Jabłońska, *Dziennik z oblężonego Przemyśla 1914–1915*, ed. Hanna Imbs, Przemyśl 1994, p. 36.

[9] Ibid.

[10] Max Ronge, *Kriegs- und Industriespionage. Zwölf Jahre Kundschaftsdienst*, Vienna 1930, p. 70.

[11] Karl Kraus, *Die letzten Tage der Menschheit. Tragödie in fünf Akten mit Vorspiel und Epilog*, Berlin 1978, p. 42.

THE HINTERLAND   165

> Eastern Galicia and Upper Hungary, spreading fear and confusion along the way.
> Not for the first or last time during the Great War did the rapid spread of informa-
> tion surpass the imagination of the authorities.

Once the soldiers had departed, civilians rarely returned to their old
rhythm of life. The biggest change was felt in Serbia, which had 4.5 million
inhabitants. In the last week of July half a million soldiers were mobilized,
followed by another 50,000 in September, in other words, over 12 per cent of
the country's population. To compare: at the end of August 1939 Poland
called up a million men or 3.0–3.5 per cent of the population. In the First
World War as a whole, Bulgaria, Germany, and France mobilized around
20 per cent of their citizens, Austria-Hungary around 17 per cent, and Russia
considerably less than 10 per cent. In Serbia the problems caused by mass
mobilization were compounded by the specific social structure. Nearly
90 per cent of the country's inhabitants were peasants. The practical consequence of calling up more than half a million men was that many farms lost
their owner, i.e. the most important person on the farm, and in the middle of
the harvest to boot. His role had to be taken over either by his father (if he was
still alive and not of conscription age) or, as was usually the case, by his wife.
Suddenly, there were far more women everywhere than men; life in the
hinterland changed gender, and not just in Serbian villages. We discuss this
in the following chapters.

Rationing and Control

The state immediately became involved in matters that in peacetime were
within the remit of municipal and economic institutions, private individuals,
and social organizations. Citizens learned about the suspension of their civil
rights. The authorities introduced censorship, abolished freedom of expression
and assembly, restricted the sums that could be withdrawn from personal bank
accounts, deferred debt repayments, and outlawed strikes. Prohibition was
introduced here and there, and curfews were established in border towns.
Subsequent announcements restricted freedom of travel, including by rail, and
requisitioned public buildings for military use. This was soon followed by the
rationing of goods and all kinds of services. In the first week of the war
a Warsaw journalist wrote:

> Something big, something awful and ghastly is happening in the
> world, and yet it seems inevitable, as if necessary [...]. The cannons
> are still to be fired. At present, all we have witnessed is mobilization,
> yet this sudden and unexpected interruption of daily life had already
> brought incalculable changes in its wake. Modern industrialism has
> complicated the economic side of humanity's existence to such

a degree, has merged and shackled everything together so profoundly, that the whole world has been derailed and finds itself on the cusp of economic catastrophe.[12]

As early as in August 1914 the Warsaw journalist had identified the fundamental problem of the new war: the structural contradiction between maximizing the number of conscripts and maximizing war production. In the Czech metals industry in the north of the country the number of skilled workers fell by 60 per cent in a single month; a few months later the Habsburg authorities began to release workers who were needed in the armaments industry from military duty, and sent 1.3 million men to the factories. It was probably only thanks to this that Austria-Hungary survived the first three years of the war.

The orders issued by local authorities introduced major changes, which people perceived as a source of great confusion – the very thing the orders were supposed to prevent. In the last days of August 12,000 people fled to Danzig from Königsberg, a city of 250,000 inhabitants that was the nearest major

Fig. 39   The manufacture of shells (1915).

[12] Z. Dębicki, 'Wojna!', *Tygodnik Ilustrowany*, no. 32, 8 August 1914.

THE HINTERLAND 167

urban centre to the Russian border. At the same time a mass of refugees arrived in the capital of East Prussia from districts on the eastern border that the Russians had occupied. The city authorities decreed that accommodation was to be provided for 50,000 new arrivals. Children were delighted by this, no doubt, since it was always simplest to turn schools into temporary lodgings. But the changes must have been felt by every resident of the royal city. The same was true in Lwów, where less ambitious orders were issued and suddenly hordes of refugees appeared: in August a reported 100,000 gathered in the Galician capital, which had a population of just over 200,000. A year later, in the smaller city of Vilnius, the authorities had to deal with 50,000 refugees.

However, the decrees on accommodation (in Königsberg it later transpired that there would be fewer refugees than initially feared) were merely a foretaste of the new, daily reality of wartime. On 5 September – just before the Germans began their counter-offensive that would push the Russians out of East Prussia within a week – the authorities of Königsberg, for the first time in decades, set maximum prices for forty-eight foodstuffs. The effect was minimal. As in other cities of the hinterland, the shop queues in Königsberg got even longer, and on 15 March 1915 the first ration cards were introduced – for bread. No one could have predicted that prices would increase more within a single year than in the forty-five years since the unification of the Reich in 1871. School pupils had reason to be happy in subsequent years, too – classes became shorter because in summer the older boys would be sent to the countryside to help with the harvest, while in winter schools would often be closed due to the lack of fuel. Citizens, particularly female citizens, also became involved in other types of campaigns: 'wartime' cookery courses, in other words, the art of preparing meals from waste and weeds (or 'wild vegetables' as these were known in the Reich and Austria) and the collection of secondary raw materials and scrap. The latter could involve the identification and gathering of metals – the tin lids of tankards and even the copper pipes to which beer barrels were attached soon began to disappear from taverns, while residential homes were deprived of lightning rods and churches and historic tenements lost their copper roofs. Pupils were roped into all the campaigns: the collection of waste paper, leaves, stinging nettles, rubber, tin cans, coffee dregs, acorns, chestnuts, fruit seeds, and other materials which, given the food crisis and the lack of imports, had suddenly become essential. Whereas the collection of secondary raw materials and scrap was organized from the top down, the transformation of flower beds and other public green spaces into vegetable gardens, mentioned earlier, was always initiated from the bottom up.

However, the conversion of flower beds and the collection of secondary raw materials and scrap were, at best, sticking plasters for a great gaping wound. From Berlin to Budapest, officials in the ministries soon arrived at the same conclusion: if peasants and proletarians could not work as producers because they had been conscripted into the army, and if imports of raw materials had stopped and services were no longer being provided by foreign subcontractors, then soon everything would be scarce and it would be impossible to maintain existing supply. Both responses to this new challenge were logical. First, only the state would be able to effectively manage a crisis caused by a drastic and prolonged reduction in supply. Second, the main task would be to distribute, in a rational manner, the meagre resources that were vanishing with each passing month.

ERSATZ

It all began with a poor harvest, that is, a lack of flour to make bread. From December 1914 bakers in the Habsburg monarchy were obliged to add various new ingredients to their bread, including barley flour, potato flour, potato pulp, and maize flour. A month later a novelty known as *K-Brot*, in other words, 'war bread' (from the German word *Krieg*) or 'potato bread' (from the German word *Kartoffeln*), appeared in the Reich. Apart from potato flour, a mixture of ground oats, barley, beans, and peas eventually came to be added to *K-Brot*. Less than two years later, in October 1916, the authorities of the monarchy decided that the product was not to contain more than 60 per cent wheat flour or rye flour; the rest of it was to be made up of the aforementioned new ingredients. In 1916 Austria-Hungary (mainly Cisleithania) suffered a famine, which Germany experienced a little later, in the winter. The potato harvest decreased from 122 million quintals (1913) to 50 million, while the cereal harvest fell to around 60 per cent of its pre-war level. Two 'no-meat' days were introduced in the monarchy, as well as one 'no-fat' day, which was Saturday. The first regulation was clear, and it will also be familiar to those who experienced communism after 1945: the 'no-meat' day meant that there was a ban on the sale of fresh and processed meat in shops and restaurants. What is more interesting is the official interpretation of the concept of 'no fat' issued by the Ministry of the Interior in Vienna in October 1916:

> On no-fat days it is prohibited to serve dishes cooked in melted fat or oil (e.g. fried schnitzel or chicken); it is permitted, however, to serve pudding prepared with the addition of fat, but not baked in fat. Next, it is forbidden to serve fish in the preparation of which butter or oil was used; it is, however, permitted to serve processed fish that has already been seasoned with oil (e.g. sardines). On no-fat days it is forbidden to serve potatoes with fat or butter, fried potatoes, or bread and butter. Lastly, it is permitted to serve meat dishes where the meat has been

THE HINTERLAND   169

> fried in its own fat, such as roast beef or beefsteak; it is forbidden,
> however, to serve roast meat stuffed with giblets.[13]
>
> In the autumn of 1916 very few of Franz Joseph's subjects ate chicken or schnitzel (the weekly ration of meat was enough for a single potion), let alone roast beef or beefsteak. Real butter was also a pre-war memory. The Imperial–Royal Ministry of the Interior clearly tried to modify the eating habits of rich and poor alike, yet the result was probably the same as it ever was.
>
> Given that everything was in short supply, the authorities intensified the introduction of ersatz (i.e. substitutes) into just about any kind of food or stimulant: acorns, chicory, and beech nuts replaced coffee; later, even beetroot extract was added to the mixture. Instead of tea, a mixture of barley and grass was used. The aromas were provided by a variety of wild flowers. Powdered hay was added to wheat flour and rye flour. Butter gave way to a mixture of milk, sugar, and food colouring. Sausage consisted mainly of the remnants of ground animal tendons and fibres (which had previously been deemed inedible) as well as water and plant supplements.
>
> In 1916 Austria-Hungary, and even more so Germany, proved to be thoroughly modern civilizations. Chemists not only manufactured ever-more-lethal gases for use in combat but also had an increasing influence on the food eaten by their fellow subjects. They provided the scents and colours that were needed to mimic original products and, as the supply of staples diminished from month to month, added their latest inventions to them. An English duchess, who had contracted the flu in Berlin in March 1916, was rightly suspected of having fallen victim to 'Ersatz illness': 'Everyone is feeling ill from too many chemicals in the hotel food. I don't believe that Germany will ever be starved out, but she will be poisoned out first with these substitutes'. Ersatz had indeed replaced the pre-war reality. Holger Herwig, who has studied this issue, claims that, in the Reich alone, 11,000 ideas for various kinds of ersatz were patented, including over 800 for 'war sausage' and over 500 for 'war coffee'.[14]

Thus, in response to the growing shortages of everything except patriotic poetry, the authorities introduced a succession of new restrictions, 'improvements', injunctions, and prohibitions. The system used to control society and the economy was not, of course, confined to the hinterland of the Eastern Front and was also practised in Western Europe. It was particularly effective in Great Britain, where the imperative to look after the health of citizens who were needed to sustain war production proved to be their salvation: despite the losses at the front the average life expectancy of women, and even more surprisingly of men, increased. At the same time, infant mortality and the

---

[13] *Kurjer Lwowski*, 17 October 1916.
[14] Holger H. Herwig, *The First World War. Germany and Austria-Hungary 1914–1918*, London 2014, p. 285.

threat of disease decreased among the lower social strata, while real wages rose and diets improved for the poorest members of society.[15]

Like France, and unlike the Central Powers, Great Britain was not cut off from the supply of imported food, which it obtained from the Americas. Moreover, because it was untouched by war on its own territory, Great Britain produced more food than it did prior to the conflict and thus food rationing did not begin until 1918. In France there were more or less importunate shortages, but ration cards were not introduced until 1917 and only in the following year did the system of restrictions become widespread.

The situation in Germany and Austria-Hungary was very different. During the war German farmers produced around a third less than in 1913. In the Habsburg monarchy before 1914 the division of labour was clear: in Cisleithania, 72 kilograms of grain per capita were harvested as compared with 203 kilograms in Transleithania. Hungary survived by exporting agricultural produce to the Austrian part of the empire. In 1914 it was decided that the Kingdom of Hungary should use its surplus to feed the army, and this is what did indeed happen. In addition, already in the first year of the war the government in Budapest reduced its supplies to Cisleithania to one-sixth of the pre-war level; the remaining surplus was sold to Germany. In return Hungary received steel and other raw materials needed by its armaments industry. During the tough negotiations both sides – Hungary and the Reich – were not afraid to use blackmail. But, as on the front, Berlin held the stronger cards. Trade was conducted by means of the German mark, which was a more resilient currency than the Austro-Hungarian crown. In the end Budapest and Vienna had to take out loans to bolster the unfavourable balance of payments. Not without reason, the Habsburg monarchy felt increasingly exploited by its ally.[16]

It is small wonder, then, that the supply of food from Hungary to Cisleithania decreased over time. Internal imports from Galicia and Bukovina also fell due to the hostilities. Austria proper, Bohemia, and Moravia struggled with a lack of fertilizer and horses as well. In 1917 the grain harvest in Cisleithania – according to perhaps overestimated figures – was 12 per cent of its pre-war level. The disaster particularly affected the cities, to which several hundred thousand refugees fled from Galicia and Bukovina in the autumn of 1914.

The lack of food soon became the most pressing problem. In the capital of the monarchy the police recorded the first queues for bread and flour in the autumn of 1914; for milk and potatoes, at the beginning of following year; for

[15] Alan G. V. Simmonds, *Britain and World War One*, London and New York, NY 2012, pp. 202–218.

[16] József Galántai, *Hungary in the First World War*, translated by Éva Grusz and Judit Pokoly, Budapest 1989, p. 191.

oil, in the autumn; for coffee, in March 1916; for sugar, in April; for eggs, in May; for soap, in July; and for beer, cigarettes, plums, and cabbage, in September 1916. Children were eventually sent to stand in the queues. Their fathers were at the front and their mothers, who before the war had been employed in light industry or in the service sector, now worked twelve hours a day in the armaments factories. On the black market, where one could get everything, prices jumped by 600 per cent during that time compared with their pre-war levels. When a tuberculosis epidemic broke out, it was named the 'Viennese disease'. The situation in Hungary was marginally better: workers' wages increased by roughly 50 per cent up to 1916, food prices rose 'only' three-fold, and the cost of supporting a five-person family more than doubled. The prices of clothes broke all records, however, rising more than twelve-fold by the beginning of 1917.

RATION CARDS

'There was such fear of this unknown thing, never before used in the history of the world: the ration card for bread.' This is how the *Ilustrowany Kuryer Codzienny* (*Illustrated Daily Courier*) reported the incredible situation that had arisen in Cracow: every day the bakeries had enough bread.[17] It was indeed an unusual tale. In the autumn of 1915 Cracow began to run out of flour and the bread queues became ever longer. People were outraged. Very quickly the authorities came up with a solution which would be copied throughout war-torn Europe that year: ration cards for food. The *Illustrated Daily Courier* was right: even the elderly could not remember there ever having been such a thing. The idea was simple: when something is scarce, its price rises. While the wealthy can afford to buy at the higher price, the poor stare hunger in the face. In this situation the authorities intervene. They set the ration to which each citizen is entitled (in Cracow this was nearly 1 kilogram of bread or 700 grams of flour per week), decide on a reasonable price for it, and order the producer to sell the product at that price – in an amount not exceeding the quota allocated to the individual concerned. The system is fair in principle: the insufficient supply is divided by the number of inhabitants, and each person (or at least each working person) is able to buy their quota because the price is significantly lower than the previous, free market price. The reality can be somewhat different, though, since the quotas may vary depending on a person's age or the type of work they perform. However, the principle of more or less equal division is neither stupid nor merely fair only in theory. The snag is that the top-down introduction of a fixed price is tantamount to interference in the market, which reacts to this in its own way: because the same product can be sold for a higher price, the producer will try to sell as much of it as he can on the free market. The next logical step is to deceive the 'ration card customer' by concealing products from him or offering him merchandise of inferior quality.

---

[17] *Ilustrowany Kuryer Codzienny*, 16 November 1915.

172   THE REAR

> Almost every rationing system encounters the same problems: first, as time passes, there is less and less of the product, supply shrinks, and thus the quotas become smaller and less certain. The queues return – no one knows when the quota allocated to a given shop will run out, hence people begin to queue in advance so as not to be left empty-handed. Second, every rationing system produces a black market, where the same product (or one of better quality) is available semi-legally or illegally at a much higher price, but without the need to queue and without any restrictions on quantity. Third, the authorities, aware of the situation, try to plug the holes in the rationing system by issuing regulations that are increasingly detailed and increasingly ineffective, because they are always one step behind human ingenuity that is focused on finding ways to circumvent the law and make more profit. In Vienna, at the end of the war, the authorities, producers, agents, and retailers had to navigate twenty-four separate regulations pertaining to the purchase, distribution, and sale of flour, only one fewer pertaining to bread, fourteen to milk, thirteen to sugar, and eight to alcohol.
>
> Between 1915 and 1918 all cities in Central and South-Eastern Europe experienced the same phenomena: a collapse in supply and a lack of food; a short-term improvement in provisioning following the introduction of ration cards; an expansion of the rationing system to cover an increasing number of commodities; a flourishing black market where prices ceased to bear any relation to workers' wages; aggression towards peasants – and even more so towards Jewish intermediaries – who could buy a piano for the price of a piglet; and finally, hunger, poverty, and cold.
>
> Ration cards for food were a new and frightening invention. In Cracow the sudden success of provisioning after the introduction of ration cards in the autumn of 1915 resulted from the fact that in the week before the rationing system went into effect people bought up all the bread they could get their hands on. They feared what was new. In the short term the ration card system proved highly beneficial: the shops were full of rationed bread. Later, the situation was the same as everywhere else, and the same as for (almost) every other product: the supply of flour decreased and a black market appeared. People learned to live with the ration card system, but in truth they overcame it by sidestepping and violating wartime regulations.

In the Reich the ration card system was introduced successively from 1 February 1915. Here and in the monarchy all major foodstuffs were entered on the list of rationed products during the course of that year; rationing was apparently in rude health. In Hungary, which was relatively well-provisioned, the first ration cards to appear were for milk (November 1915), then bread (January 1916), and then soap (March 1917). From April 1917 potatoes were also rationed. Here, too, the ration card system proved leaky and was defenceless against human cunning and resourcefulness. Some time later, the authorities became cognizant of the situation and issued a new regulation that aimed to 'tighten' the previous one. Offices issued countless decrees and orders designed to regulate the sale, purchase, and consumption of particular products.

THE HINTERLAND 173

'The provisioning crisis', notes Maureen Healy writing about Vienna, 'resembled a dance in which the rule-making authorities, unable to secure adequate supplies, lagged one step behind the rule-breaking population, which resorted to illegal means to find them. As this dance sped up, and previously law-abiding residents grew increasingly willing to break laws in order to satisfy needs, "governing" became an exercise in wringing hands and issuing empty decrees.'[18]

Regulatory madness was not the sole domain of either the Austro-Hungarian or the German authorities. In a Baltic city far from Vienna an undoubtedly intelligent and mischievous German observer noted two similar examples: 'The governor of Livonia has ordered the price of sugar to be set at 19 kopecks a pound and has threatened traders who demand a higher price with a fine of up to 3,000 roubles. As a result of this regulation the price of sugar in Riga has risen from 80 kopecks to 1.5 roubles.' Equally terse was his comment on the attempts by the head of the local Czarist police to ensure public order in the city: 'He detained over 1,000 young women, uncovered hundreds of bordellos and moonshine factories, compiled more than 10,000 reports on alcohol trading and gluttony, and at the end of the year was forced to admit that life in Riga had never been as immoral as in 1916.'[19]

'Governing' also required a major ramping up of the inspection regime. Bakeries were a magnet for professional and volunteer inspectors, who considered bakers to be just as devious as 'speculators'. Then, because many of the semi-commercial food retailers moved out of the shops and into the markets and bazaars, the state and local administration sent thousands of inspectors to monitor legality, ethical standards, and hygiene in those places. The inspectors' capacity to act is illustrated by a note from the city department:

> Never before has Cracow witnessed such turbulent scenes as those at the market yesterday. Groups of ladies began to gather from 6.00 a.m. onwards. They were waiting for the peasant women, who came in small numbers and brought only geese, hens, mushrooms, and fruit. Barely one in ten of them brought eggs and butter, and it was they who were immediately surrounded by the ladies and cooks. The turmoil intensified. Every now and then the municipal market inspector, Mr Zagórski, and the auxiliary staff and police officers were forced to intervene. The peasant women, realizing that there was a huge demand for butter, did not want to sell it at the maximum price of 5.40 crowns per kilogram. The bidding soon resulted in a price of 10 crowns per kilogram, which the market commissioner was forced to approve: otherwise, the women would have run off into the side streets and sold their butter there for a higher price.[20]

---

[18] Maureen Healy, *Vienna and the Fall of the Habsburg Empire*, Cambridge 2004, pp. 10, 40, and 64.

[19] Alfred von Hedenström, *Rigaer Kriegschronik 1914–1917*, Riga 1922, pp. 110, 118.

[20] *Ilustrowany Kuryer Codzienny*, 7 October 1915.

174   THE REAR

Let us not forget that the above quote about the bedlam on market day originates from October 1915; the war would last another three years, and at the moment the monarchy collapsed most of those 'ladies and cooks' would probably have remembered 1915 as an idyllic time, one worthy of a nostalgic sigh.

Restrictions, inspections, limits, and prohibitions did not apply solely to food, of course. Next on the list of goods in short supply was the primary energy source, i.e. coal, which power stations and industry and, to a lesser extent, municipal heating plants and private homes were forced to use. There were also shortages of gas, oil, cotton, and paper – the list was endless. Soon limits and prohibitions applied to almost everything: from time to time further restrictions were imposed on the use of electricity, primarily lighting. This led, among other things, to shorter opening hours for shops, theatres, cafés and pubs, and to dark streets and stairwells. Schools, offices, and theatres were sometimes left unheated; in larger apartments people became accustomed to generating heat from only one stove, which meant that the temperature in other rooms dropped to a few degrees above zero. When it came to public services, municipal transport (trams) and rail travel were the first to be affected: trams were less frequent and ran on shorter routes. Later on, another energy-saving solution was introduced: in 1916 the trams in Vienna stopped running after 9.00 p.m. In the vicinity of the capital, the Vienna Woods were ravaged by the fuel crisis: trees were mercilessly cut down during private raids undertaken by the city's inhabitants.

The number of trains also dwindled, as did their average speed. In July 1915 the journey from Cracow to Dąbrowa Górnicza, which was 77 kilometres away, took 6 hours and 16 minutes. Sometimes it was quicker to travel on routes that were important for the army and therefore better maintained: on the newly restored Warsaw to Brest route (approximately 200 kilometres), a train could cover the distance in 'only' 5.5 to 6 hours in the autumn of 1915. The war also meant that insignificant towns that had never before enjoyed such a privilege acquired direct rail links to the capitals of the Central Powers. From the late summer of 1915, for instance, trains ran between Kovel (Kowel) and Vienna. Fast trains needed ten hours to reach Vienna from Cracow, in other words, the travel time was no worse than in the 1980s. It was possible to get from Warsaw to Berlin by train within thirteen hours.[21] There were many exceptions, however: equally important for the army was the connection between Vienna and Lwów (600 to 700 kilometres depending on the choice of route), yet, six months after the recapture of the Galician capital, trains carrying refugees back home took around forty-eight hours to complete the journey. From the autumn of 1915 the press reminded passengers to wear warm clothing as trains were increasingly left unheated. In Russia, where the

---

[21] *Ilustrowany Kuryer Codzienny*, 1 September 1915 and 6 September 1915.

THE HINTERLAND

transport crisis was much more serious than the food crisis, from the summer of 1915 rail travel turned into a kind of lottery. Passengers never knew where or when they could travel. At around this time Eugeniusz Romer attempted to travel from Dryssa (now Verkhnyadzvinsk in Belarus) to Vitebsk along with some fellow Lithuanian landowners. The ticket offices at the station were closed and there was no information to be had. A train eventually appeared, but it turned out that, instead of being seated in passenger cars, the travellers were offered spaces on open freight cars. On a journey that before the war would have taken four hours, the train experienced a thirteen-hour delay. Most surprising, perhaps, was that even under such difficult conditions the conductor managed to check all the tickets and fine passengers who had not bought theirs in advance.[22]

Women

Universal shortages affected the everyday life of all people: men, women, and children. It was women who increasingly had to combine professional work (which nearly always attracted lower pay than men's work) with standing in queues, travelling to the countryside in search of food (or the reverse: travelling to the city in order to sell food), engaging in illegal trade that often involved barter, and, later on, stealing fuel and vegetables. With each passing month the situation of female workers deteriorated, especially in the big cities. As one woman employed in a Berlin munitions factory recalled:

> We, the women and girls, were driven like cattle. Among the ubiquitous coal smoke, we had to contend with dirt, unbridled brutality, and a barbaric work-rate. There were no safety measures, and even when someone tried to apply them, there was no point due to the frenzied nature of the work. Within one week alone, three women in the cartridge production department had all the fingers on their right hand severed by a lathe. These accidents merely gave the foreman an excuse to hurl abuse at us; no protection was introduced and nor did the work-rate diminish. [...] The working hours were from 6.00 a.m. to 6.00 p.m. with a half-hour break for lunch and fifteen minutes for breakfast. One did a week on the day shift or a week on night shift.[23]

And yet those women also had to feed their families. In this regard, too, conditions increasingly deviated from pre-war standards. The Danish silent movie star Asta Nielsen described a scene she witnessed on a Berlin street in 1916:

---

[22] Eugeniusz Romer, *Dziennik 1914–1918*, vol. 1, Warsaw 1995, p. 284.
[23] Cited in Dieter Glatzer and Ruth Glatzer (eds.), *Berliner Leben 1914–1918. Eine historische Reportage aus Erinnerungen und Berichten*, Berlin 1983, pp. 161–162.

176   THE REAR

> One day, on the street, I saw a terribly emaciated horse fall to the ground
> dead. In the blink of an eye, as if they had been waiting for that moment,
> women from the nearby tenements, armed with long kitchen knives, ran
> towards it. Shrieking, they fought over the best morsels. The steaming
> blood bespattered their clothes and faces. Other gaunt figures, with bowls
> and cups in their hands, joined the fray. They began to gather up the warm
> blood, which had stained the street red. The crowd only dispersed when
> the horse looked like a skeleton in the desert. As the women scattered, they
> held the scraps of meat close to their flat chests in fear.[24]

The more time one had to spend queuing, the less certain was the outcome. Women in the occupied territories faced the greatest challenge, since the evacuation, destruction, and occupation policies brought about deindustrialization. Jobless working-class women and their children were among the first to starve.[25] The first revolt of female 'queuers' occurred in Kraslice in western Bohemia on 16 February 1915. Despite this, provisioning in the town did not improve in the weeks that followed. In March, women openly threatened the local prefect and threw stones at his offices. The town of Trieste, as distant from the front as Kraslice, witnessed hunger riots on 20 April that lasted several days. In May, for the first time, a mass of enraged women attacked shops in Vienna. These scenes were repeated in October in Berlin. By the end of the year, in Bohemia and Moravia alone, thirty-one demonstrations against hunger had been reported. Violent outbursts became more frequent in subsequent years, reaching an apex in the final months of the war. In early 1918 Austria-Hungary was shaken by a wave of strikes and demonstrations led by factory workers, many of them women. Towards the end of that year,

> approximately 30,000 people entered the rural parishes in the north of
> Vienna to acquire potatoes from the farmers, who refused to sell any,
> pointing out that it was prohibited by the government. Thereupon, the
> crowd of mainly women and children went to the fields and took for
> themselves what the farmers refused to give them. Uniformed soldiers on
> leave tried to protect the women and children from the attacks of the
> peasants and the police. Finally, the crowd was dispersed with the help of
> the army and some police units.[26]

In Russia, different causes led to the same outcome. Up until 1916 food supplies remained at a fairly decent level. This was especially appreciated nearer to the front, where locals were aware of the threat of hunger and poverty

---

[24] Cited in Glatzer and Glatzer (eds.), *Berliner Leben 1914–1918*, p. 265.
[25] Katarzyna Sierakowska, 'Women on War and Women: Polish Lands 1914–1918', in *The First World War on Polish Lands: Expectations – Experiences – Consequences*, ed. Włodzimierz Mędrzecki, Warsaw 2018, pp. 141–159, here pp. 148–150.
[26] Reinhard Siedler, 'Behind the Lines: Working Class Family Life in Wartime Vienna', in *The Upheaval of War: Family, Work and Welfare in Europe, 1914–1918*, ed. Richard Wall and Jay Winter, Cambridge 1988, pp. 109–138, here p. 126.

THE HINTERLAND   177

hanging over them. The wealth of the Czarist state stood in stark contrast to the frugal economies of the Central Powers. As Cezary Jellenta noted in early 1915, 'Today, we feel more than ever that Russia feeds and satiates us, that it is an inexhaustible breadbasket.'[27] Russia's problem lay elsewhere. Since the beginning of the war the transport and fuel crises had been worsening. The consequence of this was that, although food was abundant, it too was becoming more expensive. Supplies to the cities were erratic. In the summer of 1915 riots broke out in Moscow: women surrounded the main bazaar and occupied it until the sellers had reduced the price of potatoes. A year later, riots at the bazaar were a regular occurrence. This time the women reacted violently to another price increase: traders were beaten up along with the police officers who tried to protect them.[28] In 1916 the crisis enveloped all the major cities of the empire and a wave of 'women's revolts', as they were known, spread throughout the country.[29]

In parallel with the top-down management of hunger, energy, and transport, the state turned its attention to another activity: mobilization of the labour force. In Germany and Austria-Hungary, right at the beginning of the war, Sunday was designated as a working day (initially only in the war industry) and women had to go to the factories at night and during public holidays as well. In Russia night-time work became legal both for women and for children. Shifts were extended everywhere. Soon an eighty-five-hour working week and an eleven-hour working day were no longer considered shocking.

In the cities women generally took over not their husband's former job, but the jobs of other men called to the front: they became shop assistants, waitresses and conductors, and were employed *en masse* as clerks in the municipal administration (and, to a lesser extent, as clerical staff in the army) – wherever conscription had caused a labour shortage. Employment also increased in typically 'female' occupations. One example was nursing, a profession directly related to the war. Many public buildings behind the lines became makeshift hospitals, each of which required not only doctors and trained medical personnel but also nurses. British nurses in Serbia, dedicated to helping their country's ally, received the highest recognition from the authorities, including the military authorities. Away from the front, nurses inspired rather more mixed feelings. In the besieged town of Przemyśl they were accused of prostitution. Of course, when such accusations fall from the lips of people as

---

[27] Cezary Jellenta, *Wielki zmierzch. Pamiętnik*, Warsaw 1985, p. 231.

[28] Tammy M. Proctor, *Civilians in a World at War, 1914–1918*, New York, NY and London 2010, p. 93.

[29] S. V. Tiutiutkin, 'Россия: от Великой войны – к Великой революции [Rossiia: ot Velikoi voiny – k Velikoi revoliutsii]', in *Война и общество в XX веке*, vol. I. *Война и общество накануне и в период Первой мировой войны* [*Voina i obshchestvo v XX veke*, vol. 1. *Voina i obshchestvo nakanune i v period Pervoi mirovoi voiny*], ed. B. A. Zolotarev and L. V. Pozdeeva, Moscow 2008, pp. 120–160, here pp. 138–140.

178   THE REAR

mischievous as Helena Jabłońska née Seifert, mentioned earlier, they have to be
treated with caution. But similar opinions were expressed by other eyewitnesses. As a Hungarian military doctor serving in the Przemyśl fortress noted:

> [...] they are recruiting teenage girls as nurses, in some places there are up
> to 50 of them! They get 120 crowns a month and free meals. That comes to
> 17,000 crowns a month! They are, with very few exceptions, utterly
> useless. Their main job is to satisfy the lust of the gentlemen officers
> and, rather shamefully, a number of doctors, too.[30]

The farther away from the front lines, the greater was the antipathy towards
independent young women, who, on account of their occupation, were in
constant contact with soldiers and doctors. Eugeniusz Romer recalled with
indignation a loud party organized by the director of the military hospital in
Polotsk, Dr Iwanowski, in November 1915:

> In the corridors and empty wards, and in rooms that were completely dark
> or lit by a pair of bulbs with green lampshades, officers cavorted with the
> nurses, and since the orchestra was playing the mazurka, a cheerful
> colonel started dancing with one of the sisters along the corridors; this
> only encouraged the others, and soon one of the larger wards was turned
> into a kind of ballroom: the beds were pushed into the corners and piled
> up on top of one another, with the remainder being thrown into the
> corridor. In this dimly lit ward the officers and the sisters of mercy began
> to dance, accompanied by boisterous laughter and ribald jokes. I was
> flabbergasted to witness that scene. Although [...] the sisters' reputation
> was widely known, I could not countenance the thought that such a thing
> could happen in the presence of senior military officers and the hospital's
> supposedly respectable matrons. [...] Apparently, some of the more
> seriously wounded patients asked the revellers to calm down, which
> only provoked displeasure at their capricious and unfriendly attitude.
> The senior doctor had himself danced the night away and was delighted
> with all the merry-making, which, he said, kept the soldiers' spirits up.[31]

Although certainly not all the accusations about the moral conduct of nurses
were fabrications, many suggested a degree of vicarious criticism. The chan-
ging situation of women was almost everywhere to be seen and resulted from
the strategic needs of the state. Outrage at the presence of women in occupations hitherto reserved for men had to be curbed, for their presence had
a patriotic sanction. The 'moralists' could only vent their spleen when the
situation allowed.

In Germany's largest constituent territory, Prussia, the number of men
employed in manufacturing, including forced labourers and prisoners of
war, fell by a quarter, whereas the number of women working on the factory

---

[30] Proctor, *Civilians in a World at War*, p. 163.
[31] Eugeniusz Romer, *Dziennik 1914–1918*, p. 321.

Fig. 40   Russian graduates of nursing courses, autumn 1914. Courtesy of Mariusz Kulik.

lines increased by three quarters. The pay women received for the same job was a third or even a half lower than 'men's' pay. In 1916 women in Hanover could buy less than half a chicken for a day's wages. Nevertheless, judging by the newspaper reports of local male journalists, women were managing just fine.

'In today's time of war everything is possible and nothing should surprise us any more,' commented a local reporter in *Scenes from the City*. 'A few years ago a woman driving a coach would have caused a sensation in Cracow: she would have been the subject of mockery, taunts, and jokes. Yet today, given the shortage of men to perform work, in almost every occupation we see their place being taken by women, who – one has to admit – are working diligently, reliably, and above all efficiently. We have become completely accustomed to women conductors on trams and every office now has many more women than men; even in the factories one encounters young girls and women performing the hardest work with energy and enthusiasm'.[32]

[32] *Ilustrowany Kuryer Codzienny*, 23 June 1915.

In Cracow, where there was hardly an armaments industry to speak of, relatively few women worked on the factory lines; most were employed in the local tobacco factory. Many hundreds of thousands went to work in the imperial centres of Petrograd, Moscow, and Vienna, and in the Ruhr. If they did not live in the city where they worked, accommodation could be desperately unhygienic: the double occupancy of straw mattresses (when one woman worked, the other slept) and the absence of soap, showers, and toilets were as common as lice.

In the metals industry located in the Czech district of Plzeň, where Škoda, the monarchy's largest industrial enterprise, had its headquarters, the proportion of women among the workforce rose from 2.4 per cent at the beginning of the war to 20 per cent in 1916. Paradoxically, women enjoyed certain privileges: the Austrian War Requirements Act of 1912 introduced draconian penalties for labour protests, but it applied only to men; the legislature had simply not envisaged that women could be employed in the armaments industry. And it was here, at the lathe or on a Fordist production line, that images which proved shocking for contemporaries emerged: externally at least, Eve was becoming similar to Adam. After numerous accidents in the factories, women were forced to dress in men's work clothes, including trousers (which had hitherto been worn exclusively by urban feminists), and to have their hair tucked under a headscarf or other covering. Since breasts began to disappear due to permanent malnutrition, women and men, when dressed in work clothes, became difficult to distinguish.[33] On the other hand, it is doubtful whether this process also applied to country women. They neither had to wear boiler suits nor suffered from hunger.

The emancipation of rural women, although not as noticeable, altered relations in the provinces at least as profoundly. Wincenty Witos, member of the *Reichsrat* for the Polish agrarian party, wrote:

> [...] The countryside had become deserted in an unprecedented way. There was hardly a house from which at least one family member had not gone off to the war. In many cases both a father and a son, and sometimes a few sons, had been conscripted into the army, so their farms were left to the care of women, children, and the elderly. This was a time of great trial. Women in the countryside, burdened with household chores and duties, never paid attention to the horses, carts, ploughing or sowing, because that is what the men did. Some of them not only had no idea how to harness a horse, but ran away from it in fear. Needs must when the devil drives, however, and here too came a change, almost unexpectedly. Left alone on their farms the women at first began to cry and lament. They looked for help and protection where they could find it and when this failed they got down to work themselves. Often it was a very hard

[33] Rudolf Kučera, 'Losing Manliness: Bohemian Workers and the Experience of the Home Front', in *Other Fronts, Other Wars? First World War Studies on the Eve of the Centennial*, ed. Joachim Bürgschwentner, Matthias Egger, and Gunda Barth-Scalmani, Leiden 2014, pp. 331–348, here pp. 338–342.

THE HINTERLAND

experience, but they showed extremely strong will and perseverance. On more than one occasion I saw a woman being thrown by a plough. She did not know how to handle it, or how to cope with the hard, neglected earth. Battered, sweaty, and grimy, she did not allow herself to be frightened by anything, though, and in the end managed to perform the task no worse than a man. It is thanks to the superhuman work of women that many farms were saved from total ruin.[34]

Both types – the 'city' women who worked in industry, services, and transport or in offices, and the resourceful countrywomen – became, like the mothers who stood in queues to buy food for their children, a permanent fixture of daily life in the hinterland in the first years of the war. There were also millions of them during the occupation.

ECATERINA TEODOROIU

The three powers whose armies systematically trampled over Central and Eastern Europe from the summer of 1914 were a bulwark of social conservatism. For them, the established order of the sexes was as fundamental a principle as the institution of the monarchy. No one doubted that war was a domain to which women should not have access, and the notion of women's military service was, at best, a bad joke. One of the few German commentators to consider the issue seriously came to the conclusion that the conscription of women was impossible due to menstruation and the nervous tension that preceded it. How could discipline be maintained, he rhetorically asked, in a unit of ill-tempered women?[35]

Reality was less clear-cut than ideology, however. First and foremost, in the Russian army, women disguised as men served not only as rank-and-file soldiers but even as officers. They were especially common in the Cossack regiments. After the February Revolution of 1917, several assault units consisting exclusively of women were formed. Germany and Austria-Hungary were more restrained when it came to the military service of women. It was only the gigantic scale of the losses on the fronts that forced both states to tap this human resource. Beginning in late 1916, women in uniform began to work behind the lines as auxiliary staff – office workers, technicians, telephone and telegraph operators. Although the self-styled defenders of morality were indignant at the alleged sexual freedom of the so-called *Etappenhelferinnen*, without their help the general staffs would not have been able to send thousands of military clerks and other male workers to the front.

From the outset the smaller participants of the conflict in the East had a more liberal attitude towards the involvement of women in the war effort. Austria-Hungary provides

---

[34] Cited in Jan Molenda, *Chłopi, naród, niepodległość. Kształtowanie się postaw narodowych i obywatelskich chłopów w Galicji i Królestwie Polskim w przededniu odrodzenia Polski*, Warsaw 1999, p. 294.

[35] Fritz Giese, *Die Idee einer Frauendienstpflicht. Tatsachen und Möglichkeiten*, Langensalza 1916.

several excellent examples in this regard. While the auxiliary service of women remained a controversial and hotly debated subject in the German-language press,

Fig. 41   A Bulgarian propaganda postcard depicting Lance Corporal Donka Bogdanova from the 60th Infantry Regiment, a veteran of the Macedonian conflict, the First and Second Balkan Wars, and also the First World War. Courtesy of Mr Peyo Kolev, lostbulgaria.com.

Polish and Ukrainian volunteer units in the Habsburg army tolerated the presence of women and sometimes even boasted about it. The Ukrainians Olena Stepanivna and Sofia Halechko even commanded detachments of the Sich Riflemen, while the Pole Wanda Gertz distinguished herself in the battles fought by the Polish Legions on the Styr and Stochod (Stokhid) rivers. In the Serbian army the British woman Flora Sandes reached the rank of captain, and in Bulgaria the infantrywomen Donka Bogdanova and Donka Ushlinova became war celebrities. Propagandists printed photographs of them with descriptions of their heroic deeds, yet none of these brave women achieved nationwide cult status.

Such was the fate, however, of a young Romanian woman by the name of Ecaterina Teodoroiu. Similarly to the Polish and Ukrainian women soldiers, she had been a member of the Scouts before the war. In 1916 she volunteered to work in a field hospital, but, when she learned that both of her brothers had been killed, she

THE HINTERLAND   183

asked to be admitted to their battalion. A few weeks later she was taken into German captivity, from which she escaped, before being wounded. Having recovered from her injuries, she returned to the front and took part in the biggest battle of the campaign, fought against the combined German and Austro-Hungarian forces at Mărăşeşti, where she was promoted to the rank of second lieutenant. She died during the fighting that took place just after the battle, which ended in success for the Romanians. Almost immediately Teodoroiu was recognized as a national heroine and accorded cult status that persists to this day. She became the protagonist of numerous poems, novels, and feature films, and had several monuments raised in her honour. In her native town of Târgu Jiu a magnificent tomb was erected bearing the inscription *Fecioara Eroină* (virgin heroine).

The virginity of this Romanian heroine was an obvious reference to Joan of Arc, 'The Maid of Orléans'. We do not know whether Ecaterina Teodoroiu died a virgin. The American researcher Maria Bucur points out, however, that the word is more likely to have had a symbolic purpose: to distinguish a national heroine from women in general and to include her in the national pantheon. The constant emphasis placed on Teodoroiu's masculine characteristics served the very same purpose. In a declaration by the Romanian army in Teodoroiu's honour, for instance, it was rather deftly stated that 'Ecaterina Teodoroiu was on the same level with the bravest defenders of her country, whom she surpassed with the strength she used to suppress her female weakness, knowing how to prove the vigour of her manliness (*bărbăţie*) in body and soul.'[36] On the one hand, such deftness testified to the greatest admiration for Teodoroiu's heroism, but on the other, it revealed a complete lack of interest in the fate of other, ordinary women.

There was one area of shortage management that was willingly and consistently delegated to local government and civic organizations: social care. Societies and associations sprang up, providing shelters as well as soup kitchens and tea rooms for the unemployed, children, and refugees. Volunteer women's organizations were very active in this regard. On 4 August 1914 the National Women's Service (*Nationaler Frauendienst*) was established in the Reich. German women attempted to provide those most in need with a bowl of soup or a cup of tea as well as a roof over their head. They also took on structural tasks: the Women's Service mediated in the recruitment of people for agricultural work and helped find accommodation for refugees; it also ran houses for midwives and nurseries. The Patriotic Women's Association (*Vaterländischer Frauenverein*), in turn, looked after troops on the move by setting up medical aid posts and kitchens at railway stations.

[36] Cited in Maria Bucur, 'Between the Mother of the Wounded and the Virgin of Jiu: Romanian Women and the Gender of Heroism during the Great War', *Journal of Women's History* 12, 2 (2000), pp. 30–56, here p. 48.

184 THE REAR

Similar forms of organization and activity were adopted by women's organizations in the Habsburg monarchy. Within a year of its establishment (in the spring of 1915) the Polish Women's League of the National Committee in Galicia had set up more than 100 regional groups with more than 12,000 members. In district towns these groups comprised several hundred people and had their own local branches. The League ran its own shops, kiosks, and tea rooms. Like many other organizations in the monarchy, it catered exclusively to members of its own nation. What was unique about it, however, was that it gave assistance primarily to only one part of that nation, and not a particularly numerous part: the Legionnaires, in other words, volunteers fighting for Polish independence.

Ethnicization

The example of the Galician Women's League points to a phenomenon known to historians as ethnicization, which was present in various forms and with varying intensity throughout the hinterland. Before the war it was possible to be a subject loyal to the emperor or king without being a member of the dominant national group, since it was not the latter that determined one's social status or job opportunities. A Ukrainian employee of the Habsburg monarchy's railway system could be as confident of receiving his salary as his Croatian counterpart. A Polish peasant in Prussia received the same price for his grain as his German neighbour, while a Latvian labourer in Riga earned the same wages as the Jewish labourer working alongside him. The war of the empires, which both sides presented as a historic confrontation between the Germanic and Slavic worlds, soon triggered an avalanche of changes that shattered the rules that applied up to 1914.

The mechanisms were different, but the outcome was similar. Trieste, which experienced an economic boom at the turn of the century, attracted a mass of Slovenes from the surrounding countryside. Nevertheless, the vast majority of the city's 230,000 inhabitants were Italian. The growing tensions between Italy and the monarchy in the spring of 1915 led to a mass exodus not only of the Italian population but also of its leading representatives – subjects of Franz Joseph. Rome declared war on the monarchy on Sunday 22 May. On the same day, in the afternoon, the police struggled to prevent an attack on the Italian consulate. In the evening the crowd attacked everything Italian – the offices of newspapers and associations, shops, and cafés. The unrest and looting lasted through the night. On the following day the authorities replaced the existing city council with a commissioner, and the police arrested and interned scores of people. Italian social organizations were outlawed and Italian officials dismissed from their posts. Simultaneously, local authorities in the surrounding municipalities were dissolved and all street names that alluded to the idea of the Italian nation-state were changed. Thoroughly

THE HINTERLAND 185

cleansed of its elites and superficially cleansed of enemy symbolism, Trieste, now ostensibly de-Italianized, became another Habsburg city behind the lines.

A similar situation developed at the other end of Central Europe. The Germans in the Baltic provinces of Russia occupied a much more prominent position than the Italians in Istria. This was not because there were more of them on the Baltic coast in absolute and relative terms than there were Italians on the Austrian Adriatic coast. The Baltic Germans had until the 1880s been not just loyal but also privileged subjects of the Czar: they played a major role in the ministries in Petersburg and *de facto* held power in the coastal provinces. Although in the previous quarter of a century their position had been substantially undermined, they nevertheless pledged their undying loyalty to the Czar in the summer of 1914, as did all his other subjects. The wave of Russian nationalism reached the Baltic with lightning speed. As early as in the autumn the authorities banned the use of German in public places. The ban was enforced by the police and, above all, by members of the public eager to inform on their Teutonic neighbours. 'Denunciation is flourishing as a second profession,' noted a German resident of Riga in November.

However, the ban on the use of German on the street and in parks, at meetings and in offices, in barristers' chambers and in courts, was only part of the Russification campaign that Germans remembered as 'the time of the muzzle': schools were closed (some continued to teach in Russian), followed by libraries. The German Club was suspended, the post office refused to accept letters addressed in German, telephone conversations in German were forbidden, and the existing names of shops disappeared. The last refuge of the German language was the Lutheran Church. Sunday services were now attended by more churchgoers than before the war; they prayed, no doubt, not just for their sons and brothers who were dying in Russian uniform at the front but also for a swift end to 'the Russian times', which had made them foreigners in their own homeland.

The decline in the status of the Baltic Germans had its counterpart in the social degradation of the Jews, which we write about in later chapters. Jews everywhere (also in Britain and France) came to symbolize the degeneracy of war, rapacious profiteering, the avoidance of national service, and the abuse of social care. In Riga their special position was reflected in the fines imposed for particular types of offences, which the police clearly treated as an excellent source of additional income. The table of fines for 'drawing curtains inadequately' was reconstructed by a local witness as follows: 'The fine is assessed according to nationality. Jews pay 100 to 200 roubles – or a month's detention. For Germans the punishment is one half, and for Latvians and Russians one quarter, of the fine imposed on Jews.'[37]

---

[37] Von Hedenström, *Rigaer Kriegschronik 1914–1917*, pp. 76 and 86.

Riga, which was as good an example of ethnicization as Vilnius, Czernowitz, Vienna, or Trieste, had its own unique features: here, in October 1915, there took place the solemn funeral of three Latvian volunteer riflemen, the first heroes to die for their imperial and national homeland simultaneously. The ceremony emphasized the nationality of the soldiers – Latvians who perished both for the Czar and for their country; if the latter had not been more important they would not have been buried separately from their Russian comrades. At exactly the same time in Poland an idea emerged that was formally modelled on the German commemoration of those killed in the war of 1870:

> Embedded into the wall of every parish church shall be a marble plaque similar to those found abroad. First it shall bear the **names of all the Legionnaires** who have perished in the war or who have died from their wounds [...]. The Legionnaires shall be followed by **all other Polish soldiers** from that place who have perished or died from their wounds while serving in the armies.[38]

As in Riga, ethnicization in the Polish lands went beyond the standard set in the autumn of 1915: Latvian volunteers and Polish Legionnaires suddenly became heroes who were more important than their compatriots fighting in other units and dying exclusively for Nicholas II and Franz Joseph. Operating within the symbolic space of the national community could take different forms; the stigmatization of a national group was as common as the sacralization of its most heroic members.

Let us return for a moment to the Baltic Germans. Their fate was atypical in that they were reduced to the rank of unreliable, suspect individuals already in the first months of the war. The authorities took advantage of the conflict to accelerate the implementation of plans that had existed for quite some time. Somewhat similar was the situation of the Armenians in the north-eastern part of the Ottoman Empire, whose expulsion began in the spring of 1915. Here, too, the aim was to get rid of an unwanted minority, although all the other circumstances were different: some Armenians participated in the anti-Ottoman uprising in Van in April, which gave the authorities an ideal pretext to commence deportation. The Baltic Germans suffered discrimination, but violence against them was rare and required at least some sort of legal justification (such as a court ruling against alleged spies or speculators). In contrast, the Armenians were murdered *en masse* and the expulsion of hundreds of thousands of people across Anatolia to the opposite end of the empire, i.e. to present-day Syria, had even more catastrophic consequences. Estimates of the number of people who perished due to fighting, execution, hunger, thirst, illness, or exhaustion vary between 500,000 and one million. Whether

---

[38] *Ilustrowany Kuryer Codzienny*, 3 October 1915.

THE HINTERLAND   187

we describe the massacre of the Armenians as a genocide or as a war crime depends on whether the Ottoman authorities wanted to exterminate the Armenians or whether the killing of a significant proportion of them was in some measure a by-product of ethnic cleansing motivated by the reality of war. The concept of genocide, which was introduced into international and criminal law after the Second World War, owes much to the public reaction to the butchery in Anatolia, news of which filtered into Europe and the United States during the First World War.

THE ARMENIAN MASSACRE

At a time when ethnic conflict was intensifying in the Balkan *vilayets* (provinces) of the Ottoman Empire, and the Internal Macedonian Revolutionary Organization (IMRO) was opening a new chapter in the history of political terrorism, the example of Macedonia was being closely monitored by the Armenians, too. Not without reason, the Armenian minority which inhabited the north-eastern fringes of Turkey saw an analogy between its own situation and that of the Bulgarians and Serbs. The Armenians were also Orthodox, also counted on Russian support, and, like the inhabitants of the Balkans, lived in a foreign ethnic environment. By the end of the nineteenth century the *vilayets* in which they lived had become a scene of constant fighting, pogroms, and clashes with armed militias.[39] The main dividing line was between Dashnak – an Armenian social democratic party that was predominant in the area – and local Kurdish tribes. The two rival powers in the region, Russia and Turkey, became involved in the local conflict, supporting sometimes the Kurds and at other times the Armenians. The Young Turk revolution did nothing to calm the situation; it merely changed the configuration of local alliances. The Dashnaks, who were initially in favour of the revolution, clashed with the Ottoman 'counter-revolutionaries' supported by the Kurdish tribes. In 1913 Armenian militias assisted government forces in quelling the Kurdish rebellion. The Czarist empire added fuel to the smouldering ethnic conflict. During the Balkan Wars Turkish Armenia was flooded with supplies of Russian weapons. At the outbreak of the Russo-Turkish war, in the last days of October 1914, the entire region was ready to explode.

Both Russia and Turkey counted on support from minorities across the border. The Ottoman Empire supported Islamic irredentism in the Caucasus, while Russia organized the Armenian Legion, comprising tens of thousands of volunteers who were Turkish citizens, and sought to gain control of the Armenian conspiracy in Anatolia. On both sides of the border massacres occurred as early as in 1914 – of Muslim civilians in Russia and of Christian civilians in Turkey. At the end of the year Enver Pasha decided to launch an

---

[39] Vakhan Dadrian, *Histoire du génocide arménien*, translated by Marc Nichanian, Paris 1996, pp. 82–105.

attack on the town of Sarıkamış in Eastern Anatolia. The idea was as disastrous as the Austro-Hungarian offensive in the Carpathians, which took place at the same time. In the high mountains, during the exceptionally cold winter, whole units of Turkish soldiers froze to death. Those who managed to reach the Russian positions were no longer able to fight effectively. The Turks had to retreat, and as spring arrived they expected a Russian offensive.

Even before it started, armed rebellions broke out in the towns of eastern Turkey inhabited by Armenians. The biggest of these took place in Van, whose residents repelled the onslaught by the Ottoman army for over a month before the Russians came to the rescue. At the end of May, when General Yudenich liberated Van, the town was already monoethnic. The population that remained consisted of local Armenians and Armenian refugees from nearby villages. Local Muslims had been either killed or expelled. After two months of Russian occupation, a Turkish counter-offensive reached Van in August 1915. Most of the Armenians fled in panic, while those who stayed fell victim to retribution.

The Van rebellion prompted the Turkish authorities into swift and radical action. At the end of April 1915 the decision was taken to intern Armenian political activists and officials. A month later the Minister of the Interior, Mehmed Talaat Pasha, decided to deport Armenians from provinces where the rebellions had taken place, in other words, not just from areas near the front but also from Central Anatolia. To this day, there is debate as to whether Talaat had genocidal intent from the outset; but even if he didn't, the 'evacuation' to Syria had appalling consequences. Already during the war, newspapers in the Entente countries described the suffering of the Armenian population:

> Many people were expelled on foot and not permitted to take any money with them. They had to carry their remaining possessions on their backs. Of course, they soon began to weaken and lag behind, whereupon the gendarmes would skewer them with their bayonets and throw them into the river. Their bodies floated into the sea or got stuck in the shallows and rocks, where they lay rotting for up to two weeks.

Hungry and emaciated, the Armenians were easy prey for Kurdish tribesmen, gendarmes, and bandits. Their property was appropriated by their Muslim neighbours, themselves often 'repatriates' recently expelled from villages in the Balkans. The younger and healthier 'evacuees', especially the women, were treated as commodities: 'Caravans of women and children are put on show before government buildings in every town and village they pass through, so that the Muslims can choose.' As the journey continued, it became clear that death awaited the 'evacuees' at their final destination:

> There are very few men among them, as most have been killed on the road. All tell the same story of having been attacked and robbed by the Kurds. Most of them were attacked over and over again, and a great many of them, especially the men, were killed. Women and children were also killed. Many died, of course, from sickness and exhaustion

THE HINTERLAND

189

> on the way, and there have been deaths each day that they have been here.[40]
>
> Most of the victims died of hunger and thirst. According to recent estimates over 660,000 people perished.[41] Their fate was not a mystery to European public opinion. The above descriptions appeared in the Western press and in high-circulation brochures and were also cited by leading politicians. Even in Germany, which was allied with the Ottoman Porte, Karl Liebknecht protested in the Reichstag about the extermination of the Armenians. Responsibility for the slaughter certainly lay with the decision-makers – members of the Young Turk government, local governors, and Talaat Pasha in particular. At the end of 1918, under pressure from the Western powers occupying Istanbul, this fact was officially confirmed by the Turkish parliament, and the Turkish courts convicted the main perpetrators. What appears more complicated is the political responsibility for the Armenian massacre. Perhaps the Armenians fell victim to the weakness of two disintegrating powers: Russia, which encouraged them to rebel yet was unable to support them effectively, and Turkey, which blamed its failures at the front on the alleged treason of its Christian citizens.
>
> Sentenced to death, Talaat managed to escape from the country in time, but was murdered in exile in 1921 by an Armenian student in Berlin. Although there was no doubt as to the perpetrator's identity, the court acquitted him after a brief two-day trial. Formally, it was adjudged that the assassin had not been of sound mind when committing the act. In reality the trial was a verdict on the crimes perpetrated by Talaat, and the defence – with the participation of a responsive public – managed to portray the murder as an act of justice.

For the victims, the legal classification had no importance whatsoever, yet for Armenians and Turks today it clearly remains key. From our point of view, we shall confine ourselves to the assertion that, first, this form of ethnicization was unique in terms of the war as a whole; with the exception of Russia after 1917, a comparable crime against a civilian population was not committed anywhere else. Second, it was a crime committed behind the Ottoman Empire's front lines and against its own citizens – not in occupied territory.

Much milder forms of ethnicization resulted from great migrations, mass escapes, and deportations. In August 1915 the *Ilustrowany Kuryer Codzienny*, a Galician daily, lured readers with the headline 'War Gives Rise to Polish Small-Scale Trade'. What the newspaper failed to explain was the cause of this development, namely, the mass flight of Jews before the Russian army. Nevertheless, its explanation for the huge increase in the number of Polish

---

[40] Arnold J. Toynbee, *Armenian Atrocities. The Murder of a Nation*, London 1915, pp. 46–50.

[41] Sean McMeekin, *The Russian Origins of the First World War*, Cambridge, MA 2011, p. 172.

190 THE REAR

shops was fairly accurate: after their existing owners had fled, 'whole districts were suffering from hunger because there was nowhere to buy goods. But necessity is the mother of invention. **Wives** whose husbands had gone off to the front, as well as **professors, bankers, craftsmen, and peasants,** deprived of bread, threw themselves into the setting up of shops.'[42] For now, the future of these 'true pioneers of Polish commerce' was somewhat opaque. Soon the shortage of credit could prove catastrophic, and the prospects for small-time traders in other provinces must have seemed similar. Nevertheless, Christian men and women, working as sellers or proprietors in regions where services had hitherto been provided by Jews, were a new element of the landscape.

Military Government and Civilian Rule

Many large cities on the Russian front, from Łódź, Riga, Königsberg, and Warsaw to Cracow, Lwów, and Czernowitz, became, briefly or for several months, cities that found themselves immediately behind the front lines. In these places, requisitioning, inspections, prohibitions, and restrictions on all manner of freedoms were especially common. Travelling elsewhere became difficult on account of the suspension of rail traffic, and it was almost impossible to find other means of transportation; a trip required a lot of additional paperwork and obtaining it depended on the benevolent consent of the authorities (which they were no doubt unlikely to give).

The military had the final say on everything. Civilizational decline was evident at every step – in some cities of the hinterland even the telephone lines were disconnected for reasons of security. The lack of gas and coal meant that municipal heating plants were often forced to shut down. Tram services were less frequent or stopped altogether, and in time the glowing street lamps provided the only respite in an otherwise moribund city.

Civilizational decline had its counterpart in the abandonment of cultural norms, in other words, the demise of common sense and decency. What with rumours about spies dressed as nuns, and about Jews using prayer to direct enemy aircraft to attack sites (Jews were routinely accused of treason because they used their own language), pathological distrust became the norm, and not only on the eastern fronts; in France and Germany there was a similar culture of distrust, as exemplified by the fatuous rumour about gold-laden cars travelling from France to Russia. Also in Western Europe, no doubt, one could find an order equivalent to the one issued by the military authorities in Riga in October 1915, which decreed the killing of all pigeons. By way of evidence – if the memoirist is to be believed – residents were ordered to hand in the severed heads of pigeons to the police.[43]

---

[42] *Ilustrowany Kuryer Codzienny*, 15 August 1915.
[43] Von Hedenström, *Rigaer Kriegschronik 1914–1917*, p. 79.

THE HINTERLAND   191

Distance from the fighting is a transnational criterion that can be used to
categorize the experiences of hinterland inhabitants. The Habsburg monarchy's administrative authorities divided territory into three zones. The first
zone encompassed areas adjacent to the front, which were under the exclusive
control of the army. In areas more distant, military commanders were the
supreme authority vis-à-vis the state and local administration. Finally, in the
peace zone, power remained in the hands of civilians and it was they who
enforced the provisions of martial law. In the Habsburg monarchy, where local
government was of a high European standard, administration became an
insuperable problem for local authorities faced with sudden and widespread
shortages. Citizens accustomed to dealing with their local authority, rather
than with the state, accused their municipal representatives of inefficiency, ill
will, and a lack of compassion. The Mayor of Vienna quite rightly complained
in 1916 that the local authority had never been responsible for provisioning:
'It's strange, I think, in peacetime nobody demanded from me that I should get
him potatoes. It didn't occur to anybody that I should provide flour or meat; it
was never the legal duty of the municipality to do so. [...] It is neither in
a statute nor found in law that it is the city's duty to take care of food.'[44]
Between the Scylla of hungry citizens and the Charybdis of the state authorities, for whom the needs of the front were more important than the needs of
civilians, local government was doomed to fail. In any case, from the point of
view of the engaged petitioners, the plight of local authorities was of no
importance.

The situation in Russia was different. Municipal governments and district
and provincial assemblies (*zemstva*) had long demanded representation at the
state level. In the face of wartime challenges, as early as in August 1914 the Czar
permitted the establishment of the All-Russian Union of Zemstva for the Care
of Sick and Wounded Soldiers and the All-Russian Union of Towns, which less
than a year later formed a joint committee known as the Zemgor. Local
government suddenly became a key institution in the functioning of
Czarism; inevitably, it soon turned into a forum for criticism of the state
administration. On the other hand, in July 1914 the Czar removed the western
part of his European provinces from civilian control, entrusting to the army (of
which he became commander-in-chief in 1915) all territories that lay to the
west of the St Petersburg–Smolensk–Dnieper line. In theory, at the outbreak of
the war the army governed an area that was larger than Germany and Austria-
Hungary combined. The situation on the ground varied, however. In the vast,
sometimes inaccessible rural areas the army had no means of exercising its
power, and life tended to carry on as before. In the larger towns, in turn, the
army was overwhelmed by the sudden rise in unemployment, ubiquitous
shortages, and the mass of refugees, which left it paralysed.

---

[44] Cited in Maureen Healy, *Vienna and the Fall of the Habsburg Empire*, p. 59.

192   THE REAR

The desire to ensure the loyalty of foreign-language-speaking subjects, to whom the Czarist authorities had hitherto denied even the most basic representation, also played a role. Thus, in Warsaw – where the most popular nineteenth-century mayor of the city, Sokrates Starynkiewicz (Сократ Старынкевич, Sokrat Starynkevich), had been a Russian military man solely answerable to his Russian superiors – the Governor-General recognized within forty-eight hours the Civic Committee established on 1 August 1914, which soon became a kind of Polish city council. The committee took over from the state authorities responsibility for, among other things, food distribution and social care as well as looking after employment and health. Granting such rights to a 'civic', i.e. public, organization was something of a sensation, but the novelty did not end there: in parallel with the eight male sections, eight women's sections were set up within the committee. These dealt with roughly the same issues as the male sections, but in addition assumed responsibility for the care of children – from crèches and orphanages to schools and workshops. The wives and daughters of venerable 'citizens' entered the public sphere, for now occupying traditional female domains but as an organized and separate group.

The example of the Civic Committee, which was financed mainly from Russian sources (government subsidies accounted for almost 70 per cent of its budget in 1914–1915, with another 17 per cent being provided by the Committee of the Grand Duchess Tatyana[45] in Petrograd), was also interesting for another reason: early in the summer of 1915 it became an organization that covered the entire Kingdom of Poland, comprising over 550 branches coordinated by the Central Civic Committee in Warsaw. In the capital alone it provided three million dinners per month.[46] This meant that Russia effectively transferred the most problematic competences of the state authorities in its hinterland to the Polish elites, who until 1914 had been refused even a modicum of self-government. A similar phenomenon occurred under different systemic conditions in the Czech lands, where self-government did not need to be created: here, too, the state willingly gave up some of its existing competences and handed them over to local authorities, which were for the most part controlled by Czechs.

Local governments and social organizations faced similar problems everywhere: hunger, the need to integrate refugees with the local population (at least superficially), rising poverty, the disintegration of infrastructure, and the breakdown of public order. One of the principal causes of anomalies in the

---

[45] Żabko-Potopowicz, Antoni, Marceli Handelsman, Władysław Grabski, and Kazimierz Władysław Kumaniecki, *Polska w czasie wielkiej wojny (1914–1918)*, vol. 2. *Historia społeczna*, Warsaw 1932, pp. 18–21. The series was published by the Carnegie Endowment for International Peace.

[46] *Dziennik Zarządu Miasta Stołecznego Warszawy*, 1 August 1915.

THE HINTERLAND 193

hinterland was unemployment. In the countryside, following the exodus of conscripts and the resulting labour deficit, unemployment was at worst mild; in general it simply did not exist. In the towns and cities, especially in modern industrial centres, the situation was very different. On the one hand, every country experienced a vast increase in war production. Mining and metallurgy also usually increased employment (though not necessarily production) in the hinterland. In the short term the Russian authorities proved the most effective: the number of weapons manufactured in 1916 was several dozen times higher than in 1913. Industrial production increased by 17 per cent in the first two years of the war. By the end of 1916 employment in the metals industry had increased by 66 per cent and employment in the chemicals industry had increased by 14 per cent. Germany, in contrast, recorded a decline in production in 1915 to four-fifths of its pre-war level; in Austria-Hungary the situation was similar.

The Decline of Cities

From the summer of 1914 nearly all branches of industry – except for those connected with the war – experienced recession, and in some cases the decline was catastrophic. The direct impact of the front in the form of bombardment or attempts to capture cities was of least significance in this regard (as we mentioned earlier, the cities mostly remained open). The indirect impact was far more serious: according to Bloch's prediction, even a geographically distant war would deprive civilian production of raw materials and exports, remove skilled and unskilled workers to the front, and destroy the foundations of the economy: the domestic and financial markets.

In the early months of the war Łódź experienced the disaster nowadays known as deindustrialization. As a major industrial centre, the city had huge reserves of raw materials. From August onwards business was done in cash, since both manufacturers and intermediaries rightly distrusted credit. A few months later, cut off from raw materials, credit, and markets, the 'Manchester of the East' ground to a halt and the textile mills closed their gates. The local situation seemed unique: during the fighting that took place in the vicinity of Łódź, not a single shipment of food entered the city for five weeks (allegedly). According to various estimates, between 35,000 and 50,000 men lay wounded in the municipal and field hospitals. Quite accidentally – although the victims were convinced there was a causal link – the final demise of Łódź, a city based on an industrial monoculture that was already in decline, coincided with the entry of the Germans into the city in early December 1914. This was the final nail in the coffin because reserves of raw materials quickly became exhausted and manufacturers could no longer export to their main market – Russia. So industrial production collapsed. During the same period, i.e. towards the end of 1914, unemployment rose. Six months later a quarter of a million men and women were out of work.

The city took a long time to recover. It would be a good fifteen years before the population reached its 1913 level. In other cities the economic downturn was more protracted, but the end result was just as catastrophic. When German troops entered the so-called Warsaw Industrial District, for instance, there were half as many industrial workers employed there as in the previous year. The port in Riga was mined in October 1914 and consequently the city lost one of its major employers. Six months later two-thirds of the workforce was still employed in industry. The real catastrophe came in the summer of 1915, when the main means of production – factory equipment and raw materials – were removed from the city along with the workers.

Other Baltic cities did not fare much better. In Königsberg, which remained relatively safe throughout the war, maritime trade fell in 1917 to 12 per cent (imports) and 5 per cent (exports) of its pre-war level. In Prussian Elbing, a city that was never close to the front lines, only one ship carrying cargo docked in 1915 (as opposed to ninety-three in 1913). The economic slump affected wages and living standards even in regions where a relatively high number of industrial plants catered for the front: in Bohemia and Moravia, in 1915, the real wages of workers fell to around three-fifths of their pre-war level.

Up until 1917 the industrial centres in the Grand Duchy of Finland were a bright spot among the general misery of cities in Central and Eastern Europe. The rise in unemployment in the summer of 1914 was short-lived, and Finland soon led the way in winning government orders for the production of armaments and strategic goods. The country took advantage of its geographical location. It was both far away from the front and close to the insatiable imperial capital of St Petersburg, soon to be renamed Petrograd. The value of the goods it exported to Russia rose more than two-fold in 1915 and doubled again in 1916. Besides armaments, Finland re-exported goods that were produced in Sweden. Traditional domestic industry also fared well. Until 1917 virtually all Russian newspapers were printed on paper imported from Finland. Economic collapse arrived only with the announcement of independence.[47]

The inhabitants of the hinterland experienced new surprises at every turn. First there were the throngs of refugees – for the most part ethnically foreign, except in the Reich – who, as fellow citizens, expected board and lodging. Then there was the tension caused by the worsening employment situation, the breakdown in provisioning, and increasing uncertainty about the future.

---

[47] I. N. Novikova, 'Великое княжество Финляндское в годы Первой мировой войны: от автономии к независимости [Velikoe kniazhestvo Finliandskoe v gody Pervoi mirovoi voiny: ot avtonomii k nezavisimosti]', in *Война и общество в XX веке*, vol. I. *Война и общество накануне и в период Первой мировой войны* [*Voina i obshchestvo v XX veke*, vol. 1. *Voina i obshchestvo nakanune i v period Pervoi mirovoi voiny*], ed. B. A. Zolotarev and L. V. Pozdeeva, Moscow 2008, pp. 186–231.

THE HINTERLAND   195

Likewise unexpected were the equally real conflicts that emerged in people's apartments and on manorial estates: hitherto obedient servants suddenly started to complain and make demands. Surreptitiously, domestic staff began to inform on their employers; we shall never know how common an occurrence this was, and whether it was motivated by personal grievances or by the class struggle. In any case, unlike in the aforementioned example of Riga, the rise in denunciations did not need to be centred on ethnicity. The police, for their part, probably preferred to rely on traditional sources of information, i.e. the caretakers of tenements, since the accusations made by domestic staff and neighbours were less credible. In time denunciations became the scourge of the local administration, which simply could not resolve matters quickly enough. In June 1915, five days after the Galician capital had been restored to the monarchy, when the most pressing concern was the loyalty of the Ukrainians, *Kurjer Lwowski*, a Lwów daily, paraphrasing an order issued by the Archduke Friedrich, reminded readers that:

1. [...] it is absolutely wrong to consider every Ruthenian a traitor.
2. It is likewise wrong to regard all arrested persons as traitors, since many are arrested on the basis of false allegations.
3. False allegations will cease if the informant is detained (where possible) along with the arrested person.[48]

We do not know whether denunciation flourished in the countryside as vigorously as it did in the cities.

The Transformation of the Countryside: Peasant Becomes Lord

At the same time, further differences emerged between the countryside and the cities that would undo the latter's civilizational advantage for at least the duration of the war. Food prices grew faster than any other prices. 'Today the peasant is God [...] we have never had it so good as during this war,' said a peasant woman to herself in a Czech tavern as she ostentatiously unpacked a delivery of white bread and roast chicken.[49] The previously cited Cracovian columnist noted a similar scene:

> Venturing out into the city in the mornings, one notices peasant carts carrying milk and vegetables on almost every street, the carts being driven almost exclusively by women. Brandishing whips, the wives of stablemen who have been called up to the army are even to be seen sitting in the driver's seat of the special vehicles that bring milk into the city from the surrounding farms and manors. On market days, traversing the squares

---

[48] *Kurjer Lwowski*, 27 June 1915.
[49] Cited in Rudolf Kučera, *Život na příděl. Válečná každodennost a politiky dělnické třídy v českých zemích 1914–1918*, Prague 2013, pp. 36–37.

used as parking spots by visiting locals, one encounters, here and there, young lads or elderly country fellows: without exception all of them are chauffeured by women, already well-versed in their profession.[50]

The entry of peasant women into the cities reflected the rising status both of women and of the countryside. Women were increasingly to be seen 'with a cigarette in their mouth',[51] which at that time was a hallmark of gender equality. While there is little indication that contemporaries resisted the idea of women playing an active and visible occupational role in the absence of men, the sudden dominance of the countryside over the cities did arouse considerable resentment. The image of well-fed peasants buying up furniture, pianos, and other bourgeois accessories pervaded the hinterland: '[...] while we, the intelligentsia, all look like beggars now, the peasants have transformed themselves into lords', complained a participant of a Sunday tea gathering on the old German–Russian border. 'Who drinks champagne nowadays? The peasants. Who smokes expensive cigars? The peasants. I even read recently that a peasant woman whose husband had died in a Warsaw hospital had buried him with great pomp and ceremony.' Members of the intelligentsia could not believe their eyes and ears, yet as progressive people they treated the material advancement of the countryside less as a reflection of their own decline and more as a foretaste of the positive changes that would ensue:

> The enrichment of the Polish peasantry is not a scourge that will consign our country to ruin. Indeed, affluence will bring cultural and economic progress to our peasant population. [...] The same cannot be said of speculation in the cities. Like a malignant cancer it is spreading throughout the social organism, sowing iniquity and oppressing most severely those urban workers whose pay is entirely dependent upon monthly salaries, such as teachers, civil servants, employees of industry and commerce, etc.[52]

Such opinions revealed a great deal of sympathy for the people. Political calculation played a role too, however. The process of ethnicization meant that it was considered necessary to nurture the national consciousness of the lower social classes. For supporters of the national cause, the conflict between town and country was beneficial only if one or the other side was ethnically alien. No one was interested in fomenting discord between Czech peasants and Czech city dwellers. This was the political background to initiatives (especially common in the Czech lands) that aimed to bring urban and rural inhabitants closer together: educational campaigns for farmers, excursions to Prague and other major cities, summer camps for village children.

---

[50] *Ilustrowany Kuryer Codzienny*, 23 June 1915.
[51] *Ilustrowany Kuryer Codzienny*, 13 August 1915.
[52] *Kurjer Łódzki*, 14 September 1917.

On the other hand, these efforts to improve relations between the country-side and the cities show that there was indeed a problem, and the frustration felt by the hungry urban population could not simply be reduced to ethnic categories. A similar mood prevailed in Vienna: the capital's inhabitants blamed the allegedly incompetent authorities, the refugees from Galicia and Bukovina who were billeted in the city, the 'treacherous Hungarians' who had stopped supplying food, and last, but by no means least, their fellow country-men from nearby Lower Austria who sold food at ever-increasing prices; but, above all, they hated the speculators, who were often their neighbours.

For villages in the hinterland the war was a relatively mild experience, which is not to say that the lot of agricultural workers suddenly improved. However, for farmers who produced food, the profits to be made at fairs and on the black market probably compensated for the losses they suffered due to lower crop yields. Joseph Held claims that angry murmurings were not heard in the Hungarian countryside until 1917, and that the 'façade of normality' generally lasted until the end of the war.[53] What is even more surprising is that historians similarly assess the mood in rural Russia. They claim that up to 1917 the hardships (but also the joys) of everyday life were more important than the war: harvests, weddings, and work in the fields, even in the revolutionary year of 1917, meant more to the Russian peasant than wartime events that were external to his or her rhythm of life.[54] At first sight this seems paradoxical, but perhaps one of the newspapers was on the right track when it tried to explain the growing antagonism between town and country in the fourth year of war as follows. Meat and fats existed 'IN SUFFICIENT QUANTITIES IN THE COUNTRYSIDE', but the peasants did not wish to sell. The 'Polish Association of Cattle and Swine Traders', intermediaries known to the farmers by face and by name, had to become involved in the purchasing of food. 'One must be able to delve into the psyche of the Polish peasant, who resents all constraints and coercion, and who will be more willing to sell to his former customer than to an official agent armed with signatures and assisted by a gendarme.'[55] There is much optimism in this view as well as a bit of enforced national solidarity and perhaps even a touch of peasant idealization. Nevertheless, it pinpoints the weakest element of the wartime system of provisioning: coercion quickly and brutally replaced the market, with its reliance on mutual trust between buyers and sellers.

---

[53] Joseph Held, 'Culture in Hungary during World War I', in *European Culture in the Great War. The Arts, Entertainment and Propaganda, 1914–1918*, ed. Aviel Roshwald and Richard Stites, Cambridge 1999, pp. 176–192, here pp. 177–181.

[54] Igor' Narskij, 'Zehn Phänomene, die Russland 1917 erschütterten, in *Schlüsseljahre. Zentrale Konstellationen der mittel- und osteuropäischen Geschichte. Festschrift für Helmut Altrichter zum 65. Geburtstag*, ed. Matthias Stadelmann and Lilia Antipow, Wiesbaden 2011, pp. 255–272, here p. 256.

[55] *Ilustrowany Kuryer Codzienny*, 2 January 1918.

Beyond areas visited by occupying forces, the countryside of Central and South-Eastern Europe survived the 1914–1916 period in relative peace. Aggressive reactions did not emerge until the year of the Russian revolutions, and not necessarily under the direct influence of the events in Russia. Aside from the stigmatization of Jews and of course the ideological declarations of the nationally conscious intelligentsia, ethnicization remained almost invisible, belonging more to the towns and cities than to the countryside. In rural areas there was no dividing line based on nationality. The aforementioned peasant woman in the Czech tavern infuriated her fellow countrymen. The Viennese felt cheated by the Hungarians, but they had at least as much animosity towards local, German-speaking peasants. Slovak peasants did not revolt against the King in Budapest, while Latvian peasants even distinguished themselves in the Czarist army. Ruthenians/Ukrainians were persecuted by successive military administrations, but seldom by people in their village. Polish peasants in the eastern provinces of the Reich or in Galicia did not even think of behaving differently from their neighbours. We know least about peasants in Bohemia and Moravia, but here, too, it was only much later that nationality triumphed over citizenship and loyalty to the state.

6

The Hunger for Information

The spy craze that consumed the authorities of the combatant states was based on the belief that certain groups of civilians were privy to secret information that they were eager to pass on to the enemy. This proposition may have been true in regard to a few individuals, but in relation to society as a whole, or even a part thereof, it was nonsense. There is no better proof of this than the enormous hunger for up-to-date information that was felt by the populations of all the warring states. Civilians generally did not possess or provide the enemy with valuable information, yet they themselves often felt confused and were keen, if not desperate, to satisfy their own curiosity. This is evidenced by the extraordinary popularity of the newspapers (so-called war tourism) and all manner of rumours and gossip. Relatively new media – cinema and modern museums – were also harnessed in the service of information and propaganda.

The Press

The metamorphosis of the European press in the summer of 1914 was all the more conspicuous because it happened virtually overnight. The war, although anticipated by many, still managed to take newspaper editors by surprise because they were focused on other problems and not the worsening diplomatic crisis. In Russia, for instance, news of the Sarajevo assassination went largely unanswered, at least initially. The press was more interested in the wave of workers' strikes that spread throughout the empire in the summer of 1914. The August events thus came as a profound shock. From the moment war was declared the newspapers changed unrecognizably. First of all, their number multiplied. Within a very short period more and more issues appeared, including special supplements and evening and afternoon editions. Despite the censorship restrictions, the 'removal' of certain articles, and sometimes the withdrawal of the entire issues, this was a golden age for the press. The war years witnessed a huge increase in the sale of books and brochures, which were published not by traditional publishing houses but by press syndicates.[1] The

---

[1] Mary Hammond and Shafquat Towheed, 'Introduction', in *Publishing in the First World War: Essays in Book History*, ed. Mary Hammond and Shafquat Towheed, London

200

THE REAR

demand for information was so great that it led to the emergence of a completely new kind of criminality: unscrupulous news-vendors would dupe their customers with old newspapers masquerading as new ones.

Given this extraordinary growth of the media, reading the content of newspapers published in the first weeks of the war is something of a disappointment. The similarities are so strong that one gets the impression that newspaper editors in all the belligerent countries had the same modus operandi. When the cable under the Atlantic Ocean was cut, the Central Powers no longer had access to the bulletins put out by international telegraph agencies. World news had to be culled from the press in neutral states. Fortunately, readers were most keen to hear about events in their own country and at the front. Initially, dailies were filled with descriptions of patriotic demonstrations and farewells to soldiers heading for the battlefields as well as information about skirmishes and troop movements. Later these were supplemented by letters from citizens who had been interned and updates for families who had been separated by the front. For those who remained behind the lines, lists of the fallen, published in the local press, were especially important. Aleksander Majkowski recalled a daily gathering of reservists at the editorial office of the *Culmer Zeitung*, where such lists could be read prior to their publication. The same scene was played out in hundreds of other towns and cities.

Announcements and advertisement columns were also adapted to the needs of the moment. Readers were encouraged to buy items that could come in handy for relatives at the front: cigarettes, medicines, newspaper subscriptions, and 'trench' editions of books. Several Austro-Hungarian insurance companies offered a new type of life cover that included injuries suffered at the front.

Dry and informative statements mixed with jingoistic exhortations did not, however, satisfy readers' appetites. People wanted to know what was really going on. Enigmatic news items were formulated in such a way as not to betray any war secrets. The West European press was effectively out of bounds. Although Russians did have access to it, the information that reached them via Russian newspapers was selective, censored, and, most importantly, out-of-date. To overcome this barrier people perfected the art of reading between the lines. On the eve of Warsaw's capture by the Germans, Father Józef Rokoszny noted: 'There must be panic in Warsaw, for all the newspapers are urging us to remain calm.'[2] Majkowski was a true expert in this field. During the debacle of the first Austro-Hungarian invasion of Serbia, he commented: 'There is not even the slightest morsel of news about the Austro-Serbian theatre of war. My

---

2007, pp. 1–8; Kurt Koszyk, *Deutsche Pressepolitik im Ersten Weltkrieg*, Düsseldorf 1968, pp. 253–256; Anton Holzer, *Die andere Front. Fotografie und Propaganda im Ersten Weltkrieg*, 2nd ed., Darmstadt 2007.

[2] Józef Rokoszny, *Diariusz Wielkiej Wojny*, ed. Wiesław Caban and Marek Przeniosło, Kielce 1998, vol. 2, p. 26.

conclusion is that things are not going too well for German's ally.'[3] When Field Marshal Potiorek's subsequent offensive was in its death throes, and the attempt to liberate Przemyśl had failed, Majkowski noted:

> What is striking is that despite the cities being festooned in flags, and the elation of the newspapers about the victory, nothing has been written about the gains. Previously, the number of prisoners of war and the amount of captured war material would have been listed, and the place to which the enemy had retreated would have been mentioned. All this jubilation in the newspapers gives an impression of artificiality. Perhaps it is meant to distract attention from a defeat that has occurred elsewhere. Could it all be about Przemyśl?[4]

Although it was intellectually stimulating, reading between the lines was exhausting in the long run. Alternative sources of information were therefore sought. Near to the front this usually meant the newspapers of the enemy. In their memoirs, inhabitants of the Polish Kingdom often mention the war reports in the Galician *Nowa Reforma*, the Viennese *Neue Freie Presse*, and even the German *Kattowitzer Zeitung*. The Galicians, in turn, read the newspapers that were published in Russian-occupied Lwów: *Słowo Polskie*, *Wiek Nowy*, *Gazeta Wieczorna*, and *Gazeta Narodowa*. When the Reich and Austria-Hungary divided the Kingdom of Poland into occupation zones, the norm for inquisitive readers was to seek out material published in other zones. In the Austro-Hungarian occupation zone, *Dziennik Poznański*, a daily published in the German city of Posen (Poznań), enjoyed great popularity. Although citizens of the Central Powers had no access to the French and British press, they were able to subscribe to newspapers published in neutral countries. In Germany and Austria-Hungary the Swiss newspaper *Neue Zürcher Zeitung* was widely read, also by Poles who were German citizens.

The authorities were concerned about the undesirable impact of newspapers, especially in territories regarded as suspect, such as the Kingdom of Poland, Eastern Galicia, and Serbia. For this reason, too, although every place was subject to military censorship when a state of war was declared, control of the press in occupied territories was particularly strict. Both at home and in territories seized during the course of the war, the censors concentrated on safeguarding military secrets and preventing manifestations of 'defeatism' among the civilian population. In practice much depended on the character of the censor and on local conditions. In Germany the press was generally eager to help maintain enthusiasm for the war, hence there was no need to overly discipline journalists. Even where interventions did occur, efforts were made to keep them secret. White spots, which were frequent in Austrian newspapers, were much less common in the Reich. The differences between

---

[3] Aleksander Majkowski, *Pamiętnik z wojny europejskiej roku 1914*, ed. Tadeusz Linkner, Wejherowo and Pelplin 2000, p. 67.
[4] Ibid., p. 157.

the policies of the two allies became particularly evident at a critical moment for the Austro-Hungarian monarchy. When the Brusilov Offensive threatened to cause the complete disintegration of the Austro-Hungarian army, the occupying authorities in the Kingdom of Poland blocked the distribution of newspapers from the Reich. German journalists reported much more frequently, extensively, and impartially about the failures of the Habsburg monarchy than they did about the defeats of their own army. Interestingly, though, there were clear differences between the Austrian press and the Hungarian press. In the first two to three years of war, the tone of Hungarian reports from the front was calm and matter-of-fact compared with the German-language press.[5] The enemy was not demonized, and journalists wrote openly about German and Austro-Hungarian military defeats and the growing crisis behind the lines.[6] Hungarian reporters described in sympathetic terms the terrible effects of the German bombing of Britain, focusing on its civilian victims. This was not so much a manifestation of a particular Hungarian liberalism as a combination of other causes, three of which seem to be most important. First, even during the war the main concern of the Hungarian authorities was to keep a lid on growing public discontent. Unlike Austria, Transleithania still had an undemocratic electoral system before the war that denied influence not only to non-Hungarian ethnic groups but also to the lower social classes of the ruling nation. Second, Hungary clearly emphasized its autonomy and independence from Austria, also in wartime. A separate information policy was an excellent means of expressing that autonomy. Third, the internal situation of Transleithania was such that control of the press did not need to be tightened. Although a war was under way in which Hungarians too were dying, the country enjoyed economic benefits and provisioning was far better than it was in Austria.

The press in occupied territories found itself in the worst situation. Here the censors were definitely less forgiving than in the big cities. Whereas satirical magazines in Berlin, Vienna, Prague, Budapest, Moscow, and Petrograd were sometimes treated as safety-valves and were allowed to criticize provisioning, internal relations, and war-related pathologies, for instance, their counterparts in Warsaw had no such freedom. This is illustrated by the fate of three newspaper jokes thought up by editorial offices in 1916. At roughly the same time, *Humoristické Listy*, *Nowyi Satirikon*, and *Mucha* joked about the problems of the war economy. In the Russian newspaper *Nowyi Satirikon* the censors allowed a story about an increasingly pregnant woman who, when asked whether she feared how her husband would react upon his return,

---

[5] Tamara Scheer, *Die Ringstraßenfront. Österreich-Ungarn, das Kriegsüberwachungsamt und der Ausnahmezustand während des Ersten Weltkrieges*, Wien 2010, pp. 145–166.

[6] Joseph Held, 'Culture in Hungary during World War I', in: *European Culture in the Great War*, pp. 176–192, here pp. 186–190. See also Eszter Balázs, '"War Stares at Us Like an Ominous Sphynx": Hungarian Intellectuals, Literature and the Image of the Other (1914-1915)', in: *The New Nationalism and the First World War*, edited by Lawrence Rosenthal and Vesna Rodic, London 2015, pp. 95–120.

THE HUNGER FOR INFORMATION   203

replied: 'He'll never find out: by the time he comes back it will all be over [. . .].
I sent him out to buy sugar.'[7] The Prague newspaper *Humoristické Listy* had an
answer as to why shoes were so expensive: 'because the price of paper has gone
up again'.[8]

Meanwhile, the Warsaw newspaper *Mucha* was temporarily shut down
when it published a joke about the campaign to collect metals. On the orders
of the Governor-General, and on pain of heavy fines, Varsovians were meant
to surrender chains, knobs, doorplates, bannisters, hat-stands, taps, pipes,
gutters, and door handles to the authorities. *Mucha* allowed itself the following joke: 'What does someone do when he is about to leave? He grabs the
handle!'[9]

The press policy of the Germans in Warsaw was still not the worst thing that
could have happened to journalists. There were times when the occupying
regime deliberately restricted or eliminated the entire press market in areas
under its control. After the final capture of Belgrade, the Austro-Hungarian
authorities did not allow any Serbian newspaper to open an editorial office. For
six months the only newspaper to appear was the regime-approved *Belgrader
Nachrichten*, which was later also published in Serbo-Croat as *Beogradske
Novine*. The versions of this publication in the two languages, which contained
official notices, classified advertisements, and messages from people searching
for their relatives, had a total circulation of 150,000. Permission to publish any
other newspaper in Belgrade was not given consideration until just before the
end of the war. The Russian occupation of Eastern Galicia, although brief, had
an even more destructive influence on the Ukrainian press. In Lwów the main
Ukrainian-language daily, *Dilo*, was closed immediately after the capture of the
city. There was no question of any newspaper being allowed to appear in
Ukrainian, since according to official Russian doctrine the language itself had
no right to exist. 'Little Russians' were treated as a Russian 'tribe' and therefore
expected to read the Russian press. In the slightly longer term this Russian
nationalities policy was defeated by Ukrainian culture in Galicia. As one can
infer from literary reminiscences, for countless military men from the Russian
part of Ukraine it was precisely their stay in occupied Lwów that proved to be
the turning point. When exposed to Ukrainian literature and to the vibrant,
albeit now severely restricted, cultural life of Eastern Galicia they rediscovered
their Ukrainian identity. Meanwhile, however, Ukrainian editorial offices,
bookshops, associations, libraries, and schools were being closed.

---

[7] Cited in Lesley Milne, '*Novyi Satirikon*, 1914–1918: The Patriotic Laughter of the Russian
Liberal Intelligentsia during the First World War and the Revolution', *The Slavonic and
East European Review* 84, 4 (2006), pp. 639–665, here p. 648.

[8] *Humoristické Listy* 59, 2 (1916), p. 19.

[9] Rokoszny, *Diariusz Wielkiej Wojny*, vol. 2, p. 219.

204   THE REAR

Russian policy towards the Polish press in Lwów was somewhat different. Publication was permitted but was subject to strict, if inconsistent censorship (the censors changed every few weeks). It was not censorship, however, that presented the biggest problem for professional journalists. Józef Białynia Chołodecki witnessed the beginnings of a new chapter in the history of the Lwów press:

> Those Polish dailies were immediately forced to trim their content, not just on account of the difficulties and costs of publishing, but also due to the lack of material and new topics to write about. Initially, the source of all news was the Town Hall; everyday life in the city was slowly returning to normal, and amidst the sound of heavy guns a new group of gentlemen had come to take control. Wishing to provide readers with at least a modicum of news about the war, journalists tried various methods, such as gleaning information from Russian officers in private or conducting interviews with chosen dignitaries. Soon the Lwów press got its information about external events from Russian newspapers and magazines shown to journalists or given to them by higher-ranking officers or their orderlies (in the latter case, not disinterestedly, of course). The Lwów journalists likewise bought all sorts of publications discarded by individual officers from hotel staff. It was sometimes also possible to peruse or copy news from Russian newspapers while waiting in the censorship office. From the beginning of October it was possible to purchase newspapers brought in from Russia. They were obtained by some cunning yid [sic] who used paperboys to distribute them and charged sky-high prices. Apparently, Viennese newspapers also appeared occasionally, for which the owner demanded a price of one or two crowns.[10]

Information was not just a sphere in which the authorities intervened; it was also a business, as the quoted fragment of Chołodecki's memoirs clearly shows. Readers and journalists alike craved fresh news. The war greatly increased the popularity of the press, but it also accelerated its visual evolution. This is evidenced by the richly illustrated publications devoted exclusively to operations at the front, such as the Budapest weekly *A világháború képes krónikája* (*Illustrated Chronicle of the World War*). In 1914, it was still dominated by illustrators. A few months later the number of published photographs began to rise, and by 1915 photographs had almost completely replaced drawings. Editorial staff called on the services of illustrators only when photographic documentation was not available. As the visual language changed, so did the nature of the information communicated to readers. Colourful stories about heroic deeds were gradually supplanted by hard facts, because that is what the public wanted.

[10] Józef Białynia Chołodecki, *Lwów w czasie okupacji rosyjskiej (3 września 1914–22 czerwca 1915). Z własnych przeżyć i spostrzeżeń*, Lwów 1930, pp. 89–90.

Gawkers and Gossip

People also tried to dig out the hard facts on their own. A new phenomenon emerged in the vicinity of battlefields: war tourism. In the autumn of 1914 German troops were pushed back from the suburbs of Warsaw. Clashes with the Russians took place in and around the town of Brwinów, which could be reached by narrow-gauge railway from the capital. Hobbyists took advantage of this opportunity to collect souvenirs such as buttons, bayonets, helmets, and shell cases, but so did looters, who robbed the dead. A side effect of this activity was that people began to view the war in a different way. The well-known Warsaw literary critic Cezary Jellenta, who also visited Brwinów, was surprised at how 'sparse' the battlefield looked compared with the 'dense' (i.e. intense) descriptions of the fighting that had appeared in the newspapers. The bombastic reportage in the Russian press of events at the front belied the scene he witnessed with his own eyes.[11]

Curiosity also prompted many thousands of onlookers to observe the hostilities at close quarters. Standard warnings made no impact on them: only sustained artillery fire would force them to take refuge in a safe place. There were no gawkers in Belgrade, which the Austrians shelled from the far bank of the Sava in the first days of the war, or in Gorlice during the May offensive of Mackensen's army. Yet there was no shortage of them in cities that were bombed from the air, such as Warsaw in the spring of 1915:

> On the eighth-floor terrace of a house overlooking Rondo Mokotowskie [now pl. Unii Lubelskiej], the Café Niespodzianka [Café Surprise] was filled to the rafters. In the evenings patrons would be on the lookout for flashes of artillery fire, while in the daytime they would practically offer coffee to the pilots of low-flying planes that passed over them.[12]

Of course, the air raids were nowhere near as devastating as they would be a few decades later. In the autumn of 1916, literally only a few bombs fell on Bucharest, and later on Warsaw, within the course of a single day. Everyone knew where the bombs had struck, especially if the place was as recognizable and popular as the Café Cristal at the corner of al. Jerozolimskie and ul. Bracka, in the vicinity of which a bomb exploded in January 1915. The casualties of such bombings were usually gawkers who had been mesmerized by the approaching aircraft. The rapid evacuation of the Russians and entry of the Germans into Warsaw in August of that year also aroused considerable interest. Stanisław Dzierzbicki noted: 'On the streets of Warsaw there are around one hundred and fifty wounded, and a few people have been killed by stray bullets. However, this

---

[11] Cezary Jellenta, *Wielki zmierzch. Pamiętnik*, Warsaw 1985, pp. 87–97.
[12] Cited in Andrzej Rosner (ed.), *Teraz będzie Polska. Wybór z pamiętników z okresu I wojny światowej*, Warsaw 1988, pp. 184–191, here p. 190.

Fig. 42 A Bulgarian pilot in front of his Albatros B.I, a German-made military reconnaissance aircraft, 1916. Courtesy of Mr Peyo Kolev, lostbulgaria.com.

has not dampened the curiosity of the thrill-seeking Warsaw public.'[13] The last few remaining residents of Belgrade responded altogether differently. As they entered the city, the Germans marched through empty streets. The only people they encountered were emaciated women in black headscarves.[14]

Neither war tourism nor swarms of curious onlookers were a match for the rapidly evolving press. Rumours and gossip were another matter, however, for they reached the places that newspapers could not. Virtually everyone – civilians, soldiers, even the authorities of the combatant states – participated in this feast of communication. As usual, the rumours had a grain of truth to them, but the facts were twisted, exaggerated, and given a wholly new meaning. Allegations that certain Czech regiments had committed treason, or that Ukrainian peasants had used secret telephone lines to relay information either to the Russians or to the Austrians, were based on unsubstantiated gossip. The impact of such information was sometimes huge. The news that a Czech regiment had gone over to the Russian side in close formation and accompanied by an orchestra was repeated by 'eyewitnesses' and soon spread throughout

[13] Stanisław Dzierzbicki, *Pamiętnik z lat wojny 1915–1918*, ed. Janusz Pajewski and Danuta Płygawko, Warsaw 1983, p. 63.
[14] Wilhelm Hegeler, *Der Siegeszug durch Serbien*, Berlin 1916, p. 29.

THE HUNGER FOR INFORMATION   207

the entire Habsburg monarchy. The claim proved highly durable, and until recently was given serious consideration by historians. The fact that nothing of the sort had happened was of little importance. Fanciful claims about atrocities perpetrated by all sides in the conflict likewise flourished. Interestingly, in Russia, it was not the misery of the Czar's subjects that caused outrage, but rather stories about Prussians cutting off the hands of unfortunate Belgian children. In September 1914, in the besieged town of Przemyśl, the otherwise level-headed Helena Jabłońska née Seifert noted with horror that 'The rumour is indeed true: one of the Muscovites taken into captivity had ten pairs of eyes hidden in his pocket.'[15]

Both official and unofficial information was permeated by the idea of betrayal lurking in one's own ranks and the barbarity of the enemy. People repeated and processed the propaganda output of the warring countries, and the authorities looked upon this with satisfaction. The belief that the enemy was murdering and mistreating prisoners of war tempered the desire to lay down arms. When skilfully managed, fear cemented the relationship between civilians and the military. This was especially important in areas close to the front. A besieged fortress such as Przemyśl was a perfect laboratory for gossip and rumours. Russian officials were just as adept in this regard, gently making it known to peasants in the Radom and Kielce provinces that the advancing Austrians aimed to reintroduce serfdom or incite another Polish insurrection.

A rumour was a double-edged sword, however. 'Defeatism' and 'spreading unverified information', for which more than one civilian was sent to the gallows, were simply gossip that did not gain official approval. In this case repressive measures were ineffective. Astonishing disclosures about the enemy's strength and its extraordinary military technology were repeated with relish, while one's own losses and failures were exaggerated. Incredible stories circulated about 'exotic' armies, both real and imagined: detachments of Asiatic nomads in the Russian cavalry, Turkish divisions (as a rule, Bosnians in the Austro-Hungarian army were suspected of being Turks), colonial troops allegedly sent to Russia by France and Great Britain, and finally Japanese soldiers who had come over on the trans-Siberian railway and were now heading for Vienna, Budapest, and Berlin. The longer the war lasted, the more often it was believed that the enemy was better equipped, better dressed, and better fed. The mood of the moment was reflected in such stories. In the summer of 1914 August Krasicki watched in admiration as the Austro-Hungarian troops marched on Przemyśl:

> [...] they looked like the guard [...]. Fresh uniforms straight from the stores, grey in colour like those of the Landwehr, with green lapels. Excellent new boots, a complete set of undergarments, all brand new; in

---

[15] Helena z Seifertów Jabłońska, *Dziennik z oblężonego Przemyśla 1914–1915*, ed. Hanna Imbs, Przemyśl 1994, p. 44.

208

THE REAR

a word: faultless. If everything in Austria is as well prepared for war, then we may be confident of the outcome.[16]

Barely a month later Helena Jabłońska made a radically different observation while working as a nurse in a Przemyśl hospital. She, in turn, was impressed by the appearance and uniforms of the wounded Russian prisoners:

> [...] I am full of admiration for them and I regret that our own soldiers pale in comparison. The Russians are all better turned out, somehow more opulent than our troops; the shirt is durable, cleaner and warmer, and everything is softer; they are less burdened. Their uniform is heavily sewn, while ours is bulky and shrivelled and chafes the skin; it lets in water and loses its shape. All of them have enough food on their person and a flask of vodka. They are tall, ruddy, and fighting fit, and appear better dressed than our officers.[17]

Was a single month, during which both armies were on the move, enough to confirm that the Russians were superior in every way – from their height and complexion to their shirts and boots? It is more likely that such observations were a result of the first defeats, of being enclosed within the walls of a besieged city and encountering supply problems for the first time. They were also a manifestation of a banal psychological mechanism – the presumption that 'others certainly have it better'. This mechanism affected military men and civilians alike. One Hungarian officer was convinced of the Russians' superiority: they apparently had warmer coats and at a distance the officers' uniforms were indistinguishable from the greatcoats worn by rank-and-file soldiers; in any case, the Russian officers did not lead their men into attack but instead brought up the rear.[18]

In the long run, rumours that affected the economic decisions of the civilian population were especially damaging from the point of view of the army and the state authorities. Even minor issues could have fatal consequences for the war economy. One example is the disappearance of small-denomination coins in all the combatant countries. This was caused by a more general phenomenon common to acute economic crises: the hoarding of all kinds of metals. Its impact on the functioning of the market was particularly destructive, however: already in the first days of the war some shopkeepers refused to accept high-denomination banknotes because they had no change. As one columnist scoffed:

---

[16] August Krasicki, *Dziennik z kampanii rosyjskiej*, Cracow 1988, p. 28.
[17] Jabłońska, *Dziennik z oblężonego Przemyśla 1914–1915*, pp. 48–49.
[18] Ferenc Pollmann, 'Die Ostfront des "Großen Krieges" – aus ungarischer Perspektive', in *Jenseits des Schützengrabens. Der Erste Weltkrieg im Osten: Erfahrung – Wahrnehmung – Kontext*, ed. Bernhard Bachinger and Wolfram Dornik, Innsbruck 2013, p. 97.

Indeed, the lack of small change has its benefits. For two days I went around the cafés drinking coffee and buying cigarettes on credit, presenting a five-rouble note everywhere I went. They all preferred to trust me rather than to give out change. This convinced me that the future was rosy, for if a single five-rouble note could bat away all my wartime troubles, then surely the economic crisis was not as bad as all that.[19]

The disappearance of coins was no laughing matter, though. As early as on 1 August 1914 the German authorities made the following threat, announced in the *Berliner Lokal-Anzeiger*:

Let no one forget that a refusal to accept our banknotes is not only unlawful and unjustified but also wicked. For anyone who behaves in this way casts doubt upon the credit of the German Reich, to which the German Reichsbank belongs, and thus displays a lack of patriotism.[20]

The inhabitants of Austrian cities faced identical problems. They solved them by, among other solutions, cutting two-crown banknotes into halves or quarters. In the autumn of 1915 the central bank relented and legalized this public practice.

In the Kingdom of Poland and in Serbia money problems were exacerbated by the hasty evacuation of the banks. At the beginning of August the State Bank in Warsaw stopped serving civilian customers, causing chaos. It took two to three weeks to bring the situation under control. Upon the return of the evacuated Russian officials, more silver roubles were issued, which calmed the public mood for a while.

In the long run, however, it was not possible to go back to pre-war norms. Time and again, news about developments at the front triggered compulsive buying on a mass scale. While groups of nationalist students sang as they marched along Unter den Linden, some Berlin shops had to close because anxious customers had bought up all their merchandise. Prices shot up, and the press and local authorities launched a campaign to combat panic buying and speculation. The setting of maximum prices, which were announced in the daily press, could not halt price inflation in the long run. Meanwhile, in early August, there was a rumour that the water supply in Warsaw had failed:

They're cutting off the water! It is not known who first uttered these words, but within ten minutes the whole city knew about it. Collect water! Everyone immediately turned on their taps and placed underneath them whatever they could find in their home: bowls, jugs, decanters, old bottles, teapots. They collected water. After an hour of this, the water flow had already started to weaken slightly.

---

[19] *Tygodnik Ilustrowany*, 8 August 1914.

[20] Cited in Dieter Glatzer and Ruth Glatzer (eds.), *Berliner Leben 1914–1918. Eine historische Reportage aus Erinnerungen und Berichten*, Berlin 1983, p. 42.

210

– What! . . .

A day later all the collected water had to be poured away. Now there was a new alarm. Never mind what it was about.[21]

In this instance, too, the problem was no laughing matter: the pressure in the network had decreased so much that the city was deprived of water. Simultaneously, the overloaded telephone network crashed. Neither people nor technology could cope with chaos of information. The state could not cope with it either.

Propaganda

At the outbreak of the war no country had specialized structures that were able to satisfy the demand for information and at the same time influence public opinion. Censorship was a one-sided tool. This was evident in the activities of, among others, the German Kriegspresseamt (War Press Office), which was established at the beginning of 1915. The Kriegspresseamt was at once a censorship office and a press agency that relayed news to the German newspapers. However, the emphasis was very much on preventing the publication of undesirable news, while the stream of news that could be of genuine interest to readers was reduced to a slow trickle. Structures responsible for disseminating propaganda that was both visually attractive and had appealing content were created with great difficulty, as is shown by the fictionalized reports of battles that occurred in the first months of the conflict. Such reports made for dull reading, and their greatest weakness lay in their lack of realism. At the beginning of the war most were written from behind a desk, and their authors usually had not the slightest knowledge of the areas in which the fighting was taking place. One of the most renowned authors in this genre, the Swiss journalist Hermann Stegemann, tormented his readers with platitudes and clichés about 'fierce battles' that invariably entailed 'heavy losses'. These reports, which were published in every issue of *Der Bund* (a Bern daily), comprise four weighty tomes in book form. Yet Stegemann, although sympathetic to the Central Powers, was a citizen of a neutral country and generally did not lapse into unbearable patriotic pathos. The reports churned out by his fellow journalists in combatant countries were even more painful to read. Cezary Jellenta had had enough of them by October 1914:

> Death no longer makes an impression and no one throws flowers at the wounded. [. . .] Every day the newspapers print a dozen or so stories about miraculous heroic deeds, but no one reads them any more. Heroism has become dreadfully cheap.[22]

---

[21] *Tygodnik Ilustrowany*, 8 August 1914.
[22] Cezary Jellenta, *Wielki zmierzch*, p. 105.

THE HUNGER FOR INFORMATION 211

In order to overcome the boring routine and capture the public imagination, new life had to be breathed into the narrative of the ongoing war. A new style of reporting and new forms of expression were needed. Austria-Hungary was a pioneer in this regard. Since 1909 the mobilization regulations had envisaged the creation of a wartime Kriegspressequartier (War Press Quarter; KPQ) composed of journalists posted by their editorial offices to work with the General Staff and with the staffs of individual armies. Of course, the dozens of journalists affiliated with the KPQ must have had a hard time retrieving any military information whatsoever. Alexander Roda Roda (whose real name was Sándor Friedrich Rosenfeld), the *Neue Freie Presse* correspondent and peerless star of war reporting, complained to his readers:

> Such interesting things are happening out there, on the outside, yet the same idyll reigns in the Kriegspressequartier as on the first day. We are still only permitted to post scant news so as not to provide information about our army to the enemy. We would gladly write something to bring cheer to our readers, but the censors keep us in check. How eagerly we would shout to the whole world about the feelings that fill our hearts, yet we must remain silent.[23]

The existence of the KPQ did not resolve the problem of how to report about successive defeats. The press releases put out by the KPQ, often written in a slapdash manner, perhaps after an evening's revelry, bordered on sabotage. When, at the end of August 1914, the Russian army was fast approaching the capital of Bukovina, the *Czernowitzer Allgemeine Zeitung* had to sell the following official communiqué to its readers: 'A great battle has been under way since 26 August. The position of our troops is favourable. The weather is warm and sunny.' The desperate editor felt obliged to provide some clarification to the city's inhabitants, who had unexpectedly found themselves on the front line:

> Let us not turn up our noses at this remark. Sunny and warm weather is a weapon, a powerful weapon, which is worth as much to the defenders of the homeland as abundant food and a favourable position. We have both of these things, and if, in the midst of this terrible struggle which makes every nerve tremble – which also stirs those who stand not on the battlefield, restless and sleep-deprived – if, in the midst of that struggle, a terse telegram adds that the weather is warm and sunny, then a ray of sunlight likewise falls on our souls, exposed to violent vagaries, in need of solace.[24]

---

[23] Alexander Roda Roda, 'Im k.u.k. Kriegspressequartier', *Neue Freie Presse*, 31 August 1914, p. 3, cited in Jozo Džambo, 'Armis et litteris – Kriegsberichterstattung, Kriegspropaganda und Kriegsdokumentation in der k.u.k. Armee 1914–918' in *Musen an die Front! Schriftsteller und Künstler im Dienst der k.u.k. Kriegspropaganda 1914–1918*, vol. 1. *Beiträge*, Munich 2003, pp. 10–38, here p. 13.

[24] *Czernowitzer Allgemeine Zeitung*, 30 August 1914.

Some of the rapporteurs, such as Roda Roda, actually worked in the same way as war correspondents, reporting from places which they had seen first-hand. Others reported from several sections of the front at once, but in reality remained in the KPQ headquarters (from 1916 located in a comfortable hotel in Rodaun near Vienna). Nevertheless, the system also gave opportunities to a new type of correspondent who was ready to share the hardships of army life; it even gave opportunities to women, such as Alice Schalek (according to Karl Kraus, the embodiment of the evil of war), who won recognition for her reports from the Italian front.

The attempts to modernize the journalistic craft were not aimed just at satisfying the general hunger for information but also at making propaganda more effective. This was likewise the aim of the KPQ, or, as the new head of the office put it in 1917: 'Pressedienst ist Propagandadienst.'[25] Reportage and fictionalized war stories were published in book form along with a huge number of brochures devoted to many aspects of the war. All aimed to bolster the fighting spirit, the will to persevere, and the readiness for sacrifice among the populations of the combatant states. Germany and (to a lesser degree) Austria-Hungary were the unrivalled leaders in this field, not only in Central and Eastern Europe, but in the world as a whole. Most of the publications appeared in German, of course, but there were also editions in Hungarian, Czech, Polish, Croatian, and Romanian.[26] The tone of the brochures was superbly captured by Jaroslav Hašek; in *The Good Soldier Švejk*, a cadet by the name of Biegler compiles a list of war publications to be written after victory:

> The Characters of the Warriors of the Great War. – Who Began the War? – The Policy of Austria-Hungary and the Origin of the World War. – War Notes. – Austria-Hungary and the World War. – Lessons from the War. – Popular Lecture on the Outbreak of the War. – Military Political Reflections. – The Glorious Day of Austria-Hungary. – Slav Imperialism and the World War. – Documents from the War. – Documents for the History of the World War. – A Diary of the World War. – A Daily Survey of the World War. – The First World War. – Our Dynasty in the World War. – Peoples of the Austro-Hungarian Monarchy under Arms. – The World Struggle for Power. – My Experiences in the World War. – The Chronicle of My War Campaign. – How the Enemies of Austria-Hungary Fight. – Who Will Be the Victors? – Our Officers and Our Men. – Memorable Acts of My Soldiers. – From the Times of the Great War. – On the Turmoil of Battle. – My Book of Austro-Hungarian Heroes. – The Iron Brigade. – A Collection of My Writings from the Front. – The Heroes of Our March Battalion. – Handbook for Soldiers in

---

[25] Jozo Džambo, 'Armis et litteris', p. 14.
[26] See Maciej Górny, *Science Embattled. Eastern European Intellectuals and the Great War*, Paderborn 2019, pp. 39–116.

THE HUNGER FOR INFORMATION   213

the Field. – Days of Battles and Days of Victory. – What I Have Seen and
Experienced in the Field. – In the Trenches. – An Officer Relates ... –
Forward with the Sons of Austria-Hungary! – Enemy Aeroplanes and Our
Infantry. – After the Battle. – Our Artillery. – Faithful Sons of the
Fatherland. – Come All the Devils in the World against Us. – Defensive
and Offensive War. – Blood and Iron. – Victory or Death. – Our Heroes in
Captivity.[27]

Publications were also produced for foreign readerships, particularly in the
neutral states. In the Reich, propaganda for foreign consumption was the first
element of information policy to come under the control of a state institution –
the Zentralstelle für Auslandsdienst (Central Office for Foreign Affairs).
Descriptions of atrocities perpetrated by Germany's enemies as well as assurances of Germany's peaceful intentions were mainly exported to neutral states.
The message directed to the societies of combatant states was naturally much
more belligerent.

Many of the propagandist publications were accompanied by photographs.
Although photography was not a completely new medium, it was during the
Great War that certain compositional techniques began to take shape.
Photographs took on a life of their own, being duplicated in their thousands,
with or without a caption, for use as postcards. The most popular images from
the Eastern Front included prisoners of war and people in occupied countries.
Indeed, the war initiated new ways of portraying defeated opponents: as an
undisciplined, filthy, and dishevelled mass, from which the photographer would
pick out 'types' that appeared especially foreign, strange, repulsive, even degenerate; or indeed exotic, since German and Austrian observers were fascinated by
the ethnic diversity of the Russian army. The Balkan peoples were viewed in
a similar manner. Ethnographic photographs depicting armed Albanian or
Macedonian 'natives' and their wives and daughters in unfamiliar folk costumes
became a popular souvenir. The head of an Austro-Hungarian research expedition to the Balkans, Arthur Haberlandt, collected many such photographs as
well as exhibits illustrating the everyday life and culture of the region. In 1917 the
Viennese could admire these exotic collections in the auditorium of Vienna
University.[28] In this instance the academic curiosity of the Austrian ethnographers took on a new meaning, becoming a tool of visual propaganda.

What attracted the greatest public interest, however, was another type of war
photography: the portrayal of battle scenes or the destructive effects of combat.
The rivalry between illustration and photography was not only technical but
also ideological. Either side in the conflict could benefit from its chosen means
of expression. Maria Bucur notes the characteristic use of illustrations in

[27] Jaroslav Hašek, *The Good Soldier Švejk*, translated by Cecil Parrott, Harmondsworth
1973, pp. 489–490.
[28] Holzer, *Die Andere Front*, p. 205.

Fig. 43 The demand for exotic 'types' sometimes had to be satisfied with rather modest means. The editors of the illustrated *Világháború Képes Krónikája* used late-nineteenth- and early-twentieth-century ethnographic postcards depicting Hasidic Jews in Hungary. They added captions to the postcards to suggest that the people shown were Jewish war refugees from Russia.

cultural and political journals in Romania, which was neutral until 1916. Most of the Romanian newspapers were Francophile and published photographs showing the destruction caused by German artillery fire on the Western Front. The photographs nearly always featured ruined monuments: churches and castles. This choice of authentic photographic evidence served to reinforce the charge of German barbarism. Interestingly, the desire for realism in showing the effects of war did not extend to its victims. In the Francophile Romanian press, corpses, battlefields, and trenches were presented by means of drawings rather than photographs. This was no accident. Ultimately, the aim was not to promote pacifism by depicting the horrors of war on photographic film, but to rally the Romanians to enter the war on the side of the Entente.[29] Images were

[29] Maria Bucur, 'Romania: War, Occupation, Liberation', in *European Culture in the Great War. The Arts, Entertainment and Propaganda, 1914–1918*, ed. Aviel Roshwald and Richard Stites, Cambridge 1999, pp. 243–266, here pp. 249–251.

THE HUNGER FOR INFORMATION   215

meant to encourage, not to deter, and all sides adhered to similar principles. As a rule, it was not permitted to publish photographs of one's own dead, hence the corpses of enemy soldiers were all the more willingly shown. Images of war damage on one's own territory depicted civilian installations but not military ones, and consequently the victims were also civilians, with a particular emphasis on women and children.

The war also found its way into cinemas. In Central and Eastern Europe and the Balkans the impact of the war on filmmaking was hard to assess unequivocally. Despite the devastation, the impoverishment of society, and the loss of artists sent to the front, cinematography flourished as never before. In some countries, such as Bulgaria, newsreels became the first indigenous film productions. But even in places where the film industry had prospered before the war, the almost complete severing of ties with Western Europe only enhanced domestic creativity. Feature film production greatly increased during the war in Russia (though heavy-handed censorship prevented the development of Russian war newsreels),[30] but access to Russian films ceased in the summer of 1915 when the success of the Gorlice Offensive and the continued progress of the German and Austro-Hungarian armies deprived the inhabitants of the empire's western provinces of natively produced films. German and Austro-Hungarian films began to dominate in Central and Eastern Europe and the Balkans.[31] Aside from feature films that tackled the subject of the war, cinemas embraced a completely new genre of documentary film: the newsreel. Initially, newsreels were exclusively made by private companies. At the end of 1916, however, with the centralization of production in Germany, cinemas began to show the first episodes of the *Deutsche Kriegswochenschau*, produced by the state-owned BUFA (Bild- und Filmamt), later renamed UFA (Universum Film AG). In Austria-Hungary the leading film production company was Sascha-Film, owned by the Czech aristocrat Alexander Kolowrat-Krakowský, which came under the control of the KPQ in 1917. The company's *Sascha-Kriegswochenbericht* (weekly war report) effectively competed with German productions, especially in neutral states and in countries allied with Austria-Hungary, such as Turkey. Newsreels were hugely popular. There was no need to make them mandatory, since cinema owners were only too eager to show them.

The year 1917 was a turning point in the wartime history of film, not just in terms of how production companies were organized but also in terms of film content. In the early war years newsreels focused on presenting the latest

---

[30] Melissa Kirschke Stockdale, *Mobilizing the Russian Nation. Patriotism and Citizenship in the First World War*, Cambridge 2016, pp. 47–48.
[31] Mark Cornwall, 'Das Ringen um die Moral des Hinterlandes', in *Die Habsburgermonarchie 1848–1918*, vol. 11, part 2. *Die Habsburgermonarchie und der Erste Weltkrieg*, ed. Helmut Rumpler and Anatol Schmied-Kowarzik, Vienna 2014, pp. 393–435, here pp. 418–422.

achievements of the armaments industry. This was partly due to the fascination with modernity and progress, but was also born of necessity. The work of cameramen at the front was extremely difficult, not least for technical reasons, since they had to cope with heavy and demanding film equipment and overcome problems with lighting. In addition, no commander wanted film-makers present and sometimes the more indefatigable ones were arrested for alleged espionage. What this meant was that film reels documented the moments before and after battles, the meals eaten by soldiers and, first and foremost, the modern weaponry that was to guarantee victory. At a certain point, however, the nature of newsreels changed. Not without significance were the critical and sometimes ironic reactions of audience members in uniform. They knew from experience that neither was their equipment as great nor was their enemy as weak as many had believed at the beginning of the war. The army command also wanted changes. Instead of a fascination with technology, it wanted filmmakers to emphasize the sacrifice and heroism of the soldiers and the competence of the commanders. The last big star of Austro-Hungarian newsreels was the young and photogenic Emperor Charles I, who from the death of his predecessor in November 1916 was ever present on cinema screens throughout the monarchy.

In 1914 the word and the image became instruments of state propaganda. Although the Balkans and Central and Eastern Europe were not at the epi-centre of propaganda production, they held an important position both as a subject-matter and as a place in which to disseminate information. It was precisely here, moreover, immediately behind the front lines, that information which was beyond state control, i.e. rumours and gossip, played an especially important role. The aim of governments was to control information flow and social mobilization. People were encouraged to do practically everything: hunt down spies, organize whip-rounds for freezing soldiers, collect secondary raw materials and scrap, purchase war bonds, care for the wounded, contribute to the Red Cross and Red Crescent, maintain public decency and personal morality, and, of course, volunteer for the army. To this end, tried and tested methods were used: press and poster campaigns. However, new tools were also used that turned out to be marketing sensations. One of the most interesting of these, though later forgotten, was the modern museum.

London's Imperial War Museum was officially founded in 1917, but did not open its doors to the public until 1920. The initial impetus came from collect-ors, who engaged in a somewhat more civilized form of war tourism than the one practised by Varsovians in 1915. Their sought-after items included news-papers, posters and notices, war-related brochures, weapons, and uniforms as well as maps, postcards, and photographs. In addition to private collectors, who had their own specialist magazines in Germany and Austria, state institu-tions got in on the act. Both in Vienna and in Berlin central libraries began to assemble international collections. One of the most complete and fascinating

Fig. 44 The fascination with war transcended the generational divide. The photograph shows children from the Bulgarian part of Thrace (1916). Courtesy of Mr Peyo Kolev, lostbulgaria.com.

collections devoted to that period is currently kept in the Staatsbibliothek in Berlin and each item bears a catalogue number that begins with the words 'Krieg 1914'. The new phenomenon attested to the demand for new types of information. A huge and insatiable market emerged that was interested in observing battlefield recreations in the most realistic terms (though not, of course, with audience participation). This need could not be satisfied by march-pasts of POWs or parades with captured munitions; war exhibitions did it much better, and the largest was opened at the Prater in Vienna in 1916.

During its first year a million people visited the Vienna exhibition. They saw not only the trophy-filled hall but also displays dedicated to war graves, medical assistance, the rapidly developing field of prosthetics, and gifts that the public had donated to the struggling army. Visitors were shown newsreels and a documentary film made by colleagues of Rudolph Pöch about anthropological research carried out on Russian prisoners of war. The highlight of the exhibition was a reconstructed section of the front, with visitors being able to enter a trench assembled in painstaking detail. Although the Viennese exhibition was notable for its size, its content was not revolutionary. In Vienna alone it had been preceded by at least fifty smaller exhibitions. Similar displays appeared in other cities of the monarchy. Hungary, which had declined to collaborate in the setting up of the Viennese *Kriegsausstellung*, presented its own exhibitions that emphasized Hungary's contribution to the joint war effort. An even bigger wave of new museums consumed the Reich. Displays appeared in almost every *Heimatmuseum*. Exhibition scripts prepared in Germany and Austria-Hungary were sent to occupied territories and to allied countries. German exhibitions were opened in Istanbul and Warsaw, for example. In places where conditions were unfavourable, such as in the capital of Montenegro, small displays of photographs, paintings, and war postcards were organized instead.

War exhibitions probably came closest to the ideal of presenting information that was both interesting and propagandist. The throngs of visitors provided the best evidence of the great public desire for news from the front. Vienna and dozens of other cities were the venues for a huge campaign in which newspaper readers, curious onlookers, war tourists, and cinemagoers participated. Later historians, cognizant of twentieth-century totalitarianism with its ubiquitous mass propaganda, tended to misinterpret this phenomenon. They confused action with reaction. Meanwhile, during the Great War no one ever felt burdened with a surfeit of intrusive information. In no way did the state have to impose its own version of wartime events. People wanted news and were ready to receive it in any form, even when it was processed by government propagandists. The civilian authorities, not to mention the military authorities, were late in adapting to the new situation. The demand for information came first, and it was this demand that forced the state to create a modern information policy.

7

Loyalties

Until recently, historians were agreed that European societies welcomed the outbreak of the Great War with near-ecstatic enthusiasm. In support of this view they could point to newspaper reports and to photographs of festive crowds thronging the streets of the belligerent states' capital cities. The consensus was also reinforced by politicians, who in their memoirs described August 1914 as a sequence of completely spontaneous patriotic manifestations that practically forced leaders to go on the offensive.

The Spirit of 1914

The streets of Paris, London, St Petersburg, and Berlin were indeed filled with joyous crowds cheering their leaders and denouncing their enemies, and as they did so, young men reported to recruiting stations. Serried ranks of students strode along Berlin's Unter den Linden, singing as they went. The participants and observers of those events had a sense that the whole nation was united in a common purpose:

> On that Saturday evening, when it became known that Serbia had rejected the Austrian note, and the Berlin population marched in front of the Austrian embassy singing the song 'Ich hatt' einen Kameraden' ['I Had a Comrade'], on that evening a population divided into classes and parties, a population divided by the striving for pleasure was suddenly welded together once again into a unit [. . .]. In this lies our rebirth through war.[1]

Enthusiasm also reigned in the Austrian capital. Here, too, unity and patriotic zeal were at the fore. In the words of Ilka Künigl-Ehrenburg:

> Never before had I seen Vienna as beautiful as in those great days. An intoxicating fervour burned throughout the city, overcoming everyone – young and old, rich and poor, tall and short, wise and foolish. No differences in rank or class could be discerned. We were one people that did not wish to be anything else or anything better. All the streets were festooned

---

[1] Oscar Schmitz, 'Die Wiedergeburt durch den Krieg', *Der Tag*, 9 August 1914. Cited in: Jeffrey Verhey, *The Spirit of 1914. Militarism, Myth, and Mobilization in Germany*, Cambridge 2004, p. 31.

with flags. Every evening throngs gathered before the imperial palace to give a rousing reception to the emperor. Archdukes in civilian attire mixed with the masses, yet they were recognized all the same and roundly cheered. [...] Foreigners [...], with tears in their eyes, shook each other by the hand. Everyone was eager to make a contribution. The money flowed, as did all sorts of other gifts. Old women from poorhouses would come with their last valuable possessions and a pair of filigree cups made of old Viennese porcelain. Exhilarated and surprised, we saw how rich we were, how rich in goodness and hearts of gold.[2]

Paradoxically, the same image of patriotic exaltation can be found in the memoirs of sceptics, the difference being that the cheering crowds filled them not with euphoria but with horror. One of the most famous was the Austrian writer Stefan Zweig, who would later become an icon of pacifism and anti-fascism. Zweig recalled the first weeks of the war as a period of increasing social isolation:

In the end [...] it became impossible to talk to anyone sensibly. Even the most peaceful and benevolent people seemed inebriated by the scent of blood. Friends I had known as radical individualists, or even spiritual anarchists, transformed from one day to the next into fanatical patriots, and then from patriots into insatiable annexationists. Every conversation would end with some idiotic phrase such as 'he who cannot hate cannot truly love' or with callous suspicion. Colleagues with whom I had not argued for years suddenly berated me that I was no longer Austrian, that I should emigrate to France or Belgium.[3]

Widespread euphoria and a few solitary outsiders baited by their former colleagues is an interpretation of the public response to the outbreak of the Great War that has many advantages. It seems to be confirmed not just by historical sources – there are hundreds of accounts similar to those presented above – but also by basic psychology. What is to be expected from a crowd if not a herd mentality and uncritical submission to the mood of the moment? Are civic courage and fidelity to one's own beliefs not the qualities of exceptional individuals, of true intellectuals? And yet, upon closer inspection, the attitudes of both the 'masses' and the elites become less unequivocal.

The 'spirit of 1914', as this outburst of collective enthusiasm was termed in the Reich, had more to do with wishful thinking on the part of governments and social elites than it did with hard facts. The noisy minority was conspicuous, of course, especially when it behaved as ostentatiously as the students in Berlin, but it would be a mistake to equate this with the feelings of the majority.

---

[2] Ilka Künigl-Ehrenburg, [Ilka von Michaelsburg] *Im belagerten Przemysl. Tagebuchblätter aus großer Zeit*, Leipzig 1915, pp. 42–44.

[3] Stefan Zweig, *Die Welt von Gestern. Erinnerungen eines Europäers*, Frankfurt am Main 1992, p. 275.

LOYALTIES

The crowds consisted of inquisitive people who wanted to get the latest news and participate in historic events. Let us start with a secondary but nonetheless important question: how typical was the behaviour of the inhabitants of large cities? In 1914, between Berlin (population 2 million) and the slightly smaller Moscow, there was just one city that had more than a million inhabitants. That city was Vienna, which was almost as populous as Berlin. Another regional metropolis, Budapest, was not even half that size and marginally bigger than Warsaw. Breslau, Łódź, and Odessa each had a population of around half a million. The remaining major cities of Central and Eastern Europe and the Balkans, such as Prague, Trieste, Lwów, and Bucharest, had at most 300,000 inhabitants. How was the declaration of war welcomed in those cities?

Two decades ago Jeffrey Verhey compared the reaction to the events of August 1914 in Berlin and in smaller towns in Germany. The scenes witnessed in the capital were not repeated anywhere else on a similar scale, and in sizeable cities such as Königsberg, Danzig, and Saarbrücken there were no large gatherings at all. In places where they did occur, they rarely took the form of patriotic demonstrations and were generally organized by students (hence the militant gatherings in small university towns like Jena or Heidelberg and their almost complete absence in the industrial centres of the Ruhr). What usually happened was that groups of bystanders would wait before newspaper offices for the latest news, and when they got it they would simply return home.[4] In Germany and Great Britain local military units would march out to loud applause, but the shouts and cheers were mostly from their friends and relatives. For its part, the press followed up every manifestation of approval, enthusiasm, or even benevolent interest, which it saw as proof of support for government policy. The situation in the Habsburg monarchy was no different. On 2 August the Austro-Hungarian newspapers reported that a torch-lit procession of 10,000 people had taken place in Budapest, culminating in an ovation in honour of the army and the Archduke Charles (the future emperor), who was visiting the city together with his wife. When the couple returned to Vienna, a group of enthusiastic students from the military academy unharnessed the horses from the couple's carriage and pulled it to the train station themselves, whereupon the Archduke and his wife continued their tour of the country.

Members of the intelligentsia were more likely than workers to volunteer for the army. Even Stefan Zweig appeared before a recruitment board in August, although in subsequent years he rarely mentioned this episode. In Bohemia and Moravia people cheered as local troops set off for the front. *Národní Politika* described the numerous ceremonies that took place, all of which followed the same format. On 3 August in Hradec Králové, for instance:

---

[4] Jeffrey Verhey, *The Spirit of 1914. Militarism, Myth, and Mobilization in Germany*, Cambridge 2004, pp. 35–36.

222 THE REAR

During a concert performed by the military orchestra, a local lawyer raised a shout in honour of the army. Many of those in attendance joined in, which prompted an ovation in honour of His Majesty the Emperor. Several times they sang the *Volkshymne* ['Gott erhalte . . .' / 'Zachovej nám Hospodine'] as well as *Kde domov můj* [the future Czech national anthem]. Throughout they shouted 'sláva!' and 'hoch!' in honour of His Majesty and the army. During the night, too, the inhabitants of Hradec Králové cheered the emperor and the army. The demonstrators arrived at the town hall and prefect's office where they sang the People's Anthem once again, accompanied by shouts of 'sláva' and 'hoch' in honour of His Majesty.[5]

The same events could be written about in different ways, especially in the multinational Habsburg monarchy, where the issue of loyalty was more complicated than in Paris, London, or Berlin. Franz Kafka witnessed the August demonstrations on the streets of Prague:

Patriotic parade. Speech by the mayor. Disappears, then reappears, and a shout in German: 'Long live our beloved monarch, hurrah!' I stand there with my malignant look. These parades are one of the most disgusting accompaniments of the war. Originated by Jewish businessmen who are German one day, Czech the next; admit this to themselves, it is true, but were never permitted to shout it out as loudly as they do now. Naturally they carry many others along with them. It was well organized. It is supposed to be repeated every evening, twice tomorrow and Sunday.[6]

Kafka's account shows that an eyewitness usually sees only a slice of reality, which he comments on in accordance with his knowledge, views, and mood. Indeed, it soon transpired that the cheering crowds in Prague posed something of a problem for the authorities: the processions and speeches were dominated by German, the portraits of Franz Joseph could not mask the shouts of 'Heil Kaiser Wilhelm!' and the route of the processions often led past several German institutions such as the Reich's consulate, the German Officers' Mess, and the editorial offices of German-language newspapers. It seemed that the German songs 'Die Wacht am Rhein' and 'Ich hatt' einen Kameraden' were sung with more gusto than the Habsburg 'Prinz-Eugen-Marsch', while their Czech counterpart, 'Hej Slované', became a symbol of treason once war had been declared against the Slavic states of Serbia and Russia. The local governor, Franz Prince of Thun and Hohenstein, had little choice: after a week of demonstrations he thanked 'the dear Czech- and German-speaking citizens of Prague' for their highly patriotic attitude and beseeched them to . . . stop gathering so as not to weaken the impression of unity that had hitherto been so

---

[5] 'Manifestace v Hradci Králové', *Národní Polityka*, 4 August 1914.
[6] Franz Kafka, *The Diaries of Franz Kafka 1914–1923*, translated by Martin Greenberg, with the cooperation of Hannah Arendt, ed. Max Brod, New York 1949, p. 78.

LOYALTIES

strong; privately, the governor feared that the Czechs and Germans would soon be at each other's throats.[7]

The Russian governor of the province of Livonia behaved in a similar, ostensibly bizarre manner. The problem was not the local Germans, whom it was hard to accuse of disloyalty. The ban on demonstrations stemmed from the fear that they were being used by local socialists to agitate against the war on the pretext of bidding farewell to soldiers heading off to the front.

The Russian partition was certainly one of the places where citizens did not necessarily identify with their own state. The proclamation of the Manifesto of 14 August 1914 by the Grand Duke Nikolai Nikolaevich triggered a wave of enthusiasm; it promised to unite the Poles under the rule of the Czar: 'Under this sceptre Poland shall be reborn, free in its religion, its language, and its self-government.' At that moment the socialist politician Tadeusz Hołówko and his wife were in the centre of Warsaw. It promised to be a beautiful day:

> My wife immediately bought a dozen gladioli as we approached the corner of al. Jerozolimskie and Nowy Świat. All of a sudden we heard the sound of a military band and some shouting. We started to walk a little faster. And it was then that we witnessed a scene that I shall never forget for the rest of my life. A Cossack regiment led by an orchestra was heading up Nowy Świat. It was surrounded by a crowd of enthusiastic Poles shouting 'Long live our army!,' 'Long live our defenders!' Impassioned ladies with burning eyes quickly bought flowers and ran in between the horses to hand them to the officers. Gentlemen emptied their cigarette cases and offered cigarettes to the Cossacks, who, sitting astride their horses, accepted this mark of admiration with a grateful smile.
>
> It was as if a dagger had been thrust into my heart. We stood with our backs against the wall of a house, wishing we could squeeze inside so as to get as far away as possible from that crowd. A mist descended over my eyes. My wife stood there completely pale, clutching the huge gladioli close to her bosom, as if wanting to hide herself from the terrible sight. The Cossack regiment passed by and the street returned to normal. We stood there, silently looking at each other.[8]

As a patriot and socialist, Hołówko was a member of a small minority for whom the obvious aim of the war was to defeat the oppressor of the Poles and of the workers, in other words, Czarism. From another perspective, that same Warsaw street was marked by restraint rather than enthusiasm in August 1914:

> I do not recall ever having witnessed such an atmosphere as on Krakowskie Przedmieście, between the Bristol Hotel and the Holy Cross

---

[7] Jan Galandauer, 'Kriegsbegeisterung in Prag', in *Magister noster. Sborník statí věnovaných in memoriam prof. PhDr. Janu Havránkovi, CSc.*, ed. Luboš Velek, William D. Goodsey Jr, and Michal Svatoš, Prague 2005, pp. 327–333.

[8] Cited in Leszek Moczulski, *Przerwane powstanie polskie 1914*, Warsaw 2010, p. 395 n.

224   THE REAR

Church, on 1 August, where a crowd had gathered for the day; a veritable throng of relatives and friends of army recruits, for whom one of the 'assembly points' was the courtyard of the university. Both pavements were full of people; a 'heartrending scene' – to use a phrase beloved of reporters – was being played out, and the mood of calm, even order, was not disturbed by the slightest excesses! And that is not all. Christian and Jewish families were literally fraternizing – in an atmosphere of shared misery. [...] Before the university itself, where the crowd was at its most dense, order was maintained by six mounted gendarmes, who enabled streetcars, carriages, and automobiles to pass along the middle of the street. I stood in the crowd and watched, rubbing my eyes. There was something inexplicably delicate about the way in which the gendarmes moved the crowd aside: with words or gestures ... they asked people to make way or to move back; they used persuasion; they did not hesitate to utter a cordial, paternalistically gracious expression; there was none of the chiding, beating, and ill-treatment we had come to expect. Slowly and carefully the gendarme would turn his horse to face the crowd that was pushing towards the street, and then, in a low voice, he would say: 'Move back, gentlemen, move back.'[9]

The descriptions of Prague and Warsaw are an accurate reflection of the mood in August 1914 in the multinational empires. As mobilization in Europe got under way, the predominant feeling was not so much war euphoria as uncertainty and fear for loved ones. This was even the case in the capitals of the great powers: London, Berlin, and Paris. Those citizens who could not always fully identify with their country had all the more reason to feel anxious. Was the potential victory of Austria-Hungary and Germany over Russia and Serbia, billed as a fight between the Germanic and Slavic worlds, an opportunity or a threat for the Slavic peoples living in the Habsburg and Hohenzollern monarchies? What could the non-Russian subjects of the Romanovs expect in the event of a Russian victory? This experience was shared by the Poles, who were divided among three warring empires, as well as by the Czechs, Lithuanians, Latvians, Estonians, Ukrainians, Transylvanian Romanians, Hungarian Serbs, Bosnians, Austrian Italians, Russian Germans, and finally the Jews. In the last weeks of the summer of 1914 the reaction of all these groups was strikingly similar. Even if they did not express particular enthusiasm, they displayed absolute loyalty. And their declared hope was that the war might improve their situation a little. In an editorial devoted to the Austro-Hungarian mobilization the Zionist weekly *Die Welt*, founded by Theodor Herzl, spoke on behalf of the monarchy's Jews, but its position was similar to that of other nationalities:

---

[9] Czesław Jankowski, *Z dnia na dzień. Warszawa 1914–1915 Wilno*, Wilno (Vilnius) 1923, p. 7.

The booming echoes of battle are upon us, and the poisoned language of the Jew-baiters, the professional anti-Semitic demagogues in the east and west of the country, must be silenced. What counts now is the husband, the armed citizen; now, in the line of fire, all are equal, likewise the Jews.[10]

If there was any regional specificity in the response to the outbreak of war in Central and Eastern Europe and the Balkans, it lay not so much in crowd behaviour as in the fact that each nationality declared its loyalty separately. Even at this early stage the ethnicization of the empires, which we discussed earlier, was noticeable. Individual ethnic groups adopted a cautious stance, even if the aim of some political movements was independence (a distant aim for the time being). Initially, it was only two vocal, albeit marginal, groups that displayed greater ambitions: the Russian pan-Slavists and the German pan-Germanists. The former hoped for the emergence of a Slavic monarchy under the leadership of the Czar that ideally would be uniformly Orthodox and, of course, Russian-speaking. Their activities were most intense during the first months of the war. For a brief period pan-Slavic slogans even found their way into the upper reaches of Russian politics. The occupation of Eastern Galicia, which in the Russian interpretation signified unification with the motherland, seemed to presage the triumph of pan-Slavism. However, in the spring of 1915 the still rather nebulous programme of the pan-Slavists began to fall apart, and instead of 'liberating' other Slavs from Habsburg and Ottoman bondage, the Russian political elites began to think about restoring the status quo.

Much more impressive was the political movement diametrically opposed to the pan-Slavists. Although the details were understood in different ways, the idea of German unity in its maximal variant encompassed practically all of Central and Eastern Europe. The key demand was the unification of Germans from the Reich with German-speaking Austrians. In 1914 this was a popular idea (though not so much with the country's elites),[11] especially in Cisleithania, and was advocated not just by nationalists but also by many liberal intellectuals. Robert Musil and Stefan Zweig also welcomed the outbreak of the war with satisfaction, seeing it as a necessary condition for the unification of the two branches of the Germanic world. With time, the enthusiasm of Austria's political leaders for anything more than an alliance diminished, though it never ceased to affect the political agenda, stoking fear among the non-Germans and causing concern among the imperial patriots.[12]

---

[10] 'Oesterreich-Ungarn unter Waffen', *Die Welt*, no. 31, 31 July 1914, p. 794.

[11] Jan Vermeiren, 'The "Rebirth of Greater Germany": The Austro-German Alliance and the Outbreak of War', in *Untold War. New Perspectives in First World War Studies*, ed. Heather Jones, Jennifer O'Brien, and Christoph Schmidt-Supprian, Leiden and Boston, MA 2008, pp. 215–228.

[12] See Richard W. Kapp, 'Divided Loyalties: The German Reich and Austria-Hungary in Austro-German Discussions of War Aims, 1914–1916', *Central European History*, 17, 2–3 (1984), pp. 120–139.

Were this aim to be realized, it would signal the end or at least the profound reconstruction of the Habsburg monarchy. It would also pose a serious threat to almost all the nationalities within it, since Germanic enclaves were scattered throughout the region. It was difficult to determine the borders of a united Germany in advance. If the borders were to include all or most of the areas densely populated by Germans, they would have to stretch a long way to the north and east. Suffice it to say that when, in November 1918, the provisional National Assembly of German Austria announced the creation of a new democratic state, its borders were to encompass not only the present territory of the Republic of Austria but also northern, western, and southern Bohemia, northern and southern Moravia, large parts of Austrian Silesia, and the capital of Bukovina (Chernivtsi), as well as other cities (including Brno, Olomouc, and Jihlava) inhabited by significant numbers of Germans. And yet these were not the postulates of the radical right, but of a broad spectrum of Austro-German politics, which was dominated by social democrats.

The prospects were even more dangerous for the Poles – the Kaiser's subjects – and for the inhabitants of the western borderlands of the Czarist empire. In Germany the outbreak of the war emboldened a relatively large group of supporters of territorial annexation. Their most ambitious plans even included the Baltic states – ideal settlement areas for future German farmers. The slightly more moderate annexationists demanded that a wide belt along the eastern borders of the Reich be incorporated into the empire and its Polish population resettled to the East. For propaganda reasons, the authorities tried to soften the annexationist propaganda somewhat. In the autumn of 1914 they banned the distribution of a memorandum authored by the leader of the Pan-German League, Heinrich Claas. However, there was no restriction on voicing such ideas at public meetings, which were then reported in the daily press.

The eruption of German chauvinism – as we have seen in the case of Prague – undoubtedly dampened the mood among the non-German subjects of Franz Joseph I and Wilhelm II. It is no wonder, then, that their reaction to the events of the summer of 1914 was decidedly reserved. Aleksander Majkowski, a writer and physician who played a prominent part in the cultural revival of the ethnically Slavic Kashubians of Pomerania, who would soon participate in the Romanian campaign before being posted to the Western Front, found himself in Sopot in early August 1914:

> [...] for the entire week that preceded Germany's declaration of war on Russia there was tremendous excitement in the air. Once the news of Austria's declaration of war on Serbia had spread, there was immediately an upsurge in patriotic German feeling, both artificial and genuine. Parades with singing, organized by youngsters in the spa gardens, took place on ul. Morska. The spa band deviated from its repertoire and played soldiers' songs interwoven with national anthems: *Ich bin ein Preuße!* [I am a Prussian!], *Deutschland über alles!*, etc. The same happened in the

LOYALTIES

cafés and restaurants. Only at Heese's did they occasionally play Polish folk melodies as well as Moniuszko and Chopin. Singularly patriotic was the Café Central, from which the singing and bellowing of drunken people could be heard, giving me no sleep . . .[13]

Majkowski's sceptical attitude obviously did not escape the attention of local patriots, because on the following day he was arrested on charges of espionage. His notes written in Polish were deemed particularly suspect by the authorities, and the situation was not resolved until the following day, when a state-appointed translator arrived to explain the misunderstanding.

Declarations of loyalty were the most common response to the outbreak of war and were soon verified in practice by the fact that mobilization proceeded smoothly. Governments also received support from non-dominant nationalities and from national and religious minorities. Even if excessive enthusiasm was the sole preserve of obliging journalists, there was no reason to fear that the subjects of the three emperors lacked patriotism – nothing pointed to a political crisis. On the contrary, relations that had been tense before the war now improved significantly, and this improvement lasted far beyond the euphoria of August that Hołówko and his wife had found so troubling. The scenes that played out in Warsaw in October 1914 astounded Cardinal Aleksander Kakowski, a man otherwise loyal to Russia:

The theatres, ballrooms, amusement halls, gambling dens, and brothels were filled with Russian officers. Polish patriots invited them into their houses, while aristocratic and bourgeois ladies, even the honourable ones, danced with the Russian officers at public and private balls; it was an unheard of situation, since prior to the war an officer in Russian uniform, even a Pole, would not have been allowed to cross the threshold of a Polish home. The friendliness shown by the intelligentsia and upper echelons of Polish society towards their Russian counterparts, the fraternization of the Polish people with 'our Slavic brothers' and 'our' army, the marriage of Polish girls to Russians, or even Cossacks, in Orthodox churches, [. . .] it was as if we had forgotten the hundred years or so of captivity and Russian's oppression of the Catholic religion and the Polish nation [. . .]. Once the Germans had been repelled from Warsaw, Polish enthusiasm for the Russian cause had no limits.[14]

Everyday Loyalties

The public reaction to the invasion of enemy troops revealed, paradoxically, that Poles in the Russian partition were law-abiding. This was particularly

---

[13] Aleksander Majkowski, *Pamiętnik z wojny europejskiej roku 1914*, ed. Tadeusz Linkner, Wejherowo and Pelplin 2000, p. 60.
[14] Cardinal Aleksander Kakowski, *Z niewoli do niepodległości. Pamiętniki*, ed. Tadeusz Krawczak and Ryszard Świętek, Cracow 2000, p. 123.

228   THE REAR

troubling for the Polish Legionnaires under the command of Józef Piłsudski. In the summer of 1914 they entered the Congress Kingdom in the hope that their presence would trigger a nationwide uprising against Russia. Instead, in countless ways, Polish peasants provided evidence of their loyalty towards ... Russia. They referred to the Russian army as 'our army' and avoided the Legionnaires as best they could. In August a rumour spread throughout the southern part of the Kingdom that the 'Falcons' (members of the Sokół youth movement) had launched another uprising and were coercing the peasants to join them. Anxieties were assuaged by the appearance of regular units of the Austro-Hungarian army, who were slightly more trusted than the Legionnaires but just as unpopular. However, the fear that the 'insurgents' could bring misfortune upon the peasants did not quickly dissipate. In the second half of September Sławoj Felicjan Składkowski witnessed how energetically a peasant woman in the village of Grotniki Małe chased some Legionnaires out of her cottage. They had wanted to set up emplacements inside, and their eviction was accompanied by yelling: 'For goodness sake, what are you doing!? You want to shoot from my cottage? Go to the forest if you want to have an uprising. When you've gone, our lot will come and burn my place down' or 'It's thanks to those "Falcons" that my cottage will go up in smoke.'[15] Many inhabitants of the Kingdom had to be forced to adopt a patriotic attitude. After they had occupied Kielce, the Polish Legions ordered all Russian signs to be removed. The shopkeepers complied, but made sure that the changes were easily reversible – just in case. When the Austro-Hungarian troops withdrew from the Kingdom in the autumn, the Russian signs were immediately visible again. 'The rain has washed away the lime,' the locals explained. In the countryside the Legions, unfairly perceived as the military arm of large landowners, were suspected of wanting to reintroduce serfdom. The mood was dangerously reminiscent of the Galician Slaughter of 1846, when Polish peasants murdered hundreds of Polish landlords. A Legionnaire recruitment officer reported in the spring of 1916 that peasants in the Sandomierz region believed that 'all their misery is due to the intelligentsia, the clergy, and the landowners, who want to sell them to the Austrians and restore serfdom'.[16] They saw Russia as their salvation. 'Long live Czar Nicholas' was scrawled onto Austrian posters by invisible hands. Father Rokoszny noted even more astonishing manifestations of loyalty to the Czar. Areas through which armies frequently marched in the first months of the war were also beset by banditry. To counter it, local communities began to organize

[15] Sławoj Felicjan Składkowski, *Moja służba w Brygadzie. Pamiętnik polowy*, Warsaw 1990, p. 25.
[16] Cited in Marek Przeniosło, 'Postawy chłopów Królestwa Polskiego wobec okupanta niemieckiego i austriackiego (1914–1918)', in *Lata Wielkiej Wojny. Dojrzewanie do niepodległości 1914–1918*, ed. Daniel Grinberg, Jan Snopko, and Grzegorz Zachiewicz, Białystok 2007, pp. 198–214, here p. 200.

LOYALTIES 229

themselves, encouraged by the Austro-Hungarian military authorities. But not all communities did so.

When peasants, citizens, and priests were to meet in the parish to discuss public order and how to defend against banditry, the peasants from Świniary said: 'We will not go. Let he who is afraid defend himself. We need no defence. Our ruler has enough troops. Let him gather them. Then he'll protect us and kick out the Austrians too.'[17]

For Legionnaire officers the attitude of Polish peasants was such a great disappointment that they sometimes concluded that the Kingdom's inhabitants were completely degenerate. One of their reports about the Piotrków province spoke of the linguistic and 'moral' Russification of the local population. The degradation of language was one example of this. 'The peasant has ceased to speak in his own dialect and now uses some sort of macaronic-Muscovite jargon. Peasants apparently asked priests to celebrate a mass for the victory of the Russian troops. They treated the billeting of Russian soldiers in their cottages as an honour and allegedly gave the soldiers their wives and daughters for the night.'[18] Although this dramatic image might say more about the author's state of mind it does about the actual behaviour of peasants, there was certainly a grain of truth to it. The conservatism of the countryside meant that people believed in a good czar, just as previously in Galicia they had believed in a righteous emperor.

The Polish lands certainly were no exception when it came to the attachment of non-dominant nationalities to the legitimate authorities. In Serbia the atrocities committed by the Austro-Hungarian army forced people to become loyal to the Serbian government. Lithuanian- and Polish-speaking Masurians from East Prussia gave proof of their loyalty to their German homeland. Eugeniusz Romer, a Lithuanian landowner and Russian subject, was taken by their attitude:

> The Prussian families in areas occupied by the Russian army, who are being removed to Russia *en masse*, also make a dreadful impression; due to espionage and the hostile attitude of those people, the military authorities do not allow them to remain in the same places as the Russian army [. . .]. There are no adult men among them or even young men – only women, children, and the elderly; all those cold and hungry people are heading for Šiauliai (Szawle); children are dying along the way. There is great poverty and misery, but also great arrogance, for instead of being grateful for the food and assistance given to them by our people, they continue to threaten us. They say that when the Kaiser comes he will make

[17] Józef Rokoszny, *Diariusz Wielkiej Wojny*, ed. Wiesław Caban and Marek Przeniosło, Kielce 1998, vol. 2, p. 85.

[18] Cited in Jerzy Z. Pająk (ed.), *Raporty i korespondencja oficerów werbunkowych Departamentu Wojskowego Naczelnego Komitetu Narodowego 1915–1916. Ziemia Kielecka*, Kielce 2007, p. 173.

230   THE REAR

our situation even worse and drive us out on foot. The attachment of these predominantly Lithuanian people to the Prussian government is indeed strange. Everything they possessed has been taken from them on account of the war and they have been denied the right to flee to safer places or to receive care.[19]

The loyalty of the civilian population was manifested in one more, particularly abhorrent way. In many places spontaneous or organized demonstrations did not express support for the authorities so much as hatred for fellow subjects of a different nationality, religion, or social class. In Zagreb and several other Croatian cities the crowds that gathered on the streets chanted 'dole Srbija!' ('Down with Serbia!'). Similar scenes were witnessed in Sarajevo. Both in Croatia and in Bosnia, shops belonging to Serbian citizens of the Habsburg monarchy were looted. Many of the demonstrators were drunken conscripts who, a few days later, would take part in the unsuccessful invasion of Serbia. In certain units of General Potiorek's army half of the soldiers were Croats and a quarter Austrian Serbs.[20] For the Habsburg monarchy's Serbian subjects, soldiers were remembered in the worst possible terms: not only as inebriated conscripts but also as the willing enforcers of martial law.

The spy craze, which taught that every Serbian man and woman should be seen as a potential traitor (women, too, were blamed and hanged for 'shots in the back'), soon spread throughout the local Bosnian and Croat population. But manifestations of loyalty were not always associated with ethnic conflict. Social groups could just as easily be seen as enemies and traitors. This was the case in those parts of the Kingdom of Poland where Poles were in the majority. Polish peasants denounced Polish priests and landowners to the Russian authorities on the grounds that they supported Austria-Hungary. Civilians – the inhabitants of towns and villages – almost always played an active role in the pogroms organized by the Russian army. In this instance the boundary between active support for government policy and common thuggery became completely blurred. In the spring of 1915 the wave of violence against fellow citizens spread from areas close to the front to Moscow and Petrograd. As a reaction to the Gorlice disaster, numerous pogroms broke out. These initially targeted Austro-Hungarian and German citizens living in Russia, but later also completely random people with German-sounding names. During the biggest pogrom on 8–9 June 1915, the crowd in Moscow destroyed several hundred shops and apartments and over 700 people were beaten up.[21] A hostile

---

[19] Eugeniusz Romer, *Dziennik 1914–1918*, vol. 1, Warsaw 1995, p. 79.
[20] Andrej Mitrovic, *Serbia's Great War 1914–1918*, London 2007, p. 67.
[21] S. V. Tiutiutkin, 'Россия: от Великой войны – к Великой революции [Rossiia: ot Velikoi voiny – k Velikoi revoliutsii]', in *Война и общество в XX веке*, vol. I. *Война и общество накануне и в период Первой мировой войны* [*Voina i obshchestvo v XX veke*, vol. 1. *Voina i obshchestvo nakanune i v period Pervoi mirovoi voiny*], ed. B. A. Zolotarev and L. V. Pozdeeva, Moscow 2008, pp. 120–160, here. pp. 130–131. See

LOYALTIES

atmosphere consumed the Central Powers, too. Repression on a smaller scale was directed at a group of Russian subjects – Poles – who were working as seasonal labourers in the Reich when war broke out. The internees were transported by train through Berlin's Silesian Station (now the Ostbahnhof), i.e. along the main line still used by commuter trains today. One witness of that journey recalled how 'the train, carrying hundreds of people in modest clothes, with all their junk, was passing through Alexanderplatz when the Berliners – among them workers – spat at the Poles and threw whatever they could find at them'.[22]

Loyalty to the state thus manifested itself in various ways and affected all social strata. Enthusiasm for the war, however, was common neither in Central and Eastern Europe and the Balkans nor in Western Europe. It was usually the elites rather than ordinary people who succumbed to euphoria. Some time later members of those very same elites began to oppose the war just as vehemently. Stefan Zweig was not an isolated case. The poems, articles, and paintings from the early months of the Great War remind us that the sense of disillusionment was delayed. It usually arrived when the loyalty of the masses had also begun to crumble.

Repression

The phenomenon of repression is one of the least intelligible and most fascinating aspects of the history of the Great War. For there is much to suggest that the combatant states were unaware of the high level of public support they enjoyed, and the reasons for this are unclear. Instead of trying to consolidate support and enhance their popularity they pursued policies that alienated everyone – from national and religious minorities to dominant national groups. At this juncture it seems appropriate to return to the recollections of Aleksander Majkowski. His arrest for the sole reason that he did not shout patriotic slogans and kept a diary in Polish is a typical example of the mindlessness of the authorities combined with the collective hysteria of a mobilized society. If we broaden the perspective from this individual case to society at large, the same phenomena can be observed. Majkowski himself mentioned the preventive arrest of Poles who were German subjects and the closure of Polish newspapers. Soon those newspapers were permitted to

---

Victor Dönninghaus, 'Der Frust einer ganzen Metropole entlädt sich – die antideutschen Pogrome in Moskau im Mai 1915. Täter – Opfer – Zuschauer', *Documenta Pragensia XXXV. Nezměrné ztráty a jejich zvládání. Obyvatelstvo evropských velkoměst a I. světová válka*, ed. Olga Fejtová, Václav Ledvinka, Martina Maříková, and Jiří Pešek, Prague 2016, pp. 235–248.

[22] Unpublished memoirs of Georg Kassler, cited in Dieter Glatzer and Ruth Glatzer (eds.), *Berliner Leben 1914–1918. Eine historische Reportage aus Erinnerungen und Berichten*, Berlin 1983, p. 56.

232   THE REAR

publish again, but only in German. The unfortunate Majkowski was also advised that, in future, his diary entries should be in German only.

Repressive measures against minorities were generally unjustified, and their effect was counterproductive. Instead of consolidating power and tightening control over society, they undermined trust in the state. Similar mechanisms were at work in the Habsburg monarchy, even in areas never under threat of Russian occupation. The worst situations were to be found in Bohemia and Moravia, on the border with Serbia, and in Eastern Galicia. In the autumn of 1914, when the first wave of patriotic demonstrations in Czech towns and cities had subsided, and the first transports of wounded had begun to arrive, with distressing stories to tell, the mood among those bidding farewell to departing troops progressively worsened. Many pointedly waved white handkerchiefs, while recruits would sometimes head off to the train station wearing black armbands. In Beroun, in central Bohemia, a group of soldiers marched under a banner that read: 'Česká krev' (Czech blood). Despite the best efforts of the officers, this 'funeral' procession managed to get all the way to the station.[23] There were more and more such cases. Although they did not visibly affect the army's behaviour on the battlefield, they undoubtedly furnished the German nationalists with arguments, and it was precisely the nationalists who did most to engender the stereotype of the disloyal Czechs. Having analysed the polemics in the press, the Czech historian Ivan Šedivý argues that Austro-Hungarian policy towards the Czechs began to lose touch with reality. The imagined betrayal of the Czech regiments combined with their glaring lack of enthusiasm for the war fostered a comfortable illusion that validated the beliefs of German chauvinists. The tragedy of the situation lay in the fact that real political decisions were made on the basis of that illusion.[24]

The alleged betrayal by Czech (and not only Czech) society became a bone of contention in the dispute between the civilian and military authorities that was to engulf the entire Habsburg monarchy. Because in terms of domestic policy the monarchy comprised two separate states, the dynamics of this phenomenon can be analysed by comparing the policies of Cisleithania and Transleithania. In the former, the demand of the military authorities for the introduction of a state of emergency appeared as early as in the autumn of 1914. Once again, events in the Czech lands were a powerful argument in favour of this. In November and December three Czech civilians suspected of distributing pro-Russian leaflets were hanged in Moravian Ostrava. The story reverberated widely, of course, particularly in the German-language press. Even more shocking was the arrest of three leading Czech

---

[23] Zdeněk Procházka, Ján Lipták, Vladislav Rybecký, Václav Čada, Miroslav Nytra, and Stanislav Mistr (eds.), *Vojenské dějiny Československa*, vol. 2. *1526–1918*, Prague, 1986, p. 496.

[24] Ivan Šedivý, *Češi, české země a velká válka 1914–1918*, Prague 2001, p. 166.

LOYALTIES

politicians – Václav Klofáč in September 1914 and Karel Kramář and Alois Rašín in the spring of the following year. In all probability only one of them – Kramář, an incorrigible Russophile – was actually guilty as charged, i.e. of treason. In any case, although he was sentenced to death a year later, Kramář avoided execution thanks to an amnesty announced by Franz Joseph's successor, the Emperor Charles. Even if most of the accusations of treason were shown to be groundless, each subsequent 'affair' led to a tightening of policy vis-à-vis the Czech lands. Civic rights throughout Cisleithania were gradually curtailed. A state of emergency was finally introduced in the spring of 1915. Additionally, in Bohemia and Moravia, decisions were taken to undermine the position of the Czechs within the state, symbolized by changes to the official name of the state and its emblem. Instead of reference to the lands and kingdoms represented in the Imperial Council, the name 'Austria' was adopted. The new emblem was devoid of any connotations with the Kingdom of Bohemia. In 1915 the Czech language was banned from offices and theatres and even some school libraries in Czech communities were closed. Austria-Hungary worked hard to create enemies in places where there had previously been none.[25]

Repression on a much larger scale occurred in Eastern Galicia. Military violence against civilians was only one aspect of the problem, although it grew to such huge proportions that it ceased to attract the attention of outside observers. Friedrich von Friedeburg, a Bavarian who fought alongside his Austro-Hungarian allies in the Carpathian Mountains, mentions it only in passing when he describes how several villages were evacuated: 'In Komarniki in the Stryj valley they hanged a priest and a precentor who had been sending signals to the Russians from the tower of the church. Even being in possession of Russian roubles was enough to raise suspicion.'[26] The violence appears completely normalized in von Friedeburg's description, and that is indeed how it was. Many such tragic stories concealed more than outsiders were able to perceive. Very often ethnic conflicts or even straightforward neighbourly quarrels were drastically resolved by an ad hoc court martial or just a soldier with a gun. This mechanism was well described by Jaroslav Hašek:

> Behind the school building in the garden was a huge funnel-shaped crater caused by the explosion of a shell of heavy calibre. In the corner of the garden stood a very large pear-tree and on one of the branches hung a piece of cut rope. Not long ago the local Greek Catholic vicar had been hanged on it as a result of a denunciation by the headmaster of the local Polish school, who accused him of being a member of the group of Old Russians and of having during the Russian occupation celebrated a mass

[25] Ibid., pp. 164–213. See also Pieter M. Judson, *The Habsburg Empire. A New History*, Cambridge 2016, pp. 391–3 93.

[26] Friedrich von Friedeburg, *Karpathen- und Dniester-Schlacht 1915*, Oldenburg and Berlin 1924, p. 56.

234 THE REAR

in the church for the victory of the armies of the Russian Orthodox Tsar. It was in fact not true, because the accused had not been there at the time but had been undergoing a cure for his gallstones at a small spa in Bochnia Zamurowana, which was untouched by the war.[27]

Indeed, Polish–Ukrainian–Jewish conflicts in Eastern Galicia became so intertwined with the military's fixation on spying that it was often difficult to separate the two. The army used the services of self-styled informants, who had no qualms whatsoever about accusing their neighbours of collaborating with the enemy. Those arrested were held and transported in makeshift conditions. The curious onlookers they passed on the way were generally hostile to these 'traitors to the fatherland' and were quick to let them know about it. One of the most tragic incidents involving alleged Russophiles took place in September 1914 in the besieged town of Przemyśl. Helena Jabłońska née Seifert gave a second-hand account of it in her diary:

> At around 5.00 p.m. a transport of Russophiles was rushed off to the station: forty-six people, including seven women from the semi-intelligentsia. [...] One young woman pulled out a revolver and shot a dragoon. They were all immediately attacked – with sabres, axes, sticks, and fists. Next came a mob carrying tree logs. They crushed the Russophiles so badly that bits of their brains bespattered the passers-by, and their blood splashed onto the walls and onto the people watching. All that was left were chunks of steaming and twitching flesh.[28]

Although the macabre nature of this scene makes it hard to believe that this was the exact course of events, in all likelihood the reality was not far removed from Jabłońska's story.[29] The Supreme Ukrainian Council, which comprised pro-Austrian politicians and which acted as patron to the Ukrainian Sich Riflemen, referred to the same event in a memorandum addressed to the commanders of the armed forces. In this document the theatre of cruelty was replaced with dry facts. According to this account, forty-five people from the village of Volytsia, among them a daughter of a Greek Catholic priest, were arrested on a charge of 'Russophilia'. As they were led through the streets of Przemyśl, they were attacked by a crowd of locals. The police did not intervene. At a certain point a nearby unit of Royal Hungarian Hussars entered the fray. They attacked the villagers on ul. Bociana and cut them to pieces with

---

[27] Jaroslav Hašek, *The Good Soldier Švejk*, translated by Cecil Parrott, Harmondsworth 1973, p. 727.

[28] Helena z Seifertów Jabłońska, *Dziennik z oblężonego Przemyśla 1914–1915*, ed. Hanna Imbs, Przemyśl 1994, p. 43.

[29] Jabłońska's thrilling story is strikingly close to the actual events as reconstructed on the basis of archival documents in Maciej Dalecki, 'Samosąd na moskalofilach w Przemyślu podczas pierwszej wojny światowej', *Rocznik Historyczno-Archiwalny* VII–VIII (1994), pp. 151–156.

LOYALTIES 235

their sabres. Only three people survived; the priest's daughter was not among them.[30]

Ukrainian activists in Austria believed that it was precisely their own national group that most often fell victim to unjustified accusations by Poles and Jews. The claim was not without foundation, although the number of victims mentioned in political pamphlets and parliamentary debates was regularly overstated. Local authorities, including the police in Eastern Galicia, were mostly in the hands of Poles, and the governor of Galicia himself, Witold Korytowski, did not hide his antipathy towards the Ukrainian national movement. Even before the war it was opposed by the so-called Podolacy (Podolians, i.e. conservatives from Eastern Galicia) and the right-wing National Democrats. Cooperation with the army presented an opportunity to resolve the conflict quickly and ruthlessly. Hence, among those accused of treason there was no shortage of Ukrainian anti-Russian activists, whose only sin was their dislike of the Polish authorities. Indeed, a Greek Catholic priest was a typical victim.

However, the victims were not only Ukrainians and the informers, onlookers, and perpetrators were not only Poles. In areas that temporarily came under Russian occupation, pogroms of Jews were commonplace. Russian soldiers were the main driving force, but Jews were also persecuted by Ukrainian and Polish peasants. As a result, after the return of the Austro-Hungarian troops, large numbers of Ukrainians were denounced by Jews. Ukrainian political activists argued that this was nothing more than an attempt to get rid of commercial rivals. Jews also took revenge on the Poles, accusing them of cooperation with the Russians. These charges were not without foundation. National Democrats and Podolians in Lwów did indeed cooperate with the Russian authorities, who in return treated Polish cultural institutions relatively better than Jewish and Ukrainian ones. It did not escape the attention of the Austro-Hungarian authorities that the Czarist army, as it retreated eastwards, took Jewish and Ukrainian activists as hostages while generally leaving the Poles alone.[31]

The Austro-Hungarian military commanders were helpless in the face of conflicting reports and mutual accusations. In many cases they simply had insufficient knowledge about Central and Eastern Europe. This was the conclusion often reached by locals who worked with their colleagues from Vienna and Berlin on a daily basis. In the autumn of 1914 Józef Piłsudski was disgusted

---

[30] Report from the Präsidium des Allgemeinen Ukrainischen Nationalrates to the k.u.k. AOK, 'Denkschrift über die Verhaftungen und Hinrichtungen zahlreicher österreichischer Ukrainer auf Grund bewußt falscher Informationen, Wien, 18. VI. 1915', in *Ereignisse in der Ukraine 1914–1922, deren Bedeutung und historische Hintergründe*, ed. Theophil Hornykiewicz, vol. 1, Philadelphia 1966, pp. 26–39, here p. 30.

[31] Christoph Mick, *Kriegserfahrungen in einer multiethnischen Stadt: Lemberg 1914–1917*, Wiesbaden 2010, p. 129.

by the ignorance of the Austrian officers, who were convinced that the areas just across Galicia's northern border were inhabited by Orthodox Russians.[32] The eastern borders of the Habsburg monarchy were no less a mystery for them. The fear and anxiety that the army felt towards civilians was mentioned earlier. This state of mind was further exacerbated by the inhabitants of Eastern Galicia informing on each another constantly. Unable to determine who was right, the army mainly concerned itself with ensuring that every suspect was detained. If there was no time or possibility to transport suspects away from the front, executions were carried out on the spot. Ultimately, the involvement of the Austro-Hungarian army in the ethnic conflicts in Eastern Galicia had catastrophic consequences for all concerned. Already by the autumn of 1914 the army had begun to take control in Galicia. Polish civil servants lost control over the province. Ad hoc military courts made extensive use of death sentences against all nationalities. Suspicion was also cast upon refugees, mainly Jews and Ukrainians. Austro-Hungarian intelligence believed that this group contained a huge number of Russian spies.[33] In the end, the emperor himself had to intervene, and not for the first or last time. In September 1914 he declared: 'I do not wish loyal elements to be pushed in a dangerous direction for the state on account of unjustified arrests.'[34]

The internal policy of the Hungarian part of the monarchy showed that repression was not necessary to ensure that subjects remained loyal. In the first months of the war the mood was as belligerent as in other regions of the country. Even in July there were so many preventive arrests of persons suspected of disloyalty, mainly Serbs and Ukrainians, that the camps and prisons ran out of space and some of the detainees had to be rapidly freed. At the beginning of September a tragic incident took place in the town of Sombor (Zombor) in Vojvodina. A protesting crowd of civilians and army recruits demanded the removal of signs written in Cyrillic script. One of the Serbian shopkeepers refused to comply and took refuge in his home from the advancing throng. Surrounded, he fired a few shots at his attackers before being arrested by the civilian authorities. The army demanded the release of the shopkeeper and threatened to imprison the public prosecutor and the head of police. When news of this reached the Hungarian Prime Minister, István Tisza, he angrily protested against the army's interference in the internal affairs of Hungary. Although his intervention did not save the life of the Serbian shopkeeper, it hardened the determination of the Hungarian authorities to maintain their independence. For the remainder of the war no military government or ad hoc courts were introduced in Transleithania in places not

---

[32] Józef Piłsudski, *Moje pierwsze boje*, Łódź 1988, p. 46.

[33] Max Ronge, *Kriegs- und Industriespionage. Zwölf Jahre Kundschaftsdienst*, Vienna 1930, p. 91.

[34] Cited in Ronge, *Kriegs- und Industriespionage*, p. 82.

LOYALTIES 237

adjacent to the front. Moreover, this decision appeared to have no negative consequences.

The policy of the Russian authorities recalled that of the Austrians rather than the Hungarians. Distrust of one's own subjects, especially Jews, was the rule. It was fuelled by the endemic anti-Semitism of Russian officers and, as in Eastern Galicia, by ethnic conflicts. Economic interests also played a major role. In the Kingdom of Poland the National Democrats continued their pre-war policy of boycotting Jewish shops. Some shopkeepers used the army to get rid of their Jewish competitors, and did so successfully. Russian warnings to the civilian population, which threatened severe penalties for the poisoning of wells, destruction of telephone lines, or spreading of defeatism, were often formulated in such a way as to seem exclusively directed at the Jews. The impression of anti-Semitic persecution was heightened by the practice of expelling Jews from areas close to the front. In May 1915 around 15,000 Jews were forcibly evacuated from the Kielce and Radom provinces to Lublin. As they fled, the Jews were attacked by peasants and Cossacks. The repression was justified on the grounds that the Jews supported the Austrians and Germans. In October 1914 the commander of the Russian 2nd Army put a price on the head of the rabbi of Tomaszów Mazowiecki, whom he accused of passing information to the Germans about the vulnerabilities in the Russian defences. In March 1915 Jews were even forbidden to settle around the Gulf of Finland on the grounds that their presence would endanger the capital of the empire. Jews were apparently a threat not just to the country's defences but also to its other inhabitants, and were accused of collaborating with the enemy during the brief Austro-Hungarian occupation of part of the Kingdom of Poland. When the commander-in-chief, the Grand Duke Nikolai Nikolaevich, issued an order to remove all Jews from the vicinity of the front and to take rabbis as hostages, he justified it by invoking the harm that Jews had done to Christians: they had frequently denounced the Czar's most faithful subjects to the Austrians. Did the behaviour of the empire's Jewish population justify the repression, at least in part? Those who witnessed the actions of the Russian authorities asked themselves and their Jewish acquaintances this very question. When interrogated, one Jew from the Congress Kingdom responded with the following anecdote:

> [...] and what about you people, whose side are you on? The Jew replied: we have a catarrh. What do you mean?, asked the priest, so the Jew explained. There's a story we like to tell about a lion. One day a horse came up to the lion, and the lion asked him: tell me, does my breath smell? The horse replied that the lion's breath did not smell, so the lion ate him. On the second day a donkey came up to the lion, and the lion asked him the same question. The donkey replied that the lion's breath was beauti-fully fragrant, so the lion ate him too. On the third day an ox came up to the lion. Once again the lion asked about his breath. The ox replied: my

238 THE REAR

dear lion, I cannot smell a thing for I have a catarrh, and the ox went quietly off home. So what I say to you is this: when the weather is so inclement, everyone should have a catarrh.[35]

One drop in this ocean of repression and harassment was the fate of foreign subjects who, at the start of the conflict, remained in enemy territory for a longer or shorter period of time. The Polish seasonal labourers transported through Berlin were mentioned earlier. A fairly large group of tourists and entrepreneurs was also interned. Their situation was unenviable. Because German banks severed ties with Russian banks, they could neither rely on their own savings nor hope to obtain credit. They tried to get permission to return home, stood in queues at station ticket offices, and waited for a decision from the authorities. The latter, however, were chaotic. For a period in the autumn of 1914 a system of dual power operated in the Reich at the local level. Civilian authorities still functioned, but military government was already in place. As a result, health spa visitors who were Russian subjects first received permission to travel to Berlin, from where they could continue their journey through Sweden and Finland to Petrograd before finally returning to the Kingdom of Poland. On the way, however, the first large group of tourists was detained in Sassnitz on the island of Rügen. Negotiations with the military headquarters in Stettin (Szczecin) lasted a long time, and it was not until December that the tourists were allowed to return home. Men of fighting age remained in internment camps in the Reich, however.[36] The travails of Russian citizens in the Reich were viewed in different ways. In the Russian press they became a theme of propaganda – shocking reports appeared under the heading of 'German depravity'.[37] In the summer of 1914 the actions of the German authorities might well have seemed depraved, particularly to the relatives of the unlucky tourists. Father Rokoszny was one of the people concerned about their fate:

> Father Ekiert came from the mountains to visit and told us of the news he had read in the Warsaw press. Apparently, the Prussians had put the people expelled from the health spas onto a boat, the men separated from the women. One of the ladies suffered a heart attack. Her companions demanded medical assistance, but the crew refused to open the door. The woman eventually died and the passengers had to remain with her for six hours. I am terrified by the thought that this woman, God forbid, was my mother. She cannot bear journeys by sea. What inexplicable beastliness and unheard of brutality! What is the purpose of such abuse? Men can be so wicked![38]

---

[35] Rokoszny, *Diariusz Wielkiej Wojny*, vol. 1, p. 146.
[36] Karol Rose, *Wspomnienia berlińskie*, Warsaw 1932, pp. 56–58.
[37] See Zinaida Gippius, *Dzienniki petersburskie (1914–1919). Dziennik warszawski (1920– 1921)*, ed. Henryk Chłystowski, Warsaw 2010, p. 31.
[38] Rokoszny, *Diariusz Wielkiej Wojny*, vol. 1, p. 40.

LOYALTIES

Polish newspapers associated with the National Democrats reacted somewhat differently. Since many of the tourists from the Kingdom were Jews, articles referred ironically to 'Russians' from Grzybów and Nalewki (Warsaw districts with a high percentage of Jews), to the 'alleged friends of the Serbs', and to 'bathers of the Mosaic faith'.[39]

It should be remembered, however, that the chicanery was directed at foreign citizens who posed a potential threat. This set Germany's policy apart from that of the other two empires – not because Berlin was more trusting of its own minorities, but simply because they were less numerous. When Austria-Hungary and Russia categorized their citizens according to the criterion of trustworthiness, the suspect groups always constituted a large proportion of the population of both monarchies. Some of these groups were stigmatized on the grounds that betrayal was expected of them. The notion of betrayal itself was understood in very broad terms. When the Russian army occupied Eastern Galicia, it distributed an information brochure among its officers about the political situation in the province. Some local politicians were seen as being well-disposed towards Russia, and it was recommended that those politicians should be invited to work with the Russian authorities after the capture of Galicia. When the brochure fell into the hands of Austro-Hungarian military intelligence, it was considered to constitute sufficient proof of treason perpetrated by the persons mentioned therein. The politicians concerned were deemed to have been 'compromised'. At best they would face trial after the return of the Austrians to Lwów. Even if it had not been their original intention, they now had no choice but to indeed commit treason and flee the country together with the retreating Russians. In doing so they confirmed *ex post* that the charges brought against them had been justified. The subsequent findings of historians add a tragicomic aspect to the whole affair, since the ill-fated brochure was virtually unknown to the Russian army. It was hardly distributed at all and the officers who did receive it had neither the time nor the inclination to read what was essentially a travel guide.[40] As can be seen, the brochure caused much more of a stir in Austria-Hungary. Its career was symptomatic not only of Austro-Hungarian public opinion, which was obsessed with espionage, but also of the professionals employed by Austro-Hungarian counterintelligence. The head of the intelligence service, Max Ronge, used equally disarming logic in relation to Greek Catholic priests in Eastern Galicia:

> We faced an outbreak of hatred that even the greatest pessimists could not have expected. Harsh measures were essential, and just as in Bosnia and Herzegovina we had to take hostages: the heads of municipalities and

[39] Cited in Aleksander Achmatowicz, *Polityka Rosji w kwestii polskiej w pierwszym roku Wielkiej Wojny 1914–1915*, Warsaw 2003, p. 171.
[40] Cited in Achmatowicz, *Polityka Rosji w kwestii polskiej*, p. 357.

240 THE REAR

Greek Catholic clergymen. Among the latter [...], by the beginning of 1916, 71 had joined the retreating Russians, 125 had been interned, 128 had been put under house arrest, and 25 had become subject to an investigation. More than one in seven pastors in the Lwów, Przemyśl, and Stanisławów dioceses had thus become compromised.[41]

Since, in addition to genuine Russophiles, 'compromised' people included those who had been preventively arrested (and quickly released) or who were merely suspects or victims of unjustified repression, the category of 'traitors to the fatherland' became completely blurred. Within it were people only suspected of treason – it is indeed hard to think of a better example of a self-fulfilling prophecy. The only victims Ronge forgot to include in his calculations were those Greek Catholic priests who 'compromised themselves' absolutely – on the gallows.

All of these activities damaged the combatant states both internally and externally. While harsh measures against foreign citizens also became the norm in Great Britain and France, which makes condemning them more problematic, the brutality the empires showed towards their own subjects should nevertheless be seen as a symptom of weakness rather than strength. By persecuting, harassing, and often murdering Ukrainians, Jews, Germans, and Poles, the multinational monarchies proved that they were unable to secure the loyalty of those groups in a civilized manner. The authorities clearly believed that terror was the best means of mobilizing people and that fear would ensure obedience. It was a tragic miscalculation. Regardless of ethnicity or religion, most subjects of both emperors remained loyal. The cruelty of the imperial armies and the indolence of the civilian authorities undermined that loyalty and provided arguments for the enemy's propaganda. In this light, it may seem surprising that until 1917 the internal situation of the three powers was stable. Repression likewise made no sense from the point of view of the combatant states' international position. This was understood by moderately liberal Russian politicians. They tried, unsuccessfully, to persuade high-ranking officers to cease their anti-Semitic excesses. The western allies also pointed out that this was the surest way for Russia to gain more enemies.

Russian and Austro-Hungarian generals laboured under the illusion that the populations of their countries were infiltrated by well-organized spy networks that were prepared to mount an effective resistance to legitimate authority and that threatened the effective conduct of the war. The reality was different, but mass repression ultimately became a self-fulfilling prophecy. Social groups habitually suspected of treason did indeed eventually succumb to it. This mechanism was destructive enough in itself, but its gross unfairness was equally damaging. When it came to the issue of treason, the authorities seemed to believe in ethnic and social predestination. Regardless of the facts, betrayal

---

[41] Ronge, *Kriegs- und Industriespionage*, p. 69.

LOYALTIES

was expected from certain nationalities and social groups, while others remained beyond reproach. Most were somewhere in the middle, such as the Polish Legionnaires who were not citizens of Austria-Hungary. In September 1914, in Kielce, Austrian officers administered the oath to these new volunteers – citizens of Russia. One of them, Wincenty Solek, recalled that none of the men repeated the oath of allegiance to Emperor Franz Joseph. Those standing at the front mumbled a few words, but the rest did not even bother. Soon afterwards a song dedicated to the event gained great popularity within the ranks.[42]

Had the Austrian officers treated these young volunteers from the Kingdom of Poland as they did Ukrainian peasants or fellow subjects from the Serbian border, in all likelihood their manifestation of disobedience would have had unpleasant repercussions. In this instance the 'apostolic general' did not order anyone to be hanged or shot, but instead decided to ignore the whole matter. And rightly so. Despite their lack of enthusiasm for 'His Imperial Majesty', many of the soldiers who took the oath in Kielce gave their lives in defence of Austria-Hungary.

---

[42] 'An apostolic general / Once swore in the oath / The Faith was very happy / Its arms and legs raised both / What a lark we had / Whether standing or reclining / On the land or on the sea / Every man to Austria / Faithful shall he be / O mercy be to Thee,' from Wincenty Solek, *Pamiętnik legionisty*, ed. Wiesław Budzyński, Warsaw 1988, p. 23.

PART III

Occupation

8

The First Moments

In 1914, 'occupation' was a concept as alien as the gas mask, ration card, or aerial bomb. In the history of Europe various territories had been repeatedly occupied by enemy armies and, after the end of hostilities, had been either annexed or returned to the defeated state. The longest such episode began in 1878, when Austria-Hungary occupied Bosnia and Herzegovina. With the consent of the international community, this occupation was euphemistically referred to as an 'administration'; it would last for thirty years. In 1908, the Habsburg monarchy annexed Sarajevo and adjacent areas, provoking a storm of protest.

Lawyers had long struggled with the problem of how to define the responsibilities of an occupier (which had no legal right to the given territory under international law) towards the population of the territory it administered. War presented an additional problem: how decent could one realistically expect a state to be if the (largely hostile) occupied territory was situated close to its front lines? A compromise solution, drawn up in The Hague in 1899, was guided by the principle that the victorious state, i.e. the occupier, was obliged where possible to protect civilians and any institutions that were neutral in respect of the war. It was obliged to maintain public order, not to confiscate private property or tolerate looting, and not to apply the principle of collective responsibility.

The rules were thus straightforward. No one could have foreseen, however, that within a decade or so occupiers would be administering territories larger than most existing states, and would be doing so throughout a long period of warfare during which the population of the (for now) victorious state was suffering from hunger. Behind the lines of the eastern fronts, occupation was experienced by many millions of people. Their number was incomparably greater than in the West, in the hinterland of the Italian front, or on the Turkish–Russian border.

Nevertheless, not every occupation can be fully described as such. Although every seizure of territory by enemy troops is referred to as an occupation, the reality is sometimes very different. This is the case when an invasion of enemy territory is brief, because victory soon turns into defeat and the invading army is forced to retreat to the original state border. A good example is the Serbian front in the first year of the Great War. The Austro-Hungarian troops failed to occupy the enemy's territory and only managed to enter sections of it at various times. Their greatest success came in December 1914, when for two weeks they occupied Belgrade – a *de facto* front-line city situated on the border.

Events in the north were somewhat different. In August 1914 Russia occupied large parts of East Prussia for ten days or so. During the hostilities, towns in the southern part of the province – Ortelsburg (Szczytno), Hohenstein (Olsztynek), and Neidenburg (Nidzica) – went up in flames. In the north and east, too, the Russians occupied several districts. After weeks of fighting the attackers withdrew from the only major territory of the Reich to be invaded during the war.

A 'normal' occupation was out of the question both in the south of East Prussia and in the north; the so-called 'Winter Battle of the Masurian Lakes' ('Winterschlacht in den Masuren') in February 1915 was the last time the eastern territories of the Reich experienced large-scale front-line action during the First World War (the only other intrusion being the four-day occupation of Memel, today's Klaipėda, in March 1915). In those few months, the territory occupied by the Russians never passed into civilian control; it was always directly adjacent to the front. The inhabitants of East Prussia were thus exposed to martial law, a huge influx of refugees, and the proximity of the front, with all its associated destruction, misery, and fear. For German propaganda, the presence of Russian troops in the north-east of the country in 1914 was its greatest trump card: stories about Cossack cruelty and cities in flames, the rape of

Fig. 45   East Prussia. A destroyed railway bridge in Darkehmen (now Ozyorsk in Kaliningrad province). Courtesy of the Herder-Institut, Marburg, Bildarchiv.

women, and the deportation of civilians to the East became part of the German war narrative.

The 'Asian' menace was effectively used to frighten the public. Yet Russian atrocities could hardly compare with crimes against civilians committed by the German military in Belgium and northern France. Up to 1915, Prussian authorities reported approximately 1,500 violent deaths of civilians, which was probably closer to reality than the roughly 100 claimed by the Russian army.[1] In any case, locals privately admitted that, while the Russians had indeed stolen a few things (mainly watches) and had caused a degree of damage, their fellow countrymen – refugees from other districts of East Prussia – had been far more guilty of pillage and destruction.

'Normal' occupation in the East lasted years rather than months: Lwów was occupied by the Russians from the beginning of September 1914 until the end of June 1915; Łódź by the Germans for almost four years; Warsaw and Lublin from August 1915 until the end of the war; Vilnius for more than three years; Belgrade for slightly less; Bucharest for two years; and Riga for the entire final year of the war. During that time the changes that occurred in the cities were incomparably

Fig. 46 A market in the town of Ortelsburg (Szczytno) abandoned by the Russians. Courtesy of the Herder-Institut, Marburg, Bildarchiv.

---

[1] Alexander Watson, '"Unheard-of Brutality": Russian Atrocities against Civilians in East Prussia, 1914–1915', *The Journal of Modern History* 86 (2014), pp. 780–825, esp. pp. 823–824.

greater than those in the countryside, where the arrival of the 'Russians', 'Germans', or 'Austrians' generally made little difference.

Retreat

Hugo Slim, the renowned British human rights expert, distinguishes among seven forms of violence perpetrated against civilians in wartime. The first includes killing, wounding, and torturing; the second, rape and sexual violence; the third, deportation and forced labour; the fourth, impoverishment; the fifth, famine and disease; the sixth, emotional suffering; and the seventh, post-war suffering and expulsion.[2] All of these calamities occurred during the First World War in Central and Eastern Europe and the Balkans, and some took on complex and diverse forms. Let us take a look at the misfortunes people suffered when the Great War appeared on their doorstep. Let us also examine how civilians tried to prevent those misfortunes or at least mitigate their effects. What happened in the period between the departure of an army and the establishment of a new administration (or the restitution of the old one)? Our guide will be diaries and memoirs that describe the short but intense period when the front shifted and occupation began.

The onset of war was preceded by grim prophecies and portents:

> When, in Myślenice [. . .], I asked one very stubborn prophet on what he was basing his assertion, he told me that for two weeks all the dogs in the village had been howling, continually turning their snouts to the east, and that this was a clear sign of impending war. Another told me that every night, for the previous few days, plumes of red smoke had been visible on the eastern horizon. The only time people had seen such plumes was a couple of weeks before the outbreak of the Prussian War. And in the Dąbrowa district, an old and very sensible peasant by the name of Mleczko told me with utter conviction that, for a month now, he had seen a huge woman dressed in red robes wandering the cemetery at night, which was an omen of a great and bloody war.[3]

The first confirmation that all these premonitions had been correct came in the form of announcements and special newspaper editions containing news about mobilization. It did not take long for far more mundane evidence of the approaching front to appear. News of battles that had been waged nearby began to filter through to people. While such information was almost always infused with bureaucratic optimism, even a mildly attentive reader could check a map to see that the front was getting closer rather than farther away. As late as on 29 August 1914, the local newspaper in the capital of Bukovina, the

---

[2] Hugo Slim, *Killing Civilians. Method, Madness, and Morality in War*, New York 2008, p. 39.

[3] Wincenty Witos, *Moje wspomnienia*, vol. 2, Paris 1964, p. 7.

Czernowitzer Allgemeine Zeitung, carried news from the front under the heading 'Victory after Victory'. Two days later, the governor of Bukovina fled the city and the Austro-Hungarian army began to blow up the bridges on the Prut River. At the beginning of September, the inhabitants of Czernowitz found themselves alone: the Austro-Hungarian soldiers had left and the Russians had not yet arrived. Looking out from the city, people could see smoke from burning villages in every direction.

During a retreat, the imperative was to blow up bridges, burn down stations, and destroy railway lines. For the sappers this was certainly easier than building bridges and roads and laying narrow-gauge track, and sometimes more pleasant. While observing his colleagues as they dynamited the goods station in Piotrków at the end of October 1914, a German officer noted: 'It is hard not to notice the sappers' delight in destroying window panes, arc lamps, clocks, etc. It is on such occasions that their inner child is set free.'[4] On the other hand, temporary track repair and the restoration of rail connections were among the first activities to be undertaken by invading forces. In areas that changed hands several times, such works – which, unlike digging trenches, attracted remuneration, at least in the first months of the war – provided employment and wages to locals and professionals alike. In August 1914 the Russians withdrew from Sandomierz in the Congress Kingdom so hurriedly that they did not have time to destroy the track and bridges. This was accomplished instead by the Austrians towards the end of their first occupation of the town, which lasted a few weeks. On 22 September, the Russians, who in the meantime had recaptured Sandomierz, managed to repair the bridge and begin work on the railway line. They also set up a second, pontoon bridge. Soon, however, they set about destroying both bridges in order to halt the advance of the returning German and Austro-Hungarian troops. In the middle of October Austrian engineers completed the makeshift track repair and opened the rail connection. A week later, as the Cossacks approached Sandomierz once again, the Austrians began to methodically destroy the track and facilities they had only just repaired. On 28 October, just before leaving the city, they blew up the railway workshops and tore down the bridges. On the following day, Father Rokoszny went out to examine the latest devastation. At the station he met railway workers brought in by the Russians from Dęblin who were already preparing for work. It took them barely a week to get the line to Radom up and running.[5]

---

[4] Harry Graf Kessler, *Das Tagebuch*, vol. 5 (1914–1916), ed. Günter Riederer, Ulrich Ott, Christoph Hilse, and Janna Brechmacher, Stuttgart 2008, p. 147.

[5] Józef Rokoszny, *Diariusz Wielkiej Wojny*, ed. Wiesław Caban and Marek Przeniosło, Kielce 1998, vol. 1, p. 170 and passim.

Fig. 47 Piotrków station in 1916.

In the end there had to come a time when the front would pass through the towns and villages of Galicia, the Kingdom of Poland, Serbia, and Romania. Reading contemporary accounts, one easily gets the impression that the devastation was all-encompassing. However, despite all its brutality, the war did not reach every place. Understandably, the strange and menacing landscape of the battlefields drew much more attention than territory that had escaped bombing and destruction. To get a sense of proportion, one has to read between the lines and focus on the details that deviate from the apocalyptic visions. The German aristocrat, writer, and patron of art Harry Kessler, who observed the desolate Congress Kingdom from the saddle of his horse, noted that 'All Poland is, it seems, a place of devastation, laid to apocalyptic waste.'[6] Nevertheless, he was rarely unable to find a place to sleep for the night. A good example of a very emotional account is that of Cardinal Kakowski, who took a train journey after the Kingdom had been occupied by the Germans in the summer of 1915. It should be remembered that areas bordering railway lines were often the most devastated:

> All the stations and railway buildings [...] are in ruin. The railway workshops in Warsaw and Pruszków and the factory buildings in Żyrardów have been gutted. Count Sobański's forests beyond Żyrardów have been partly cut down and partly damaged. [...] The closer one gets to the battle line, the greater the devastation. The standing crops have

[6] Kessler, *Das Tagebuch*, vol. 5, p. 374.

THE FIRST MOMENTS   251

been blackened by poisonous gas. In Radziwiłłów, the little church has
been bombed. Just next to the railway line, the pine trees are half broken,
stripped of bark, or have had their crowns severed by shrapnel. The earth
is riddled with shells, which have formed deep craters, each several feet
from the next. The forest has been cut lengthways and sideways by fire
trenches. On the Bzura River itself are deeper trenches, roof-covered to
protect them from shelling, and a few hundred yards across the Bzura lie
the German trenches. The fields are covered in grass and weeds that reach
to the height of a peasant. Here and there one sees the debris of ruined
homesteads and farm buildings. A veritable desert! In this place, someone
who has not seen the steppe will get an idea of what it looks like. [. . .] the
smell of corpses emanates from the earth, over which flocks of crows and
ravens circle. As one gets further away from the Bzura there is less
destruction to be seen. At Skierniewice a view of fields under cultivation
re-emerges. Despite the bombardment, Skierniewice has retained its former appearance. Łowicz has suffered little, and the collegiate church is still
standing. Behind the town are a few burned villages. Single or mass graves
stand adjacent to the railway line. The beautiful churches in Zduny and
Złaków, with their slender towers, are partly destroyed. Their shell-
shattered roofs have been patched up with straw. Only in Krośniewice
does one see people at work. Such a wonderful country, yet so melancholic
in appearance.[7]

Most vulnerable were villages situated on roads along which armies passed.
Cities, towns, and villages that lay directly on the line of the front and thus
attracted artillery fire were an extreme case. The biggest of these was Belgrade,
and the most destroyed was probably Gorlice (we have already described the
effects of the German firestorm in that town). Seriously damaged were the
Bulgarian port cities (at the time located not only on the Black Sea but also on
the Aegean), which were shelled from the sea and bombed by air by the
Russians, French, and British. The inhabitants of such places were not observers of the impending storm but its victims. Those who could flee did so,
although sometimes this only worsened their predicament. In the war diaries
and memoirs, such civilians, who escaped together with the army, were like
film extras: they did not actively participate in the fighting, but their presence
added to the drama of the situation. The Russian cavalryman Andrei Lobanov-
Rostovskii witnessed the panicked escape of Polish peasants during a battle at
Opatów in the autumn of 1914:

> The confusion of the peasants is simply impossible to describe. The
> women and children were howling in terror, while the men tried to stop
> their panicked draught-animals from escaping. A hysterical woman clung
> on to my horse and screamed: 'Officer, how can we get out of here safely?,'

[7] Aleksander Kakowski, *Z niewoli do niepodległości. Pamiętniki*, ed. Tadeusz Krawczak and
Ryszard Świętek, Cracow 2000, pp. 248–249.

252   OCCUPATION

to which, for obvious reasons, I had no answer but to wave my hand. A peasant driving three stubborn cows had barely managed to lead them onto a side road when the shells began to fall. He turned around and went off in another direction, but the artillery was firing there too. In the end he gave up and headed back to his burning village.[8]

The fate of fugitives who fled their destroyed homes only to be thrown into the whirlwind of battle was tragic, but it was the exception rather than the rule. Scenes similar to those described by Lobanov-Rostovskii were witnessed in places where the fighting was fiercest. Those places aside, however, the war had far less tragic consequences for the civilian population, especially when compared with the region's devastation during the Second World War. Although there was considerable war damage, it is worth noting that in the years 1914–1918 no major city of Central and Eastern Europe, with the exception of Belgrade and Czernowitz, became a target for systematic and sustained artillery fire. For more than a year after the outbreak of the war, the Serbian capital was repeatedly bombed and temporarily occupied by the enemy; tens of thousands of prisoners and sick and wounded soldiers languished within it. When the Austro-Hungarian army entered the city for a second time in October 1915, of the 90,000 pre-war inhabitants, only 7,000 to 12,000 remained. But Belgrade was an exception. During the First World War, larger cities usually surrendered without a fight. For the time being, military commanders could not countenance the idea of putting civilians, women, and children at risk of siege, bombardment, starvation, or door-to-door combat, the last of these being completely unimaginable. When, in June 1915, during the recapture of Lwów by the Austro-Hungarian army, there was an accidental exchange of fire between the Russian rear-guard and a Habsburg patrol, the newspapers were outraged: how could such an incident have occurred, given the danger it posed to the public? In most cities the passage of the front proceeded altogether differently, and the threat to life and property was not always a direct result of the hostilities.

When the boom of heavy artillery could be heard, and soldiers from shattered units as well as deserters began to appear on the streets, it became increasingly difficult to remain optimistic about the future. In the fraught atmosphere people would panic for the slightest reason. This is exactly what happened on 27 August 1914 in Lwów. When the cry 'the Muscovites are coming!' rang out,

> from the direction of Jałowiec and the Łyczakowska tollgate a mass of people headed into the city. Recruits and reservists ran out of their barracks, and wagons, carts and other vehicles set off. Women grabbed their children and, succumbing to the psychology of the crowd, rushed

---

[8] Cited in Peter Englund, *Schönheit und Schrecken. Eine Geschichte des Ersten Weltkriegs erzählt in neunzehn Schicksalen*, translated by Wolfgang Butt, Bonn 2012, p. 40.

THE FIRST MOMENTS 253

blindly, barefoot and semi-clothed, without thought or consideration, towards the Bernardine Church, spreading panic and terror as they went. The screech of shop blinds being hastily closed only added to the noise and confusion. In the space between St Anthony's Church and pl. Cłowy numerous men, women and children as well as armed and unarmed soldiers gathered, accompanied by carts, automobiles, trams, and unharnessed horses, forming a dense and compact whole, incapacitated by its own pressure.[9]

On this occasion it was a false alarm. It was not until a few days later that the retreating Austro-Hungarian troops, tired and beaten, marched hastily through Lwów. In the meantime, the city had been abandoned by a large group of civil servants and members of the local elites, including half of the 100-strong City Council. Only three councillors remained from the Jewish caucus, which had numbered fifteen people. Similar things happened in virtually every metropolis. As the press was quick to point out, the wealthier an individual, the more scrupulously he avoided sharing the burden of occupation with his compatriots. In the summer of 1915, for instance, several Poles from famous aristocratic families, the owners of vast landed estates, escaped along with the Russians: Włodzimierz and Seweryn Czetwertyński, Maurycy Zamoyski, Ksawery Branicki, and Józef Potocki; Leopold Julian Kronenberg also fled. The Warsaw-based *Kurier Narodowy* (*National Courier*) complained: 'Those who have remained are the none-too-wealthy and the destitute.'[10]

During the evacuation of public offices, special care was taken to ensure that the assets of state and private banks and documents did not fall into the hands of the enemy. Initially, this kind of evacuation proceeded in a fairly orderly fashion with full observance of the rules. This was the case in Warsaw in the summer of 1915:

> The evacuation, though not particularly hasty, is constant and systematic. First we sent off our hospital staff, then the officials' wives. At present, some institutions, such as the courts, the tax office, customs and excise, etc. are being gradually or partially evacuated. We proposed that the private banks and credit unions should move their cash deposits – but they all refused.[11]

The final task for departing officials was to burn documentation and pay themselves their own salaries several months in advance. As a rule, however, the settling of other accounts was forgotten. At the end of August, civil servants in Lwów did not receive their monthly pay cheque, and no pensions or

[9] Józef Białynia Chołodecki, *Lwów w czasie okupacji rosyjskiej (3 września 1914–22 czerwca 1915). Z własnych przeżyć i spostrzeżeń*, Lwów 1930, pp. 35–36.
[10] Cited in 'Opuścili posterunek', *Ilustrowany Kuryer Codzienny*, 25 September 1915.
[11] Stanisław Dzierzbicki, *Pamiętnik z lat wojny 1915–1918*, ed. Janusz Pajewski and Danuta Płygawko, Warsaw 1983, p. 55.

254　　OCCUPATION

allowances were paid out to widows and orphans. In August 1914 in the Congress Kingdom, from which the Russians had to temporarily withdraw, army officers and civil servants were paid four months' and three months' salary, respectively. Teachers and priests did not receive a penny.[12]

For civilians, the evacuation of public officials (including, for example, railway and postal workers) was a tell-tale sign that things were not going as well as the newspapers claimed. The painter Tadeusz Dowgird (Tadas Daugirdas), a native of Kaunas, witnessed the changeover of power in his city in the summer of 1915. The first German shells fell on Kaunas on 15 August. The Russian gunners in the Kaunas fortress responded with fire, and there was nothing to suggest that the defenders were thinking about retreat. By the following morning, however, doctors, post office staff, and the state and municipal police had packed their bags and were heading towards the station to catch the train to Vilnius. A few hours later they were joined by the commander of the fortress. The City Hall sent agitated queries to the military headquarters about what to do when the Germans arrived, but there was no one in Kaunas who could give a response. On the morning of the next day, when Dowgird went for a stroll to see the damage, he noticed an unusual sight:

> On the way to ul. Iwanowska, by the city park, I was passed by the fire brigade, who were driving in the direction of the Orthodox cathedral. I assumed that they were going to put out a fire [...]; the nearby barracks of the dragoon regiment were in flames. Instead, they got as far as Lewinsohn's inn before turning around and heading off towards the Wiłkomierz [Ukmergė] road. When they passed me again, I noticed that all the fire engines were loaded with belongings and that women and children were sitting in between the firefighters. In the first vehicle, standing beside the driver, was the chief of the fire brigade himself.[13]

Having realized that the enemy was fast approaching, those most in danger of maltreatment and repression at the hands of the invading forces also fled. In the first four weeks of the war approximately one-quarter of the inhabitants of Lwów, which had a population of over 200,000, escaped from the city. Most afraid were the Jews – 40,000 remained out of a community of 57,000. People fled before the occupier on an even bigger scale in Romania in the last quarter of 1916. As a result of exodus and conscription, the population of the occupied part of the country decreased from over 4.2 million to fewer than 3.5 million. In Austria-Hungary, refugees – primarily from Galicia and Bukovina – were

---

[12] See Białynia Chołodecki, *Lwów w czasie okupacji rosyjskiej*, p. 41; Rokoszny, *Diariusz Wielkiej Wojny*, vol. 1, pp. 7–8.

[13] Th. von Dowgird, 'Kownos letzte Russentage', in *Das Litauen-Buch. Eine Auslese aus der Zeitung der 10. Armee*, Wilna (Vilnius) 1918, pp. 112–115.

THE FIRST MOMENTS

proportionately fewer in number, with estimates ranging from 500,000 to 1.3 million.[14]

It is no accident that the majority of the refugees from Galicia and Bukovina who flooded Vienna and other urban centres of the Austrian hinterland in 1914 consisted of Jews who were terrified by the prospect of Cossack pogroms. Less rational were the fears harboured by the inhabitants of East Prussia. The alleged figure of 800,000 refugees who fled the 'Cossack Terror' appears to be disproportionately high when compared with the small number of confirmed war crimes perpetrated by the Russians. It is conceivable that it would have been safer for those people to stay at home. Fear gripped people on the other side of the front, too. At the news that the Austrians were approaching, entire Orthodox parishes in the Chełm region underwent voluntary evacuation. Masses of civilians took off during the second Austro-Hungarian invasion of Serbia, fearing repression as cruel as that which they had experienced a few months earlier.

What motivated people to voluntarily leave their homes or to hide in the woods until the situation had calmed down? Simple prudence was one reason, of course; panic and tales of crimes perpetrated by the advancing enemy were another. There were also quite specific fears, which are generally not stated explicitly in the historical sources. In soldiers' accounts, regardless of the front to which they relate, what is often striking is the absence of farmers and young women. Elderly farmers' wives and grandmothers are the only people who remain in cottages that have been cleared of all essential supplies and valuable belongings. This was no accident, of course. Farmers who stayed behind ran the risk of being shot or hanged for even the slightest insubordination, whether real or imaginary. Wincenty Witos, who defended his property against the Cossacks, managed to avoid this fate: 'The soldiers were about to cut me to pieces with their sabres because I had not allowed them to take my horse and because, as we tussled over it, I hit one of the Cossacks in the face so hard that he fell to the ground. Expecting further retaliation, I immediately left for Tarnów.'[15] As he departed, Witos left his wife to guard the farm. We do not know what happened to the couple next, since the wife of Poland's future Prime Minister did not keep a diary.

The frequent absence of young women when armies were on the move can in turn be explained by the threat of rape. It is difficult to say how common rape was, because neither the perpetrators nor the victims wanted to publicize the issue. One diary entry by Helena Jabłońska née Seifert appears

[14] Julie Thorpe, 'Displacing Empire: Refugee Welfare, National Activism and State Legitimacy in Austria-Hungary in the First World War', in *Refugees and the End of Empire. Imperial Collapse and Forced Migration in the Twentieth Century*, ed. Panikos Panayi and Pippa Virdee, New York, NY 2011, pp. 102–126.

[15] Witos, *Moje wspomnienia*, vol. 2, p. 45.

Fig. 48 Refugees from Máramaros (Maramureş) on the north-eastern edge of Hungary returning home after the brief Russian occupation.

characteristic in this regard. In October 1914 Jabłońska had a conversation with an elderly peasant woman who had been evacuated from Medyka together with her daughter-in-law and grandchildren. Her interlocutor spoke of the various misfortunes that had befallen the family at the hands of both the Russians and the Austro-Hungarian gendarmes. In among these stories the peasant woman briefly mentioned that when the 'Muscovites' had entered the village, they not only looted the cottage but also 'mistreated my daughter-in-law'.[16] Stanisław Srokowski recalled an event that had occurred during the first Russian occupation of Galicia:

> The hordes of Dagestan Cossacks and Chechens wounded and murdered the peaceful inhabitants and committed heinous acts of rape on the women and young girls. In Mielec alone, the Russians raped sixteen secondary school girls. They also shot at women who resisted their advances, and even at children if they screamed.[17]

Another account, relating to the environs of Tarnów during the Russian invasion, describes the following scene:

---

[16] Helena z Seifertów Jabłońska, *Dziennik z oblężonego Przemyśla 1914–1915*, ed. Hanna Imbs, Przemyśl 1994, p. 72.
[17] Stanisław Srokowski, *Z dni zawieruchy dziejowej 1914–1918*, Cracow 1932, p. 127.

THE FIRST MOMENTS 257

Women and girls were constantly exposed [...] to many dangers, but most of all at the beginning, when the Cossacks went on the rampage. They took shelter in homes where there were more people, fled to the towns, and hid in cellars – if they were assaulted they would resist in a manner worthy of the holy virgins and matrons of the early Church. There were thousands of such women, ready to risk everything, even death, so as not to offend God, not to tarnish their souls.[18]

On the basis of similar, often enigmatic accounts, historians believe that rape was widespread in Galicia and that the victims were usually Jewish women.[19] Their tragedy is revealed in memoirs and official reports, but often in the background, since it is not they who were considered the real victims of Russian barbarity; it was rather their husbands, fathers, and brothers, who stood in their defence and were killed by the Cossacks. For this reason, too, Jewish refugees crowded into the larger towns and cities, rightly believing that they would be safer there than in the shtetls. It is estimated that in 1916, 80,000 took shelter in both Vienna and Warsaw, the two cities with the highest concentration of Jewish refugees.[20]

Since Hungary accepted only a small number of refugees, the problem of 'others' was concentrated in the Danubian countries and in the Czech lands. In early June 1915, over 500,000 refugees and evacuees (170,000 Poles, 266,000 Jews, and 72,000 Ukrainians) were receiving state benefits in Cisleithania.[21] In Austrian, Czech, and Moravian towns and cities, the fear that the strangers would bring in diseases was combined with a certain resentment: the savages from the East were idle, whereas locals not only had to work on their account but also had share their increasingly meagre resources with them. As the Viennese police reported in the spring of 1915: 'People are saying that the Jewish refugees are nothing but a drain on society. They receive assistance from the state and on the whole lead a comfortable life.' To clarify: state

---

[18] Jan Borzęcki [Jan Czuj], *Moskale w Tarnowie. Od 10 listopada 1914 do 6 maja 1915 roku*, Tarnów 1915, p. 11.

[19] See Frank M. Schuster, *Zwischen allen Fronten. Osteuropäische Juden während des Ersten Weltkriegs (1914–1919)*, Cologne 2004, pp. 168–199 and Alexander Victor Prusin, *Nationalizing a Borderland. War, Ethnicity, and Anti-Jewish Violence in East Galicia, 1914–1920*, Tuscaloosa, AL 2005, p. 30.

[20] Piotr Wróbel, *Zarys dziejów Żydów na ziemiach polskich w latach 1880–1918*, Warsaw 1991, pp. 71 and 77. For a summary of recent research on First World War refugees, see Alex Dowdall, 'Citizens or Subjects? Refugees and the State in Europe during the First World War', in *Breaking Empires, Making Nations? The First World War and the Reforging of Europe*, ed. Richard Butterwick-Pawlikowski, Quincy Cloet, and Alex Dowdall, Warsaw 2017, pp. 98–122.

[21] Żabko-Potopowicz, Antoni, Marceli Handelsman, Władysław Grabski, and Kazimierz Władysław Kumaniecki, *Polska w czasie wielkiej wojny (1914–1918)*, vol. 2. *Historia społeczna*, Warsaw 1932, p. 179. The authors estimate that 40,000 Jews received state benefits in Cisleithania at that time, while another 150,000 refugees received no state support at all.

assistance for refugees amounted to 21 crowns per month; at the very bottom of the social ladder, an unskilled female worker received 50 crowns. When, in July 1917, as a result of inflation, refugees received the fabulous sum of 10.5 crowns per week from the state, a kilo of flour cost 22 crowns.[22]

In this respect the hinterland did not differ from the occupied territories: in every city, 'our people', i.e. local residents in need of state assistance or medical care, were distinguished from refugees, who were often referred to as 'fugitives'. In occupied Lwów in the spring of 1915, 'Hutsuls' (Ukrainian highlanders) became a symbol of misfortune, i.e. infectious diseases, brought in from the outside. The *Kurjer Lwowski* regularly produced statistics to show, irrefutably, that refugees were overwhelmingly responsible for the epidemiological threat to the city.[23] At the beginning of 1917 the municipal authorities in Prague banned the use of public transport by refugees from Galicia and Bukovina on the grounds that they could spread typhus. The ban was only rescinded under pressure from the state authorities and following protests by Jewish organizations.[24] In Warsaw and Vienna the authorities were asked to remove the refugees because they were spreading not only disease but also immorality. In response to one of these petitions, Franz Joseph is said to have declared that, if conditions were too cramped for his beloved Viennese, he would gladly accommodate the Galician refugees in the Schönbrunn Palace. The monarch's intervention did not calm the public mood for long.

For the time being the effects of population movements might have been seen as a temporary consequence of the turmoil of war. In reality, flight and deportations not only reduced the size of populations but also led to changes in their composition: in Warsaw the number of inhabitants decreased by around 20 per cent. Since the decline in the 'Christian' population – mainly Roman Catholics – was much greater than the decline in the Jewish population, the proportion of Jewish residents in Warsaw increased from 38 per cent (1914) to 45 per cent (1917). In the Polish–Belarusian and Polish–Ukrainian borderlands, in turn, the 'migration of peoples' affected Orthodox believers more than it did Catholics. As a result, the proportion of Poles in areas that would later be occupied by Germany and Austria-Hungary was surprisingly high.

Not everyone fled of their own accord, however. Naturally, this was not possible for prisoners and internees accused of spying for the enemy, and they were instead transported behind the lines together with administrative staff. Nor was there any question of Jews being allowed to move freely. On the orders of the Russian Chief of the General Staff, Nikolai Nikolaevich Yanushkevich,

---

[22] Data from Beatrix Hoffmann-Holter, 'Jüdische Kriegsflüchtlinge in Wien', in Gernot Heiss and Olvier Rathkolb (eds.), *Asylland wider Willen. Flüchtlinge in Österreich im europäischen Kontext seit 1914*, Vienna 1995, pp. 45–59.

[23] *Kurjer Lwowski*, spring 1915, passim.

[24] Marsha L. Rozenblit, *Reconstructing a National Identity. The Jews of Habsburg Austria during World War I*, Oxford 2001, pp. 78–79.

THE FIRST MOMENTS 259

a notorious anti-Semite, Jews were deported from areas close to the front. Such measures sometimes occurred on a massive scale, especially from the summer of 1915 onwards. After the defeat at Gorlice, the Russian authorities radically accelerated the forced repatriation of German colonists from the Chełm region; the operation encompassed tens of thousands of people. As we mentioned earlier, at that time, too, the Russians tried to persuade the entire rural population to voluntarily leave areas from which the army was withdrawing. The result of this was a mass migration of peoples, all the more tragic because more often than not the refugees' homes were burned down by Russian soldiers. Deportations of Jews presented an additional problem caused by the existence of a so-called Pale of Settlement. This limited the areas where Jews were allowed to live to the western and south-western provinces of Russia (which had once belonged to the Polish–Lithuanian Commonwealth). As the German army advanced, ever greater sections of the Pale of Settlement became occupied and the areas where Jewish deportees were legally allowed to settle rapidly shrank. In May 1915 the governors of the Mogilev, Poltava, and Yekaterinoslav provinces announced that they had no space for Jewish deportees. At that time, Jews from the Kaunas province were still stuck in railway carriages on sidings. Typhus broke out among the deportees. In the end the military authorities bowed to pressure from the civilian administration and halted the deportation of 'suspect' Jews.[25] Meanwhile, in August 1915, the Empire was forced to take a historic step and abolish most restrictions on settlement.[26] The retreating Czarist army deported at least 750,000 Poles, 300,000 Lithuanians, a quarter of a million Latvians, half a million Jews, and well over 100,000 Germans to the depths of Russia. Courland lost two-thirds of its population, the future state of Lithuania proportionately less, and Estonia and the Kingdom of Poland significantly less.[27]

Local Government's Finest Hour

Compared with rural inhabitants, the population of towns and cities was hardly evacuated at all, and it was urban residents, above all, who would learn the hard way what a sudden change of rulers actually entailed. The transformation of the hinterland into occupied territory was almost always preceded by a transitional period. Usually, several hours or sometimes days would elapse between the departure of the defenders and the arrival of the occupiers, and these were the most dangerous moments for local residents as

---

[25] Eric Lohr, 'The Russian Army and the Jews: Mass Deportations, Hostages, and Violence during World War I', *The Russian Review* 60, 3 (2001), pp. 404–419.

[26] Eric Lohr, *Russian Citizenship from Empire to Soviet Union*, Cambridge 2012, p. 123.

[27] Peter Gatrell, *A Whole Empire Walking. Refugees in Russia during World War I*, Bloomington, IN 2011, pp. 22–48.

far as their wellbeing and property were concerned. People knew each other in the countryside, and robbery or rape had a face and a name, whereas in the city one merely had to walk a few streets away to become completely anonymous. Accordingly, in almost every major town or city, the disappearance of the existing authorities was accompanied by a sudden spate of theft, burglary, and violence. Bands of young men looted as much as they could. Those who had something to lose tried to organize at least a modicum of public order and safety. Sometimes when they departed with their own troops, the municipal authorities took care to appoint successors, sometimes the existing police remained in place, and sometimes citizens were able to quickly set up a 'militia' or some sort of armed guard to protect the city from anarchy. Perpetual gossip about the eruption of violence probably exaggerated the threat, and the actual increase in crime was far from catastrophic. Nevertheless, the fear of crime was widespread.

In the Congress Kingdom the initiative was handed to the civic committees, which had hitherto provided assistance to the needy and run cheap canteens. This was the only form of self-government that the authorities had permitted in the Kingdom. In the larger cities of Galicia, Serbia, and Romania, and in the western provinces of the Russian Empire, where municipal government already functioned, the task of providing assistance was simply taken up by the incumbent mayors. In doing so, however, they exposed themselves to considerable risk. What this risk entailed is shown by the fate of the mayors of the two largest cities captured by the Russians in 1914: Czernowitz and Lwów. The Russians deported both of them to the East, from where they returned only in 1917 as part of an exchange of internees.

The mayors of these two provincial capitals, Salo Weisselberger in Czernowitz and Tadeusz Rutowski in Lwów (the latter deputizing for the absent Józef Neumann), were among the first local officials to transfer the city they administered from the rule of one emperor to the rule of another in a relatively smooth fashion. During that process, for a shorter or longer period of time, both cities practically governed themselves and did not answer to any state administration. This period of 'civil society' abounded in dangers, which the efficient local governments did their best to prevent. Weisselberger and Rutowski began their new public service by attempting to quell the chaos and panic that ensued after the army and officials had fled. To this end, they created a Civic Guard, which was usually unarmed or carried only bladed weapons, but at least its members wore armbands decorated in the colours of the city. The guard maintained public order and also ensured that traders did not sell their goods above the maximum official price. Other cities that experienced an 'interregnum' also followed suit, albeit a little later. In Warsaw, the local Civic Committee took control when the Russians departed. It was the committee that negotiated with the Germans on how power was to be transferred to the occupying forces. Meanwhile, the Civic Guard, which was subordinate

THE FIRST MOMENTS 261

to the Civic Committee, maintained public order. In Piotrków, Sandomierz, and other smaller towns, the role of police officers was played by firefighters (who, unlike their colleagues in Kaunas, had remained in their posts). The formation of similar units in the countryside depended on the initiative of local elites. In the village of Wierzchosławice near Tarnów the inhabitants could count themselves lucky: shortly after the entry of the Russians, the local prefect was able to set up a Civic Guard with the consent of the Russian army command; its presence clearly helped to limit military excesses.[28] In Belgrade, however, which was situated on the front line, no transitional administration was created. As we mentioned earlier, the city was heavily damaged by artillery fire (especially the districts bordering the Sava and Danube), and of its 90,000 pre-war inhabitants, less than 20 per cent remained. When the Germans and Austrians crossed to the other side of the Sava, they found no local government institutions there to help them communicate with the local population.

The period between the departure of one army and the arrival of the next, although generally short, frayed the nerves of even the most sanguine inhabitants. From the point of view of civilians, the moment of transition to occupation and the moment of liberation did not essentially differ. Both experiences were permeated by a sense of danger and helplessness that tended to conquer all other feelings. Against this background many welcomed the entry of troops with relief, even troops that had previously been hostile: an occupation regime was better than no regime at all. The waiting was made worse by rumours, some more fanciful than others, about defeats, disasters, and atrocities perpetrated by the approaching enemy:

> Suddenly the news spreads that they are already in Włostów and are heading for Opatów. This raises the question: why are they not coming here? The public seems to think that if they are to come, they might as well get it over with. One man, somewhat more agitated, says: let even the devil come, so long as he does it quickly. Others ask in an ironic tone: truly, will no one capture Sandomierz? What a disgrace! Sandomierz has played a leading role in so many wars – is it to be a mere extra in this one? Are they going to annex it in the same manner as all the others? Infamy! Let us provoke them![29]

Waiting for the enemy army was not the only source of anxiety. There were already many dangers to contend with. In Sandomierz, on the day after the Russians left, local peasants looted the barracks. The firefighters (i.e. the members of the newly formed Civic Guard) managed to capture only a few of the perpetrators. The same thing happened immediately after the arrival of

---

[28] Witos, *Moje wspomnienia*, vol. 2, p. 47.
[29] Rokoszny, *Diariusz Wielkiej Wojny*, p. 24.

262   OCCUPATION

the Austrians. Looting, with the participation of local peasants and urban mobs, was commonplace. One example was Lwów:

> Once the Austrian troops had marched off, the detainees and wounded had been transported out, the civilian population had departed, and the peasant wagons loaded with belongings and cattle had escaped from the vicinity of Winniki [Vynnyky], bands of thugs and ruffians rushed out to loot the houses, shops, barracks, and railway depots. Here and there fires broke out. Those groups of thugs and ruffians considerably strengthened their numbers with regiments of supposedly 'respectable' citizens drawn from the ranks of workers, watchmen, caretakers, pimps, and half-witted amateurs looking for easy spoils.[30]

In the almost completely deserted Belgrade, gangs of thieves competed with Austro-Hungarian soldiers to plunder abandoned middle-class homes. Returning a few days later, the owners were confronted with a melancholy sight:

> All of the furniture had been carried into the street [. . .] The bedroom was a shambles – everything was ransacked. Nikola's [the author's husband's] books were scattered throughout the alley way and street. [. . .] I ached inside when I saw that chaos in my house. They had left soiled underwear in the porcelain washbasin. They broke all of my cabinets [. . .]. All of the silver was taken away, as well as other valuables, including silverware and glasses.[31]

Similar scenes were frequently played out and the descriptions of them follow the same pattern. Taking advantage of the chaos in the city, local thieves, many of whom had only just been released from evacuated prisons, went on stealing sprees. They were joined by some of the local residents and later also by peasants from nearby villages. Their first target was the alcohol stores. Then, having let go of their last remaining inhibitions, the drunken gangs would engage in fighting, arson, and murder. The Civic Guard was not always able to control the situation. When power changed hands in the city again, the same story was repeated. On the eve of the recapture of Lwów from the Russians, local low-lifes and Russian marauders went on an orgy of pillage, attacking Jewish homes in particular. On the day after the capture of the city by the German and Austro-Hungarian army, the *Kurjer Lwowski* wrote:

> The last few days have been like a terrible nightmare. They shall never be forgotten by the people of Lwów who experienced them. It was as if the city had gradually frozen solid. The late June nights fell into complete

---

[30] Białynia Chołodecki, *Lwów w czasie okupacji rosyjskiej*, pp. 45–46.
[31] Cited in Jovana Lažić Knežević, *The Austro-Hungarian Occupation of Belgrade during the First World War. Battles at the Home Front*, PhD dissertation, Yale University, 2006, p. 116.

THE FIRST MOMENTS   263

darkness, wrapped in a ghostly shroud. Indeed, for several days, no rooms
that looked onto the street were lit. It felt safer to remain under the cover
of darkness, especially as the military command had ordered us to do so.
Here and there the lanterns barely glowed, emitting a dim light, like faint
oil-lamps. Even the usually lively thoroughfares were filled with the scent
of death. Taking advantage of the sepulchral mood, and certain of impun-
ity, there arose – as if from the earth – the most hideous of beasts,
a thuggish rabble. Shops and apartments, especially in the Jewish neigh-
bourhoods, were plundered; blood was even spilled. . . .

Meanwhile, continued the *Kurjer Lwowski,*

> [. . .] A rumour, spread by a coward, fanned the flames of fear with the
> products of a sick mind [. . .] some sort of slaughter was predicted, some
> sort of massacre and plunder by the rear-guard of the departing Russian
> troops, yet everything suggested that those troops had chosen a different
> route, one that did not pass through the city.[32]

On the other hand, an encroaching army also posed a threat, even if it no
longer had any enemies to fight. Soldiers felt uneasy in their new surroundings.
Often they would take a safety-first approach and fire, sometimes at their own
comrades whom they had mistaken for the enemy. Civilians ran the risk of
being accidentally shot, especially if their jobs or circumstances required them
to be outside. One of the Legionnaires recalled his baptism of fire in
August 1914 in Kielce: 'We were taken by surprise by a Russian vehicle with
two officers inside it. They fired at the station, killing a completely innocent
Jewish cab driver, and then beat a hasty retreat under a hail of bullets from our
Mannlicher rifles.'[33] Very heavy losses were suffered by the civilian population
of Belgrade, where delayed escapees often got caught up in Austrian artillery
fire.
  Despite all the uncertainties, accidents, and thuggery, an army's entry into
a city was not usually accompanied by violence. This was the case in
Czernowitz. The editor and owner of the *Czernowitzer Allgemeine Zeitung,*
a Zionist activist by the name of Philipp Menczel, was a member of the
transitional municipal authorities. As he recalled, before the Russian army
decided to enter the city, which the Austrians had abandoned, for several days
it plundered the villages and Jewish towns on the other side of the Prut River.
The first Cossack to cross the river, guided by his infallible instinct, found
a tavern, where he proceeded to drink himself unconscious. This gave the Civic
Guard in Czernowitz the rare honour of being able to take a soldier of the
regular army into captivity. It was not until the following day that a Russian
envoy arrived in the city to demand its immediate surrender. In order to sign

---

[32] 'Dni grozy', *Kurjer Lwowski*, 23 June 1915.
[33] Michał Tadeusz Brzęk-Osiński, *Ze wspomnień Legionisty i Piłsudczyka 1905–1939,*
ed. Witold Dąbkowski and Piotr A. Tusiński, Warsaw and Radom 2003, p. 1.

264 OCCUPATION

the terms of the surrender, a delegation from the municipal authority crossed the remnants of the destroyed bridge to the other side of the river and headed for the abandoned sugar factory:

> Near to the sugar factory, a young officer came out to meet us. He was accompanied by a group of Jewish soldiers, who in all likelihood, because they knew German, were there to act as interpreters. The young man, obviously expecting a long and delicate negotiation, spoke at great length. However, we interrupted his performance. When one of the soldiers asked us in German whether we would surrender the city voluntarily, I turned to the officer and answered in Russian: 'Our army has retreated. The city is in your hands. I do not believe a welcoming ceremony is necessary.' Then the mayor added in German: 'We trust that your troops will be well-disposed towards the civilians in our city; their mood is peaceful and not aggressive.' We exchanged a few minor pleasantries, and five minutes later we said goodbye. The adjutant announced that he would repeat everything to his general very precisely. We returned to the city. The main street was filled with an agitated, though silent crowd.[34]

As the guns fell silent, representatives of local civil society faced their next, and perhaps most important, task. This consisted in protecting the inhabitants against mistreatment by the invading army. Of course, the point was not to offer armed resistance but to demonstrate that, despite the evacuation of local officials, the town or village concerned was not lawless; that it had some sort of government which the occupying forces would have to reckon with. First impressions were key. The authorities also had to restrain over-zealous patriots from bringing misfortune upon their fellow citizens. In Lwów, the Civic Guard managed to prevent groups of Polish youths from launching attacks on Russian troops entering the city.

Attempts to protect the lives and property of fellow citizens were not always met with gratitude, however. In Kragujevac, during the final offensive of the Central Powers against Serbia, remnants of the retreating irregular Serb forces prepared themselves for futile resistance. Since there were large stores of explosives in the city, it was certain that there would be civilian casualties. In this situation the former Finance Minister, Vukašin Petrović, who had organized the temporary civilian authorities, took it upon himself to act as mediator between the incoming Germans and his retreating Serb compatriots. Kragujevac was thus saved, but Petrović was forever regarded as an Austrian lackey and traitor to his nation. A similar fate befell the local authorities in Tarnów, which was occupied by the Russians. The deputy mayor, Herman Mütz, a lawyer who represented Jewish residents, fled for his life before the Russians arrived. He was replaced in his post by the urban architect Janusz Rypuszyński, who, together with the mayor, Tadeusz Tertil, represented the

---

[34] Philipp Menczel, *Als Geisel nach Sibirien verschleppt*, Berlin 1916, p. 34.

THE FIRST MOMENTS   265

local authority vis-à-vis the Czarist army. Upon the return of the Austro-Hungarian forces, the military authorities forced Rypuszyński to resign. They insinuated that he had worked too closely with the Russians and had defended the property of Jewish citizens with insufficient vigour; Tertil also had to explain himself before the Austro-Hungarian prosecutors. Mütz, who spent the occupation far away from Tarnów, deserved much more credit in the eyes of the authorities. Over a dozen councillors resigned in protest at this flagrant injustice. This was just one of hundreds of cases which fuelled bitter infighting between Austrian subjects of Jewish, Polish, and Ruthenian nationality.[35]

The spy craze that had taken hold of the military establishment made the exercise of temporary authority a dangerous task. In places that changed hands during the fighting, local government committees and Civic Guard officers greeted not only the incoming occupiers but also the returning defenders with their hearts in their mouths. As transpired on many occasions, it was precisely the defenders who presented the greatest threat to local elites. In the Congress Kingdom people said, not without irony, that 'Daddy had returned'. For sixteen members of the Civic Guard in Zamość, 'Daddy's return' ended in tragedy. When the Russians returned to the city following a brief sojourn by the Austro-Hungarian forces, they unceremoniously shot all the Civic Guard members dead.[36] Life was not at all safer on the other side of the front. Here the Austro-Hungarian military courts were ferocious, meting out the ultimate punishment with exceptional zeal. Local people thus tried, whenever they could, to manifest their joy at the restitution of legitimate authority. August Krasicki described the return of Austro-Hungarian troops to the small town of Horodenka in the Hutsul region:

> As we approached Horodenka, we saw horsemen and a group of people come towards us. They were led by a Yid dressed in a dinner suit, with a huge blue-and-white flag (the colours of Zion, apparently) affixed to his emaciated carthorse. He rode up to the general and began to speak but, no doubt overcome with emotion, burst into tears and could not finish his welcoming speech. The entourage of Jews and peasants led us into Horodenka, where we stopped at around 3.00 p.m. [...] Various delegations with banners and portraits of the emperor emerged. The Ruthenians carried blue-and-yellow banners, images of St Nicholas, and portraits of the national poet Shevchenko. At the triumphal gate on the market square, the mayor offered bread and salt, and the Ruthenian delegation did likewise separately. The Jewish band played marching music.[37]

---

[35] William W. Hagen, *Anti-Jewish Violence in Poland 1914–1920*, Cambridge 2018, pp. 82–90.

[36] Jarosław Cabaj, *Społeczeństwo guberni chełmskiej pod okupacją niemiecką i austriacką w latach I wojny światowej*, Siedlce 2006, pp. 23–24.

[37] August Krasicki, *Dziennik z kampanii rosyjskiej*, Cracow 1988, pp. 184–185.

266   OCCUPATION

Despite such enthusiastic greetings, the Austro-Hungarian military courts knew no mercy. Wincenty Witos wrote about the disillusionment felt by people who, after all, were happy that the Russians had gone and that 'our boys' had returned:

> They refused to understand that, after the Austrian army had fled, life could not simply come to a standstill. The people left in charge, whether they liked it or not, had to cooperate with the Russians for the simple reason that it was they who now held exclusive power. But given their pre-existing mood, the authorities had no time for basic principles. Instead, they made traitors of the most innocent people.[38]

First Contact

Compared with 'Daddy's return' (regardless of whether 'Daddy' was the benevolent Franz Joseph I or Nicholas II), the first encounters with the incoming enemy were sometimes a pleasant surprise. It was the moment that everyone dreaded, and farmers and young women would often hide in the woods to avert danger. Father Rokoszny recalls that peasants in the Sandomierz region, convinced that the Austrians were about to strip them of all their possessions, concealed their clothes and bed linen in pits that were used for storing potatoes.[39] However, although the front-line troops often stole, they did so in moderation; more importantly, they quickly moved on, just like the Russian soldiers at Tarnów:

> They caught [...] the chickens, turkeys, and geese very skilfully, and then went off to the curate's house and forest inspectorate to take the rest of the horses and cattle. Immediately after eating dinner they left the village and headed west. The locals even began to praise the soldiers, for they had done no harm to anyone and had paid handsomely for the turkeys and geese [...] After two days the praise also ceased and complete tranquillity returned.[40]

In the second echelon there arrived baggage trains, supply officers, and the entire infrastructure of the front-line units. It was precisely in this sort of company that Aleksander Majkowski spent the Romanian campaign:

> The locals, if they remained in the villages situated on the route taken by the army, were very frightened. In one yard I saw an old woman beating her chest in the sign of the cross as she walked around it. I imagine she was praying as she did so. People had every reason to pray. Our column, which comprised only the staff wagons, had by the evening acquired a hog,

[38] Witos, *Moje wspomnienia*, vol. 2, p. 103.
[39] Rokoszny, *Diariusz Wielkiej Wojny*, vol. 1, p. 40.
[40] Witos, *Moje wspomnienia*, vol. 2, p. 44.

THE FIRST MOMENTS 267

a cow, and several ducks and chickens, although our people, on account of
their nobler disposition, were generally on their guard to prevent robbery.
[. . .] For any edible animal in the villages along the route could not be sure
of survival when the columns passed through.[41]

It is hardly surprising that civilians equated the behaviour of their conquerors with aggression and an appetite for plunder and destruction, but this
was not a completely fair assessment. In the first years of the war, when the
Germans and Austrians were already having to tighten their belts, large tracts
of Central and Eastern Europe and the Balkans still had food in abundance.
Following the entry of the German army into Warsaw, Stanisław Dzierzbicki
observed scenes similar to those that one of the new German masters of
Bucharest would record in his diary. The German soldiers:

> [. . .] ask for beer everywhere they go and, being unable to find it any-
> where, gorge themselves on cakes instead, mountains of them, while
> writing 'Gruss aus Warschau' ['Greetings from Warsaw'] postcards that
> they send to Germany. On the whole the Germans look tired, haggard,
> and unkempt. Since the main front-line forces are apparently engaged on
> the Narew and Wieprz rivers, it is mostly the Landwehr that has entered
> Warsaw. Consequently, the Germans have not impressed the Varsovians
> at all, and especially the Varsovian ladies, who have come out in their
> droves [. . .] to catch a glimpse of our not so welcome guests.[42]

The Austrians involved in the final occupation of Belgrade were no less
hungry. It may seem paradoxical that even in a war-ravaged country such as
Serbia, afflicted with epidemics, the Austrians could be envious of the food
situation. The latter had deeper, structural causes as well as short-term ones.
Like most territories on the Eastern Front, Serbia was an agricultural country
that usually had a food surplus. The Balkan monarchy specialized in pig
breeding, and indeed descriptions of the hairy, sheep-like Serbian hogs are
found in almost every German or Austrian account from that country. In the
short term, Serbia's better food supplies were due to the prudence of the
country's authorities, who halted grain exports at the outbreak of the First
Balkan War in 1912. Supplies could be found, here and there, even in the
fourth year of the war.

But let us return to the activity of local government officials. The temporary
local authorities and the Civic Guard rescued the situation at least in part. They
stopped or at least mitigated the waves of robberies and theft and mediated
with the approaching army. As we mentioned earlier, this type of public service
could, after the occupier's retreat, be regarded as collaboration (this term was
not used during the First World War, but the charges amounted to exactly

[41] Aleksander Majkowski, *Pamiętnik z wojny europejskiej roku 1914*, ed. Tadeusz Linkner,
Wejherowo and Pelplin 2000, pp. 217 and 229.
[42] Dzierzbicki, *Pamiętnik z lat wojny 1915–1918*, p. 62.

that). In the meantime, the more important citizens of local communities ran the risk of being taken hostage.

Occupiers took hostages almost everywhere. This was in line with the Hague Convention, and the fate of internees bore no resemblance to that of pseudo-hostages taken during the Second World War. In the event of treason, attacks by non-uniformed units or other civilian violations of the rules of war, hostages could be killed. Nevertheless, even when occupying forces withdrew, there were virtually no executions anywhere (let alone mass executions); the killing of innocent people – hostages are innocent by definition, a fact which is often overlooked since the experience of the Second World War – would have only exacerbated the structural conflict between the new authorities and the local population. Meanwhile, occupiers during the 1914–1918 period were genuinely concerned about their own safety. It was not their intention to get rid of the existing authorities; on the contrary, they counted on the calming effect that those authorities would have on the population at large. Therefore, occupiers preferred to threaten repression rather than to rule by terror; they chose hostages from among the local elites, rightly calculating that their incarceration would send a sufficiently strong signal to the vast majority of people. When the Russian army entered Galicia, on the orders of its commander-in-chief, Nikolai Nikolaevich Yanushkevich, it took hostages in every town and city and sometimes in the villages it occupied. In Lwów, in September, the Russians immediately took sixteen hostages (Poles, Ukrainians, so-called Old Ruthenians, and Jews, four of each), whom they installed in the George Hotel. Both the selection criteria – the threat was addressed to every major ethno-political group – and the treatment of the hostages were symbolic. So long as their compatriots and supporters remained obedient to the new authorities, the hostages would not be at risk.

Bucharest, too, after the German ultimatum, was surrendered as an open city. Before leaving for Iaşi, the Romanian government appointed politicians and other public figures known for their pro-German sympathies as the heads of ministries. The existing police prefect continued to be responsible for public order, which the occupier considered a pragmatic solution. The city was full of refugees, and the railway station was teeming with Bucharestians hoping to escape at the last moment; there was a danger of total chaos. As elsewhere, the assistance of local elites proved very useful in such a situation. Nevertheless, even here the occupier took hostages, albeit for different reasons: after declaring war on the Central Powers, the Romanians interned some of their German and Austro-Hungarian citizens, and when they abandoned Bucharest they took many of those people with them. Having captured Bucharest, the Germans took professors, local luminaries, and politicians' relatives (including the Prime Minister's sister and sister-in-law) as hostages. The men were held in the Imperial Hotel, while some of the women were sent to a convent. Others

THE FIRST MOMENTS

ended up under house arrest. After peace was declared in 1918, an exchange of hostages took place.

Not everywhere, and not always, did occupiers display moderation and treat their hostages in such a civilized manner. As we mentioned earlier, when the Russians withdrew from Lwów in June 1915, they took many of their hostages with them, including the rector of the university and the acting mayor, Tadeusz Rutowski; the two men returned to the city several months later, along with the previously deported Greek Catholic archbishop, Andrey Sheptytsky.[43] The taking of hostages during the Serbian campaign occurred on a truly grand scale. This was a new phenomenon, and not just in terms of numbers. The army commanded by General Potiorek began interning people already within the territory of the monarchy, in other words, its own citizens. Such actions were not regulated by international law. The detainees (their formal status varied) were usually chosen from among the elites of Serbian communities in border towns. Even Stjepan Grgjić, a deputy to the local Landtag (provincial assembly), was not spared. Serbian internees – citizens of the monarchy – were soon joined by citizens of Serbia. They were treated as human shields, being held in front of strategic facilities such as military outposts, railway stations, police stations, and even reservoirs that supplied drinking water. By the autumn of 1914 several thousand people found themselves in this dangerous situation. Some were hanged in retaliation for the real or imagined attacks perpetrated by the Serbian *Komitadjis*.[44]

There is another category of hostages about which we know very little. The Austro-Hungarians and Germans also took hostages in the countryside as punishment for a municipality's failure to supply a given quota of supplies or in the event of a threat from local gangs or partisan units. Of course, such people were held not in hotels but in detention cells. Although there is no evidence of executions having taken place, in the description of the drama in Korczyn later in this chapter, which had to do with the town's failure to pay reparations, the threat of hostages being hanged is all too apparent.

A String of Misfortunes

The repertoire of repression against civilians was naturally more robust, and when the front was nearby it was particularly acute. In time, as the hostilities moved further away, the nature of the repression changed and it became less intense. Most importantly, in these later periods it was even less likely to entail the loss of life.

---

[43] Mark von Hagen, *War in a European Borderland. Occupations and Occupation Plans in Galicia and Ukraine, 1914–1918*, Seattle, WA 2007, pp. 37–42.

[44] Jonathan E. Gumz, *The Resurrection and Collapse of Empire in Habsburg Serbia, 1914–1918*, Cambridge 2009, pp. 40–44.

Fig. 49 Non-uniformed Serbian prisoners of war (so-called third-line troops), in other words, the famous *Komitadjis*, whose treacherous attacks were much feared by the Austro-Hungarian military command.

The misfortunes that initially befell civilians included reparations, requisitioning, forced evacuation, labour, and 'carriage' (i.e. the service of providing free transportation). Reparations were imposed universally and especially often. In theory, they were divided into three categories: substitute (imposed exceptionally in lieu of taxes), administrative (taking the form of extraordinary taxes), and punitive reparations. Receipts were given for the first two categories, and the payer was entitled to a refund after the war. In practice, however, the third option – punitive reparations – was the most common. In this instance the boundary between punishment sanctioned by the rules of war and plain robbery became completely blurred, all the more so because there were no regulations pertaining to potential compensation for requisitions, reparations, and damages caused not by one's own army but by the enemy.

THE FIRST MOMENTS   271

During the short stay of the German troops in Piotrków Trybunalski, food and money were extorted from the town authorities under the threat of bombardment. Most frequently, however, the justification for imposing reparations was alleged treason, and, since treason was perceived to be lurking around every corner, there was ample opportunity for repression. In September 1914, when attempting to capture Sandomierz, the Austrians threatened to destroy the town. The events made a strong impression on Father Józef Rokoszny:

> The night was terrible. I fell asleep early. Just before 11.00 p.m. I heard some commotion in the corridor. The organist was banging on Father Grajewski's door, and then he came to me. I opened the door. Father Kubicki and Przyłęcki, the notary, were collecting reparations that the general had imposed on the town (20,000 crowns in total) because someone had apparently been using flags to send signals to the Russian army. The deadline was midnight. Everyone had to give what they could. I handed over 100 roubles and returned to bed without any hope of falling asleep. A quarter of an hour later there was more commotion outside the house and repeated knocking. Then some voices: 'Open the door!' They were female voices begging for help. I ran to the front door, where I was confronted by two of the Chodakowski ladies and a few servants carrying bundles. 'What's going on?,' I asked. The women told me that the bombing was going to start in ten minutes and that they had been ordered to flee the town. I assured them that it wasn't true, that it was all about the reparations, and that they should calm down.[45]

The priest's sangfroid was born of experience, for the mechanism of exacting reparations was the same everywhere and was derived from the Wild West. The message that the military authorities communicated to the civilian population took the form of a simple alternative: your money or your life. Reparations were used as punishment for actions (whether real or imagined) that municipal authorities had no chance of preventing. In Radom, in December 1915, an Austro-Hungarian outpost reported unexplained shooting to the district commander. There was no material damage, nor any wounded, but the military authorities nevertheless announced that, if any similar incident were to occur in future, reparations to the tune of 50,000 crowns would be imposed on the city. The *Gazeta Radomska* noted in its editorial, somewhat timidly, that it had learned of the shooting incident only from the announcement itself. 'The situation is all the more unfortunate', continued the editorial, 'because the city, bereft of its investigative authorities and armed police, is unable to prevent this kind of criminal activity or to pursue the perpetrators, particularly as the events in question took place beyond the city's borders.'[46]

---

[45] Rokoszny, *Diariusz Wielkiej Wojny*, vol. 1, p. 100.
[46] Cited in 'Groźba kontrybucji nad Radomiem', *Kurjer Lwowski*, 1 March 1916.

272   OCCUPATION

Just how flimsy the real reasons were for imposing reparations on towns and cities is shown, paradoxically, by those instances where reparations were avoided. This was the case when the Germans entered Warsaw, for example, although, after the destruction of Kalisz and earlier aerial bombardments, the worst was expected of them. Moreover, in such a large city, incidents of the kind normally used to justify repression were bound to occur. On this occasion, however, the German commanders decided to prioritize long-term political interest over short-term financial gain. Extorting protection money from Warsaw would certainly not have endeared the Germans to the Polish population.

Reparations spread like a tsunami. First they appeared in areas where hostilities were taking place, but soon they extended to other areas, too. As the shooting died down, reparations stopped being justified on the grounds of treason or cooperation with the enemy. Under occupation they became a means of collective punishment for various offences against the new authorities. The lower an occupier's standing, the more often reparations were used. It is no wonder, then, that, in the occupied part of the Kingdom of Poland, the Austro-Hungarian authorities resorted to reparations time and again. The reason for imposing punitive reparations could be, for instance, a refusal by certain inhabitants of a municipality to pay taxes, or the escape or failure to report for duty by the previously appointed members of a work brigade. Sometimes the reason was simply a disapproving look, as in Stawino in the district of Łuków, where 'the residents were unruly and impertinent towards the German hussars billeted there, and several peasants even spat in front of them'.[47]

Whereas reparations affected entire municipalities and above all towns and cities, requisitioning, although common, was a calamity that affected individuals. In this case, under the Hague Convention, it was possible to requisition items for a fee or for a receipt that could be redeemed at a later date. In practice, requisitioning was often tantamount to robbery, especially during the first days of occupation and when one's own army was in retreat. In a village near Przemyśl, requisitioning proceeded as follows:

> A woman from Łętownia, whose husband had also been mobilized, told me that she had been visited by two Hungarians with a cart. One of the men, armed with a rifle, stood by her elderly father, while the other man 'requisitioned'. He was looking for valuable items and something to eat and drink, and in the end he tore the beads from her neck. Many cows and

---

[47] Cited in Marek Przenioslo, 'Postawy chłopów Królestwa Polskiego wobec okupanta niemieckiego i austriackiego (1914–1918)', in *Lata Wielkiej Wojny. Dojrzewanie do niepodległości 1914–1918*, ed. Daniel Grinberg, Jan Snopko, and Grzegorz Zachiewicz, Białystok 2007, pp. 198–214, here p. 209.

horses were taken to the [Przemyśl] fortress without payment and subsequently sold for a handsome price.[48]

One of the regions acutely affected by requisitioning (which was undertaken by three separate armies) was the Chełm region, through which the front passed several times in 1914–1915. According to Jarosław Cabaj, during the first two years of the war the stock of horses in the region fell by almost 60 per cent; that of cows by more than 50 per cent; that of sheep by over 80 per cent; and that of pigs by over 70 per cent (compared with 1913). German troops were largely to blame for the plunder. More importantly, only the Russians and Austrians offered payment (although usually far below market prices). The most that peasants could expect from the Germans was receipts, and they could only hope that in future the occupation authorities would redeem them.[49] In Eastern Galicia, where the situation was equally bad, the stock of pigs decreased by over 70 per cent, that of horses by almost 45 per cent, and that of cattle by over 40 per cent during the first two years of the war.

The property most frequently requisitioned was that belonging to manorial estates. There were at least two reasons for this. First, the condition of

Fig. 50   Hungarian Hussars independently 'requisitioning' milk (1915).

---

[48] Jan Vit, *Wspomnienia z mojego pobytu w Przemyślu podczas rosyjskiego oblężenia 1914–1915*, translated by Ladislav Hofbauer and Jerzy Husar, ed. Stanisław Stępień, Przemyśl 1995, p. 39.

[49] Cabaj, *Społeczeństwo guberni chełmskiej pod okupacją niemiecką i austriacką*, pp. 90–91.

274 OCCUPATION

cattle and pigs on manorial estates tended to be better than that of animals on peasant farms. Second, many landowners preferred to move to a safe place in uncertain times and leave their estates to the care of their employees. It is hardly surprising that the latter did not wish to risk their own lives in defence of their employers' property. The losses suffered by landowners were magnified by the thefts carried out by local peasants, who in this way 'redressed' their own losses. This was a widespread phenomenon. The Lithuanian landowner Eugeniusz Romer complained about 'the light-fingered instincts that have been unleashed among the servants and among neighbours from the village, who always came to the manor house at every time of need and were never turned away, yet in the turmoil of war they are the first to cause damage and steal'.[50] The Galician politician Władysław Leopold Jaworski shared a similar reflection in his diary: 'The *szlachta* (nobility) is interested only in compensation. The peasants and city-dwellers are thieves. Who actually constitutes Poland? What small handful of people?'[51]

Nevertheless, reparations and requisitioning, although often carried out under the threat of death, did not pose as great a risk to life and wellbeing as two other woes of war: forced evacuation and 'carriage'. In contrast to the departure of officials and the voluntary or near-voluntary escape of people before the approaching front, forced evacuation affected the inhabitants of smaller regions where hostilities were planned (and where, as the evacuees themselves suspected, the intention was simply to plunder everything freely without any inconvenient witnesses). Here, too, the spy craze played a certain role. On the eve of the Gorlice Offensive, for example, residents were removed from all the villages from which the Germans were to launch their attack. Such evacuations always met with resistance from the peasants, who often had to be removed by force. Wincenty Witos witnessed the evacuation of municipalities on the left bank of the Dunajec. Despite several entreaties, the locals refused to leave their homes. This is hardly surprising, given that the evacuation took place in winter and no suitable alternative accommodation had been found. When the peasants were taken by force to villages located several kilometres away from the front line, many farmers and their wives took the risk of going back for the livestock and possessions they had left behind. In the new places the authorities were unable to provide decent living conditions. Crammed into farm buildings, people froze and fell ill. As Witos recalled, the hygiene situation among the evacuees was catastrophic:

> At some point in March 1915, after the food had been distributed, my neighbours invited me to their home so that I could see their situation at

[50] Eugeniusz Romer, *Dziennik 1914–1918*, vol. 1, Warsaw 1995, p. 193.
[51] Władysław Leopold Jaworski, *Diariusz 1914–1918*, ed. M. Czajka, Warsaw 1997, p. 12.

THE FIRST MOMENTS   275

> close quarters. They were living in Bielcza, at farmer Jan Hynek's, and were in the fortunate position of having been allowed to stay on his property. As soon as I entered the house, I was assaulted by a terrible smell reminiscent of rotting meat. I pretended not to notice and sat down on a bench. In the house, which was 30 square meters at most, lived forty-seven people, among them a dozen or so tiny children, dirty and hungry, shouting at the tops of their voices. The farmer, an old acquaintance of mine and a decent man, told me that these people were the lucky ones, for the situation of those who had been living in the barn for several weeks was far worse. I simply cannot describe that scene. Some of the people were practically barefoot; they ate once a day, had no change of under-wear, and were so infested with insects that they had turned black. As if that was not enough, the army treated them with contempt and the local peasants hated them. They themselves often made matters worse by quarrelling or committing petty theft. Unable to bear that awful stench or to witness that hellish scene any longer, after an hour I said goodbye to everyone and left. As I walked out, wailing women tugged at my sleeves.[52]

Witos was too astute an observer not to notice that the misery of the evacuees was in part a result of their own decisions. Even when the authorities finally rose to the challenge and offered the evacuees suitable alternative accommodation, many did not want to leave their temporary abode, in order to remain close to their family homes.

The same army that removed peasants under duress could also force them to act as guides or drivers (using their own horse-drawn carts). Both these roles were very dangerous. Guides who led reconnaissance units could be killed by enemy bullets or end up on the gallows if they were found to have led the troops astray.

'Coachmen' also faced danger. Sometimes they would get caught in artillery fire. If they perished, their death would not be recorded under 'own losses' in any military statistics. It is hardly surprising, then, that peasants eagerly awaited the moment when they would no longer have to render the service of 'carriage'. August Krasicki, an aristocrat sensitive to the situation of the peasants, especially those from his native region, recalled meeting a group of peasants who were returning home by train from the Eastern Carpathians. They had all been dismissed from service for the sole reason that their horses had died.[53] In any case, it was hard not to sympathize with people in such difficult circumstances, especially as the service they had been forced to render went beyond their legal obligations. Because the number of available horses and carts declined with each passing month, 'carriage' became harder to come by. As a result, once mobilized, peasants who should have been allowed to return home after a few days often found themselves travelling with the army

---

[52] Witos, *Moje wspomnienia*, vol. 2, p. 63.
[53] Krasicki, *Dziennik z kampanii rosyjskiej*, p. 118.

276   OCCUPATION

for months. Over time they became more determined to leave at any cost. A good method was to transport the wounded behind the lines – from there, with a little luck, one could go home instead of returning to the front. People devised other methods, too: 'They hide their horses in the forest, dismantle the carts, and bury the wheels in manure. Before a cart like that can be reassembled, the army will be long gone. Others spend their days skulking in the woods and return home only at night.'[54]

Those who avoided evacuation, survived requisitioning and reparations, and were neither taken hostage nor used as 'coachmen' sometimes had to perform one other type of service for the army. They did forced labour in the immediate vicinity of the front, which involved digging trenches and burying the fallen. Initially, on the orders of the military authorities, everyone reported for work, but it soon transpired that these tasks would be assigned only to certain social groups. Father Rokoszny recalled that in August 1914, when first summoned by the Austrians, 1,000 residents gathered on the market square in Sandomierz armed with shovels. The army officers conducted the selection procedure themselves, rejecting members of the local intelligentsia and taking only manual workers. In time, however, in the Congress Kingdom, in Galicia, and in the western provinces of Russia, it was local Jews who shouldered the burden of forced labour, and not only those Jews who were used to doing manual work on account of their profession. August Krasicki noted that in Kovel 'Local Jews of all classes and professions are digging trenches: bankers, merchants, hairdressers, waiters, craftsmen, and porters.'[55] This fact is not especially surprising, since after the evacuation of its Russian civilian population Kovel became an almost exclusively Jewish town. On the other hand, this is not the only evidence of unequal burden-sharing and repression. Let us take a closer look at this issue.

Social (Dis)order

In the Kingdom of Poland and Galicia, where the heaviest fighting took place in the first two years of the war, social divisions often overlapped with ethnic ones. The peasants were mostly Polish or Ukrainian, the landowners were Poles, and the towns and cities housed large Jewish populations. Victims of repression, even if they were accidental victims, always represented a specific social group. For this reason the same events can be interpreted in two different ways, and this divergence of perspective is at times clearly visible in the sources. In September 1914 the military doctor Ryszard Łączyński recorded in his journal an event that links this issue with our previous

[54] Sławoj Felicjan Składkowski, *Moja służba w Brygadzie. Pamiętnik polowy*, Warsaw 1990, p. 191.
[55] Krasicki, *Dziennik z kampanii rosyjskiej*, p. 321.

THE FIRST MOMENTS

arguments about the problems facing civilians (e.g. the brutality of the army, reparations, and hostage-taking):

> At 10.00 a.m. one of our companies set off on a patrol to hunt down the Cossacks. Because the Jews of Korczyn had provided false information about the Cossacks, reparations amounting to 10,000 roubles were imposed on them. What happened was that at night, the day before yesterday, one of our units had been first to cross the Vistula to Korczyn; its orders were to take the Cossacks with bayonets, without firing a shot. Our boys advanced with their rifles unloaded. Anyone with a loaded rifle was to get a bullet in the head – the Cossacks had to be taken without a shot being fired. The Jews forewarned the Cossacks, who managed to escape from the town, and the mission ended in failure. Previously, when our boys had asked about the Cossacks, the Jews had told them that the enemy was gone. Yet when our boys reached the market square, the Cossacks greeted them with gunfire; in other words, the Jews had misinformed us. As punishment, reparations amounting to 10,000 roubles were imposed on the Jews, which they were ordered to pay within three hours. The town has a population of around 1,500, almost all of them Jews. Twenty-three of them, including two rabbis, were taken hostage. The despair and lamentation of the Jews is indescribable. They ran around the town like madmen, terrified by the size of the sum they had to pay; in two hours they barely collected 4,000 roubles and then declared that they had no more. So our gendarmes decided to give them a lesson in morality, an object-lesson in social and political law: they started raising a gallows on the market square in order to hang three members of the Jewish community from it. A crossbeam set between two trees, with three nooses hanging from it, lent a gloomy aspect to the market square in the town of Korczyn. It worked. The Jews, or rather the gendarmes when they carried out body searches, found 8,000 roubles on a tailor and another 6,000 on his wife. From these amounts the 10,000 roubles' worth of reparations was collected. The Jews were ordered to dismantle the gallows . . .[56]

As other accounts show, a few of the Polish residents of Korczyn, not wishing to sever relations with their Jewish neighbours, contributed to the reparations. Depending on which memoirs one reads, the same event is described either as reparations imposed on the Korczyn Jews or on the residents of Korczyn. Accounts of other misfortunes that befell civilians in areas where most of Europe's Jews lived can be interpreted in a similar way.

As we mentioned earlier, the arrival of the front was associated with a crisis in public order. So far we have mainly described the behaviour of hooligans and criminals, but the disappearance of authority also triggered rapacious and

---

[56] Cited in Urszula Oettingen, *Czarkowy – na drodze do niepodległości*, part 1. *Bój 16–24 września 1914 r.*, Kielce 2002, p. 143.

278 OCCUPATION

thuggish instincts in people who in other circumstances would have probably never come into conflict with the law. Indeed, the disturbance of public order had a deeper, social dimension. In places where power changed hands, in moments of transition, the order and norms hitherto observed in a local community sometimes broke down. This phenomenon was most evident on the Eastern Front. Were it not an anachronism, one could say that the Russian army that entered Eastern Galicia in 1914, six years before the Bolshevik offensive, unleashed a class struggle in the region. The sides in this struggle were the cities and the countryside, the middle class and the lower strata. The Russian invasion signalled the triumph of the peasantry over the bourgeoisie, especially the Jewish bourgeoisie. For Helena Jabłońska née Seifert, Przemyśl under Russian occupation became a completely different town:

> The character of the town has changed so much that one would not recognize it as Przemyśl. The morning market and the town square are filled with Ruthenian [Ukrainian] carts and peddlers. All commerce is now in their hands and in the hands of tradeswomen from the country-side. Sitting on their stools or on their carts, they sell lard and sausage. Soap, halva, and all manner of confectionary can be bought everywhere. There are saltwater fish of all sizes and species, canned fish, various cheeses, and masses of white eggs sold at 40 hellers for seven items. Bread is extremely expensive. All the shops, except for the Ruthenian ones, are closed – nothing to be had there.[57]

What Jabłońska, the Przemyśl landlady, found so surprising was not just the improvement in food supplies (it would have been indeed strange had more food not been available after the end of the siege). She was also struck by the fact that the *Ruscy* (i.e. Ukrainian) peddlers had taken on a role that others had previously performed:

> Who lives in tenement houses these days? Caretakers and peasants. So duped have the peasants been by the Muscovites that they have occupied the houses by force. [...] They sit around on the balconies and sleep on Jewish bed linen. To be sure, there is no shortage of comical scenes. For instance, a plump peasant woman in church dressed in a deep-cut ball gown over a coarse smock, wearing a bead necklace and sporting a corset ripped at the waist with percale gusset, and other similar scenes.[58]

Sometimes both the 'class struggle' and anti-Semitism assumed a much more dangerous form. In August 1914 in Bychawa near Lublin, a town famous for its Talmudic school, many of the mostly Jewish inhabitants decided to flee before the approaching Austrians. As they headed north, they were pelted with stones by local peasants and then attacked and robbed by the Cossacks.

---

[57] Jabłońska, *Dziennik z oblężonego Przemyśla 1914–1915*, p. 171.
[58] Ibid., p. 190.

THE FIRST MOMENTS

Immediately after the withdrawal of the Austro-Hungarian troops, those Jews who had remained in the town fell victim to a Russian pogrom. The Russian gendarmerie, which investigated the events in Bychawa, arrested a dozen or so Jews, finding them guilty of rioting and disloyalty;[59] the local peasants got off scot-free.

In Galicia, too, there was no doubt which side the Russians were on. Although not Jewish herself, Helena Jabłońska née Seifert felt, not without reason, that she too was a victim of this conflict:

> It is unbelievable what those Muscovites have done to make the people rebel. They have presented caretakers and their cooks with formal, officially stamped documents which transfer the ownership of tenement houses to them. Today, when one of the owners returned, the caretakers, on the basis of a Russian document, did not want to let her into her own property. The matter was resolved by the police [the Austro-Hungarian police, following the Gorlice Offensive and the recapture of Przemyśl by the Habsburg monarchy], and the caretakers turned the apartment into a detention room.[60]

Smaller Galician towns, whose mainly Jewish inhabitants usually fled or were forced out, fell victim to organized robbery by local peasants. The perpetrators were not the poorest labourers, however, but rather farmers who had wagons onto which the spoils could be loaded. Many no doubt believed that they were performing a just act, i.e. taking revenge on the supposedly exploitative Jews and contributing to the boycott called for by the National Democrats. The Supreme National Committee (NKN) envoy in Western Galicia reported:

> [...] the local population was not completely disaffected by the Muscovites on account of the fact that the latter smashed up and looted Jewish shops and the homes of refugees. Indeed, the local population was pleased to see this, and the lower classes often aided the Russian soldiers in their destruction. This is because the innate hatred that our population feels towards the Jews, reinforced by the Jews' earlier military shenanigans, was greatly intensified by Russian agitation.[61]

Violence against Jews was certainly not limited to pogroms organized by the Russian army. Requisitioning, forced labour, 'carriage', evacuation, hostage-taking, and rape – all of this could, and did, assume the character of anti-Semitism under certain circumstances.

---

[59] Konrad Zieliński, *Żydzi Lubelszczyzny 1914–1918*, Lublin 1999, p. 79.
[60] Jabłońska, *Dziennik z oblężonego Przemyśla 1914–1915*, p. 213.
[61] Cited in Jerzy Z. Pająk, *Od autonomii do niepodległości. Kształtowanie się postaw politycznych i narodowych społeczeństwa Galicji w warunkach Wielkiej Wojny 1914–1918*, Kielce 2012, p. 142.

280   OCCUPATION

THE OCCUPATION OF TARNÓW

Certain events associated with the Great War have for years been unable to attract the interest of historians. Of these, the best example is the almost-six-month-long Russian occupation of Tarnów. Although it did not abound in moments that would fundamentally alter the course of the global conflict, the occupation immediately found a chronicler. Already in 1915, several weeks after the Austro-Hungarian army had returned to the city, there appeared a chronicle written by a thirty-year-old priest called Jan Czuj, which described the recent events. Father Czuj was no ordinary author. In the 1920s he became a professor at the Catholic University of Lublin and the University of Warsaw, and was the first rector of the Academy of Catholic Theology (in the 1950s he was one of the driving forces of the pro-communist 'patriotic priests' movement). In his wartime publication, Czuj went under the pseudonym of Jan Borzęcki. His description of the Russian occupation is noteworthy not only on account of the wealth of information it contains and the accuracy of some of the observations but also on account of the mentality and beliefs expressed, which were probably representative of other Galicians, too.

Tarnów fell to the Russian army on 10 November 1914. For the author, the beginnings of the occupation came as a pleasant surprise. It had been widely assumed that the arrival of the 'Muscovites' would signal ruin for all of the town's inhabitants, yet the occupiers concentrated on looting Jewish shops and apartments and behaved more moderately towards the Christian population. As the local NKN envoy reported:

> [in Tarnów] the Jews were ruthlessly terrorized. They were not even allowed to stand in the windows because stones would be thrown at them. Such wild behaviour was manifested not only by the Cossacks, but also by the infantry. One such unit was passing along ul. Krakowska towards the end of Muscovite rule in Tarnów, when it noticed an Israelite standing in the window of Mr Haller's house; the soldiers proceeded to bombard the house with stones.[62]

Contrary to this opinion, Father Czuj observed that particular Russian units behaved very differently in the occupied town. Front-line troops merely passed through and paid for the goods they wanted. The Cossacks, in contrast, committed theft and rape, and their commanding officers either did not notice or were too afraid to discipline their subordinates. One of the first decisions made by the Russian military command in the town was to force local Jews to dig trenches. A total of seven Catholics and seven Jews from among the Tarnów elites were taken hostage; the Catholics were released sooner.

During the first weeks the repression was mainly directed at the Jews. The Polish population of Tarnów felt the full force of the Russian occupation with a certain delay. It was not until the end of November that the Russian authorities banned the sale of alcohol. Supply problems arose, prices soared, and the Polish Catholic bourgeoisie was subjected to constant inspections. In late January and early February the town came under fire from the Austro-Hungarian artillery. Later

---

[62] Cited in Pająk, *Od autonomii do niepodległości*, p. 137.

that month shells launched from 'Big Bertha' howitzers began to fall on Tarnów. On 18 February the shelling was extremely heavy. As Father Czuj wrote: '[...] a second shell landed in the garden on ul. Mickiewicza opposite The Falcon. A few soldiers, who had been busy cooking a meal, perished there along with a few horses. The force of the explosion threw half a horse onto the roof of the Brodziński school, two floors up. All along ul. Mickiewicza the iron gas lamps were torn from their foundations and smashed to the ground.'[63] Four days later, a shell landed on the town brothel, killing twenty people: prostitutes and their Russian officer clients. In March Austro-Hungarian and German planes began bombing Tarnów and the Pilzno road, while down below on the streets of the town appeared destitute children. These were unmistakable signs that Russian rule in Tarnów was drawing to a close. In the first days of the Gorlice Offensive the town once again came under the control of the Habsburg monarchy.

Father Czuj proved to be an astute observer. He noticed, for instance, the propaganda manoeuvre employed by the Russians that involved marching the same prisoners of war through Tarnów several times for effect, and recounted how some of the wealthier prisoners were able to buy themselves out of captivity. Father Czuj also made some interesting observations about the Russian field hospitals (where he probably went to minister to the wounded). The hospitals subsidized by the Duma were good, but the rest were in a catastrophic state.

Fig. 51   Damage to the cathedral basilica in Tarnów.

---

[63] Jan Borzęcki [Jan Czuj], *Moskale w Tarnowie. Od 10 listopada 1914 do 6 maja 1915 roku*, Tarnów 1915, p. 39.

282   OCCUPATION

The assessments and comments that accompany the author's observations present a separate problem. Some of Father Czuj's remarks attest rather poignantly to the lack of solidarity among the various social groups in occupied Tarnów. When the prostitutes were killed by Austrian artillery fire, the chronicler recorded the event with undisguised satisfaction. He felt even less sympathy for his Jewish neighbours. Although Russian repression threatened all of the town's inhabitants, and even though it was known that once the Jewish shops had been looted the Polish ones would be next, Father Czuj felt no sense of shared fate. On the contrary, Jewish misery amused him:

> On another occasion, once again in the early morning, I witnessed an entertaining scene: a Jew was running quickly between two doorways, when a Cossack stopped him because he took a liking to the man's shoes. One should be aware that the Muscovites have excellent eyesight. In this case, however, the Cossack had made a mistake [...]. He tried on the shoes and examined them for a moment, and when he had convinced himself that his own shoes were better than the Jew's, he returned the shoes to the frightened son of Israel; for his mistake, he struck the Jew only once with his whip.[64]

The author finally sets out his main accusation against the Russian occupiers. Even in the light of the above remarks, which are a far cry from the dictum of love thy neighbour, his conclusion is surprising. Father Czuj does not begrudge the Russians for their oppression, war crimes, or even their persecution of Catholics, but rather for their overly benign attitude towards the Jews. 'They oppress the Jews', he writes, 'but only superficially, out of calculation, in order to win over our people, who have been mercilessly exploited by our Orthodox community.'[65]

Father Czuj's chronicle is one example of the power of the anti-Semitic worldview, which even the First World War was unable to shatter. It also attests to the deeper phenomena that could be observed throughout the territory that was affected by the war in one way or another. Misery and tragedy were a shared experience only in theory. In practice they exacerbated the tensions that divided particular communities prior to 1914. The calamities suffered by some were observed with satisfaction by others. From this perspective, the war took on the character of a natural disaster, one that was in its own way just, because it finally inflicted punishment upon neighbours who had long since deserved it.

One of the most moving accounts of the fate of the Jewish population during the Great War is a book by the Russian journalist and Yiddish writer Salomon Rappoport (who used the pseudonym S. An-ski), *The Tragedy of the Galician Jews during the First World War*. Written on the fly, Rappoport's account is

[64] Ibid., p. 9.
[65] Ibid., p. 39.

THE FIRST MOMENTS   283

a veritable patchwork of the horrors, tragedies, and crimes that Jews suffered
at the hands of all the warring parties. The Jews 'were always stuck between
two flames, between two hostile camps. And from both sides all they could
expect was robbery, threats, slander, and terror.'[66] However, what most
appeals to the imagination in An-ski's book is the evolution of the author's
views. An-ski came to Galicia as a Russian patriot, convinced that it was the
Poles who were trying – unsuccessfully – to implant the germ of anti-
Semitism in the Russians. Every day he remained in Galicia, and every
conversation he had with Galician Jews, convinced him that the truth was
far worse. Finally, having observed the Russian evacuation after the defeat at
Gorlice in May 1915, An-ski wrote:

> Yet here, on the blood-drenched battlefields, where the flame of hatred
> between nations burns so brightly, there is already a terrifying consensus
> that all of this has been caused by the Jews. The Pole with his false smile,
> the naïve Ukrainian refugee, the Austrian or Hungarian prisoner of war,
> and the Russian soldier – all are united in their hatred of the Jew.[67]

***

What we are investigating here are the emotions felt by civilians, for
whom the war did not begin with occupation. The beginning was
marked by manifestations of loyalty, soon to be followed by ever more
onerous restrictions. Regardless of how loyal or disloyal subjects were to
the belligerent emperors and kings, the moment of regime change was
a difficult experience for them. Even if in some places the material
damage was not as great as in the vicinity of major communication
routes or in regions where there was persistent fighting, some form of
violence affected almost every community in occupied Central and
Eastern Europe and the Balkans. It was a unique experience, different
from the police repression at the beginning of the war and different
from the subsequent order imposed by the occupying authorities and
their decrees.

In any case, the distinction between one's own authorities and those of
a foreign state did not always retain its pre-war meaning. Józef Piłsudski was
right when he described the unique situation of places that changed hands
several times:

> The look of such a 'neutral corridor' town is odd. One lot of masters has
> left, the other not yet arrived. The poor 'neutrals' count over their sins

---

[66] Szymon An-ski, *Tragedia Żydów galicyjskich w czasie I wojny światowej. Wrażenia
i refleksje z podróży po kraju*, translated by Krzysztof Dawid Majus, Przemyśl 2010, p. 72.
[67] Ibid., p. 197.

against their new lord, sins that were services to the one who has left. They are all drawn psychologically into the orbit of power of the new arrivals.[68]

For local inhabitants, 'Daddy's return' signified not so much the restoration of security as a new type of threat. It was experienced in full by the populations of towns recaptured by the Habsburg army in the spring and summer of 1915. In Rzeszów, on the day after the Russian troops withdrew, the returning local authorities introduced new maximum prices, bread-making quotas, mandatory lists of food supplies held by private individuals, and a new census (among other reasons, in order to immediately collect outstanding taxes). The gendarmerie wasted no time in searching for real and alleged spies. On the first day alone, thirty people were arrested. Equipped with its up-to-date census, the army set about conscripting men who had avoided military service during the Russian occupation. The *Ilustrowany Kuryer Codzienny* summarized its report from Rzeszów with a phrase whose irony clearly went unnoticed by the censor: 'After six months of captivity the population can take a deep breath, for now it understands the difference between Czarist and Austrian rule.'[69]

Generally, for the duration of the transitional period, occupiers tightened existing regulations and restrictions and added new ones, but it was not they who destroyed the peacetime order: in all the territories they entered, that peacetime order had already been abolished by the previous, native authorities. Millions of young men joined the army. People had far fewer rights than they did before the summer of 1914. In almost every major city the number of unemployed increased dramatically. Goods in the shops became increasingly scarce and increasingly expensive. The arrival of occupying forces, even if it changed little in the material sense, still came as a huge shock: the highest authority in the land, uniforms, customs, and the portraits hanging on the walls of offices, all changed within the space of a few days. In Galicia and Bukovina the subjects of Franz Joseph in theory held their 'own' Hussars, i.e. the Hungarian army, in the lowest possible esteem, but they feared the Russians, and especially the Cossacks, even more. Widespread anxiety was exacerbated by disillusionment – people felt helpless and let down. 'Only those who experienced it for themselves could possibly comprehend the feelings of pain, bitterness, and regret that I, and all others who remained, felt on 14 November, when we found ourselves in the town alone, with no prefect's office, no court, no army, and no gendarmerie', wrote the newly appointed mayor of Gorlice in his journal in November 1914.[70] Similar days of dread

---

[68] Joseph Pilsudski [Józef Piłsudski], *The Memories of a Polish Revolutionary and Soldier*, translated by Darsie Rutherford Gillie, New York, NY 1931, p. 251.

[69] Wacław Sperber, 'Z oswobodzonego Rzeszowa', *Ilustrowany Kuryer Codzienny*, 30 May 1915, p. 7.

[70] Bronisław Świeykowski, *Z dni grozy w Gorlicach. Od 25 IX 1914 do 2 V 1915*, Cracow 1919, p. 13 n.

were experienced by millions of people in Łódź, Lwów, and Czernowitz in 1914, in Warsaw, Grodno, Vilnius, and Belgrade in 1915, in Bucharest in 1916, in Riga in 1917, and in many cities on the western borders of Russia in 1918. In each place, and in each year, the situation was slightly different. For Tallinn or Kiev, the entry of the occupier in 1918 did not signify the destruction of the old regime, or indeed of any regime. Public order had already broken down a year earlier.

9

New Orders

In the western Russian Empire and Romania the Germans occupied territory previously unknown to them. Austro-Hungarian officials had, at least in theory, some idea about both Serbia and the Russian Polish lands.[1] Regardless of the starting position, however, each occupier had its own idea of the new regime it wanted to establish. To do so it would need the assistance of local people, but it had little or no intention of consulting them on the appropriateness of its plans.

The question of official time is a good illustration of the approach taken by the occupiers. It so happened that the countries participating in the war were not only located in different time zones (Russia did not ratify the international agreement on this matter and left the setting of local time to municipal authorities) but also used different calendars. Every occupier put the clocks either forward or back, which was not devoid of symbolic meaning. The Russians introduced the Julian calendar and Petersburg time in Eastern Galicia and Bukovina, while the Germans introduced the Gregorian calendar and Central European time in the East. In Sandomierz, which was occupied by the Austrians, the clocks were put back by thirty-five minutes to synchronize them with Viennese time, while the switch to the Gregorian calendar moved the date forward by a full thirteen days. The same happened in Serbia. In Russian-occupied Lwów, in turn, the Julian calendar was introduced (which moved the date back by thirteen days). In Warsaw, as in other territories they occupied, the Germans imposed Berlin time. But regardless of what new official time was introduced in Warsaw, Lwów, or Belgrade, and by whom, there was more to it than just moving the hands on the clock. The residents of those cities took a very dim view of changes that disturbed the way in which they measured the rhythm of their everyday lives. Under German and Austrian occupation the problem was further complicated by the distinction between

---

[1] Stephan Lehnstaedt, 'Das Militärgouvernement Lublin im Ersten Weltkrieg: Die "Nutzbarmachung" Polens durch Osterreich-Ungarn', *Zeitschrift für Ostmitteleuropa-Forschung* 61, 1 (2012), p. 6, points out, however, that the top posts in the general administration and in the gendarmerie were occupied by non-Poles. In 1916 the Foreign Ministry in Vienna wrote about 'a well organized clique [. . .]; the behaviour of that clique is capricious, but it is always guided by the greatest possible distrust of the Poles'.

NEW ORDERS

summer time and winter time, and was met with a similar lack of understanding. The changes were justified by the need to improve efficiency in the army and civil service, but in reality they only led to chaos and disorganization and did not make life any easier. This was largely because locals continued to tell the time in two different ways. In Romania, after the switch to Central European time (i.e. from *timp român* to winter *timp german*), by the middle of September it was already dark at 5.30 p.m. and the evenings became 'unbearably long' for Romanians and Germans alike.[2]

The point, therefore, was rather to demonstrate the power of the new regime. In Belgium, where the German occupiers approached the matter in the same way as in the Congress Kingdom, 'civilians delighted in keeping "Belgian time" on their watches (which was an hour earlier than German time), as a sort of manifestation of patriotism'.[3] In Central and Eastern Europe such protests were less common, although they did occur, particularly under Russian occupation and in Serbia. In May 1916 the Austrian writer Friedrich Wallisch, who was serving as an officer in the Balkans, noted:

> The new summer time has also been introduced in Serbia. Although this arrangement had been accepted even in countries that were hostile to us, the Serbs did not entirely subscribe to this 'Swabian' idea of moving the clocks forward. However, just as those who doubted in our victory, being convinced that the Serbian army would return, were eventually forced to accept our position in this war, so too in this case the distinction between 'our time' and 'your time', between *našo vrijeme* and *vašo vrijeme*, will soon be consigned to history. It was not easy to explain to the peasants the purpose of this new system of measuring time and how it would be carried out. It was simplest in places where, on the morning of 1 May at 8.00 a.m. according to the old time, for instance, an order was issued to the effect that it was now 9.00 a.m.[4]

Ultimately, the Reich's political dominance when it came to the issue of time affected not just the occupied territories but also Germany's allies. In the spring of 1916, under pressure from Berlin, Bulgaria reformed its calendar. The date of 31 March was to be immediately followed by 14 April. The change was announced in the manner of a diktat.

The next stage in the imposition of a new regime was the change of alphabet, and also the change of language, which was only partly related to it. Sometimes, where an occupied territory was to be incorporated into the victorious state or separated from the empire as a new nation-state, this change was of strategic

---

[2] Gerhard Velburg, *Rumänische Etappe. Der Weltkrieg, wie ich ihn sah*, Minden 1930, p. 196 n.

[3] Tammy M. Proctor, *Civilians in a World at War, 1914–1918*, New York, NY and London 2010, p. 134.

[4] Friedrich Wallisch, *Die Pforte zum Orient. Unser Friedenswerk in Serbien*, Innsbruck 1917, p. 95. Wallisch used the Croatian spelling of the word 'time' (*vreme* in Serbian).

Fig. 52 The front page of a newspaper published by the Russians in occupied Lwów. The title above the illustration reads: 'Today's Street Traffic in Lwów'. Courtesy of Mariusz Kulik.

importance, but in most cases it was a practical matter: it was difficult for an occupier to move around a territory if the signage was incomprehensible. Nor was the problem limited to language and alphabet: for the first few months in occupied Warsaw the Germans did not know how to use the trams. The Russians had removed all the notice boards containing information about tram routes and destinations. For Warsaw residents, knowing the number of the line was enough. The occupiers' efforts to become accustomed to their new surroundings often made life more difficult, in turn, for the locals. In Ober-Ost (the territory controlled and administered by the German army in Lithuania, in Belarus, and in the eastern part of Congress Poland) all railway stations received new signs with the local place names transcribed into German. In

NEW ORDERS

289

many cases this linguistic challenge proved beyond the capabilities of the translators in the German army. As a result, even locals found it difficult to guess the original names from the appalling transcriptions.

The alphabet problem did not arise in German-occupied Romania. Everywhere else, when the new authorities introduced the Latin alphabet to replace Cyrillic or vice versa, they soon had to ask whether this was to their own advantage or not. Russian was not widely known in Galicia and Bukovina, although of course it was better understood by Ukrainians than by Poles, Romanians, and Jews. The Russians were well aware of this, but they left themselves with no alternative: since they had 'liberated' territories that were 'eternally Russian', the Russification of public space, and to some extent of education, was essential in order to emphasize the gravitas of their programme. To this end the Russians could count on the supranational opportunism of private entrepreneurs, in other words, all manner of intermediaries who jumped at the chance of removing German shop signs and putting up Cyrillic signs alongside the Polish ones. It was local governments that resisted the changes. They explained that there was no one to manufacture the Russian signage and that the project would be an expensive eyesore. In Lwów this sabotage proved so effective that Russian street signs did not appear until six months into the occupation.

Relations were quite the opposite in the occupied Kingdom of Poland, where the Germans did not have to put much effort into removing Cyrillic from public spaces; the Poles did this quickly and eagerly as soon as it became clear that their new masters were not about to leave. Things were altogether different in Serbia. The Austro-Hungarian occupiers changed the traffic regulations without too much bother: from driving on the right to driving on the left, the latter being the rule in the monarchy. However, time and the alphabet presented a much bigger challenge. As we mentioned earlier, the Serbs incorporated 'Swabian' summer time by using, depending on the circumstances, one of two concurrent systems – 'our' time and 'their' time. They did the same with the Gregorian calendar, which meant that both the day and the year were expressed in two different ways. Eventually, the Austrians decided to respect the traditions of the vanquished Serbs. They tolerated the 'old style' and did not force the Serbs to celebrate church holidays, for example, in accordance with the new calendar. From the outset they also recognized that it would be impossible to remove Cyrillic from public spaces. Only a minority of Serbs could read and write; if one wanted to communicate with that minority, then a compromise was necessary. The orders of the occupation authorities were thus published in Cyrillic, and petitioners could send correspondence in Cyrillic to the occupier's institutions. The military authorities went even further. In 1917 they published a trilingual calendar (in German, Hungarian, and Serbo-Croat) that contained both the Gregorian calendar and the Julian calendar, 'the latter being in Cyrillic script, in which some of the lighter and more informative texts are also printed'.[5]

Another problem concerned the presence of the occupier in public places. In the countryside no one was surprised when a local army unit was billeted at the home of the village bailiff, at the local manor, or with the richest peasants. Similarly, it was taken for granted that a Russian 'gradonachalnik' (town commandant) would move into the imperial–royal prefect's office, and that a German regional commander would take over the headquarters of the local governor. Things became a bit more complicated when the German authorities in Bucharest requisitioned an existing royal residence. When, in turn, the German Governor-General installed himself in the Royal Castle in Warsaw, he occupied the seat of his equal-ranking Russian predecessor only in theory; the place had for decades been contaminated with the toxic memory of Russian repression of the Polish national movement, although it remained a national shrine.

Fig. 53   Austro-Hungarian soldiers visiting the throne room of the Skupština (Serbian parliament).

---

[5] Cited in Tamara Scheer, 'Manifestation österreichisch-ungarischer Besatzungsmacht in Belgrad (1916–1918)', in *Der Erste Weltkrieg auf dem Balkan. Perspektiven der Forschung*, ed. Jürgen Angelow, Gundula Gahlen, and Oliver Stein, Berlin 2011, pp. 211–239, here p. 230. On the structure of occupation authorities, see Tamara Scheer, *Zwischen Front und Heimat. Österreich-Ungarns Militärverwaltungen im Ersten Weltkrieg*, Frankfurt am Main 2009; and Mark von Hagen, *War in a European Borderland. Occupations and Occupation Plans in Galicia and Ukraine, 1914–1918*, Seattle, WA 2007, pp. 23–28.

NEW ORDERS

However, the change was drastic not when an occupier took over a prominent public space from its predecessor, but when the new occupier wilfully downgraded it. In Belgrade the Austrian authorities converted the parliament building (begun in 1907 but never completed) into food stores. The yellow-and-black flag of the Habsburg monarchy was raised above the Kalemegdan Fortress overlooking the floodplain of the Danube and Sava rivers. In a park on the same hill the Austrians dismantled a monument to Serbia's wars of independence (and then melted it down to extract the precious raw material). They had every reason to be ashamed: the Military Government General in Belgrade knew that the Austrians had violated the Hague Convention and, from then on, categorically opposed both the destruction of old monuments and the raising of new ones. Thus, the plan to decorate the city with busts of Franz Joseph, as proposed by some Austrian officers, also had to be shelved. After the destruction of the Kalemegdan monument, the Governor-General's chief of staff, Colonel Hugo Kerchnawe, criticized the act as a 'pointless assault on the military pride of the Serbian people'.[6]

Other experiences, seen by the inhabitants of occupied territories as typical examples of the occupier's brutality, were familiar to the inhabitants of the hinterland as well. This is best illustrated with reference to the sensitive area of religious worship. In Bucharest, during the short campaign of 1916, Roman Catholic masses became a problem as they had previously been celebrated for, among others, the informal protector of the Catholic faith in Romania, i.e. Franz Joseph. In Lwów, a year earlier, a similar problem arose when the Russians demanded that the Catholic archbishops (Roman Catholic, Greek Catholic, and Armenian) order their congregations to pray for the Czar. The hierarchs refused, and so negotiations began. Under the compromise that was reached, worshipers were to pray for the emperor without naming either Franz Joseph (as they had done in recent decades) or Nicholas II (as the new authorities wanted).

Another example of a similar conflict also concerned the religious sphere. One of the most common experiences to the west and east of the front line was the dismantling of copper roofs. Prominent and stately buildings were the principal targets. Urban residents were unhappy to witness the aesthetic degradation of city centres, but their opinion counted for little. In any case, over time, the need for raw materials and scrap led to a much more serious conflict. The authorities set their sights on churches, where it was possible to recover metals not only from the roofs but also from the bells. Despite the resistance of congregations and clergy, local

---

[6] Cited in Scheer, 'Manifestation österreichisch-ungarischer Besatzungsmacht in Belgrad', p. 229.

Fig. 54 The Kalemegdan monument shortly after the capture of Belgrade by the Austro-Hungarian and German armies.

construction companies carried out various commissions and were not at all secretive about them: the process of dismantling a church roof could hardly be concealed and often lasted weeks. Worse still, the belfries were stripped during the day in the presence of onlookers and passers-by, while the bells were broken up on the spot to make them easier to transport. It was a clear case of desecration. The reaction to the demolition of Orthodox churches in Polish areas occupied by the Central Powers was in all likelihood different, since the new authorities were destroying the shrines of a religion that was alien to the majority of local residents. Virtually every Orthodox believer left Warsaw. When the Germans ordered the demolition of the roof of the Alexander Nevsky Cathedral – a great symbol of Russian power in the 'Privislinsky Krai' ('Vistula Land') – neither Roman Catholics nor Jews protested.

NEW ORDERS

Local communities tried to resist the requisitioning of church bells as they did other calamities caused by the war and occupation. Paradoxically, such resistance had the best chances of success in areas through which the front passed repeatedly over a short period of time. When power changed hands very quickly, the new rulers did not always have time to undertake an operation that entailed considerable organizational effort and cost. In Sandomierz the retreating Russians abandoned their plans when they were presented with a cost estimate amounting to several hundred roubles that included photographic documentation of the historic belfry.[7] A while later, Father Rokoszny noted in his diary:

> They are pulling down the bells in the Opatów district; in one parish, as they did so, a crowd looked on in silence; after removing the bells the soldiers said: 'What fools you are! If you had got in our way and caused a scene, we would not have taken your bells.'[8]

The Central Powers used the same procedure to recover valuable raw materials from sacred buildings both at home and in occupied territories. In every place, local governments and residents regarded the dismantling of historic roofs and bells as nothing short of barbarism; protest committees were established and public-spirited citizens submitted complaints and appeals. In Lwów the authorities removed the copper roof from, among other buildings, the Armenian Cathedral, but after an intervention by the church authorities they left the Boim Chapel intact. One can only speculate whether the residents of Lwów might have achieved more success had they been dealing with the occupier and not their own authorities.

This same conflict was repeated in the provinces, where congregations were just as attached to their places of worship as the residents of capital cities. In the municipality of Fetești, 150 kilometres east of Bucharest, a soldier by the name of Tilka was surprised when, one day, he heard the bells of the Orthodox church ringing out in a strangely discordant fashion. It turned out that the bells were being taken down. A group of despairing believers had gathered around the church, among them the equally dejected and silent priest. The bells would no longer be heard, noted Tilka:

> Their metal will pierce the bodies of warriors still warm with life; warriors who are perhaps from here and whose baptism that metal announced. What can I tell these people? Is there any point in telling them that in Germany all the bells have long since been melted down into a deadly ore? Ordinary villagers will never forgive us for taking their bells.[9]

---

[7] Józef Rokoszny, *Diariusz Wielkiej Wojny*, ed. Wiesław Caban and Marek Przeniosło, Kielce 1998, vol. 2, p. 20.

[8] Ibid., p. 226.

[9] Cited in Lisa Mayerhofer, *Zwischen Freund und Feind – Deutsche Besatzung in Rumänien 1916–1918*, Munich 2010, p. 167 n.

In occupied Romania 4,340 bells, weighing 454 tonnes in total, were melted down.

Territories

Russia occupied Eastern Galicia, part of Western Galicia, and Bukovina in the late summer of 1914. In September the Russians set up a conventional occupation administration, in which, as usual, the interests of the military and civilian authorities diverged, i.e. the desire to pacify areas adjacent to the front *versus* strategic plans to transform enemy territory into lands that would in future be incorporated or at least remain friendly. These aims were partly compatible when it came to positive actions such as encouraging collaboration or creating local structures well-disposed to the new authorities, but they could also be completely contradictory. Imposing Russian as the language of instruction encroached on the rights of Poles and Ukrainians; Jews also had cause for concern. The closure of potentially disloyal public organizations or newspapers had the same effect. As a result, in less than a year the Russians managed to alienate practically everyone – Poles, Ukrainians, and Jews. When, in July 1916, they recaptured part of Eastern Galicia and Bukovina, those areas remained in the front-line zone. The army would not even hear of an occupation policy that went beyond maintaining peace behind the lines and engaging in economic exploitation. In any case, the latter was difficult to do in areas close to the fighting.

Austria-Hungary occupied a more extensive territory – and for longer. In the summer of 1915 the Imperial–Royal Military Government General for the lands of the Kingdom of Poland, with headquarters in Lublin (Militärgouvernement Lublin, MGG/L), was established. At the end of that year the armies of the monarchy occupied much of Serbia and Albania as well as Montenegro. In 1917 and 1918 parts of Ukraine – around 400,000 square kilometres with a population of 20 million – were also occupied.

Bulgaria seized much less territory – Romanian Dobruja (Dobrogea) and the Serbian and Greek parts of Macedonia. Sofia wanted to annex all these lands permanently, and, perhaps because of this, among all the occupiers of the 1915–1918 period the Bulgarians stood out for their brutality. Many of Bulgaria's actions were guided by the prospect of revenge for the defeat of 1913. Indeed, units consisting mainly of Macedonian Bulgarians were sent to protect the most important of the conquered provinces. The new masters began by interning all former soldiers of the Serbian army. They also tried to eliminate the local intelligentsia. 'Going to Sofia' was a phrase used to describe the process by which a local teacher, clergyman, or lawyer, whether Greek, Serbian, or Muslim, would be taken from his home by a patrol of Bulgarian soldiers or gendarmes. A while later the patrol would return without the prisoner, who had 'gone to Sofia', never to return. According to conservative

NEW ORDERS

estimates, around 2,000 members of the intelligentsia in the occupied Serbian lands fell victim to these semi-secret executions. The aim was to reverse the nationalities policy that had been pursued by Serbia and Greece. Those former occupiers had tried to persuade Macedonian children that they were Greek or Serbian. Now their names were changed to Bulgarian ones and foreign textbooks were confiscated.

In the area of provisioning, too, the Bulgarians were remembered in the worst possible terms, although the fault was not entirely theirs. Berlin forced Sofia to supply increasing amounts of food, and as a result shortages began to emerge in the country in 1916. In response the Bulgarians treated their occupation zone as a form of compensation and ruthlessly exploited it. At the beginning of 1918, when hunger in Macedonia had become widespread, the Germans had to lend their own food supplies to the Bulgarians to prevent mass starvation, the first victims of which were recorded in 1917.[10]

The biggest occupier in the East was the German Reich. In 1914 it seized the western part of the Kingdom of Poland along with the city of Łódź (which had a population approaching half a million) – the province of Piotrków generated 4 per cent of Russia's pre-war GDP. In the summer of the following year the Germans occupied the majority of the Kingdom and, further to the east, Vilnius and the lands up to Riga. Now Russia lost over 12 per cent of its GDP, and one-third of all its factories, which in 1913 had accounted for a fifth of industrial production.

The Russians tried to minimize their losses. During the 'great retreat' in the summer of 1915 they tried to evacuate anything of productive value. Besides people, the Czarist authorities mainly evacuated factories – from Warsaw and Riga (the latter lost two-thirds of its population of half a million) they removed everything that could in theory be of use when production was resumed somewhere in Russia. By the end of 1915 the number of refugees and evacuees in Russia had risen to 3.3 million; a year later there were 6 million, including more than 3.5 million who were included in the official statistics of charitable organizations. With every defeat of the imperial army a new wave of refugees traversed Russia. In Kharkiv (Kharkov), a major railway junction, precise statistics were kept of the transports that passed through it: in July 1915 only 2,565 evacuees were recorded; in August, when the Germans entered Warsaw, the number rose to 43,606; and in September the statistics revealed as many as 233,419 evacuees.[11] Evacuation was accompanied by the mindless destruction of infrastructure on a grand scale. Stanisław Dzierzbicki, who witnessed the

---

[10] Björn Opfer, *Im Schatten des Krieges. Besatzung oder Anschluss – Befreiung oder Unterdrückung? Eine komparative Untersuchung über die bulgarische Herrschaft in Vardar-Makedonien 1915–1918 und 1941–1944*, Münster 2005, pp. 96–101.

[11] Liubov Zhvanko, Біженство Першої світової війни в Україні. Документи і матеріали (1914–1918) [*Bizhenstvo Pershoi svitovoi viiny v Ukraini. Dokumenty i materialy (1914–1918)*], Kharkiv 2010, pp. 39–41.

last days of Russian rule in Warsaw, observed not only the chaotic removal of steam engines and boilers from factories but also the dismantling of the popular narrow gauge railways – Kolejka Grójecka and Kolejka Wilanowska: 'Suburban residents were allowed to plunder the Belvedere station, the workshops, and the locomotive sheds. Several people were injured, crushed by beams falling from the roofs.'[12]

The Germans occupied depopulated regions with ruined industry, mass unemployment, and widespread poverty. In September 1917, when the Russian army existed only on paper, they captured Riga, which was in an even worse state after three years of war and two years as a front-line city. Without encountering much resistance the Germans captured Estonia, the rest of Belarus, and Ukraine in March 1918. They now controlled the entire western part of the Russian Empire – one-quarter of its land and rail network, one-third of its population, 73 per cent of its steel industry, and 89 per cent of its coal mines.

In the south, from the end of 1916, the Germans controlled 80 per cent of Romania, including its oil deposits. It was not until 1942 that the Reich managed to occupy a larger territory. At that time, with its troops stationed

Fig. 55 The German and Polish text below the photograph reads: A railway bridge during an explosion. Courtesy of the Herder-Institut, Marburg, Bildarchiv.

---

[12] Stanisław Dzierzbicki, *Pamiętnik z lat wojny 1915–1918*, ed. Janusz Pajewski and Danuta Płygawko, Warsaw 1983, p. 59.

on the Atlantic, Germany ruled or controlled Norway, Denmark, and nearly all of Central and South-Eastern Europe, and the front line ran more or less between Petrograd and Rostov-on-Don.

The Economy

Serbia supplied the monarchy with 170,000 head of cattle, 190,000 sheep, and 50,000 hogs. Albania supplied 50,000 turtles to the Reich and Cisleithania, while in 1916–1917 Poland surrendered 6,000 freight cars of grain, 14,000 freight cars of potatoes, 1.9 million eggs, and 19,000 horses.[13] In 1917 the occupiers exported almost 1.7 million tonnes of grain from Romania to Germany and Austria-Hungary. We do not know how many of these products ended up in field kitchens and messes, and how many reached the increasingly hungry residents of cities in the hinterland.

In mid 1917 roughly 60,000 Lithuanians, Latvians, and Belarusians worked as forced labourers for Ober-Ost, while another 34,000 were recruited to work in the Reich. At the end of 1916 a total of 70,000 Poles and Ukrainians worked for Austria-Hungary. This figure includes 52,000 who did forced labour in the territory administered by the Military Government General in Lublin and 15,000 who worked 'voluntarily' in other parts of the monarchy; another 5,000 people employed in the monarchy had the status of 'internees', i.e. forced labourers. From the autumn of 1915 between 200,000 and 240,000 Poles went to work in the Reich. There they joined a similar number of compatriots and other Russian subjects who in the summer of 1914 had signed up for work on the harvest (as they had done every year for generations). The German authorities deemed them to be potential Russian conscripts and prevented their return home.[14]

Any number with several zeros makes an impression. In the case of the German and Austro-Hungarian occupations, the figures can be multiplied almost without end: Romania provided millions of tonnes of oil, while the western provinces of the Russian Empire supplied (besides labour) huge quantities of food and wood; the traditional hunting ground of the Russian czars – the Białowieża Forest – was almost completely devastated as a result. Everywhere they went, the occupiers plundered machinery, natural resources, and secondary raw materials. Economic exploitation reached hitherto unknown heights. Historians have (understandably) focused on it when writing about the economy.

---

[13] Holger H. Herwig, *The First World War. Germany and Austria-Hungary 1914–1918*, London 1996, p. 278.

[14] For more on this subject, see Christian Westerhoff, *Zwangsarbeit im Ersten Weltkrieg. Deutsche Arbeitskräftepolitik im besetzten Polen und Litauen 1914–1918*, Paderborn 2012.

298   OCCUPATION

However, there are other data for the same period that challenge the figures cited above. Work for an occupier was not tantamount to repression. The Jews of Łódź complained to the Polish city council when the latter awarded construction jobs on local roads exclusively to Poles.[15] In the German-occupied Kingdom of Poland in 1918 the total stock of hogs was 124 per cent of its 1912 level;[16] ration cards appeared in Warsaw in October 1915, two months after the city had been captured by the Germans and a good six months after rationing had been introduced in the Reich. In Bucharest in June 1917 the weekly bread ration was over 3 kilograms, while in Berlin it was about half that, and in Vienna it was lower by two-thirds. This list is likewise not exhaustive.

Several factors contributed to these evident contradictions. First, and most important, was the subjective sense of harm felt by all people under occupation. They had little idea about the problems that the new authorities faced and probably did not care much about them either. Tilka's (Velburg's) reaction on the day the church bells were dismantled at Feteşti, his inability to explain that the occupier was not behaving any better than or any differently from back home in Germany, is very telling: since people were living under occupation, they had to blame the authorities for every misfortune, whether the authorities were culpable or not. Indeed, civilians in the hinterland did exactly the same. People denounced 'them', regardless of the actual situation on the ground.

The second factor concerns the deliberate choices of the occupiers. The occupiers were always underprepared when it came to exercising power, and usually did not know how to deal with their acquisitions. The plans in the drawer were missing. Sometimes the occupiers were aided by experts who were fellow citizens, and in Łódź in the spring of 1916 these experts expressed a total lack of interest in continuing local textile production. The interest of the state, claimed the representatives of German industry, 'is simply to employ the largest number of workers in whatever way possible'. For this reason it was 'quite possible', they continued, 'to employ a great many of these workers in German factories, which are suffering today on account of the desperate lack of manpower'.[17] After eighteen months of war, it was not even necessary to deal the finishing blow: Łódź had already ceased to be an important industrial centre some time earlier. The verdict of the German experts drove a nail into the coffin and gave a guarantee to the German textile industry that, at least until the end of the war, its competitor would not be reborn. The second aim of this policy proved harder to fulfil. Instead of coming to the rescue of German

---

[15] Ibid., p. 132. The appeal was successful.

[16] Data provided by Zbigniew Landau and Jerzy Tomaszewski, cited in Marian M. Drozdowski, *Warszawa w latach 1914–1939*, Warsaw 1990, p. 89.

[17] Cited in Antoni Żabko-Potopowicz, Marceli Handelsman, Władysław Grabski, and Kazimierz Władysław Kumaniecki, *Polska w czasie wielkiej wojny (1914–1918)*, vol. 2. *Historja społeczna*, Warsaw 1932, p. 85.

NEW ORDERS   299

industry *en masse*, the workers of Łódź dispersed into the villages of central Poland, the very places from which they had arrived not so long ago.

Similar logic did not apply in the case of the Romanian and Galician oil fields, the Białowieża forests, or the Dąbrowa coal basin. Nor did it apply to Serbian animals marked for slaughter or to railway lines in all occupied territories. In each of these cases the occupier invested considerable sums in the hope of making a return within a year at most. 'Robber economy' is an apposite phrase in this context. However, it is worth remembering that – contrary to the investor's intentions – some of the outlay was recovered only after the war had been lost, and by then it was not the investor who benefited from it. Lithuania, Latvia, and Poland did not need to convert their railway track from Russian to European gauge after 1918, since they inherited the 'normal' gauge from the occupier. In Lithuania, Ober-Ost built an additional 200 kilometres of track. One line connected the south-west of the country to a network of iron roads; the other connected Kaunas with Riga.[18]

Between Plans and Reality: Conflicting Aims

The lawyer from Jena we cited earlier, Bogislav Tilka (pseudonym Gerhard Velburg), spent the war years as a private. He did not help to prepare plans as an employee of the ministerial bureaucracy or general staff. Instead, his role was to implement those plans at the lowest level, where he had to negotiate both with local peasants and with dim-witted superiors:

> [...] on every table lies one regulation on top of another, orders upon orders, forms upon forms [...]. 'Report immediately,' 'Report every three days,' 'Carry out the census as accurately as possible,' 'It is strictly forbidden' – these are some of the other orders and decrees. Is there anything at all that we are not supposed to count?! Every new-born calf, every chick, every goose, every piece of curd cheese.
>
> On a desk at the local military headquarters lay stacks of documents: Logbook of Army Decrees, Logbook of Decrees Issued by Mackensen's Forces, Logbook of Decrees Issued by the Military Government in Romania, and so on. These documents regulated the following issues, among others: the collection of coffee dregs, officers' baggage allowances when travelling, and forbidden outfits for German soldiers. They also contained administrative queries, such as: 'What are the present whereabouts [in August 1917] of Lieutenant Otto Ephraim, who in October 1914 received an overpayment of 25 marks from the payroll office of the 52nd Regiment? 'Honestly', groaned Tilka at one point, 'if

---

[18] Christopher Kopper, 'Der Erste Weltkrieg als Eisenbahnkrieg', in *Neue Wege in ein neues Europa. Geschichte und Verkehr im 20. Jahrhundert*, ed. Ralph Roth and Karl Schlögel, Frankfurt am Main 2009, pp. 222–234, here p. 232.

300   OCCUPATION

the war could be won by regulations we would have sealed victory long ago.'[19]

There were many things that the occupier could plan and imagine. At the very bottom of the social ladder, where the issue concerned a specific chicken or piece of cheese, the occupier was confronted with defenceless citizens only in theory. In reality the occupier had to deal with a community and with individuals who had known each other for years and who used all their considerable cunning to temper, circumvent, or neutralize – for instance, by means of a suitable gift or hearty meal – the initially energetic and self-confident *Kulturträger* ('bearers of civilization'). The situation on the ground was quite different from the way the generals perceived it; every new regulation that left their desks complicated matters still further and, in the main, did not produce the desired or anticipated effect.

The monarchy faced similar dilemmas. In 1916 it occupied the southern part of the Kingdom of Poland as well as Serbia and Montenegro. Being wholly dependent on supplies from the monarchy, Montenegro did not play a role economically. In Serbia the issue was food. The reserves that had been built up during the Balkan wars were already coming to an end. In any case, there was no good way of distributing the food, and in the countryside there were labour shortages. In this situation, despite pressure from Vienna, the Military Government General in Belgrade (Militärgouvernement Serbien, MGG/S) did not allow the remnants of the Serbian economy to be exploited in order to save its own hinterland. On the contrary, in the face of the catastrophic shortage of male workers (due to the huge numbers of men conscripted in 1914, the epidemics at the beginning of the following year, the 'Golgotha' of 1915–1916, and the exodus of over 150,000 soldiers to Corfu), the occupier even tried to bring in Russian prisoners of war to work in the fields. Until the harvest of 1916 relatively little food found its way to the monarchy's hinterland, but in the autumn of that year, despite the poor harvest, the situation was brought under control: hunger ceased to be a social problem. In defiance of some decision-makers, the occupier usually paid peasants for the food they supplied. Requisitioning was less common, and coercive measures in the form of hostage-taking were more of a threat than a reality. In the following year the Vienna dailies compared prices with amazement: 'beef cost three times as much in Vienna as in Belgrade, lamb twice as much, whereas pork cost roughly 30 per cent more in Vienna than in Belgrade'; Serbian flour and fat rations were still higher than Austrian ones, etc. And so it was to remain until the end of the war: in Serbia the occupiers fed themselves (naturally, the officer corps got the lion's share), ensured that the locals had enough to eat, and sometimes shared food with their comrades

---

[19] Gerhard Velburg, *Rumänische Etappe*, passim, here pp. 109, 177.

Fig. 56 A street scene in occupied Šabac.

elsewhere. But they saved virtually nothing for their own hinterland: in the summer of 1918 'three different officers' messes in Belgrade regularly used over 16,000 eggs per month'. At the same time, the hungry population of Vienna received 'occasional one-time shipments of 1,000 eggs or fewer per month'.[20]

In Serbia, unlike in the Kingdom of Poland, Lithuania, or Romania, there was little need to cooperate with local elites. On the contrary, if the authorities encountered any attitude that smacked of Serbian nationalism or political thought, they reacted immediately and brutally. After Romania's attack on the monarchy, the MGG/S, faced with the potential danger of a Serbian uprising, carried out possibly the largest police operation in the history of occupied lands during the First World War; it interned tens of thousands of people, mainly 'suspect' men and sometimes members of their families too. Along with those incarcerated a year earlier, 70,000 Serbs found themselves in internment camps. What began as an attempt to subjugate the intelligentsia – 'leaders, agitators, and other helpers' – turned into a mass deportation of men aged seventeen and over, i.e. men of fighting age.

At that time, around 1.4 million people lived in the Austro-Hungarian occupation zone. The disastrous effect of depriving the economy of approximately 5 per cent of the population – men of conscription age, i.e. potentially

---

[20] Jonathan E. Gumz, *The Resurrection and Collapse of Empire in Habsburg Serbia, 1914–1918*, Cambridge 2009, pp. 140–192, data from pp. 171, 189.

the most productive workers – was all too apparent: in the summer of 1917 Austro-Hungarian soldiers could be seen working the fields in the company of prisoners of war and a few internees brought in from the hinterland.[21] A minor consolation – though probably not regarded as such by the MGG/S – was that Serbian internees and prisoners of war were working in the hinterland at the same time as agricultural labourers.[22] In Romania the occupiers were more sensible, freeing tens of thousands of men from captivity. As prisoners 'on leave' they returned to their farms and got to work, thus reducing the labour shortage in agriculture on the one hand and easing the burden for the German camp administration on the other. Their return also improved the mood in local communities; the benefit was therefore mutual.

Relations were different in the Kingdom of Poland and Lithuania, where the occupiers solicited the cooperation of local elites and institutions, the latter having been brought into existence by the occupiers themselves. Nevertheless, the two German administrations were very different: Ober-Ost believed in the effectiveness of coercion much more than did the General Government of Warsaw (Generalgouvernement Warschau). Since it was based on cooperation with local elites, the Warsaw model – explained the authors of a 1926 study for the German parliament – was clearly more efficient than the Lithuanian one: 'Ober-Ost administered much of its territory on paper only, since there was no real contact with the lower levels of the administration and absolutely no contact with the local population.'[23]

The examples of Warsaw and Vilnius in the autumn of 1916 may serve to illustrate this 'lack of contact' combined with a need to consider the views of an occupied population as expressed through its legitimate representatives. In October, the authorities asked the newly appointed local government of Warsaw to provide lists of unemployed people who could be sent to work in the Reich. The City Hall refused and did not budge even when the Germans repeated their demand. The Germans, in turn, realized too late that they had chosen the worst possible moment for forced recruitment: hectic preparations were under way for the proclamation of a manifesto by the two emperors, which came to be known as the Act of 5 November. Polish goodwill mattered more during those few weeks than at any other time. The Germans thus decided not to repeat their demand for a third time.

This was a rare example of open and effective resistance by dependent elites. In Vilnius the situation was more typical. Here the city representatives formally protested against the introduction by the occupier of a universal obligation to work to which all men were subject. However, the occupier took no notice and proceeded to implement the new regulations. The city

---

[21] Scheer, 'Manifestation österreichisch-ungarischer Besatzungsmacht in Belgrad', p. 224.
[22] Gumz, *The Resurrection and Collapse of Empire in Habsburg Serbia*, pp. 96–101.
[23] Cited in Christian Westerhoff, *Zwangsarbeit im Ersten Weltkrieg*, p. 80.

representatives ceased their protest, but instead began – surreptitiously, illegally, and effectively – to encourage their fellow citizens to boycott the order.[24]

The examples of Warsaw and Vilnius show that local elites had some room for manoeuvre even when a theoretically omnipotent occupier had clearly defined priorities. In both cities the elites adopted the tactic of passive resistance. This decision was characteristic of relations with the occupier in the third year of the war: military resistance and political terrorism were, for the time being, not on the horizon, but by the same token ruthless coercion was not an option for the occupier. The previously mentioned Hugo Kerchnawe, Chief of the General Staff of the Military Government General in Serbia and an influential historian after the war, later regretted, not without reason, that 'political considerations' had always been a hindrance, even in sectors of the economy that were vital to the war effort.

In the Kingdom of Poland the occupier lacked experts first and foremost. The army pretended to be *au fait* with matters, but at every step it realized that the instrument it knew best – coercion – did not produce the desired results. In the summer of 1916, a year after the establishment of the Military Government General in Lublin, the Austrians finally accepted that they could not expect larger surpluses from what was essentially an agricultural region. The exception was potatoes, but poor rail connections made transporting them difficult, and it was decided instead to process them on the spot for alcohol. In this situation the Military Government General focused on two objectives: first, to feed its own bureaucracy; and second, to distribute produce in such a way as to prevent famine in the region. The export of surpluses to the hinterland came third.

In the end, the Lublin authorities chose a mixed model of exploitation: while the rationing of raw materials and labour and the regulation of prices were dominant, peasants were given incentives in the form of perks and bonuses to supply products over and above the official quotas. Agricultural workers were assembled into 'harvest brigades'. District commanders counted up the people and horses, and determined what each would receive under the rationing system. It turned out that 80 per cent of the harvest would be retained locally as food or seed, while only 20 per cent would be consumed by the monarchy's army or – in last place – by fellow citizens in the hinterland. Even this pessimistic balance sheet proved fanciful, however, since citizens of Cisleithania received even less than the MGG/L officials had calculated. Barely 240,000 tonnes of agricultural produce found its way to the hinterland in 1916–1917. This was not an isolated case: from beginning to end, i.e. from the capture of Łódź until the capture of Kiev, the occupation of Russia's western territories came as a disappointment for both Germany and Austria-

---

[24] Christian Westerhoff, *Zwangsarbeit im Ersten Weltkrieg*, pp. 206 n., 228 n.

304   OCCUPATION

Hungary. Over the course of four summers, the General Government of Warsaw supplied less than 1 per cent of the total number of potatoes gathered in Germany during the exceptionally bad harvest of 1916. Four consecutive harvests in the Generalgouvernement Lublin increased the monarchy's net reserves of grain by 0.5 per cent. Subsequent exports from Ukraine provided 10 per cent of what the Central Powers had been expecting.[25] From the point of view of the occupier, the mobilization of the labour force mentioned earlier was hardly more successful: at the end of 1916, of the 3.5 million people living in the territory administered by the Military General Government in Lublin, only 4 per cent of men were mobilized for forced labour – in a country in which no one had been conscripted to the army since the summer of 1915.

In Romania the occupier opted for a mixed system. Requisitioning was sometimes tantamount to plain robbery – the army took what it considered useful and did not issue receipts. Far more common was requisitioning that had the trappings of legality. The eminent Romanian conservative Alexandru Marghiloman summarized the results of a meeting between local landowners and representatives of the German occupier thus:

> [...] no price shall be entered on the receipts for wheat from the 1916 harvest. The assumption is that the price will be 1,600 lei per wagon. The owner is to receive an advance payment of 800 lei. As for the remainder, who pays, and how much, will be decided once peace is declared. Quite simply, the grain is being acquired for 800 lei per wagon. [...] For the Germans the calculation is straightforward: in 1916 we paid 3,200 lei per wagon plus taxes; in 1917 we will pay 800 lei, which over the two years gives a 'Durchschnittspreis' [average price; in German in the original] of 2,000 lei.[26]

Landowners were in any case treated better than peasants, and peasants were treated better than city dwellers. Craftsmen, manufacturers, and merchants had their entire stocks of raw materials and finished goods taken by the occupier (and usually received less money for them than was due). The occupiers requisitioned whatever they could – from metals to leather and textiles. In Romania the textile industry suffered a collapse analogous to that of Łódź.

In the more transparent urban environment, enforcing orders was much easier. Here it was possible to place factories under temporary administration, restrict the use of energy, introduce ration cards and curfews, and, most importantly, confiscate goods. Private cars, bicycles, carts, and horse-drawn carriages steadily vanished from the streets of Bucharest; the chronically

---

[25] Lehnstaedt, 'Das Militärgouvernement Lublin im Ersten Weltkrieg', pp. 1–26. See also Stephan Lehnstaedt, *Imperiale Polenpolitik in den Weltkriegen. Eine vergleichende Studie zu den Mittelmächten und zu NS-Deutschland*, Osnabrück 2017, pp. 322–346.

[26] Cited in Mayerhofer, *Zwischen Freund und Feind*, p. 164.

NEW ORDERS 305

overcrowded trams became less and less frequent. It was only then that the Germans realized that by paralysing all forms of transport except walking they were acting against their own interests: the staff of the numerous offices set up by the occupier faced exactly the same difficulties as the civilian population. Another problem was the requisitioning of items made of copper, brass, and tin. The consumption of vegetable preserves prepared in zinc-plated iron pots led to cases of poisoning, as did the consumption of plum brandy distilled by a new method; people cursed the occupier.

In the countryside it was much harder to execute orders. In any case, the Germans were aware that if they deprived a peasant of his life's possessions the chances of benefiting from next year's harvest would fall to zero. The occupier therefore bought produce from farmers at a set price, and usually in an amount that allowed them to continue their work, i.e. sow seed and feed livestock. Whereas initially the occupiers paid for food using vouchers (and paid relatively high sums, as described above), after the 1917 harvest they switched to cash payments. In addition, vegetables, fruit, and, to some extent, dairy products and eggs were excluded from the quota system, under which items were bought at official prices. In this instance, the occupier behaved rationally: there was no way of transporting perishable food to the Reich and the local food industry was unable to process it. As a result, the army and civilians subsisted on dairy products, vegetables, and fruit purchased locally at roughly free market prices. These were lower than the black market prices for products that were subject to quotas, such as meat, wine, and plum brandy. As mentioned earlier, the creation of vegetable plots on urban green space was another way of improving supply. In Bucharest's oldest public park, the elegant Cişmigiu Gardens, cabbage was planted next to the carefully manicured shrubs and flowers, while pumpkins and cucumbers were grown on the lawn in front of the royal palace.

The mixed system of requisitioning, rationing, and free market forces worked reasonably well in Romania during the first year of occupation: although the hinterland received a lot, both occupiers and occupied were much better off than the inhabitants of Cisleithania and the Reich. The system also worked because, apart from those aspects of it that were decreed and partially enforced, everyone involved had a good deal of room for manoeuvre. Soldiers, for instance, were allowed to send 5-kilogram food parcels to their loved ones. The Romanians later calculated that these parcels – during the first nine months of the occupation alone – weighed the equivalent of 1,000 railway carriages or more. In addition, a soldier going on leave had the right to bring food to his family – in practice as much as he could carry. Again, the Romanians later estimated that soldiers on leave had exported 18,000 tonnes of food from the country. Some soldiers used their salaries to buy food on the free market, but supplies were also amassed in other ways. On hearing that Tilka was about to go on leave, his hosts slaughtered a sheep, two geese, and

306 OCCUPATION

four ducks, and a friend of theirs built some crates in which to transport them. Aside from meat, the crates were filled with over 35 kilograms of flour, a bag of beans and lentils, and a kilograme each of butter, tobacco, garlic, and onions. As a result, Tilka set off on his journey to Jena encumbered by a large wooden chest, four smaller crates, a bag of flour, a knapsack, and two haversacks. His family was delighted, of course, but that is beside the point.

We could of course speculate that the author lied, and that the sheep and poultry were slaughtered because he had coerced and threatened his hosts. It seems far more likely, however, that he didn't. It was the hosts who took the initiative. It was they who filled the crates and bags with goods in the hope that this satisfied representative of the local occupation authorities would not forget their gesture when stocktaking took place on the farm the following year, and when (no doubt) this or that did not tally with the previous year's records. The inspector could easily fail to notice such an error if he remembered the hosts' generous gift. Lurking in the background, too, is the supposition that if the inspector wanted to be excessively zealous he could easily mention the meat, flour, beans, butter, and tobacco that he had confiscated from potential suspects . . .

This last option – blackmail – seems unlikely, however. The arrangement was clear to both parties – to the person giving the bribe and to the person taking it. It was the representative of the occupier who took the bribe, and unless he was a scoundrel he would fulfil his part of the bargain. One can only guess (research is lacking) that this was the broadest common denominator in relations between occupiers and occupied from Livonia to Montenegro. In Romania many traces of this mechanism for correcting the theoretically strict demands of the occupier survived until 1918, but it is hard to imagine that the situation was radically different from that of occupied Poland, Serbia, or Lithuania. Peasants in Bucharest could expect to make a profit of between 200 and 500 per cent on the black market.[27] It seems unlikely that the margin for risk was any lower elsewhere. The new prices were paid by the middle and upper strata of society. Both lost out, the former incomparably more than the latter, but even impoverished officials and teachers were a world away from the real misery to be found in soup kitchens and 'tea rooms', in shelters and heated halls, and in other places for the poor.

In the third year of the war, mortality among the lowest social strata increased everywhere. In Vilnius the city population declined by 30 per cent. Three-quarters of the 140,000 inhabitants relied on soup kitchens. Among Jews, who in 1914 accounted for almost half the population, mortality increased three-fold, while the number of births fell to one-third of its pre-war level. At the beginning of 1917 there was a two-fold increase in mortality

---

[27] Mayerhofer, *Zwischen Freund und Feind*, p. 231.

NEW ORDERS 307

among local Poles compared with 1915.[28] Help for the growing number of destitute people came from various sources. As mentioned earlier, much of this assistance was provided by the belligerent states, with Russia being the most generous by far. In Western Europe and America dozens of charities tried to ease the misery of the poor in Serbia and Poland by organizing food supplies from the United States. However, the results fell far below expectations. Although the Rockefeller Foundation launched a campaign that saw every child in Warsaw receive a weekly tin of condensed milk for three months, in March 1917 the shipments stopped – the Swiss market ran out of goods and new problems arose with rail transportation. The planned import of American flour to occupied Poland did not materialize at all due to the opposition of Great Britain. Even a dramatic appeal by the Noble Prize-winning author Henryk Sienkiewicz, who coordinated the charitable activities of the so-called Vevey Committee, did not manage to loosen the blockade on the Central Powers. In June 1916, in a letter to the prominent charity activist Laurence Alma-Tadema, Sienkiewicz complained:

> I would like the English precisely to understand that Germany's main goal is to exterminate the Polish nation though hunger in order acquire free land for colonization. That is why all assistance offered to the Poles in provinces currently in the hands of the Germans helps to restrict Germany's growth and weaken her power.[29]

However, the reality of occupation was much more complicated than the Polish writer imagined.

Life under Occupation

For the middle and lowest strata of society a new front opened after 1915 in territories under occupation. On this occasion the line of division was not between rulers and their subjects, but within society itself and especially in places where large Jewish communities existed. It was the occupation authorities who decided which local entrepreneurs would receive a quota of rationed goods, a work commission, or a commercial licence. Bribery was rife. In the Kingdom of Poland, however, this otherwise trivial phenomenon took on political significance depending on who was doing the bribing. According to the recruitment officer for the Polish Legions in Piotrków, Tadeusz Hartleb, in Busko it was the Jews who were the culprits:

---

[28] Theodore R. Weeks, 'Vilnius in World War I, 1914–1920', *Nordost-Archiv* NF XVII (2008), pp. 34–57, here p. 46 n.

[29] Cited in Danuta Płygawko, *Polonia devastata. Polonia i Amerykanie z pomocą dla Polski (1914–1918)*, Poznań 2003, p. 197.

308   OCCUPATION

Licences for the import and export of certain goods, so-called commercial patents, applications for exemptions from requisitioning, billeting, and carriage, etc. are all arranged through Miss Preis, while the discretion characteristic of the Jews when it comes to bribing officials means that one can never be sure whether a matter has been successfully resolved merely due to an 'acquaintance' with an adjutant or because a bribe has been paid. [...] The group most disadvantaged by this is the Polish petite bourgeoisie, which generally behaves in a proper manner [...], is increasingly dependent on the Jews economically, and is very pessimistic about its future.[30]

Economic rivalry between Christians and Jews was a universal phenomenon. Despite the imagined domination of commerce by Jews, it was usually Poles, Ukrainians, Lithuanians, or Belarusians who held the upper hand. In the Russian Empire, Jews were clearly under-represented in local authorities, and this lack of representation was also later reflected in civic committees and aid organizations that were not based on faith. In the provinces, supplies of rationed goods rarely reached Jewish businesses, as is shown, for instance, by the complaints of Jewish bakers and confectioners.[31] Jews likewise found it more difficult to receive support from charitable organizations. They were always in the minority in organizations that operated across the Polish Kingdom, while their own organizations were hampered by civilian authorities at the local level. Besides, the view that help for Poland should above all go to ethnic Poles was also endorsed by Sienkiewicz.[32] It was against this background that frictions between the Rockefeller Foundation and other charitable organizations arose.

Faced with local conflicts over rations, licences, and aid, the occupation authorities had no chance of satisfying all the parties involved. On the other hand, they could easily lose authority with the local population and were thus cautious, sometimes overly so. When, for instance, the Austro-Hungarian military authorities were looking for a synagogue for their Jewish soldiers in occupied Lublin, they proceeded with great sensitivity. Although there were was no shortage of synagogues and prayer halls in the city, the majority were in areas affected by a typhoid epidemic and for that reason were off-limits to the army. From September 1915, therefore, the Oasis cinema on ul. Radziwiłłowska served as a temporary synagogue. Local civilians also participated in the services. Meanwhile, the National Democrat newspaper *Głos Lubelski* (*Voice of Lublin*), and a similar publication called *Ziemia Lubelska*

---

[30] 20 June 1916, Busko. Report of warrant officer Tadeusz Hartleb to the Central Recruitment Office in Piotrków, in Jerzy Z. Pająk (ed.), *Raporty i korespondencja oficerów werbunkowych Departamentu Wojskowego Naczelnego Komitetu Narodowego 1915-1916. Ziemia Kielecka*, Kielce 2007, pp. 24–28, here p. 25.

[31] Konrad Zieliński, *Żydzi Lubelszczyzny 1914-1918*, Lublin 1999, p. 102.

[32] Pływawko, *Polonia devastata*, p. 200 (letter to Bishop Adam Sapieha).

NEW ORDERS

(*The Lublin Lands*), unleashed a campaign to condemn the special status that was allegedly being given to Jewish merchants. In no uncertain terms they accused the occupier of favouring the Jews:

> It is well-known that before the war various government institutions in Austria were heavily infected with Jewry. Now, fearing that they might be called to the front, the Jews have begun to barge their way into various offices and institutions, especially the army commissariat. This has made it much easier for local Jews to quickly forge relationships with officials responsible for military procurement and the distribution of various rationed goods. [...] As a result, Polish merchants have nothing to sell in their shops, while the Jews have no shortage of products.[33]

As the atmosphere of the anti-Semitic campaign grew more febrile, the owner of the Oasis severed his contract with the occupation authorities. His justification was that 'members of the intelligentsia, who constitute the majority of patrons' had begun to boycott the cinema due to the 'stench' of Jews.[34] The Austrians accepted the decision, thus displaying their respect for property rights and their extreme caution in dealing with the local population.

In the countryside the transfer of power had another aspect. Once the front had moved on, the new masters appeared no more frequently than the old ones, i.e. very rarely. But here, too, both sides, occupiers and occupied, had to become accustomed to the new reality. The occupiers were omnipotent only in theory. Just as often they were helpless, and in this regard Tilka's experiences are pertinent. In Romania in 1917 the Germans tried to carry out a census: the name, date of birth, and place of birth of every peasant was to be entered onto the appropriate form at the registration office. People in the countryside were afraid of registration because it could lead to conscription or to deportation to Germany for work.

The initial results, which were delivered by local mayors and village bailiffs, drove the Germans into a fury. Many families did not have surnames. When asked for his details, a peasant would state his given name (e.g. Radu), which he would sometimes supplement with his father's given name (e.g. Ion) to distinguish himself from neighbours who also bore the name Radu. Other peasants were known by names that were completely different from the ones that figured in the official documents. Gypsies did not appear in any records at all and did not have birth certificates. Local officials drew up lists of inhabitants according to their own inscrutable criteria. On some of the lists people's given names were entered first, while on others they were entered second, and there was a host of other minor problems to boot. The German head of the local registration office ran around shouting: 'Radu Ion, Ion Radu, Serban Nicolai,

---

[33] Cited in Mieczysław Ryba, *Środowiska i ugrupowania polityczne na Lubelszczyźnie 1914–1918*, Lublin 2007, p. 152.

[34] Zieliński, *Żydzi Lubelszczyzny 1914–1918*, p. 134.

310   OCCUPATION

Nicolai Serban, Constantin Gheorghe, Gheorghe Constantin, and so on! One *primar* [mayor] writes in one way, the other in a different way, and sometimes the same person writes in two different ways. [...] How are we to know what he is called? My name is Emil Kießler, in other words, my given name is Emil and my surname is Kießler. That is what I call German orderliness.'

The unfortunate Kießler tried to introduce 'German orderliness' by summoning all the registrees to a single location. His subordinate remembered how the day began:

> None of the 500 people summoned to appear in Dudeşti-Feteşti turned up, despite the fact that we had posted our order everywhere, clearly and in big letters, in both languages, and the crier had announced it as well. Kießler was in a rage, cursing [...] unleashing his anger onto me and onto our translators: had we translated it properly? Had we not confused the Gregorian calendar with the Julian calendar? Central European time with East European time? Summer time with winter time? Even the *primar* and the notary, who were required to attend every meeting, failed to show up. Kießler sent for the *primar*, who was still in bed. He cheerfully turned up at 7.00 a.m. and reminded us that we had set aside two days for the meeting, today and the following day. Knowing his people as he did, he explained that they would only come on the second day because they would wait to see if anything bad happened to the people who came on the first day.

Kießler, beside himself with fury, changed his decision and ordered the crier to gather everyone together immediately. The interpreter, apparently adept in the use of Romanian expletives, instructed those present about their obligation to register. Then, several Germans began to verify the details of the 300 men – after all, that is why the meeting had been convened. Many of the men could not be found on the lists provided by the *primar*. Half of them gave dates and places of birth that did not correspond to the details on the list. Some said that they had been born 'at home' or 'in the marshes', while others did not know their own surname or were ashamed to admit that they did not know their date of birth. Half the men were unable to sign the protocol. As the day drew to a close even Kießler fell silent; it finally dawned on him that to fully execute the registration order would mean having to struggle with the locals until the end of the war. Three months later Kießler's subordinate remarked with some astonishment that, while he coped with office boredom by reading novels, his boss spent his time playing cards: 'There is absolutely nothing to do. We have long since abandoned our efforts to register people accurately with their real names and more or less correct date of birth.' When the new German boss arrived in Feteşti a month later, he could not understand why orders were not being carried out. 'In every respect one could see that ten days ago he was still in Germany,' commented Tilka on the newcomer's unshakable enthusiasm for work.[35]

---

[35] Gerhard Velburg, *Rumänische Etappe*, pp. 111, 116 nn., 167 n., 185.

It was not just Romanian peasants who played dumb, cursed their luck, and took pity on poor soldiers, offering them small practical benefits in lieu of big ones (which were unfortunately out of reach). In distant Kyrgyzstan, in 1916, the Russian authorities abandoned their unsuccessful attempts to carry out censuses and instead handed responsibility for conscription to councils of elders. The lists compiled by the elders proved just as useless as the official ones – thirty-year-olds supposedly capable of serving in the army turned out to be sixty-year-olds and vice versa. Quite reasonably, officials suspected the tribal leaders of corruption. However, such allegations did not appear to make much of an impression on the suspects.[36] Peace, the price of which was a certain hypocrisy, lasted only until the authorities decided to mobilize the inhabitants of Central Asia for forced labour. When the spectre of conscription no longer affected just a few individuals but became a widespread fear, an uprising broke out in the region. Nomads, mainly Kyrgyz and Kazakh, turned against the local authorities and Russian colonists. The latter organized armed raids on their rebellious neighbours. It was not until the end of 1916 that the army managed to suppress the uprising in Central Asia. Several hundred thousand of its participants took refuge beyond the borders of the empire, and an unknown number suffered repression or died of starvation after their cattle herds were slaughtered.[37]

The relative peace in the countryside was probably connected with conscription. In Serbia the last soldiers to be mobilized were called up in the autumn of 1915; in Romania conscription was carried out only once (in the summer of 1915), while in the Kingdom of Poland and Courland young men could likewise sleep peacefully. In these cases occupation did not dramatically worsen the situation. On the contrary, it conferred a privilege: the avoidance of conscription, which meant that millions of fathers, husbands, sons, and brothers were saved from death in the trenches.

Order persisted in the countryside so long as these gains outweighed the losses caused by exploitation of the occupied territory. Turning the screw caused this mechanism to fail. The historian Jan Molenda, an expert on the issue, has described the transformation of peasant attitudes during the war in Galicia and the Congress Kingdom:

> When adversity and repression escalated, the peasants usually responded according to the same pattern. First, they tried to appeal to the authorities by means of petitions and applications and through the mediation of rural institutions and organizations. When this approach failed, and especially when repression and hardship intensified, they switched to passive

---

[36] Joshua A. Sanborn, *Drafting the Russian Nation. Military Conscription, Total War and Mass Politics 1905–1925*, DeKalb, IL 2003, p. 35.

[37] Elizabeth E. Bacon, *Central Asians under Russian Rule. A Study in Culture Change*, Ithaca, NY 1980, pp. 115–116.

312 OCCUPATION

resistance. This increased from 1917 onwards. At that time the police and army sent requisition squads into villages. Faced with the prospect of force being used, the peasants usually relented, especially in the years 1916–1917. Gradually, however, as material resources diminished, they switched to active forms of resistance. Clashes with the police and army requisition squads became more widespread in 1917 and intensified in the following year.[38]

In parallel, and for the same reasons, peace in the countryside came to an end in occupied Serbia and Montenegro. The new authorities were approaching the border, and beyond it the only instrument of effective policy appeared to be violence.

The Growth of Cities

Quite frequently, occupiers enabled and implemented structural changes that had been under discussion for a long time. Throughout the Polish Kingdom, the Germans created a legal framework for municipal government and were probably the catalyst for a second, fundamental reform: the incorporation of municipalities situated close to large urban centres. In many places this issue had been debated for decades. For a long time cities had suffocated within borders that were determined by imperial defence needs. Here and there, in Königsberg or Cracow for instance, the abandonment of old forts in favour of modern fortifications on the city outskirts opened up new areas for urban development before the war. Elsewhere the situation was less favourable, particularly in Warsaw, where expansion to the west or north was prohibited. The effect of this was even reflected in the statistics: in 1910, 116 people on average lived in a Warsaw tenement house; in St Petersburg the number was 52, and in Moscow 38.[39] The record numbers of tenants translated into a worse quality of life, less capacity for work, lower hygiene standards, and higher mortality; in a situation of rising hunger and disease this state of affairs was of great significance to the occupier.

The expansion of city borders always encountered obstacles: who was to bear the cost of extending urban infrastructure to hitherto rural areas? How could the changes in taxation be fairly distributed? In principle, cities were of course interested in acquiring new land for housing and industrial develop-ment, whereas nearby municipalities – faced with the prospect of incorpor-ation into a much larger organism – were far less keen; city residents in the monarchy were subject to higher taxes ('excise duty'), which meant that long-

---

[38] Jan Molenda, *Chłopi, naród, niepodległość. Kształtowanie się postaw narodowych i obywatelskich chłopów w Galicji i Królestwie Polskim w przededniu odrodzenia Polski*, Warsaw 1999, p. 285.

[39] Malte Rolf, *Imperiale Herrschaft im Weichselland. Das Königreich Polen im Russischen Imperium (1864–1915)*, Göttingen 2014, p. 260.

term negotiations between cities and suburban municipalities became necessary. In Lwów the negotiations failed, but in Cracow several municipalities were incorporated in 1910–1912; an agreement with the neighbouring town of Podgórze was approved in April 1913 and implemented soon after the Battle of Gorlice, i.e. on 1 July 1915. For a while, Cracow, with a population of fewer than 200,000, occupied an area that was one and a half times bigger than Warsaw, which had a population of nearly a million.

Clearly, the occupier understood and was able to untie local Gordian knots: under the cover of top-down orders, Łódź increased in area by more than 50 per cent in 1915; a year later the area of Warsaw increased threefold. Lublin also made huge gains. The enthusiasm for reform was probably all the greater because in these cases the cities were located in occupied territory. However, the experiment proved so successful that immediately after the war it was repeated on a massive scale. In April 1920 the Prussian parliament voted to establish a Greater Berlin. The new capital of the Weimar Republic had twice as many inhabitants as the pre-war city and at least thirteen times more space.

10

Mission civilisatrice

The soldiers and officers who went off to fight in the summer of 1914 not only had modern weapons but also held certain beliefs about the enemy and the territories in which the hostilities were to take place. For the most part they had scant information about the specific characteristics of Galicia, Serbia, the Kingdom of Poland, East Prussia, Lithuania, and Belarus, but they did not go there free of prejudice or lacking in a priori judgments. Sometimes their ideas combined to form a very precise image of a place. These fixed notions, which had little to do with reality but were nonetheless enduring, came to be known as stereotypes shortly after the end of the war. The American journalist and adviser to President Wilson who coined the term 'stereotype', Walter Lippmann, based his theory on an analysis of the American press during the Great War. It is likely that the Eastern Front, and especially the ways in which the Germans and Austrians perceived the East, would have provided Lippmann with even more interesting data.

The importance of stereotypes is not limited to the history of culture. During the First World War in particular, stereotypes would sometimes affect the behaviour of the occupiers and even the policy of the Great Powers in conquered territories. This was mainly true of the Germans and Austrians and to a lesser extent the Russians, Bulgarians, and Turks. An extreme example of the power of stereotypes was the spy craze. The persecution of Jews or Ukrainian peasants did indeed have more to do with prejudice than with hard facts. But the problem was not limited to the fear, founded on prejudice, that betrayal was lurking around every corner. The stereotype of the East was both well developed and deeply ingrained, and was rarely challenged by objective knowledge about the region and its people. In essence, many of the participants of the campaigns in Eastern and South-Eastern Europe were completely ignorant. Already during the first weeks of the war Józef Piłsudski observed that his Austrian colleagues were convinced that in the Kingdom of Poland they would encounter an Orthodox, Russian-speaking people, at once primitive and hostile. His attempts to show that these fears had no basis in fact (especially in relation to the Kielce and Sandomierz regions to

MISSION CIVILISATRICE 315

which the Austro-Hungarian army was headed) fell on deaf ears.[1] What was the origin of such beliefs?

Semi-Asia

In the German understanding of the East, the entire region was seen as a homogeneous entity. One of the most popular geographical and ethnographical descriptions of the world in German, August Wilhelm Grube's *Geographische Charakterbilder*, whose twenty-first edition appeared on the eve of the First World War, depicted the East as follows:

> Its great unity and uniformity in national terms is due largely to the dreariness of the land, a diffuse space devoid of difference, no part of which is distinguishable, in which everything – man and plant, animal and soil, wind and weather – wears the same uniform.[2]

The monotony masked any differences between particular lands and nations. In the eyes of the German geographer the Polish lands were as homogeneous as the whole of Russia:

> 'The entire Polish Republic can be seen within one square mile'. This popular saying is true insofar as it would be difficult to find another country in the world as uniform and unified as Poland as regards the customs, dialect, and lifestyle of the inhabitants, the shape of the land, the crop culture, and the fertility of the soil. The homogeneity of the peasant estate is even more striking: the fate of one peasant – in happiness or misfortune, at work or at rest, as proprietor or labourer – is the fate of all, and sadly it is certain to be a miserable fate. As soon we step across the German border (going directly from German soil and therefore not through the Grand Duchy of Poznań or Galicia), we immediately find ourselves in an altogether different world.[3]

It would be hard to find a better illustration of how a stereotype functions than in the enduring belief in a boundless and monotonous space held by people who – unlike Grube – got to know the East at close quarters as German or Austro-Hungarian soldiers. Whether in the Polesie marshes or in the Bolimów forests, among the Lithuanian lakes or in the Carpathian mountains, observers

---

[1] Józef Piłsudski, *Moje pierwsze boje*, Łódź 1988, p. 46.
[2] In 1913–1916, the twenty-first edition of the two-volume work, edited by Hans Stübler and published by Friedrich Brandstetter, appeared under the abbreviated title of *Geographische Charakterbilder*. We refer here to one of its earlier editions: A. W. Grube, *Geographische Charakterbilder in abgerundeten Gemälden aus der Länder- und Völkerkunde nach Mußterdarstellungen der deutschen und ausländischen Literatur für die obere Stufe des geographischen Unterrichts in Schulen, sowie zu einer bildenden Lectüre für Freunde der Erdkunde überhaupt*, Leipzig 1878, vol. 1, p. 83.
[3] Ibid., p. 156.

316   OCCUPATION

invariably experienced the 'endless space'. As their letters, diaries, and memoirs emphatically show, the stereotype took precedence over their own observations. Having experienced the campaign in the Congress Kingdom for a few weeks, Count Harry Kessler sighed: 'There is nothing flatter, nothing more devoid of form and history, than Radom, Tomaszów, Ostrowiec, Zwoleń, Kielce, and all these Polish provincial towns, with their multitudes of Jews and locals, and puddles instead of pavements.'[4] The newcomers did not remain indifferent to the monotonous space, however. They gave it human characteristics, usually negative ones. As the historian Charlotte Heymel notes, German soldiers, in their reports from the front, treated the East European landscape as yet another enemy, almost as if this enemy had donned a green Russian uniform.[5]

The Germans encountered another phenomenon in the East that they found difficult to reconcile with the monotony: chaos. Their bleak image of the region was reinforced with ideas about an absence of tradition and civilization and a detachment from history. These features were especially apparent when – as Grube noted – observers arrived from the German cultural sphere and compared the latter with what they saw. From this perspective the contrasts were all the more sharp. And again, the observations of participants of the Great War faithfully reproduced the image of the East that had taken shape earlier, not just in academic and popular works but also in belles-lettres. At the end of the nineteenth century the liberal Austrian novelist and journalist Karl Emil Franzos (who was born in Podolia) wrote about 'semi-Asia', a space that was neither Europe nor the Orient:

> Whoever takes the fast train from Vienna to Iaşi, for instance, travels twice through the semi-Asian area and twice through the European one: from Vienna to Dziedzice (Europe); from Dziedzice to Śniatyń (Semi-Asia); from Śniatyń to Suceava (Europe); and from Suceava to the Pontus or the Urals (Semi-Asia, deep Semi-Asia), where everything, not just the military roads in autumn, is caked in mud. No art or science will evolve from that mud, and especially no white tablecloths or washed faces.[6]

In 'semi-Asia' Franzos had a particular antipathy towards Galicia and the Poles. For him, lack of civilization, superstition, poverty, and corruption combined to form an image of backwardness that could only be overcome through 'German cultural work' that kept the Poles well away from local government.[7]

---

[4] Harry Graf Kessler, *Das Tagebuch*, vol. 5 (1914–1916), ed. Günter Riederer, Ulrich Ott, Christoph Hilse, and Janna Brechmacher, Stuttgart 2008, p. 140.
[5] Charlotte Heymel, *Touristen an der Front. Das Kriegserlebnis 1914–1918 als Reiseerfahrung in zeitgenössischen Reiseberichten*, Berlin 2007, p. 253.
[6] Karl Emil Franzos, *Aus Halb-Asien. Culturbilder aus Galizien, der Bukowina, Südrußland und Rumänien*, vol. 1, Leipzig 1876, pp. 95–96.
[7] Karl Emil Franzos, *Aus der großen Ebene. Neue Kulturbilder aus Halb-Asien*, vol. 1, Stuttgart 1889, p. xvii.

MISSION CIVILISATRICE

Kessler knew nothing of Galicia, but he was ready to corroborate Franzos's notion of 'semi-Asia' from the moment he crossed the German–Russian border between Neudeck (now Świerklaniec in the Tarnowskie Góry district) and Nowa Wieś:

> The roads are pockmarked with holes and no longer bordered by trees, while in the village houses, usually wooden and painted light blue, seem poorer than in our country. Women in colourful shawls, but barefoot, stand by their front doors or wade through puddles. Along the way numerous crosses and chapels are to be seen. Soon cultivated fields become a rare sight; to the right and left extend meadows, bald and abandoned, fringed by tracts of forest. [. . .] The Polish and Jewish inhabitants vegetate here in the same squalor; beyond that they are strangers to one another.[8]

Kessler's final remark is revealing: despite everything, people in the East are sometimes different and the Jews are more than just incidental folklore. Below we discuss the significance of this revelation.

At around the same time General Max von Gallwitz also entered enemy territory in pursuit of Rennenkampf's army, which was fleeing East Prussia:

> By car to the customs house, then onwards on horseback. Our boys, most of whom have never been as far the eastern border posts, are aghast. The road up to the border is excellent, but beyond it is a dirt road full of potholes. The crops are worthless, the houses miserable, and the people dirty and poor! This is where Semi-Asia begins.[9]

It could be reasonably argued, of course, that both Gallwitz and Kessler were simply describing what they saw. However, the terrible state of the roads and the squalor and poverty of the villages were still not enough to justify the view that chaos and backwardness were the defining features of Central and Eastern Europe. Yet this is the conclusion that German and Austrian observers usually drew from their observations. Several scholars have attempted to investigate this phenomenon in the West European and American history of ideas. Larry Wolff writes about an Eastern Europe which, to enlightened Western minds, occupied an intermediate position on the mental map. Being neither Europe nor Asia, it belonged neither to the group of regions that were fully civilized nor to those that were completely barbarous. Its most important feature was that it was suspended in an undefined space, somewhere between known quantities.[10] Hubert Orłowski, in turn, draws attention to a specific motif in the German stereotype of Poland, especially during the period of rapid

---

[8] Kessler, *Das Tagebuch*, vol. 5, pp. 116–117.
[9] Cited in Kessler, *Das Tagebuch*, vol. 5, p. 39.
[10] Larry Wolff, *Inventing Eastern Europe. The Map of Civilization on the Mind of the Enlightenment*, Stanford 1995, p. 13.

318 OCCUPATION

industrialization. For the unified, victorious Germany, with territorial ambitions not just within Europe, its eastern neighbour did not seem worthy of special interest, but nevertheless played an important role. In the German stereotype Poland became the 'crooked mirror of modernization', a 'repository of modernization deficits', an instructive example of a wretched fate that the Germans had managed to avoid thanks to their own efforts.[11] The theme common to Wolff and Orłowski is that Poland, or Eastern Europe in general, was seen as an unfinished, unformed, and amorphous project.

Lack of order and structure supposedly characterized not just the region's landscape and material culture but also its ethnic make-up. In a report from the German HQ in Marijampolė this problem surfaced even in regard to the origin of three people who bore the name 'Smith' in its Polish, German, and Russian variants:

> [...] We discover, with a sense of distress, that all three have distanced themselves far from their national identity. Because ... Mr. Schmidt, who on top of everything else carries the [German] given name Heinrich, professes himself an incarnate nationalist Pole, Mr. Kowalski as a thorough Russian and the apparently Muscovite Mr. Kusnjetzow as a genuine German. And the situation is no better with the confessional identity of the three. The Pole Schmidt is Roman Catholic, the Russian with the Polish name of Kowalski is Orthodox, while Mr. Kusnjetzow, in spite of his Russian name, belongs to the Evangelical community.[12]

This anecdote is too wonderful to be completely true. The German official in Marijampolė clearly had a didactic purpose in mind, namely, to persuade his superiors that local ethnic and religious and consequently political relations could not be measured in the categories used hitherto. Knowing the mentality of his superiors he curbed his imagination and did not burden them with further annoying details about 'local' people or Lithuanians, for instance. Yet this pedagogical anecdote concealed some very important questions. In what way was the East different? Was there a force that could bring structure to the chaos? What role should Germany play in the East? The answers to these questions were not clear-cut, nor were the motivations and attitudes of the people who asked them.

Even before the outbreak of the war, increasingly vocal nationalist groups in Germany postulated expansion to the East. The aim was not political dominance but the acquisition of territory for a surplus German population. So-called pan-Germans, represented by the *Alldeutscher Verband* (Pan-German League), enjoyed growing popularity during the war. Previously an

---

[11] Hubert Orłowski, *Z modernizacją w tle. Wokół rodowodu nowoczesnych niemieckich wyobrażeń o Polsce i Polakach*, Poznań 2002, pp. 103–105.
[12] Vejas Gabriel Liulevicius, *War Land on the Eastern Front. Culture, National Identity, and German Occupation in World War I*, Cambridge 2000, p. 53.

elitist organization, it doubled its membership to around 50,000. Its leaders were wedded to the idea of a second German colonization, just like the one in the Middle Ages, which had changed the character of Central and Eastern Europe. This colonization would primarily involve the settlement of rural areas in accordance with the ideal of a healthy life – one that was free of modern pathologies and in harmony with proto-Germanic traditions (however these were imagined). The Reich authorities were flooded with projects that proposed the annexation of ever greater expanses of territory. The more moderate projects envisaged a wide belt along Germany's eastern border, but the appetite of the armchair imperialists was whetted by the first military successes on the fronts. Shortly before his death in the trenches, the eminent nationalist activist Professor Friedrich Waterstradt sent a memorandum to the authorities, in which he stated:

> The survival of our nation and, to that end, the creation of an efficient peasant estate, are existential questions for us. They justify even blatantly harsh and ruthless interference in the rights of nations that inhabit conquered territories. Since we are universally hated, we must, once and for all, rid ourselves of the cosmopolitan sense of justice and engage all our forces and efforts in the preservation of our national strength.[13]

The successes of the German army in the East left the annexationists ecstatic. Shortly after the victory at Gorlice, Friedrich von Schwerin, the leader of the local administration in Frankfurt an der Oder, proposed the colonization of Courland and the Kaunas and Suwałki regions. A few months later, he set off on a study visit to the Baltic with his friend, Max Sering, a professor from Berlin. Sering's ideas went even further: the Reich should absorb all the land between East Prussia and Finland.

Although the pan-Germans were a vociferous group, they did not wield the reins of power. The position of the government in this matter was quite sceptical, and the more audacious memoranda were intercepted by the censors. The pan-Germans were thus unable to dominate the public debate. Their annexation proposals also met with scepticism among the expert community, which pointed to the practical difficulties of territorial expansion. Josef Partsch, a geographer from Leipzig and a former rector of the University of Breslau, countered Waterstradt's reckless plans and those of his fellow nationalists:

> Even the most daring optimists should banish any hope of a major shift in Germany's eastern border. [. . .] We must not forget that the annexation of larger territories, inhabited by other nationalities, will not strengthen the

---

[13] Cited in Imanuel Geiss, *Der polnische Grenzstreifen 1914–1918. Ein Beitrag zur deutschen Kriegszielpolitik im Ersten Weltkrieg*, Lübeck 1960, p. 50.

320 OCCUPATION

Reich but, to quote Bismarck's apt phrase, will strengthen centrifugal forces in its own lands.[14]

Liberals believed that no force would be able to Germanize millions of new, mostly Slavic citizens of the Reich. The leading spokesman of the liberals during the war, Friedrich Naumann, sighed: 'How beautiful it would be if one could Germanize the Czechs. But one cannot.'[15] In response to such doubts, the pan-Germans proposed that the problem of Germanization be sidestepped. After all, the objective was territorial gains and not population growth. Inhabitants of the East who were unlikely ever to become Germans could simply be displaced in favour of settlers from the Reich. The liberals considered this solution, in turn, to be unfeasible. They could not yet imagine resettlement on such a gigantic scale, while the experience of German colonization in the formerly Polish Wielkopolska region was discouraging, to say the least. Despite their chauvinism, Germans who already resided in areas earmarked for colonization often voted with their feet against German settlement of the East. While eulogists could exhort others to 'endure in the bastion of the German language', very few of them rushed to participate in the undertaking themselves. The war strengthened this phenomenon still further. When Waterstradt was writing his memorandum, hundreds of thousands of refugees from East Prussia were in temporary shelters in the western part of Germany. Many would remain there despite being encouraged to return to the 'borderlands' to endure.[16]

MITTELEUROPA

When, in 1915, the most important publication devoted to Germany's war aims appeared, the idea of a Central European federation was not a novelty in German political thought. Versions of the idea had already appeared in liberal publications just prior to the Springtime of Nations. For German patriots who dreamed of unification, a voluntary federation seemed a relatively easy and, more importantly, peaceful solution to their problem. Most German authors, notably Lujo Brentano and Walther Rathenau, who dominated this debate, envisaged a customs union based on an agreement between the German Reich and Austria-Hungary and subsequently joined by the Balkan states. In their view, access to the markets and natural resources of the region could, if only partly, make up for the unsatisfactory development of German imperialism.

---

[14] Cited in Janusz Pajewski, *'Mitteleuropa'. Studia z dziejów imperializmu niemieckiego w dobie pierwszej wojny światowej*, Poznań 1959, p. 94.

[15] Ibid., p. 121.

[16] Dieter Herz-Eichenrode, *Politik und Landwirtschaft in Ostpreußen 1919–1930. Untersuchung eines Strukturproblems in der Weimarer Republik*, Wiesbaden 1969, pp. 101–110.

The outbreak of the Great War accelerated the debate on Mitteleuropa. Drafts of various projects for a future customs union were forged by the Austrian social democrats and the think tank around Joseph Maria Baernreither, a member of both chambers of the Austrian parliament (the Abgeordnetenhaus and the Herrenhaus). Austro-Hungarian responses varied. On the one hand, German nationalists, notably Heinrich Friedjung, supported closer ties with Germany in the belief that they would strengthen the Germans at the expense of the Slavs within the monarchy. On the other hand, Austria's industrial circles feared the competition with German industry (and, correspondingly, Germany's major agricultural producers demanded that high tariffs be maintained to protect their incomes). During the First World War, Austria-Hungary's attitude to the project was rather lukewarm. In addition to other problems, the Habsburg partner in the planned union was largely preoccupied with negotiating a renewal of the Austro-Hungarian compromise. In effect, wartime discussions between the two allies did not lead to any practical outcome.

The issue of economic expansion played an important role in all such plans; it was also central to Friedrich Naumann's concept of *Mitteleuropa*. His book of the same name became one of the biggest bestsellers of the Great War: from its first edition in 1915 until Germany's capitulation in 1918 almost 200,000 copies were sold.

Naumann was a Lutheran pastor and left-liberal politician. Both these professions inclined him to reject the many annexation projects that emerged at the beginning of the war. In his book *Mitteleuropa*, Naumann countered the annexationists by proposing instead a voluntary union of Central and Eastern European countries (in later editions he added Bulgaria to the list) that would rest on two pillars: a common culture and economic interest. He believed that the historic moment when Germans could have effectively Germanized their Slav neighbours had gone forever. However, German culture was still dominant in the region, and German was the *lingua franca* of various nationalities. More importantly, the countries and nations of Central and Eastern Europe were a natural economic area. The establishment of an economic and customs union between the Reich and the Austro-Hungarian monarchy would create a central point to which neighbouring states would naturally gravitate. And only on the basis of the economic union would it be possible to secure political unity. In this context Naumann wrote of a 'Middle European body economic' (*das mitteleuropäische Wirtschaftsvolk*). Thanks to the idea of *Mitteleuropa*, Germany would finally become a legitimate partner for the British Empire, the United States, and Russia.[17]

During the war, Naumann tried to influence not just German public opinion but also other members of the future federation. To this end, he travelled to areas controlled by the Central Powers. On one of these trips, in March 1917, Naumann visited Poland, where he spent a fair amount of time in Łódź; he held talks there with representatives of the city's Polish and Jewish

---

[17] Moshe Zimmermann, 'A Road Not Taken: Friedrich Naumann's Attempt at a Modern German Nationalism', *Journal of Contemporary History* 17, 4 (1982), pp. 689–708, here p. 690.

communities. The visit led to the publication of a brochure entitled *Was wird aus Polen?* (Berlin 1917), in which Naumann criticized the excessive requisitioning that the occupiers had enforced in Poland. Naumann's supporters believed that only his project could restore independence to the nations of Central and Eastern Europe under the Russian yoke.[18]

The chaotic nature of German policy in the region proved an insurmountable barrier to the realization of Naumann's programme. A Polish expert on the problem illustrates this chaos with reference to statements made over several months in 1918 by Georg Cleinow, the German press superintendent in the occupied Polish, Lithuanian, and Belarusian territories:

> In February 1918, for example, Cleinow argued that the establishment of a 'bulwark' against Russia lay in the interests not only of Germany but also of her neighbours; in March he proclaimed that the Poles were an obstacle [...] in relations between Germany and Russia; and in June, hence already after the annexation of Livonia and Courland had been announced, he advised that the Polish Kingdom should be treated as if it were still in Russian possession.[19]

Berlin's vacillation on whether to implement the ambitious plan for a Central European federation, or to annex as much territory as possible, or to return to the old monarchical policy and come to an arrangement with Russia deprived Naumann's concept of the gravitas it needed in order to materialize.

Post-war historiography saw Naumann's project as one of the varieties of German imperialism. During the war, however, such opinions were rare. On the contrary, the author encountered strong resistance from German chauvinists, who accused him of attempting to water down national identity by associating it with other (naturally inferior) peoples. In the post-war era the idea of economic cooperation between independent political entities in the region had to give way in Germany to the nationalist programme of the struggle for *Lebensraum*. After Naumann hardly anyone treated the Central and Eastern European nations as political partners; instead they were seen as an obstacle to German greatness.

Because, despite the sincere intentions of German nationalists, the plans for mass population exchanges proved unrealistic, those who took a different view on the nature and purpose of Germany's presence in the East came to the fore. It was from this realization that the project to civilize by conquest was born, which followed in the wake of the German army's triumphs. This project was

[18] Hermann Oncken, *Das alte und das neue Mitteleuropa. Historisch-politische Betrachtungen über deutsche Bündnispolitik im Zeitalter Bismarcks und im Zeitalter des Weltkrieges*, Gotha 1917.

[19] Pajewski, '*Mitteleuropa*', p. 368.

based on the assumption that 'semi-Asia' could be occidentalized, made into Europe proper, and at the same time turned into a German sphere of influence. Its advocates shared the critical image of the East in many respects, but they drew different conclusions from those of the pan-Germanists. They wanted to change the region along with its inhabitants rather than to transform it into a zone of German settlement. This is how German and Austro-Hungarian politicians interpreted their occupation policy overall and in particular any concessions that were made to the conquered nations. The vision of the 'Europeanization' of the East remained attractive almost until the very end of the war. A few months before the Reich's capitulation, during a debate in the Reichstag on the peace treaties with Russia and Finland, Friedrich Naumann argued:

> If the brilliant cultural historian Viktor von Hahn once said that the Elbe marks the border between Europe and Asia, then the bill we now have before us is an attempt to move Hahn's border eastwards – up to the line connecting the White Sea with the Black Sea. Whether this border shall become a great historical border for centuries to come, none of us knows.[20]

While Naumann's speech was directed against Czarism and the Bolsheviks, its primary target was the German annexationists. As a liberal, Naumann regarded nation-building processes in the East to be inevitable. Annexation would delay those processes, antagonizing the populations of the emerging Baltic republics and at the same time depriving the Reich of its character as a nation-state. The experience of Austria-Hungary in March 1918 suggested that the multinational empire model was no longer viable. The paradox was that the German and Austro-Hungarian project to bring civilization to the East rested in the hands of the same military and civilian apparatus that was responsible for economically exploiting the conquered territories and disciplining their populations. The strategic idea of modernizing and occidentalizing Central and Eastern Europe thus became an appendage to the practice of occupation that often ran contrary to current objectives.

The Balkans

Many of the remarks made above could also be applied to the German and Austrian stereotype of the Balkans, both in its pre-war version and in the version that permeates war diaries, memoirs, and letters. In the Balkans the Germans and Austrians encountered the same squalor, ethnic chaos, and poverty as in the East. But whereas the East was a remote space located

---

[20] *Verhandlungen des Reichstags*, vol. 311. 1917/1918, 142. Sitzung, 18. März 1918, Spalte 4442. Cited in Pajewski, '*Mitteleuropa*', p. 306.

somewhere between Europe and Asia, the Balkans were a 'hideous mixture' of European and Oriental cultures and races.[21] These two regions had a similar level of backwardness. 'There is nothing more pathetic', grumbled one Austro-Hungarian soldier, 'than Serbian roads. They epitomize what this nation has come to regard as culture; how wretched, how vile, how unreliable and superficial.'[22] His German comrade, a participant in the Romanian campaign, had a similar impression:

> Whoever has crossed the imposing mountains along the border, as I have, and several days later finds himself in this place, down below on the Wallachian Plain, confronted with the Romanians' appalling lack of culture [...] will scratch his head in bewilderment. What madness has driven this miserable nation to put its dirty paws on lands from which it is separated by such a mighty bulwark?[23]

The images of the Balkans and of Central and Eastern Europe were nevertheless different. First, there were nation-states in the south-eastern part of the continent. Their specificity, however, lay in the fact that no one in the imperial capitals took them seriously. Seen from Vienna or Berlin, they were comical and in some sense similar to each other. In August 1914 the head of the German Supreme Army Command (OHL), Helmuth von Moltke the Younger, was probably being candid when he gave the following advice to an Austrian colleague: 'Unleash the Bulgarians against the Serbs; let those two mobs rip each other to shreds.'[24] Second, the peninsula's mountainous terrain could hardly be seen as monotonous. On the contrary, the landscape was as diverse as the ethnic structure. Third, the shock caused by the presumed lack of culture and civilization confirmed, explained, and strengthened the deep revulsion that the Germans and Austro-Hungarians had towards the Balkans peoples, who were allegedly cruel and perfidious, aggressive and deceitful, corrupt and superstitious. The civilized, European sense of superiority found additional justification in a fourth respect. The Serbs, soon to be followed by the Romanians, were the enemies of the Central Powers. This meant they were viewed not only with aloofness and contempt – as were the Jews, Poles,

---

[21] Maria Todorova, *Imagining the Balkans*, New York, NY 1997.

[22] Cited in Mechthild Golczewski, *Der Balkan in deutschen und österreichischen Reise- und Erlebnisberichten 1912–1918*, Wiesbaden 1981, pp. 135–136 (from the memoirs of Josef Neumair).

[23] Cited in Golczewski, *Der Balkan in deutschen und österreichischen Reise- und Erlebnisberichten 1912–1918*, p. 155 (from the memoirs of Alfred Olberg).

[24] Cited in Björn Opfer, *Im Schatten des Krieges. Besatzung oder Anschluss – Befreiung oder Unterdrückung? Eine komparative Untersuchung über die bulgarische Herrschaft in Vardar-Makedonien 1915–1918 und 1941–1944*, Münster 2005, p. 143; see also Stefan Minkov, 'Der Status der Nord-Dobrudscha im Kontext des deutsch-bulgarischen Verhältnisses im Ersten Weltkrieg', in *Der Erste Weltkrieg auf dem Balkan. Perspektiven der Forschung*, ed. Jürgen Angelow, Berlin 2011, pp. 241–255.

MISSION CIVILISATRICE

Belarusians, Lithuanians, and Ukrainians – but also with hatred. The notoriously 'regicidal' Balkan 'thugs' were responsible for the murder of Franz Ferdinand and had caused the war. In Vienna the war against the Serbs was initially envisaged as a punitive expedition under the slogan of 'Serbien muß sterbien' ('Serbia must die') – a slogan as telling as it is clumsy in German. It was only after the thrashing that the Serbian 'shepherds' and 'swineherds' meted out to the invaders in 1914 that the Austrians changed their opinion.

And yet, in relation to the Balkans as well, the idea emerged that the Austrians and Germans were on a civilizing mission. Moreover, in this case, unlike in Poland or Belarus, the project could rely on several decades of experience. Bosnia and Herzegovina had been under Austro-Hungarian occupation and administration since 1878, being formally annexed by the Habsburg monarchy in 1908. Vienna's quasi-colonial policy towards Sarajevo set the framework for subsequent attempts at cultural occidentalization and political domination in the Balkans. Suzerainty over the province's civilian administration was exercised by the Austro-Hungarian Minister of Finance. In 1882 this task fell to the Hungarian aristocrat Béni Kállay, and it was he who devised a liberal programme for the peaceful conquest of the Balkans:

> To make the people contented, to ensure justice, to develop agriculture, to render communication easy and cheap, to spread education, *to retain the ancient traditions of the land vivified and purified by modern ideas* – that is my administrative ideal. [...] Austria is a great Occidental Empire, charged with the mission of carrying civilization to Oriental peoples.[25]

The message had to be clear to any reasonably well-informed reader of the European press. The Habsburg monarchy was trying to assume the role of a colonial power. Its civilizing mission in Galicia, pursued since the Partitions of Poland, had, in the opinion of liberals, been an utter failure.[26] Hence Bosnia now took on the role of Africa, just as the Russian provinces occupied by the Reich and Austria-Hungary would do later. The mission undertaken by both powers during the war in the East was the regional equivalent of the 'white man's burden': political dominance in the name of civilization and progress, in the name of expanding the borders of West European civilization. Yet the two best-known examples of this project – Ober-Ost and Serbia – contained an element that precisely contradicted these principles, namely, the army's antipathy towards constitutional monarchy and parliamentarism, indeed its

---

[25] Cited in Diana Reynolds Cordileone, 'Swords into Souvenirs: Bosnian Arts and Crafts under Habsburg Administration', in *Doing Anthropology in Wartime and War Zones. World War I and the Cultural Sciences in Europe*, ed. Reinhard Johler, Christian Marchetti, and Monique Scheer, Bielefeld 2010, pp. 169–190, here p. 176.

[26] Marcin Siadkowski, *Szlachcicen. Przemiany stereotypu polskiej szlachty w Wiedniu na przełomie XIX i XX wieku*, Warsaw 2011.

326   OCCUPATION

aversion to all political modernity that emerged after 1848. In the occupied territories the generals – at last, just like in the good old days! – were *de facto* not answerable to politicians, were not threatened with investigations by deputies from the Reichsrat and Reichstag, and did not have to reckon with the opinions of socialists and pacifists of every hue. They were able to carry out their plans for an ideal European order unhindered, where necessary give local elites a consultative role and a degree of self-government, and improve infrastructure in accordance with the interests both of the rulers and of the ruled; for now, the danger that this patriarchal modernization project might turn into a modern democracy seemed completely abstract – just as in Africa.

New Governments

The conquered lands were not owned by African tribes, however, but by European monarchs. Although Western public opinion found it difficult to accept that countries as young as Serbia and Romania should be taken seriously, there were no such doubts when it came to the Russian Empire. To justify a change of ruler it had to be shown that the incumbent was not doing his duty vis-à-vis the local population. Journalists, politicians, and propagandists from the Central Powers thus tried to outdo each other in condemning the uncivilized nature of the governments and political elites of Russia, Serbia, and Romania in the provinces those countries had lost. A columnist for the professional medical weekly *Deutsche Medizinische Wochenschrift*, for example, made the tart observation that, while the Russian authorities had 'delighted' Varsovians by building new Orthodox churches, the Germans had focused on more earthly concerns, creating hospitals for infectious diseases and carrying out epidemiological screening of prostitutes.[27] In the seventh week of the occupation, the *Deutsche Warschauer Zeitung* proudly reported that, whereas the Russians had denied the Poles local government for decades, the Germans had given it to them straight away.[28] Summing up the first two years of its tenure, the Governor-General's office in Warsaw noted that: 'The German administration, aside from measures to meet the country's needs, has also undertaken cultural tasks neglected by the Russians for almost a century.'[29]

The German and Austrian authors of the report were particularly fond of irony. They sneeringly referred to the Serbs, Russians, and Romanians as *Kulturträger*, while describing their own civilizational achievements as 'the

---

[27] J. Schwalbe, 'Deutsches Militärgesundheitswesen in Warschau', *Deutsche Medizinische Wochenschrift* 42, 22 (1916), pp. 673–674. This text notes the obligation for 'Frauenspersonen, die der gewerbsmäßigen Unzucht nachgehen' (prostitutes) to be registered.

[28] 'Die Städteverordnung für Russisch-Polen', *Deutsche Warschauer Zeitung*, 19 September 1915.

[29] *Zwei Jahre deutscher Arbeit im Generalgouvernement Warschau*, Berlin 1917, p. 22.

Huns' work' – in reference to the slogans of French and British propaganda. In a journalistic account from occupied Smederevo in Serbia, Wilhelm Hegeler described the work of Bavarian sappers who were fixing the destroyed water supply system with the aid of machine parts and entire machines appropriated from Brest and Valenciennes. The smiling NCO, showing Hegeler the make-shift installation, declared: 'We are continuing our barbaric activities in France and Russia to supply Smederevo with decent waterworks.'[30] A Viennese colleague of Hegeler's was completely serious when he spoke of the Austrians' Balkan mission as follows:

> While the remnants of the Serbian army-in-exile, like an emasculated Antaeus deprived of his earth, are fed horrific lies from Paris and London about the cruelty of our occupation forces in Serbia, the Austro-Hungarian military administration is effectively pursuing its goal: not just to restore peaceful relations in the sphere of cultural and economic life, which Serbia has not known for four years, but to do far more – to bring the country into the Central European cultural community in every respect.[31]

The height of criticism of the civilizational failings of enemies in the East became their symbolic removal from Europe. Intellectual chicanery of this kind most often concerned Russia. Indeed, there was a fairly simple logic to it. Since the areas captured from the Russians were considered 'semi-Asia', the real Asia had to be located somewhere further east. In German-language publications the war with Russia was seen as a defence of Western civilization against Eastern barbarity, its vanguard being the Cossacks – the 'modern Huns'.[32] The Protestant theologian Reinhold Seeberg put it this way:

> Culture [in Russia] is trodden into the ground by heavy Cossack boots, while freedom and a higher personal morality are destroyed with the aid of the whip. Any country over which Russia gains control is at risk of barbarism. Over there, in the East, we are fighting savages in order to defend culture; a man like Hindenburg is guarding European and German culture against Russian barbarism.[33]

In any case, it soon transpired that to identify Russia with the Cossacks did not do enough to emphasize the country's Asiatic character and origin. Accordingly,

---

[30] Wilhelm Hegeler, *Der Siegeszug durch Serbien*, Berlin 1916, p. 52.

[31] Friedrich Wallisch, *Die Pforte zum Orient. Unser Friedenswerk in Serbien*, Innsbruck 1917, p. 58.

[32] Hans-Erich Volkmann, 'Der Ostkrieg 1914/15 als Erlebnis- und Erfahrungswelt des deutschen Militärs', in *Die vergessene Front. Der Osten 1914/15. Ereignis, Wirkung, Nachwirkung*, ed. Gerhard P. Groß, Paderborn 2006, p. 265.

[33] Reinhold Seeberg, *Geschichte, Krieg und Seele. Reden und Aufsätze aus den Tagen des Weltkriegs*, Leipzig 1916, p. 59, cited in Günter Brakelmann, *Protestantische Kriegstheologie im Ersten Weltkrieg. Reinhold Seeberg als Theologe des deutschen Imperialismus*, Bielefeld 1974, p. 99.

German and Austro-Hungarian authors (and, taking their lead, journalists in the occupied territories: Poles, Ukrainians, Lithuanians, and Jews) began to write about 'Tatars', 'Scythians', 'Mongols', and 'Bashkirs'. The Russians were supposedly characterized by 'eastern' apathy and their rule by 'eastern' despotism. Once they had been removed from Europe, they should never be allowed to return.

The propaganda potential of the project to civilize the East was greatest in places where the armies of Central Powers could act as liberators, such as in the Polish lands and Lithuania in particular. In those territories the occupation administration could appeal to the patriotic feelings of Poles and Lithuanians, and of Jews and Belarusians, which had been quashed by the Czarist regime. This was not without its consequences. The revival of 'national life' was especially noticeable in the larger cities, such as Warsaw and Vilnius. After the entry of the Germans into Warsaw, the city was consumed by a frenzy of national celebration. As a manifestation of anti-Russian feeling, this was a desirable phenomenon; nevertheless, it was potentially dangerous because it could easily be directed against the Germans, too. Obliging journalists tried to build a bridge between patriotism and loyalty to the new regime by pointing to the indigenous roots of the great changes that were taking place: Prince Leopold of Bavaria – the commander of the army that entered the former capital of the Polish–Lithuanian Commonwealth in August 1915 – suddenly turned out to be a descendant of the seventeenth-century Polish monarch Jan III Sobieski. Being a member of the Wittelsbach dynasty, Leopold's pedigree was beyond doubt, but the Germans knew that it was not enough to legitimize their rule. They skilfully nurtured the public mood, for instance by allowing a Polish university and polytechnic to be opened, and by removing famous Russians from street names and replacing them with Poles (e.g. Berg Street was renamed Traugutt Street to commemorate the leader of the January Uprising of 1863). Names that referred to Russian or Russified towns and cities also vanished, hence Erywańska (Yerevan) Street became Kredytowa Street, and Nowoaleksandryjska (New Alexandria) Street became Puławska Street (this was logical given that the town of Puławy had its historical name restored), etc. A few months after the establishment of the new regime, a Galician visitor to the city noted:

> The shop signs are all in Polish. Very occasionally, somewhere high up on a wall, a Russian sign can still be seen. On the lanterns that display house numbers the Russian street names have been covered up; they remain only on street corners. All the new street names are exclusively Polish: Aleja 3-go Maja (an extension of Aleje Jerozolimskie up to the Poniatowski bridge), pl. Warecki, and ul. Stanisława Małachowskiego.[34]

---

[34] August Krasicki, *Dziennik z kampanii rosyjskiej*, Cracow 1988, p. 461.

MISSION CIVILISATRICE 329

Russian monuments also disappeared, though not all at once. In monarchical Europe no one was in a hurry to tear down monuments in honour of crowned heads of state or imperial armies. Initially, they were removed rather than destroyed. In Vilnius the retreating Russians dismantled the monuments to Catherine the Great, General Muravyov, and Pushkin (this event inspired the German poet and playwright Herbert Eulenberg to produce a short story about monuments pushing each other off their plinths).[35] The floodgates opened upon the abdication of Nicholas II. In 1917 a wave of devastation swept through the former provincial capitals, destroying many of the Czarist monuments still present within them. The remainder were removed in the inter-war period.

In the urban space cleansed of the symbols of Russian rule, cultural and political activity licensed by the German authorities flourished. During a visit to Warsaw, August Krasicki went to the summer theatre to see

> [. . .] a play called *Medal 3-go maja* [Third of May Medal] by Kozłowski. It is a satirical piece set in Warsaw twenty-five years ago under Muscovite rule. The actors are Lew Juchtin (Apuchtin), the school superintendent Iwan Tulio (Jankulio), Professor Ochorowicz, and Eusapia Palladino. They are all characterized as archetypes. A play such as this would have been unthinkable a year ago. The theatre shook with applause every time Russian rule was criticized or denounced.[36]

The initial reaction of the Warsaw public to the new nationalities policy was indeed positive. City residents welcomed the opening of the university and polytechnic in November 1915 with great enthusiasm. At both institutions Polish replaced Russian as the language of instruction. For the first time in history women were not discriminated against and enjoyed the same rights as men. Within two years female students made up almost 20 per cent of the student body at the university.[37] All these changes were perfectly in tune with how the Germans imagined their civilizing mission. At the same time, the opening of Warsaw University and Warsaw Polytechnic was a highly political and therefore sensitive issue in everyday life. From 23 September public meetings and marches were banned in Warsaw. It was easy to imagine that the new milieu, comprising hundreds if not thousands of students, i.e. young, relatively well-educated people who were often energetic and even more often patriotic, would bring a new atmosphere to the streets of Warsaw; an atmosphere which, from the point of view of the occupier, was completely

---

[35] 'Die verschwundenen Denkmäler in Wilna. Eine mitternächtliche Szene', in Hermann Struck and Herbert Eulenberg, *Skizzen aus Litauen, Weissrussland und Kurland*, Berlin 1916, unpaginated.

[36] Krasicki, *Dziennik z kampanii rosyjskiej*, p. 460.

[37] Robert Blobaum, *A Minor Apocalypse. Warsaw during the First World War*, Ithaca, NY and London 2017, pp. 190–192.

330   OCCUPATION

unnecessary. Both sides were aware of the risk. For this reason the future rectors of the university and polytechnic – introduced to Hans von Beseler by the German-appointed official responsible for Polish affairs, Count Bogdan Hutten-Czapski, who was also vice chancellor of both institutions – made an official announcement that the new institutions 'would exclusively serve science and learning'.[38] Governor Beseler pretended to believe them.

The news that the aforementioned meeting had taken place was released on the same day as another, equally bureaucratic announcement that all fur was to be requisitioned from Varsovians. Hutten-Czapski nevertheless believed that, when it came to propaganda, the Germans had succeeded in achieving their goal:

> The opening of the university and polytechnic has made a deep impression on Polish public opinion. It is now a fact that the Germans, although they made no assurances and even tried to supress political activity when the two institutions were opened, within a few months of capturing Warsaw gave the country the opportunity to promote national high culture, whereas the Russians gave us nothing but beautiful-sounding promises.[39]

A while later, in a old town house once belonging to the Mazovian Dukes (now housing the Institute of History of the Polish Academy of Sciences), an exhibition of memorabilia from the November Uprising of 1830 was opened. Governor Beseler graced the exhibition with a visit, accompanied by several officers. The apogee of Polish–German cooperation was to occur about a year later. On 5 November the creation of a Polish state was officially announced. The setting of the ceremony, during which a fairly run-of-the-mill document was read out, reflected both the magnanimity of the occupiers and their strength:

> The weather was clement; it was an unusually lovely day for the time of the year. The city was festooned in national flags and banners. In the castle courtyard, and in front of the castle, students from the university and polytechnic, secondary school pupils, and a host of associations and organizations waited in anticipation. [...] About 600 invited guests gathered in the castle's great columned hall. The cordon was policed by the Legionnaires. Beseler, surrounded by dignitaries and his entire military staff, read out the proclamation act, which was then repeated in Polish by Count Hutten-Czapski and also read from the castle balcony. At that moment Polish banners were unfurled on the castle walls alongside the German ones. A huge cry: 'Long live an independent Poland!,' issued by

[38] *Deutsche Warschauer Zeitung*, 12 November 1915.
[39] Cited in Marta Polsakiewicz, 'Zapomniana okupacja. Niemieckie wojska w Warszawie 1915–1918', *Dialog – Magazyn Polsko-Niemeckie* 90 (2009–2010), pp. 59–61, here p. 61.

MISSION CIVILISATRICE

a thousand voices, resounded through the hall and courtyard and pl. Zamkowy (Castle Square).[40]

The Central Powers did not pursue their nationalities policy solely in areas they had already occupied, however. Beginning in 1916 a campaign funded by the Reich's Ministry of Foreign Affairs to support irredentism among non-Russian nationalities in the Czarist empire gathered pace. In June of that year activists from Poland, Ukraine, Estonia, Latvia, Lithuania, Kalmykia, Kazakhstan, Kyrgyzstan, Georgia, Tatarstan, Azerbaijan, and Dagestan, as well as a group of Baltic Germans, met at a conference in Lausanne in neutral Switzerland. Their joint declaration condemning Russia for violating the rights of non-Russian nationalities was addressed to President Wilson by name. The text, which was also disseminated in Scandinavia, met with a lively response and placed the Entente Powers in an awkward position. The allegations made by the participants of the Lausanne conference were justified, and the suspicion that German intrigue lay behind everything, although correct, was not officially confirmed until after the war.[41]

Jewish political circles, and not just in the Central Powers, vested great hopes in a war against Russia. The Czarist state was rightly regarded as a mainstay of European anti-Semitism, while at the beginning of the war both the German and the Austro-Hungarian governments strove to suppress domestic anti-Semitic propaganda. For politically active Jews, these facts were logically coherent: to them the Great War was primarily a crusade against Russia. No wonder, then, that Jewish organizations in the Reich and in the Habsburg monarchy gave a cool reception to the slogan 'God, punish England' (*Gott, strafe England*) and instead replaced it with another: 'Revenge for Kishinev' (*Rache für Kischinjow*, the city in Russia where in 1903 one of the biggest pogroms in history took place). Jewish soldiers who fought for the Central Powers marched eastwards to defend their brothers from persecution and also to civilize them – to bring those gabardine-wearers closer to the ideal of enlightened German Jewry. The Jewish question was no less part of the civilizing mission than the Polish, Ukrainian, or Lithuanian question, even if the rules were different.

In areas that they captured from Russia, the Central Powers could play the role of liberators without too much difficulty, and could do so at least until economic exploitation had dispelled any remaining sympathy for them. It was different in Serbia and Romania. There, playing with local nationalism was too dangerous: the Serbian and Romanian armies, though defeated and exiled, had

---

[40] Stanisław Dzierzbicki, *Pamiętnik z lat wojny 1915–1918*, ed. Janusz Pajewski and Danuta Płygawko, Warsaw 1983, p. 192.

[41] Seppo Zetterberg, *Die Liga der Fremdvölker Russlands 1916–1918. Ein Beitrag zu Deutschlands antirussischem Propagandakrieg unter den Fremdvölkern Russlands im Ersten Weltkrieg*, Helsinki 1978.

not laid down their arms. Therefore, in the Balkans, the Austro-Hungarian and German occupiers tried to suppress national sentiment and undermine solidarity among social groups. They blamed former rulers and elites for all the misfortunes associated with the war. Addressing the 'people' directly, they gave assurances that the 'people' were 'a thousand times better than their leaders'.[42] Since the local elites had failed, the empire had to take on the role of patron. Characteristic of this position was a sentence in an official report by the Austro-Hungarian Military Government General in Belgrade: 'Let this work cover the Austro-Hungarian armed forces with eternal glory and be a lasting gift to the indigenous people.'[43] At least for a while it might have seemed that the gambit had paid off. In the Romanian countryside German soldiers took control so smoothly that there was no major social unrest there until the summer of 1918. In Serbia, and especially in Montenegro, armed resistance appeared sooner, but its causes should be attributed to the deteriorating supply situation rather than to policy.

Conquest by Science

Science, especially ethnography, anthropology, and geography, became one of the means to 'occidentalize' Central and Eastern Europe and the Balkans. The populations of conquered territories (and of the Balkan ally, Bulgaria) were of interest to the conquerors as a research problem. There was no lack of opportunity to learn about local peculiarities. During the war the number of Germans and Austrians who became acquainted with these hitherto exotic regions grew rapidly, and they usually experienced these regions in military uniform:

> Thanks to the war, thousands of Germans have come to know the Balkans. Our soldiers waded through snow and mud during the Serbian–Macedonian campaign. Later on, German doctors and nurses reached Bulgaria via Romania. German signal units (telegraph and rail) did a great service to their ally by reaching every nook and cranny of that beautiful country. Then, German troops helped to repel General Sarrail's offensive in the south and took part in the victorious advance through Dobruja (Dobrogea) in the north. German pilots defended the capital's airspace against French bombardment and protected Varna against enemy attack from the sea. German zeppelins took off from Hungary and crossed the entire Balkans. Even a few Reichstag deputies finally took the opportunity to embark on fruitful trips to Bulgaria.[44]

[42] Wallisch, *Die Pforte zum Orient*, p. 35.

[43] *Bericht über die Verwaltung des Kreises Belgrad-Land in der Zeit vom 1. November 1915 bis 31. Dezember 1916*, Belgrade 1917, p. 6.

[44] Arthur Dix, *Zwischen zwei Welten. Die Völkerbrücke des Balkan*, Dresden 1917, p. 9.

MISSION CIVILISATRICE

Among the participants of the Balkan campaign were many people who took a keen interest in the local landscape and culture and in the inhabitants of the region. Beginning in 1915, in the wake of the Central Powers' military successes, increasingly large tracts of Central and Eastern Europe and the Balkans became a location for geographical, anthropological, and ethnographic research. Army scientists and amateur photographers were especially interested in collecting 'typical' images of locals in folk costume. They also collected all sorts of artefacts. In several cases the state participated in these initiatives. The Bulgarian government financed two scientific expeditions to investigate the populations and geography of Dobruja and Macedonia. In the latter province German scientists from the Mazedonische Landeskommission (Malako) were also active. The Austrians, in turn, undertook zoological and ethnographic field trips around Serbia and Montenegro. All the findings appeared in German and Austrian publications already during the war. Their purpose was to provide clear evidence of the occupiers' contribution to civilization. Sometimes ethnologists in uniform were indeed the first people to investigate little-known cultures, but this was rare.

HANDBUCH VON POLEN

Less than half a year after the German army had occupied Warsaw, Governor Beseler set up the Geographical Commission (*Landeskundliche Kommission*). The organization, whose first chairman was the geographer Max Friederichsen, consisted exclusively of German scientists. In the first year of their activity they focused on collecting materials: books and journals on the geography and ethnography of the Polish lands as well as photographs, maps, soil samples, and minerals. From 1917 the initial results of their work began to appear in print. The governor himself attached greatest importance to a huge collective work that bore the ambitious title of *Handbuch von Polen* [*Handbook to Poland*]. He saw it not only as a scholarly work but also as a political act – a symbol of the superiority of civilized German government over Czarism. In the preface, he declared:

> Apart from offering scientific and practical findings, this work shows that the German administration, operating in what is a conquered and occupied country, pays attention not just to military, political, and administrative tasks, but also to scientific ones, responding to local needs and inspired by local conditions. Let this book, therefore, be a contribution towards a proper understanding of the German spirit.[45]

In a very positive review of the work in the *Geographische Zeitschrift*, Joseph Partsch hit a similar tone:

---

[45] Hans Beseler, 'Geleitwort', in *Handbuch von Polen. Beiträge zu einer allgemeinen Landeskunde*, ed. E. Wunderlich, Berlin 1917, unpaginated.

334 OCCUPATION

Abounding in material, this work is a rich source of invaluable knowledge for the inquiring and enterprising spirit. It is undoubtedly an important gift not just for the German people, but certainly also for the educated population of Poland; a gift for which no nation has ever been so indebted to those who liberated it from the darkest bondage.[46]

The response of the Polish academic community fell far below these expectations. Published with a two-year delay, the 1917 Yearbook of the Lwów-based popular science magazine *Kosmos* contained extensive descriptions of all the articles in the *Handbuch von Polen* together with summaries in German. The assessments were withering, the principal accusation being that the *Handbuch* had completely ignored not just Polish, but also foreign authors of studies on the Polish lands. Only Germans were cited in the book. An insight into the tone of the reviews is provided by Jan Stanisław Bystroń, who assessed the ethnographic part of the German publication:

In the forests live goblins, witches, werewolves, and nymphs; the Woodland Spirit reigns over them. How strange is Mother Nature that she cannot envisage anything without a hierarchy, and a foreign hierarchy to boot, for the Woodland Spirit is clearly a native of Russia. [...] I imagine that an essay entitled 'Das Erntefest bei den Wasserpolen' ('The Harvest Rituals of the Upper Silesians'), written by eight-year-old Hans at a primary school in Hohensalza (Inowrocław) or some other proto-Germanic town, would be similar.[47]

. Why were the reactions of Polish scholars so caustic? There were at least two reasons. First, the *Handbuch* piqued their professional pride. Not without reason, they perceived its lofty judgments about the lands and people of Poland, about which they had never been consulted, as a manifestation of academic imperialism. The professional shortcomings of the *Handbuch* allowed them, in a spectacular fashion, to take on the competition in the form of German scientists who were essentially amateurs convinced of their own superiority. Second, the vehemence of the Polish protests had a political backdrop. The Poland referred to by the authors of the *Handbuch* was limited to the Congress Kingdom and was in addition separated from the eastern territories by a natural border. Moreover, the authors considered the region to be a transitional area, open on all sides and lacking a specific character; its political destiny was that it would be included in a German *Mitteleuropa*. This position undoubtedly corresponded to the existing policy of the Reich. Thus, the main charge levelled by the Polish reviewers was that the *Handbuch* subordinated science to politics. In the assessment cited above,

---

[46] J[oseph] Partsch, 'Das Handbuch von Polen', *Geographische Zeitschrift* 24, 2–3 (1918), pp. 68–76, here p. 76.
[47] Jan Stanisław Bystroń, review of A. Schultz, 'Volkskunde', *Kosmos* XLII (1917), pp. 145–149, here pp. 147–148.

Bystroń criticized Arved Schultz's attempt to correlate ethnographic groups with existing political borders as 'regional gymnastics':

> Just as the 'westliche Gruppe' aims to identify Poles living under Prussian rule as a separate entity, having no desire to merge with the nucleus of Poles living in the Kingdom and being significantly different from them, so the division into northern and southern groups corresponds more or less to the current borders of the German and Austrian occupations. Whether this division is intended to justify certain *faits accomplis*, or whether it is evidence of a certain mental paralysis and an inability to look at ethnic relations beyond the prism of state policy, I cannot say.[48]

Of all the German and Austro-Hungarian cultural and scientific initiatives in the occupied territories, the *Handbuch von Polen* is a classic example of how the project to civilize the East was flawed. The lofty aims of this project were not reflected in the expertise of its originators, whose political constraints and often nationalistic views irritated the very people who were expected to be grateful: the intellectual elites of Central and Eastern Europe. It turned out that in this part of the world it was too late for colonialism.[49]

Recognition for the wartime research done by German and Austrian ethnographers fades dramatically when one takes a closer look at the specific outcomes of their scientific work. Their studies, unsupported by solid research (for which there was no time during the war), are quite superficial, and more reminiscent of travel writing than scholarship. No wonder, then, that the authors hardly ever went beyond the pre-war stereotype of the East and the Balkans. Montenegro is an extreme case. This poor, backward, mountainous country, inhabited by a warlike people, aroused both interest and disgust. Authors were fascinated by the mythologized figure of the Balkan highlander – a born warrior, a living fossil of the clan system – and even by the 'healthy' patriarchal relations that prevailed in the country as reflected in the extremely low social status of women.[50] Anthropologists wanted to find specific racial features in the local population that accounted for the lifestyle of the Montenegrins. They were guided by the principle that a nation whose main occupation was constant war must have an exceptionally valuable

---

[48] Ibid., p. 146.

[49] Maciej Górny, *Science Embattled. Eastern European Intellectuals and the Great War*, translated by Antoni Górny, Paderborn 2019, pp. 119–161.

[50] Ursula Reber writes about the Austro-Hungarian ethnographic fascination with Montenegro in 'The Experience of Borders: Montenegrin Tribesmen at War', in *Doing Anthropology in Wartime and War Zones. World War I and the Cultural Sciences in Europe*, ed. Reinhard Johler, Christian Marchetti, and Monique Scheer, Bielefeld 2010, pp. 191–205.

set of inherited features. Their interest did not always go hand-in-hand with sympathy and empathy, however. The very same anthropologists, ethnographers, and geographers celebrated the successes of the monarchy in its mission to civilize a wild and inhospitable country and often devoted more attention to those successes than to the actual subject of their research. In his report to the Imperial–Royal Geographical Society, one of the most renowned scientists to visit the area occupied by Austria-Hungary during the war, the Viennese geographer and anthropologist Eugen Oberhummer, focused on the most recent investment in the country's transport infrastructure: a freight cable car connecting the Austro-Hungarian port of Kotor with Cetinje via Mount Lovćen.[51]

Expeditions to Macedonia, by far the most popular 'destination' for scientists from the Central Powers, brought no major breakthroughs either. Field work merely confirmed the pre-existing belief that the region had not yet been touched by civilization. As one German zoologist in uniform observed, in Skopje 'Only the houses built or renovated by the German army are bearable to look at.'[52] In anthropological terms, the warlike, semi-wild Albanian highlanders elicited a degree of interest among German scientists, who suspected them of having a distant racial affinity with the Bavarians. Aside from the highlanders, the province was a 'racial mixture' that could not be disentangled, since it was covered, just like the whole of the East, by a thick layer of dirt:

> The streets of Prilep are swarming with children. With their bright blue eyes and sun-bleached flaxen hair, they could be taken for Germans. This is not a mistake one could make in the long run, however, for nowhere in Germany would one find children so grimy, dirty, and neglected.[53]

The interest of German and Austrian scientists in the ethnography of Central and Eastern Europe and the Balkans fell sharply after the end of the war. There is no better proof than this as to the opportunistic character of their work. When writing about nationalities, cultures, and even about the natural world in foreign countries, German and Austro-Hungarian authors affirmed, first and foremost, the civilizing impact of the occupation. Civilizational change interested them much more than the facts on the ground.

---

[51] Eugen Oberhummer, 'Montenegro und Albanien unter österreichisch-ungarischer Verwaltung', *Mitteilungen der k.k. Geographischen Gesellschaft in Wien* 61, 7 (1918), pp. 313–346.

[52] Franz Dorflein, *Mazedonien. Erlebnisse und Beobachtungen eines Naturforschers im Gefolge des deutschen Heeres*, Jena 1921, p. 248.

[53] Ibid., pp. 271–272.

MISSION CIVILISATRICE

BULGARIA'S FIVE MINUTES

At the outbreak of the Great War, no Balkan state was well-regarded in the European press. During the First Balkan War, which was fought between the Balkan League (Bulgaria, Serbia, Greece, and Montenegro) and the Ottoman Empire, news filtered through about civilian massacres. Soon afterwards, the Carnegie Endowment for International Peace published a comprehensive report that held all the belligerents equally responsible. Such news merely confirmed the entrenched stereotype of the savage Balkan peoples, known for their 'primitive disputes and primitive ways of resolving them'.[54] The assassination in Sarajevo, which was received with indignation around the world, worsened the image of the region still further. No wonder, then, that Austria-Hungary's 'punitive expedition' to Serbia appealed to that stereotype and treated its opponent not as a rival but as a common criminal. It was not until Bulgaria entered the war on the side of the Central Powers in 1915 that the situation fundamentally changed. Now, assessments of the nations and states of South-Eastern Europe became more problematic.

During the 1915–1918 period both Central European monarchies became vastly more interested in their Balkan ally. Contempt gave way to admiration – for the bravery of the Bulgarian army, the dynamism of the fledgling state, and the national character of the Bulgarians:

> The Bulgarian's character is widely praised. His distinctive features are simplicity, modesty, prudence, patriotism, geniality, and a readiness for sacrifice [...]. Furthermore, the Bulgarian is distinguished by diligence and attentiveness combined with great perseverance. Finally, his powerful need for education is striking. As regards temperament, he is serious and systematic, but also willing to rise to the great challenges facing his nation.[55]

Such qualities could in no way be reconciled with the stereotype of the Balkan savage. It thus became logically necessary to show that the Bulgarians were different from their less virtuous neighbours, above all the Serbs and Montenegrins:

> Among the diverse Balkan peoples the Bulgarians surely occupy top spot, for there is no other nation that rises so conspicuously above all others for its valour, patriotism, intelligence, and willingness to embrace the highest values. [...] This nation of the European Orient has rightly earned the watchful attention of people in the West. It desires that we should take a greater and deeper interest in it, become familiar with and understand it, and that we should cultivate our alliance on the basis of mutual understanding.[56]

---

[54] Božidar Jezernik, *Dzika Europa. Bałkany w oczach zachodnich podróżników*, translated by Piotr Oczko, Cracow 2007, p. 16.

[55] Georg Buschan, *Die Bulgaren. Herkunft und Geschichte. Eigenschaften, Volksglaube, Sitten und Gebräuche*, Stuttgart 1917, pp. 1 and 23.

[56] Ibid., p. 1.

This profound interest in Germany's Balkan ally, postulated by the anthropologist Georg Buschan, was not limited to the benign observation of culture and customs; it also penetrated a sphere invisible to the eye: the interior of the human body. The logical consequence of the idea that the Bulgarians were the exception among the Balkan peoples in almost every respect was the overwhelming desire to peek under their skin, in other words, to examine their racial and ethnic origins. The 'Prussians of the Balkans', as they were referred to in German-language publications, supposedly had different racial origins from the peninsula's Slavic inhabitants, although the proponents of this claim often disagreed about the details. In keeping with historical knowledge, the Bulgarian ethnos was said to be composed of, among others, Asian Proto-Bulgarians. What is telling is that this ethnic component was emphasized by, for instance, the Budapest orientalist Adolf Strausz,[57] who drew attention to the similarities between the frugal and hard-working Bulgarian peasant and his Hungarian counterpart (who likewise claimed descent from the Volga nomads). Some German anthropologists advanced bolder arguments, claiming that the Bulgarians were the original Thracian inhabitants of the Balkan Peninsula. A few German and Bulgarian eccentrics went even further, arguing that the Bulgarians were the descendants of the Germanic Goths. In works published during the war by German publishing houses, Gancho Tsenov, the *enfant terrible* of Bulgarian archaeology, sought to prove that the Thracians, Goths, Illyrians, Macedonians, and even the Huns (hence practically all the ethnonyms associated throughout history with the lands of modern-day Bulgaria) constituted a single ethnic group that was identical to the Bulgarians.[58] The alleged kinship between the Bulgarians and Germans, which was confirmed by observations and measurements carried out by physical anthropologists in Macedonia and other places, greatly facilitated the work of war journalists. It would have been unseemly to accuse descendants of the Goths of squalor and barbarity.

The exceptionally good press that Bulgaria enjoyed in the Reich and Austria-Hungary during the war years emboldened Sofia to pursue its ambitious programme of territorial expansion. Indeed, many of the publications devoted to the Bulgarian ally dealt with the country's 'natural' borders. A whole galaxy of ethnographers from the Central Powers became interested in Macedonia, for example, and tried to prove that it was inhabited solely by Bulgarians.

However, the Balkan ally's ambitions went much further. In January 1916 the parliament in Sofia set out its war aims. Naturally, the objective was to unify all Bulgarians – including those who did not yet consider themselves Bulgarian – within the borders of a single monarchy. The country's territorial scope was symbolized by a new flag: black, white, and blue. The black symbolized the Black Sea, the white the Aegean, and the blue the Adriatic. Neither the Reich nor the

---

[57] Adolf Strausz, *Großbulgarien*, Leipzig 1917.
[58] Gantscho Tzenoff, *Geschichte der Bulgaren*, Berlin 1917; Gantscho Tzenoff, *Goten oder Bulgaren. Quellenkritische Untersuchung über die Geschichte der alten Skythen, Thraker und Makedonier*, Leipzig 1915.

> Habsburg monarchy approved of such far-reaching annexation by their ally. The friendship declared in wartime publications was also put under strain when German and Bulgarian soldiers met in the trenches. In their letters home, officers sent to the Salonika Front expressed their disgust at the cruelty of the Bulgarians. Seen at close quarters, the 'Prussians of the Balkans' did not exactly live up to their idealized propaganda image. Even when feasting together, many new arrivals from the Reich felt uneasy when their Bulgarian hosts broke out into one of the most popular military songs of the Second Balkan War: *Our Allies – Our Traitors.*[59]

Education and Hygiene

Because Germany and Austria-Hungary tried to assume the position of an enlightened colonial power in the territories they occupied, they were practically forced to pursue educational activity in the broad sense. This aspect of their occupation policy was likewise approached with missionary zeal. Schools and universities were opened, and, since there was no mandatory schooling in the Czarist empire, for many the occupation signalled a breakthrough – the beginning of a journey towards (West) European standards. In Warsaw the local Civic Committee introduced universal schooling on the day the Military Government General was formed, i.e. eighteen days after the Germans had captured the city.

In Romania and in areas seized from Russia, classes were held in native languages and in German, and the staff were often locals. Although teachers were required to quickly learn German and to swear allegiance to the new regime, they were generally left to their own devices. The creation of teaching seminars for women caused indignation among local conservatives, but the occupiers were not overly concerned with this kind of resistance to social and cultural progress. Austro-Hungarian educational policy in Serbia was different. The occupation authorities deemed state schools to be breeding grounds of nationalism and hence did not allow them to continue in their existing form. Instead, they replaced all the staff and introduced a completely new curriculum. The former Serbian teachers were re-employed only in exceptional cases. There were no women among them, however, because Conrad von Hötzendorf considered women to be particularly ardent and incorrigible Serbian chauvinists.[60] The Austrians also undertook spelling reform and banned the use of Cyrillic in schools. The new teachers were soldiers,

---

[59] Oliver Stein, '"Wer das nicht mitgemacht hat, glaubt es nicht". Erfahrungen deutscher Offiziere mit dem bulgarischen Verbündeten 1915–1918', in *Der Erste Weltkrieg auf dem Balkan. Perspektiven der Forschung*, ed. Jürgen Angelow, Berlin 2011, p. 282.

[60] Jonathan E. Gumz, *The Resurrection and Collapse of Empire in Habsburg Serbia, 1914–1918*, Cambridge 2009, pp. 75–76.

340   OCCUPATION

whose skills were usually limited to knowledge of the language. Such staff could not, of course, provide a decent level of education, and so the positive impact of Austrian education policy on Serb civilians was sought elsewhere. Pupils and society alike were to imbibe 'Central European values': diligence, order, cleanliness, and reliability. This was the kind of curriculum that the NCOs from reserve units were no doubt able to implement.

The education of new citizens did not take place solely at school. Austrian propagandists praised, for example, the successful popularization of new forms of intensive farming:

> Under gentle pressure and thanks to the good example that has been set for him, the Serbian peasant, who has much oriental laziness in his blood, has now been forced to perform honest work in the fields. No longer does he wait until the cattle have eaten their fill in the meadows and the sun has warmed the plums and corn. And, to his great surprise, he sees that in many regions more land has been sown this year than ever before.[61]

Germans and Austrians exploited the occupied countryside with great energy. However, they also tried to improve the quality of crops and husbandry. In this respect the actions taken by the Austrian authorities in the part of the Kingdom of Poland they controlled were typical. On the one hand, the supply of food, and especially of meat, deteriorated with each passing month. On the other hand, the authorities did a lot to help local farmers. In 1916 breeding bulls, new medicines, and specialists in animal diseases were brought in from Germany. Meat markets and fairs, abattoirs, and the disposal of animal by-products – i.e. all the stages in the production and sale of meat – came under the control of the sanitary authorities. At the same time, the administration tried to publicize what it was doing for the benefit of the local population and to quell rumours about food being exported to Germany and Austria-Hungary.

The sphere in which the occupiers' achievements were particularly visible was hygiene, and it was this that the propaganda of the civilizing mission referred to most often. Vejas Gabriel Liulevicius goes as far as to claim that it was the leading metaphor used by the military administration of Ober-Ost. Czarist rule, in contrast, was identified with dirt.[62] 'Cleanliness and order are transforming the face of the city', wrote Friedrich Wallisch, 'and even our fiercest enemies must admit that Belgrade has never been so clean.'[63] This was not just propaganda. Even observers ill-disposed to the Germans and Austrians conceded that the problem had been taken seriously. Cardinal Kakowski recalled one of the characteristic orders of the occupation authorities:

---

[61] Wallisch, *Die Pforte zum Orient*, pp. 63–64.
[62] Liulevicius, *War Land on the Eastern Front*, p. 199.
[63] Wallisch, *Die Pforte zum Orient*, p. 52.

MISSION CIVILISATRICE

Infectious diseases were successfully and meticulously controlled. Rail passengers had to produce a card to show that they had been 'deloused'. Surprisingly, I too had such a card, which was sent to me *ex officio*. Without a delousing card no one could enter a railway carriage.[64]

'Normal' passengers did not receive delousing cards '*ex officio*'. The system was thorough and effective. It was also aided by the delousing stations brought in from German ports, which prior to 1914 had been used by emigrants en route to America. Eighteen delousing stations were set up behind the lines on the Eastern Front, serving soldiers, workers, and other rail passengers. Their daily capacity was 45,000 people.

Protective vaccinations were introduced in all areas under German and Austro-Hungarian occupation. Epidemiological laboratories were also set up. In Serbia the Austrian authorities considered their successful fight against typhus fever, which until recently had decimated Serbian soldiers and Austro-Hungarian prisoners alike, to be especially deserving of praise. Every municipality in the country was ordered to set up an epidemiological hospital in a self-contained building. Soldiers guarded the entrances, and the doctors (brought in from Austria-Hungary) who worked there maintained daily contact with the headquarters in Belgrade. In the Congress Kingdom the German army relied on the help of rabbis, who promoted hygiene among the faithful. They also resorted to more severe methods. Vaccination and delousing campaigns, especially in the countryside, were compulsory. Doctors, with military assistance, quite often took the opportunity to immediately vaccinate patients who had been deloused.

GERMANY FIGHTS TYPHUS FEVER

Dr Gottfried Frey (1871–1952) was born in Świecie (Schwetz), a town on the Vistula. Before the war he was a district doctor in Upper Silesia, and that is probably why he was appointed head of the Medical Board of the Generalgouvernement Warschau in 1915. He considered his main task to be the combating of infectious diseases in the occupied territory. Typhus fever seemed especially dangerous to him. As Frey recounted after the war, the disease was 'a great threat to the Prussian border provinces, to the occupying forces, and to front-line units. It was therefore necessary to undertake quite unusual measures in order to reduce the risk of infection to a minimum [...]. Equipped with the paraphernalia of German anti-epidemic campaigns, we did not have to fear infectious diseases; we were able to avert the danger everywhere. Except for the incredibly unhygienic Jewish quarter in Łódź, there were few places where we had to fight typhus fever systematically.'

---

[64] Aleksander Kakowski, *Z niewoli do niepodległości. Pamiętniki*, ed. Tadeusz Krawczak and Ryszard Świętek, Cracow 2000, p. 281.

342

OCCUPATION

From the turn of the century, typhus fever (*Typhus exanthematicus*) was regarded as a plague worse than cholera. In the Reich it was present only as a memory: the last recorded epidemic had taken place in 1881 in West Prussia (Pomerania). When lice appeared on soldiers on the Eastern Front in the autumn 1914, doctors were initially helpless. They soon came up with a solution, however, which was to delouse soldiers' clothing using steam. Civilians presented more of a problem. In freezing weather conditions and with hunger rife, a typhus epidemic broke out in Łódź in December 1915, prompting Dr Frey and his colleagues to take radical action. The 'scheduled delousing of infected districts' took the form of *Entlausungskolonnen* (de-lousing columns) combing entire districts, including apartments and people. Particular attention was paid to local Jews: the parts of the city they inhabited became, in the official parlance, 'typhus streets' or even 'typhus districts'.

The most important carrier of the disease was the clothes louse. Typhus quickly came to be seen as a 'Jewish disease', born of the dirt allegedly endemic to that community. Dr Frey and colleagues distinguished Jewish dirt from Christian dirt and Jewish lice from Polish lice:

> Our observations from the last epidemic [i.e. in Łódź in the winter of 1915/1916] show that head lice – very common among the Polish population – do not carry the germ of typhus fever. Clothes lice were found only on people from the lowest social strata. Generally, in our territory, such people are Jews, and not Poles.

Dr Frey was shocked at the resistance of the Jewish community and its aversion to the *Entlausungskolonnen* – by stubbornly sabotaging the idea that the sick and the healthy should be treated differently, it simply did not understand the needs of modernity. Between 1 July 1916 and 1 October 1918 the Germans deloused 3.25 million people and over 480,000 apartments. However, their efforts proved unsuccessful as 50 per cent of the confirmed cases in the short history of the Generalgouvernement Warschau were recorded in the winter of 1917/1918.

Elsewhere, the Austrians considered typhus to be a disease that was endemic to the local population in their part of the Kingdom of Poland, i.e. the MGG/L. They did not have the resources to run a major sanitation campaign and instead disinfected individual houses and apartments rather than whole streets or districts. As a rule, they did not isolate the sick, but tried to provide them with continuous medical care. The results of their approach were no worse than those of Dr Frey.

Nor could any occupier win the battle against the most serious plague, i.e. tuberculosis, which claimed more victims than either typhus or dysentery. However, it was not considered public enemy number one until after the hostilities had ended and the Spanish flu epidemic had subsided.[65]

---

[65] For more on Dr Frey, see Christian Teichmann, *Krieg und Ethnizität in Warschau, 1915–1918. Das jüdische Beispiel*, Master's dissertation defended at the University of Leipzig in 2002. We would like to thank the author for sharing the manuscript.

The sickness statistics for the whole territory occupied by the Central Powers show that – aside from endemic tuberculosis – typhus fever was initially the biggest threat to the local population, giving way to influenza in the final years of the war. The exceptions were Macedonia and Romania, where malaria raged, but where typhus also remained a threat. Yet the reports of the sanitary services, the discussions among doctors and hygienists, and the press articles published at the time often give the impression that the occupiers were mainly concerned with a completely different epidemic: venereal disease. Syphilis and gonorrhoea became new enemies to be overcome on the victorious march to the East.

Observers who described the region's squalor with such revulsion never ceased to be amazed by the seductive power of the local women: 'Venereal disease is very widespread among the Gypsies, and though it is truly hard to believe, many of our soldiers and officers have returned from that district [the Gypsy district in Skopje] with a nasty infection.'[66] Even scientific ventures, which consisted in zoological, geographical, and ethnographic studies of the region, were not free of risk: 'A certain Gypsy woman, who held a certain status during the occupation as a courtesan, was often photographed. She now figures in more than one album from Macedonia as a typical Gypsy woman.'[67]

It was not just in Macedonia that the occupation authorities had to deal with syphilis and gonorrhoea. Throughout the occupied East the fight against venereal disease was often associated with the hygiene measures that were introduced. There were several reasons why these two concepts were linked. The occupied territories of Central and Eastern Europe and the Balkans were, in the general opinion of the conquerors, especially contaminated – not just by ordinary dirt, but by moral filth. For this reason it was necessary to proceed with extreme caution. On the other hand, gonorrhoea and syphilis entailed hospitalization, which meant that soldiers undergoing treatment had to be removed from front-line duty at least for a period of time. Venereal disease thus became a problem not just for its victims but also for the state. Finally, as the supporters of the eugenic movement in Reich were quick to point out, soldiers who became infected in the occupied territories would, while on leave, spend time at home with their German wives: this would only spread the disease and bring the terrifying spectre of racial degeneration ever closer. Furthermore, one of the effects of the disease was infertility – another heavy blow to the future defence of the state. All these factors led to a major distortion of perspective and to hygiene and health care being frequently identified with the prevention of venereal disease. This mechanism is perfectly captured in Rudolf Lennhoff's account of the German medical congress that took place in Warsaw in 1916:

[66] Dorflein, *Mazedonien*, p. 252.
[67] Ibid., p. 253.

344

OCCUPATION

In Warsaw itself an energetic fight against the threat of infection has been undertaken. In such a big city in the East, where in addition to those willing to work as prostitutes there are many girls who are pushed into the profession by abject poverty, it is hardly surprising that there is a huge risk of infection. All the more so as sanitary supervision and care have been hitherto unknown. That is why it was necessary, first of all, to create a morality police whose task it was to identify prostitutes and to diagnose, isolate, and treat the infected.[68]

The German occupation authorities did indeed go about their task with gusto. They soon realized that there were over 10,000 women in Warsaw infected with syphilis who were either prostitutes or occasionally practised prostitution. The experts calculated that each of those women infected between three and ten men within a short period of time. Two completely different strategies were necessary in order to prevent further infection. German soldiers were gently persuaded that masturbation was far more hygienic than casual sex, and those who could not be persuaded were given condoms by the army. They also had the right to visit military or officers' brothels (during the war there was an ongoing debate in the German medical press about whether this was a good solution; despite moral reservations, the majority view was that soldiers should not be deprived of the privilege of visiting the so-called *Puff*). The women who worked for the German army were, of course, subject to screening and medical care. Observing all these activities from the outside, allies could not help making the odd caustic remark:

> The amorous relations of the German soldier do not cease even after he has left the apartment of his temporary mistress: he is still obliged to record her name and address accurately and to give these details to the authorities in the event he becomes infected.[69]

Women and girls suspected of prostitution were treated differently. Units of the morality police arrested women on the street and in their homes even when there was no certainty that they were actually involved in prostitution. Mistakes were common, and sometimes resulted from allegations made by spiteful neighbours. It is easy to imagine how difficult it was for a girl to salvage her reputation after the police had escorted her out of her house on suspicion of prostitution. German policy was so draconian that there were even rumours that prostitutes whose syphilis was too advanced were being shot.[70]

However, although the problem of prostitution was widespread, it was not always as straightforward as the German and Austro-Hungarian hygienists

---

[68] Rudolf Lennhoff, 'Kongreßtage in Warschau', *Medizinische Reform* XXIV, 12 (1916), p. 119.

[69] Sławoj Felicjan Składkowski, *Moja służba w Brygadzie. Pamiętnik połowy*, Warsaw 1990, p. 313.

[70] Ibid.

MISSION CIVILISATRICE 345

wanted to believe. Soldiers' memoirs are full of anecdotes about brief dalliances or even longer-lasting relationships, especially in places where the front did not move for a while or to which it quickly returned. As Sławoj Felicjan Składkowski recounts, in the vicinity of Kovel the Legionnaires tried to find accommodation in the same cottages where they had once stayed in order to rekindle earlier acquaintances.[71] During the fighting in the Podkarpacie region, highland women treated sex with Polish soldiers serving in the Austro-Hungarian army as a sort of patriotic duty. Those same memoirs also mention peasant women and city women prostituting themselves for money or food. Often they were the so-called reservists, in other words, the wives of soldiers serving in the Russian army who had no means of supporting themselves or their children. A Legionnaire doctor, who had treated more than one embarrassing affliction, was decidedly sceptical about the romance of soldierly love:

> Well, perhaps I should mention wartime 'love affairs'?! [...] They were a good thing when the uhlans wore beautiful lapels, just as in 1830, and when fifty or a hundred of them arrived in a village. Nowadays most of us are dirty, louse-infested, and exhausted from marching, and when we enter a village there are two or three thousand of us! What chance of romance when you have twenty soldiers crammed into a hovel?![72]

Obviously, large-scale prostitution mainly affected women in the bigger towns and cities, and it was there that the occupiers' health policy was most likely to have a real impact on the phenomenon. Women in Warsaw were by no means the first victims of the German campaign against syphilis and gonorrhoea. The procedure for dealing with such cases had been transferred wholesale to the Congress Kingdom from Brussels, where the morality police had begun operating earlier. A few months later the Austro-Hungarian occupation authorities introduced similar methods in Belgrade. In none of these cities did the police display any degree of kindness. Suspects were detained and then transported *en masse* to a German or Austro-Hungarian hospital, where military doctors examined them in front of other women. The sick were forcibly hospitalized, as were the 'doubtful cases'. People who had already been cured were sometimes held in the hospitals and forced to do ancillary work. Every woman treated for venereal disease in a German military hospital was registered as a prostitute. The social consequences of registration were problematic, especially in the case of minors. For some, getting rid of the stigma proved too difficult. A girl with the 'official' status of prostitute would often become one in reality.

In the occupied territories the reactions of the public to the hygiene aspect of occupation policy were extreme. Some people readily engaged with the

---

[71] Ibid., p. 257.
[72] Ibid., p. 312.

moralizing discourse of the German and Austro-Hungarian authorities. From this perspective, women were treated as a threat to soldiers and their families and not as victims of illness. In Belgrade this was the position taken not just by the local pro-Austrian elites but also by representatives of the women's movement who collaborated with the Croatian magazine *Ženski svijet*, published in Zagreb. Rumours abounded that Serbian women who practised prostitution would be punished by having their bodies tattooed as a permanent reminder of their moral demise.[73] In Warsaw the German point of view was adopted by doctors and hygienists from the Polish Society for the Struggle against Prostitution and Venereal Disease, whose spokesman was Leon Wernic. 'Love for the Fatherland', said Wernic in reference to the German policy on prostitution at a meeting of the Polish Society for Social Medicine in 1916, 'necessitates [...] the adoption of new measures to prevent depopulation and racial degeneration on account of venereal disease.'[74] On the other hand, separate initiatives emerged in Warsaw that aimed to protect the rights of women. The Equality League interceded on behalf of arrested women, and its activists succeeded in having almost 1,000 women deleted from the register of prostitutes. Alfred Sokołowski, the renowned Warsaw physician and editor of the *Gazeta Lekarska* (*Journal of Medicine*), suggested how to control the problem of prostitution and the epidemic of venereal disease in the long run:

> It is necessary to change the way girls are brought up and, above all, to prepare them to be financially independent. In this regard professional schools for girls would be of the greatest service.[75]

In a situation of ubiquitous mobilization, economic exploitation, and poverty, the occupation authorities naturally were not able to heed the advice of the doyen of Warsaw's medical community. It is doubtful, however, whether they would have done so even under more favourable conditions. To change the strategy in regard to venereal disease would have required abandoning the stereotype of the dirty and dangerous East. Yet, from the occupiers' point of view, the threat to health and morality derived precisely from that stereotype. In any case, it was certainly not caused by the presence of the armies of the Central Powers or by the disadvantageous social position of women. Indeed,

---

[73] Jovana Lažić Knežević, *The Austro-Hungarian Occupation of Belgrade during the First World War. Battles at the Home Front*, PhD Dissertation, Yale University 2006, pp. 162–163.

[74] Leon Wernic, 'Zarys walki z chorobami wenerycznymi i nierządem w czasach ubiegłych i dzisiaj, w czasie wojny i pokoju', in *Medycyna społeczna. Prace Polskiego Towarzystwa Medycyny Społecznej*, vol. 1 (1916), Warsaw 1917, p. 149.

[75] Alfred Sokołowski, *Wielkie klęski społeczne (ospa – choroby tyfusowe – dżuma – grypa – cholera – choroby zakaźne, właściwie wiekowi dziecięcemu – suchoty płucne – choroby weneryczne – alkoholizm) i walka z niemi*, Warsaw 1917, p. 329.

the war was meant to bring the torch of civilization to 'semi-Asia'. Neither the Germans nor the Austrians were prepared to admit that it was only after their arrival in the region that some of its civilizational deficiencies emerged.

***

Historians differ in their assessment of the intentions and consequences of the German and Austro-Hungarian *mission civilisatrice* in the East. During the inter-war period and up to the 1960s, researchers were divided more or less according to their nationality. German and Austrian authors took seriously the occupier's programme to modernize the barbaric regions of Eastern Europe and the Balkans. Other authors either ignored it completely or considered it a propaganda gimmick. In their view, the German spiel about a cultural mission was simply a tactic designed to mask the fact that the region's inhabitants were ruthlessly exploited by the occupiers. Later, in the 1960s, the situation changed and the number of scholars who defended the Central Powers' civilizing mission sharply declined. The assessments of the occupation made by academics on both sides of the Iron Curtain ceased to be substantively different. Likewise today, the maelstrom of negative emotions contained in the German stereotype of the East inclines the majority of researchers to critically evaluate the whole phenomenon; all the more so because the authoritarian practices and frequently racist language of the German occupiers evoke clear associations with the Third Reich. In more recent works the point of reference for the civilizing mission in the East is the German occupation during the Second World War. This idea has been most emphatically developed by the American historian Vejas Gabriel Liulevicius in his outstanding book on the Ober-Ost dictatorship in Lithuania and Belarus:

> Rather, the eastern front experience of the First World War was an indispensable cultural and psychological background for what came later in the violent twentieth century, a pre-existing mentality.[76]

In short: the Germans and Austrians knew in advance that in the East they would encounter 'semi-Asia'. The experiences they gained there only strengthened that belief and radicalized their thinking about the region and the people who inhabited it. They were ill-disposed towards them from the outset, and the power the occupiers exercised in the East for several years deprived them of any moral inhibitions. Two and a half decades later the inhabitants of Central and Eastern Europe and the Balkans would pay a high price for that lack of moral restraint.

Is such a harsh assessment justified? In relation to certain individuals and some of the more fervent nationalist circles, certainly yes, but in relation to the entire undertaking described above, no. First and foremost, it is important to

---

[76] Liulevicius, *War Land on the Eastern Front*, p. 1.

consider the intentions behind the mission to civilize the East by conquest. Paul Weindling, the renowned British medical historian, writes about this. He draws attention to the fact that the tone of the Austro-Hungarian and German military doctors 'tended to be moralistic and they were often more moralistic and indeed religious than racial in spreading their gospel of hygiene'.[77] At least at the beginning of the eastward march, many of its participants believed in the liberal utopia of shifting the borders of European culture. This programme consisted in the revival of cultural and political life among the non-Russian nations of the Romanov empire, the scientific investigation of conquered territories, and the promotion of education and hygiene among the occupied populations. Naturally, the Central Powers saw the propaganda value of all these activities, but this does not invalidate the fact that the German and Austro-Hungarian presence in the East, aside from its nationalist, imperialist, and racist elements, also had a liberal component. Historians should focus on the moment when the liberal project proves unsuccessful – when faith in it disappears and when the concomitant hope that the savages can be civilized likewise vanishes. Both these concepts give way to a conviction that the East can only be tamed by force. The belief in the efficacy of violence opens the door to the deportation and mass extermination of the region's inhabitants. It is only after their removal that the East will be weighed and measured once again as a more or less uninhabited *tabula rasa* ready for colonization by the civilized people of the West.

During the First World War, German and Austro-Hungarian military men were as far removed from such thoughts as can be imagined.

---

[77] Paul Weindling, 'A Virulent Strain: German Bacteriology as Scientific Racism, 1890–1920', in *Race, Science and Medicine, 1700–1960*, ed. Waltraud Ernst and Bernard Harris, London and New York, NY 1999, pp. 217–233, here p. 230.

Afterword

On 21 November 1916, the octogenarian Emperor Franz Joseph died. His reign had lasted sixty-eight years. On 30 November, the funeral procession carried his remains to St Stephen's Cathedral, and then to the nearby Habsburg family vault, the Capuchin crypt. A sense of bereavement pervaded even those who did not support the monarchy. The future social-democratic Chancellor of Austria (from 1970) Bruno Kreisky, who was five years old in 1916, recalled feeling bereft and desolate. No one remembered any other ruler. Before his demise, the Emperor supposedly confided to his valet that he feared his funeral toll would also signal the end of the Empire. Indeed, the new Emperor and King of Hungary Charles I ('and the last', many sneered) had slim chances of saving the monarchy, even if he proved to be a genius.

Meanwhile, in Berlin, Wilhelm II had managed to spoil everything he touched during the twenty-eight years he spent on the throne. Since the start of the war, the heir to the Hohenzollern crown had been overshadowed by the popular Marshal Paul von Hindenburg (chief of staff since August 1916) and his deputy, Erich Ludendorff. Wilhelm knew that, upon crossing the threshold of the military headquarters, he turned into 'Hindenburg's adjutant' with no say over anything. While his Viennese associate departed, the German Emperor was forced to relent in a matter of symbolic politics which he had tackled successfully for over twenty years with the same unyielding and pointless persistence. On the western façade of the Reichstag building, inaugurated in 1894, the giant inscription 'Dem deutschen Volke' (To the German nation) had been intended from the outset, but Wilhelm had successfully blocked its inclusion, believing that this symbolic recognition of the sovereign would indicate a lessening of his prerogatives as a monarch. Now, over two years into the war, pushed to the margins, he withdrew his opposition in the misguided belief that this would appease the left and the centre of the political spectrum.[1]

The Russian Emperor found himself in an even more unenviable position. Nicholas II had governed Russia for about as long as his cousin from Berlin –

---

[1] See, for instance, Piotr Szlanta, *Wilhelm II. Ostatni z Hohenzollernów*, Warsaw 2015, pp. 255–259.

Fig. 57   The façade being installed on the Reichstag.

since 1894. After the Gorlice debacle in 1915, he came up with a terrible idea: against the sound advice of his ministers and generals, he made himself commander-in-chief. From that point on, his reputation was tarnished not only by his perceived ineptitude as heir to the throne but also by military reverses. Russia put tremendous effort into increasing the output of its armaments industry in the first years of the war. Meanwhile, agricultural production declined by a fifth – about a half of all peasants and agricultural workers had been conscripted, providing the vast majority of the regular troops. By the end of 1916, 1.7 million soldiers had died of combat injuries and disease; 8 million were wounded or ill; and 2.5 million (including at least several hundred thousand deserters) had become prisoners of war. The state was forced to manage 6 million refugees and deportees from the westernmost parts of the empire. By 1916, the system for providing food to urban populations was seriously failing, and workers of both sexes felt ruthlessly exploited – especially compared with the 4 million employed directly or indirectly by the military administration, who could maintain secure and relatively opulent lifestyles in the Russian hinterland. The inefficiency of the administration, high levels of corruption, inflation, and the lack of food exacerbated the social conflict, made

AFTERWORD   351

worse by the equally fundamental dispute over Czarism and, consequently, the
shape of the state.[2]

On 1 November 1916, Pavel Miliukov, leader of the Party of Constitutional
Democrats, delivered a speech in the Duma. His preparation was exceptionally
meticulous. He piled one example on top of another – of incompetence and
corruption in the administration, of neglect and incomprehensible actions, of
unusual relations at the court. Every example was bookended with the question
'Is this stupidity, or is this treason?' Liberal deputies were not alone in sharing
this critical view of the situation. So did the generals, the court, and the
conservative politicians, who bemoaned the ineptitude of their ruler. A full
month after the funeral of Franz Joseph, they took matters into their own
hands, murdering Grigory Rasputin, the infamous favourite of the Czarina.
They were too late, though; for the workers of Petersburg and Moscow, and for
the millions of refugees and soldiers, personal vendettas at the court no longer
made any difference.

The Czar abdicated on 15 March 1917, when he realized that the generals
would not, and could not, follow his orders. His brother, the Grand Duke
Mikhail Alexandrovich, refused the crown. In other words, after 300 years of
Romanov rule, the Russian monarchy was over. The Czar would be murdered
in July 1918 by the Bolsheviks.

Franz Joseph I, Wilhelm II, and Nicholas II forsook the idea of monarchy in
different circumstances. The king has two bodies, wrote Ernst Kantorowicz,
a native of Posen, in 1957 – an earthly body and a body representing the
kingdom.[3] Of the three, Franz Joseph was the only one not to have compromised the notion of monarchy. His successor, Charles I, was forced to abdicate
concurrently with Wilhelm II, in November 1918. He was expelled from his
country, and the Republic of Austria then nationalized the Habsburg proper-
ties. Charles died aged thirty-seven, a penniless exile on Madeira, having been
invited to live there by a wealthy local. Neither of them knew that the climate
on the island would prove deadly to the former emperor.

The empires fell. The era of nation-states began.

---

[2] Boris Kolonitskii, *«Трагическая эротика». Образы императорской семьи в годы
Первой мировой войны* ['*Tragicheskaia erotika'. Obrazy imperatoskoi sem'i v gody
Pervoi mirovoi voiny*], Moscow 2010.

[3] Ernst Hartwig Kantorowicz, *The King's Two Bodies. A Study in Mediaeval Political
Theology*, Princeton, NJ 1957. In his youth, Kantorowicz was a German nationalist who
fought against the Poles. As a Jew (in the light of the Nuremberg Laws), he emigrated to the
United States. Mindful of his experiences in Germany, he refused to submit a loyalty oath
in line with the requirements of Senator Joseph McCarthy.

SELECT BIBLIOGRAPHY

Contemporary Periodicals

Czernowitzer Allgemeine Zeitung
Deutsche Warschauer Zeitung
Dziennik Zarządu Miasta Stołecznego Warszawy
Humoristické Listy
Ilustrowany Kuryer Codzienny
Krytyka
Kurjer Lwowski
Kurjer Łódzki
Medycyna społeczna. Prace Polskiego Towarzystwa Medycyny Społecznej
Mitteilungen der k.k. Geographischen Gesellschaft in Wien
Národní Politika
Tygodnik Illustrowany

Primary Sources

An-Ski, Szymon *Tragedia Żydów galicyjskich w czasie I wojny światowej. Wrażenia i refleksje z podróży po kraju*, translated by Krzysztof Dawid Majus, Przemyśl 2010
Bericht über die Verwaltung des Kreises Belgrad-Land in der Zeit vom 1. November 1915 bis 31. Dezember 1916, Belgrade 1917
Bernhardi, Friedrich von *Vom heutigen Kriege*, Berlin 1912
Białynia Chołodecki, Józef *Lwów w czasie okupacji rosyjskiej (3 września 1914–22 czerwca 1915). Z własnych przeżyć i spostrzeżeń*, Lwów 1930
Bloch, Jan G. *Przyszła wojna pod względem technicznym, politycznym i ekonomicznym*, ed. Grzegorz P. Bąbiak, Warsaw 2005
Bratek-Kozłowski, Franciszek *Życie z bagnetem i lancetem. Wspomnienia – refleksje*, Toronto 1989
Borzęcki, Jan [Jan Czuj] *Moskale w Tarnowie. Od 10 listopada 1914 do 6 maja 1915 roku*, Tarnów 1915
Dąbrowski, Jan *Dziennik 1914–1918*, ed. Jerzy Zdrada and Elżbieta Dąbrowska, Cracow 1977
Dix, Arthur *Zwischen zwei Welten. Die Völkerbrücke des Balkan*, Dresden 1917

SELECT BIBLIOGRAPHY 353

Dorflein, Franz *Mazedonien. Erlebnisse und Beobachtungen eines Naturforschers im Gefolge des deutschen Heeres*, Jena 1921

Dyboski, Roman *Siedem lat w Rosji i na Syberii (1915–1921). Przygody i wrażenia*, ed. Tomasz Bohun, Warsaw 2007

Dzierzbicki, Stanisław *Pamiętnik z lat wojny 1915–1918*, ed. Janusz Pajewski and Danuta Płygawko, Warsaw 1983

Flemming, Jens, Klaus Saul, and Peter-Christian Witt (eds.) *Lebenswelten im Ausnahmezustand. Die Deutschen, der Alltag und der Krieg, 1914–1918*, Frankfurt am Main 2011

Franzos, Karl Emil *Aus der großen Ebene. Neue Kulturbilder aus Halb-Asien*, vol. 1, Stuttgart 1889

Friedeburg, Friedrich von *Karpathen- und Dniester-Schlacht 1915*, Oldenburg and Berlin 1924

Gerlach, Hellmut von *Die große Zeit der Lüge. Der Erste Weltkrieg und die deutsche Mentalität (1871–1921)*, ed. H. Donat and A. Wild, Bremen 1994

Giese, Fritz *Die Idee einer Frauendienstpflicht. Tatsachen und Möglichkeiten*, Langensalza 1916

Gippius, Zinaida *Dzienniki petersburskie (1914–1919). Dziennik warszawski (1920–1921)*, ed. Henryk Chłystowski, Warsaw 2010

Glatzer, Dieter and Ruth Glatzer (eds.) *Berliner Leben 1914–1918. Eine historische Reportage aus Erinnerungen und Berichten*, Berlin 1983

Hašek, Jaroslav *The Good Soldier Švejk*, translated by Cecil Parrott, Harmondsworth 1973

Hedenström, Alfred von *Rigaer Kriegschronik 1914–1917*, Riga 1922

Hedin, Sven *Nach Osten!*, Leipzig 1916

Hegeler, Wilhelm *Der Siegeszug durch Serbien*, Berlin 1916

Hindenburg, Generalfeldmarschall von *Aus meinem Leben*, Leipzig 1920

Hochwächter, G[ustav] von *Mit den Türken in der Front im Stabe Mahmud Michtar Paschas. Mein Kriegstagebuch über die Kämpfe bei Kirk Kilisse, Lule Burgas und Cataldza*, Berlin 1913

Hohenborn, Adolf Wild von *Briefe und Tagebuchaufzeichnungen des preußischen Generals als Kriegsminister und Truppenführer im Ersten Weltkrieg*, ed. Helmut Reichold, Boppard am Rhein 1986

Hornykiewicz, Theophil (ed.) *Ereignisse in der Ukraine 1914–1922, deren Bedeutung und historische Hintergründe*, vol. 1, Philadelphia, PA 1966

Immanuel, [Friedrich] *Der Balkankrieg 1912/13*, Berlin 1914

Jabłońska, Helena z Seifertów *Dziennik z oblężonego Przemyśla 1914–1915*, ed. Hanna Imbs, Przemyśl 1994

Jankowski, Czesław *Z dnia na dzień. Warszawa 1914–1915 Wilno*, Wilno (Vilnius) 1923

Jaworski, Władysław Leopold *Diariusz 1914–1918*, ed. M. Czajka, Warsaw 1997

Jellenta, Cezary *Wielki zmierzch. Pamiętnik*, Warsaw 1985

Kafka, Franz *Tagebücher 1910–1923*, Frankfurt am Main 1983

354   SELECT BIBLIOGRAPHY

Kakowski, Aleksander *Z niewoli do niepodległości. Pamiętniki*, ed. Tadeusz Krawczak and Ryszard Świętek, Cracow 2000

Kawczak, Stanisław *Milknące echa. Wspomnienia z wojny 1914–1920*, Warsaw 1991

Kennan, George F. (ed.) *The Other Balkan Wars. A 1913 Carnegie Endowment Inquiry in Retrospect*, Washington, DC 1993

Kennard, Dorothy *A Roumanian Diary 1915, 1916, 1917*, New York, NY 1918

Kessler, Harry Graf *Das Tagebuch*, vol. 5 (1914–1916), ed. Günter Riederer, Ulrich Ott, Christoph Hilse, and Janna Brechmacher, Stuttgart 2008

Knox, Alfred *With the Russian Army 1914–1917*, vol. 1, London 1921

Kraus, Karl *Die letzten Tage der Menschheit. Tragödie in fünf Akten mit Vorspiel und Epilog*, Berlin 1978

Kraushar, Aleksander *Warszawa podczas okupacji niemieckiej 1915–1918*, Lwów 1921

Künigl-Ehrenburg, Ilka [Ilka von Michaelsburg] *Im belagerten Przemysl. Tagebuchblätter aus großer Zeit*, Leipzig 1915

Kuropatkin, A[leksei] *The Russian Army and the Japanese War*, vol. 2, London 1909

Das Litauen-Buch. Eine Auslese aus der Zeitung der 10. Armee, Wilna (Vilnius) 1918

Ludendorff, Erich *Meine Kriegserinnerungen 1914–1918*, 9th edition, Berlin 1926

Majkowski, Aleksander *Pamiętnik z wojny europejskiej roku 1914*, ed. Tadeusz Linkner, Wejherowo and Pelplin 2000

Menczel, Philipp *Als Geisel nach Sibirien verschleppt*, Berlin 1916

Meyer, Alfred *Der Balkankrieg 1912/13 unter Benutzung zuverlässiger Quellen kulturgeschichtlich und militärisch dargestellt*, Berlin 1913

Musil, Robert *The Man without Qualities*, vol. 1, translated by Sophie Wilkins and Burton Pike, New York, NY 1995

Netzhammer, Raymund *Bischof in Rumänien. Im Spannungsfeld zwischen Staat und Vatikan*, vol. 1, Munich 1995

Pająk, Jerzy Z. (ed.) *Raporty i korespondencja oficerów werbunkowych Departamentu Wojskowego Naczelnego Komitetu Narodowego 1915–1916. Ziemia Kielecka*, Kielce 2007

Pilsudski, Joseph [Józef Piłsudski] *The Memories of a Polish Revolutionary and Soldier*, translated by Darsie Rutherford Gillie, New York, NY 1931

Piłsudski, Józef *Moje pierwsze boje*, Łódź 1988

Rokoszny, Józef *Diariusz Wielkiej Wojny*, vol 1 (1914–1915); vol. 2 (1915–1916), ed. Wiesław Caban and Marek Przeniosło, Kielce 1998

Romer, Eugeniusz *Dziennik 1914–1918*, vol. 1, Warsaw 1995

Ronge, Max *Kriegs- und Industriespionage. Zwölf Jahre Kundschaftsdienst*, Vienna 1930

Rose, Karol *Wspomnienia berlińskie*, Warsaw 1932

Rosner, Andrzej (ed.) *Teraz będzie Polska. Wybór z pamiętników z okresu I wojny światowej*, Warsaw 1988

Składkowski, Sławoj Felicjan *Moja służba w Brygadzie. Pamiętnik połowy*, Warsaw 1990

SELECT BIBLIOGRAPHY 355

Sokołowski, Alfred *Wielkie klęski społeczne (ospa – choroby tyfusowe – dżuma – grypa – cholera – choroby zakaźne, właściwe wiekowi dziecięcemu – suchoty płucne – choroby weneryczne – alkoholizm) i walka z niemi*, Warsaw 1917

Solek, Wincenty *Pamiętnik legionisty*, ed. Wiesław Budzyński, Warsaw 1988

Srokowski, Stanisław *Z dni zawieruchy dziejowej 1914–1918*, Cracow 1932

Starzyński, Roman *Cztery lata w służbie Komendanta. Przeżycia wojenne 1914–1919*, Warsaw 2012

Stegemann, Hermann *Geschichte des Krieges*, vols. 1–4, Stuttgart and Berlin 1917

Struck, Hermann and Herbert Eulenberg, *Skizzen aus Litauen, Weissrussland und Kurland*, Berlin 1916

Świeykowski, Bronisław *Z dni grozy w Gorlicach. Od 25 IX 1914 do 2 V 1915*, Cracow 1919

Toynbee, Arnold J. *Armenian Atrocities. The Murder of a Nation*, London 1915

Velburg, Gerhard *Rumänische Etappe. Der Weltkrieg, wie ich ihn sah*, Minden 1930

Vit, Jan *Wspomnienia z mojego pobytu w Przemyślu podczas rosyjskiego oblężenia 1914–1915*, translated by Ladislav Hofbauer and Jerzy Husar, ed. Stanisław Stępień, Przemyśl 1995

Wallisch, Friedrich *Die Pforte zum Orient. Unser Friedenswerk in Serbien*, Innsbruck 1917

Witos, Wincenty *Moje wspomnienia*, vol. 2, Paris 1964

Zweig, Stefan *Die Welt von Gestern. Erinnerungen eines Europäers*, Frankfurt am Main 1992

Zwei Jahre deutscher Arbeit im Generalgouvernement Warschau, Berlin 1917

Secondary Sources

Achmatowicz, Aleksander *Polityka Rosji w kwestii polskiej w pierwszym roku Wielkiej Wojny 1914–1915*, Warsaw 2003

Angelow, Jürgen (ed.) *Der Erste Weltkrieg auf dem Balkan. Perspektiven der Forschung*, Berlin 2011

Arendt, Hannah *Elemente und Ursprünge totaler Herrschaft. Antisemitismus, Imperialismus, totale Herrschaft*, Munich 1986

Bachinger, Bernhard and Wolfram Dornik (eds.) *Jenseits des Schützengrabens. Der Erste Weltkrieg im Osten: Erfahrung – Wahrnehmung – Kontext*, Innsbruck 2013

Balázs, Eszter '"War Stares at Us Like an Ominous Sphynx": Hungarian Intellectuals, Literature and the Image of the Other (1914–1915)', in *The New Nationalism and the First World War*, ed. Lawrence Rosenthal and Vesna Rodic, London 2015, pp. 95–120

Bator, Juliusz *Wojna galicyjska. Działania armii austro-węgierskiej na froncie północnym (galicyjskim) w latach 1914–1915*, Cracow 2005

Bauerkämper, Arnd, and Elise Julien (eds.) *Durchhalten! Krieg und Gesellschaft im Vergleich 1914–1918*, Göttingen 2010

356 SELECT BIBLIOGRAPHY

Bihl, Wolfdieter *Der Erste Weltkrieg. Chronik – Daten – Fakten*, Vienna, Cologne, and Weimar 2010

Biondich, Mark *The Balkans. Revolution, War and Political Violence since 1878*, Oxford 2011

Blobaum, Robert *A Minor Apocalypse. Warsaw during the First World War*, Ithaca, NY and London 2017

Boemke, Manfred F., Roger Chickering, and Stig Förster (eds.) *Anticipating Total War. The German and American Experiences, 1871–1914*, Cambridge 1999

Borodziej, Włodzimierz, Jochen Böhler, and Joachim von Putthamer (eds.) *Legacies of Violence. Eastern Europe's First World War*, Munich 2014

Brakelmann, Günter *Protestantische Kriegstheologie im Ersten Weltkrieg. Reinhold Seeberg als Theologe des deutschen Imperialismus*, Bielefeld 1974

Broadberry, Stephen, and Mark Harrison (eds.) *The Economics of World War I*, Cambridge 2005

Bucur, Maria 'Between the Mother of the Wounded and the Virgin of Jiu: Romanian Women and the Gender of Heroism during the Great War', *Journal of Women's History* 12, 2 (2000), pp. 30–56

Bucur, Maria *Heroes and Victims. Remembering War in Twentieth-Century Romania*, Bloomington, IN 2010

Cabaj, Jarosław *Społeczeństwo guberni chełmskiej pod okupacją niemiecką i austriacką w latach I wojny światowej*, Siedlce 2006

Chwalba, Andrzej *Historia Polski 1795–1918*, Cracow 2000

Clark, Christopher *The Sleepwalkers. How Europe Went to War in 1914*, New York, NY 2013

Cornwall, Mark 'Das Ringen um die Moral des Hinterlandes', in *Die Habsburgermonarchie 1848–1918*, vol. 11, part 2. *Die Habsburgermonarchie und der Erste Weltkrieg*, ed. Helmut Rumpler and Anatol Schmied-Kowarzik, Vienna 2014, pp. 393–435

Czerep, Stanisław *II Brygada Legionów Polskich*, Warsaw 1991

Dąbrowski, Jan *Wielka Wojna 1914–1918 na podstawie najnowszych źródeł*, vols. 1–2, Warsaw 1937

Dadrian, Vakhan *Histoire du génocide arménien*, translated by Marc Nichanian, Paris 1996

Dalecki, Maciej 'Samosąd na moskalofilach w Przemyślu podczas pierwszej wojny światowej', *Rocznik Historyczno-Archiwalny* VII–VIII (1994), pp. 151–156

Dietrich, Elisabeth 'Der andere Tod. Seuchen, Volkskrankheiten und Gesundheitswesen im Ersten Weltkrieg', in *Tirol und der Erste Weltkrieg*, ed. Klaus Eisterer and Rolf Steiniger, Innsbruck and Vienna 1995, pp. 255–275

DiNardo, Richard *Breakthrough. The Gorlice–Tarnow Campaign, 1915*, Santa Barbara, CA 2010

Diner, Dan *Cataclysms. A History of the Twentieth Century from Europe's Edge*, Madison, WI 2008

SELECT BIBLIOGRAPHY 357

Dornik, Wolfram *Des Kaisers Falke. Wirken und Nach-Wirken von Franz Conrad von Hötzendorf*, Innsbruck 2013

Dowling, Timothy C. *The Brusilov Offensive*, Bloomington, IN 2008

Doukelli, Kyriaki *Geschichte Makedoniens und Thrakiens von den Balkankriegen bis zum Ersten Weltkrieg. Außenpolitische Ereignisse und ihre innenpolitischen Rückwirkungen*, PhD Dissertation, Universität Mannheim 2008

Dowdall, Alex 'Citizens or Subjects? Refugees and the State in Europe during the First World War', in *Breaking Empires, Making Nations? The First World War and the Reforging of Europe*, ed. Richard Butterwick-Pawlikowski, Quincy Cloet, and Alex Dowdall, Warsaw 2017, pp. 98–122

Dönninghaus, Victor 'Der Frust einer ganzen Metropole entlädt sich – die anti-deutschen Pogrome in Moskau im Mai 1915. Täter – Opfer – Zuschauer', in *Documenta Pragensia XXXV. Nezměrné ztráty a jejich zvládání. Obyvatelstvo evropských velkoměst a I. světová válka*, ed. Olga Fejtová, Václav Ledvinka, Martina Maříková, and Jiří Pešek, Prague 2016, pp. 235–248

Drozdowski, Marian M. *Warszawa w latach 1914–1939*, Warsaw 1990

Džambo, Jozo (ed.) *Musen an die Front! Schriftsteller und Künstler im Dienst der k. u.k. Kriegspropaganda 1914–1918*, vol. 1. *Beiträge*, Munich 2003

Engelstein, Laura '"A Belgium of Our Own": The Sack of Russian Kalisz, August 1914', *Kritika: Explorations in Russian and Eurasian History* 10, 3 (2009), pp. 441–473

Englund, Peter *Schönheit und Schrecken. Eine Geschichte des Ersten Weltkriegs erzählt in neunzehn Schicksalen*, translated by Wolfgang Butt, Bonn 2012

Erős, Ferenc 'Gender, Hysteria, and War Neurosis', in *Gender and Modernity in Central Europe. The Austro-Hungarian Monarchy and Its Legacy*, ed. Agatha Schwartz, Ottawa 2010

Ersoy, Ahmet, Maciej Górny, and Vangelis Kechriotis (eds.) *Discourses of Collective Identity in Central and Southeast Europe (1770–1945). Texts and Commentaries*, vol. 3, part 2. *Modernism: Representations of National Culture*, Budapest and New York, NY 2010

Evans, Andrew D. *Anthropology at War. World War I and the Science of Race in Germany*, Chicago, IL and London 2010

Facon, Patrick 'Le soldat français d'Orient face à la maladie', in *The Salonica Theatre of Operations and the Outcome of the Great War*, ed. National Research Foundation 'Eleftherios K. Venizelos', Thessaloniki 2005, pp. 223–235

Fischer, Fritz *Griff nach der Weltmacht. Die Kriegszielpolitik des kaiserlichen Deutschland 1914/18*, Düsseldorf 1967

Fučík, Josef *Osmadvacátníci. Spor o českého vojáka Velké války*, Prague 2006

Galandauer, Jan 'Kriegsbegeisterung in Prag', in *Magister noster. Sborník statí věnovanych in memoriam prof. PhDr. Janu Havránkovi, CSc.*, ed. Luboš Velek, William D. Goodsey Jr, and Michal Svatoš, Prague 2005, pp. 327–333

Gatrell, Peter *A Whole Empire Walking. Refugees in Russia during World War I*, Bloomington, IN 2011

Galántai, József *Hungary in the First World War*, translated by Éva Grusz and Judit Pokoly, Budapest 1989

Gawlitta, Severin *Zwischen Einladung und Ausweisung. Deutsche bäuerliche Siedler im Königreich Polen 1815–1915*, Marburg 2009

Geiss, Imanuel *Der polnische Grenzstreifen 1914–1918. Ein Beitrag zur deutschen Kriegszielpolitik im Ersten Weltkrieg*, Lübeck 1960

Gilchrist, Harry L. *A Comparative Study of World War Casualties from Gas and Other Weapons*, Edgewood, MA 1928

Ginio, Eyal 'Paving the Way for Ethnic Cleansing: Eastern Thrace during the Balkan Wars (1912–1913) and Their Aftermath', in *Shatterzone of Empires. Coexistence and Violence in the German, Habsburg, Russian, and Ottoman Borderlands*, ed. Omer Bartov and Eric D. Weitz, Bloomington, IN and Indianapolis, IN 2013, pp. 283–297

Golczewski, Mechthild *Der Balkan in deutschen und österreichischen Reise- und Erlebnisberichten 1912–1918*, Wiesbaden 1981

Gorgolini, Luca *I dannati dell'Asinara. L'odissea dei prigionieri austro-ungarici nella Prima guerra mondiale*, Turin 2011

Gorgolini, Luca *Kriegsgefangenschaft auf Asinara. Österreichisch-ungarische Soldaten des Ersten Weltkriegs in italienischem Gewahrsam*, translated by Günther Gerlach, Innsbruck 2012

Górny, Maciej *Science Embattled. Eastern European Intellectuals and the Great War*, translated by Antoni Górny, Paderborn 2019

Grinberg, Daniel, Jan Snopko, and Grzegorz Zachiewicz (eds.) *Lata Wielkiej Wojny. Dojrzewanie do niepodległości 1914–1918*, Białystok 2007

Groß, Gerhard P. (ed.) *Die vergessene Front. Der Osten 1914/15. Ereignis, Wirkung, Nachwirkung*, Paderborn 2006

Gumz, Jonathan E. *The Resurrection and Collapse of Empire in Habsburg Serbia, 1914–1918*, Cambridge 2009

Hagen, Mark von *War in a European Borderland. Occupations and Occupation Plans in Galicia and Ukraine, 1914–1918*, Seattle, WA 2007

Hagen, William W. *Anti-Jewish Violence in Poland 1914–1920*, Cambridge 2018

Hall, Richard C. *The Balkan Wars 1912–1913. Prelude to the First World War*, London 2000

Hammond, Mary and Shafquat Towheed (eds.) *Publishing in the First World War. Essays in Book History*, London 2007

Hatlie, Mark R. 'Bevölkerungsverschiebungen in Riga während des Welt- und Bürgerkrieges 1914–1919', in *Der ethnische Wandel im Baltikum zwischen 1850–1930*, ed. Heinrich Wittram, Lüneburg 2005, pp. 53–80

Hatlie, Mark R. 'Riga und der Erste Weltkrieg: Eine Exkursion', *Nordost-Archiv*, NF XVII (2008), pp. 13–33

Healy, Maureen *Vienna and the Fall of the Habsburg Empire*, Cambridge 2004

Heiss, Gernot and Olvier Rathkolb (eds.) *Asylland wider Willen. Flüchtlinge in Österreich im europäischen Kontext seit 1914*, Vienna 1995

Heppner, Harald (ed.) *Czernowitz. Die Geschichte einer ungewöhnlichen Stadt*, Cologne, Weimar, and Vienna 2000

SELECT BIBLIOGRAPHY

Herwig, Holger H. *The First World War. Germany and Austria-Hungary 1914–1918*, London 1996

Herz-Eichenrode, Dieter *Politik und Landwirtschaft in Ostpreußen 1919–1930: Untersuchung eines Strukturproblems in der Weimarer Republik*, Wiesbaden 1969

Heymel, Charlotte *Touristen an der Front. Das Kriegserlebnis 1914–1918 als Reiseerfahrung in zeitgenössischen Reiseberichten*, Berlin 2007

Holzer, Anton *Die andere Front. Fotografie und Propaganda im Ersten Weltkrieg*, Darmstadt 2007

Holzer, Anton *Das Lächeln der Henker*, Darmstadt 2008

Holzer, Jerzy and Jan Molenda, *Polska w pierwszej wojnie światowej*, 3rd edition, Warsaw 1973

Jeřábek, Rudolf 'Taktische Voraussetzungen der Brusilowschlacht Juni 1916', in *Schlachtfeld Galizien*, ed. Claudia Reichl-Ham, Irmgard Nöbauer, and Werner Fröhlich, Vienna 2016, pp. 157–185

Johler, Reinhard, Christian Marchetti, and Monique Scheer (eds.) *Doing Anthropology in Wartime and War Zones. World War I and the Cultural Sciences in Europe*, Bielefeld 2010

Judson, Pieter M. *The Habsburg Empire. A New History*, Cambridge 2016

Kapp, Richard W. 'Divided Loyalties: The German Reich and Austria-Hungary in Austro-German Discussions of War Aims, 1914–1916', *Central European History* 17, 2/3 (1984), pp. 120–139

Kłańska, Maria *Daleko od Wiednia. Galicja w oczach pisarzy niemieckojęzycznych 1772–1918*, Cracow 1991

Knežević, Jovana Lazić *The Austro-Hungarian Occupation of Belgrade during the First World War. Battles at the Home Front*, PhD Dissertation, Yale University 2006

Kopper, Christopher 'Der Erste Weltkrieg als Eisenbahnkrieg', in *Neue Wege in ein neues Europa. Geschichte und Verkehr im 20. Jahrhundert*, ed. Ralph Roth and Karl Schlögel, Frankfurt am Main 2009, pp. 222–234

Koszyk, Kurt *Deutsche Pressepolitik im Ersten Weltkrieg*, Düsseldorf 1968

Kramer, Alan *Dynamic of Destruction. Culture and Mass Killing in the First World War*, Oxford 2007

Kroh, Antoni *O Szwejku i o nas*, Nowy Sącz 1992

Kučera, Rudolf *Život na příděl. Válečná každodennost a politiky dělnické třídy v českých zemích 1914–1918*, Prague 2013

Kučera, Rudolf 'Losing Manliness: Bohemian Workers and the Experience of the Home Front', in *Other Fronts, Other Wars? First World War Studies on the Eve of the Centennial*, ed. Joachim Bürgschwentner, Matthias Egger, and Gunda Barth-Scalmani, Leiden 2014, pp. 331–348

Lehnstaedt, Stephan 'Das Militärgouvernement Lublin im Ersten Weltkrieg: Die "Nutzbarmachung" Polens durch Osterreich-Ungarn', *Zeitschrift für Ostmitteleuropa-Forschung* 61, 1 (2012), pp. 1–26

Lehnstaedt, Stephan *Imperiale Polenpolitik in den Weltkriegen. Eine vergleichende Studie zu den Mittelmächten und zu NS-Deutschland*, Osnabrück 2017

Leidinger, Hannes '"Der Einzug des Galgens und des Mordes": Die parlamentarischen Stellungnahmen polnischer und ruthenischer Reichsratsabgeordneter zu den Massenhinrichtungen in Galizien 1914/15', *Zeitgeschichte* 33, 5 (2006), pp. 235–260

Leidinger, Hannes, Verena Moritz, Karin Moser, and Wolfram Dornik *Habsburgs schmutziger Krieg. Ermittlungen zur österreichisch-ungarischen Kriegsführung 1914–1918*, St Pölten 2014

Lein, Richard *Pflichterfüllung oder Hochverrat? Die tschechischen Soldaten Österreich-Ungarns im Ersten Weltkrieg*, Vienna 2011

Leonhard, Jörn *Die Büchse der Pandora. Geschichte des Ersten Weltkriegs*, Munich 2014

Lewandowski, Jan *Królestwo Polskie pod okupacją austriacką 1914–1918*, Warsaw 1980

Liulevicius, Vejas Gabriel *War Land on the Eastern Front. Culture, National Identity and German Occupation in World War I*, Cambridge 2000

Livanios, Dimitris '"Conquering the Souls": Nationalism and Greek Guerrilla Warfare in Ottoman Macedonia, 1904–1908', *Byzantine and Modern Greek Studies* 23 (1999), pp. 195–221

Lohr, Eric 'The Russian Army and the Jews: Mass Deportations, Hostages, and Violence during World War I', *The Russian Review* 60, 3 (2001), pp. 404–419

Lohr, Eric *Russian Citizenship from Empire to Soviet Union*, Cambridge 2012

Malinowski, Andrzej *Kwestia macedońska w Bułgarii w latach 1878–1918*, Toruń 2006

Marton, Kati *The Great Escape. Nine Jews Who Fled Hitler and Changed the World*, New York, NY 2006

Mayerhofer, Lisa *Zwischen Freund und Feind – Deutsche Besatzung in Rumänien 1916–1918*, Munich 2010

McMeekin, Sean *The Russian Origins of the First World War*, Cambridge, MA 2011

Mick, Christoph *Kriegserfahrungen in einer multiethnischen Stadt: Lemberg 1914–1947*, Wiesbaden 2010

Mick, Christoph 'Krieg und Ethnizität: Lemberg im Zeitalter der Weltkriege', in *Stadt und Krieg im 20. Jahrhundert. Neue Perspektiven auf Deutschland und Ostmitteleuropa*, ed. Christoph Cornelißen, Václav Petrbok, and Martin Pekár, Essen 2019, pp. 173–189

Milne, Lesley '*Novyi Satirikon*, 1914–1918: The Patriotic Laughter of the Russian Liberal Intelligentsia during the First World War and the Revolution', in *The Slavonic and East European Review* 84, 4 (2006), pp. 639–665

Mishkova, Diana 'Friends Turned Foes: Bulgarian National Attitudes to Neighbours', in *Pride and Prejudice. National Stereotypes in 19th and 20th Century Europe East to West*, ed. László Kontler, Budapest 1995

Mitrović, Andrej *Serbia's Great War 1914–1918*, London 2007

Moczulski, Leszek *Przerwane powstanie polskie 1914*, Warsaw 2010

SELECT BIBLIOGRAPHY 361

Molenda, Jan *Chłopi, naród, niepodległość. Kształtowanie się postaw narodowych i obywatelskich chłopów w Galicji i Królestwie Polskim w przededniu odrodzenia Polski*, Warsaw 1999

Mommsen, Hans, Dušan Kovač, and Jiří Malík (eds.) *Der Erste Weltkrieg und die Beziehungen zwischen Tschechen, Slowaken und Deutschen*, Leipzig 2001

Narskij, Igor' 'Zehn Phänomene, die Russland 1917 erschütterten', in *Schlüsseljahre. Zentrale Konstellationen der mittel- und osteuropäischen Geschichte. Festschrift für Helmut Altrichter zum 65. Geburtstag*, ed. Matthias Stadelmann and Lilia Antipow, Wiesbaden 2011, pp. 255–272

Nedorost, Libor *Češi v 1. světové válce*, vols. 1–2, Prague 2006 and 2007

Opfer, Björn *Im Schatten des Krieges. Besatzung oder Anschluss – Befreiung oder Unterdrückung? Eine komparative Untersuchung über die bulgarische Herrschaft in Vardar-Makedonien 1915–1918 und 1941–1944*, Münster 2005

Oettingen, Urszula *Czarkowy – na drodze do niepodległości*, part 1. *Bój 16–24 września 1914 r.*, Kielce 2002

Orlevych, Iryna 'The Thalehof Tragedy in the Intellectual Thought of Galician Russophiles in the Interwar Period', in *Intellectuals and World War I. A Central European Perspective*, ed. Tomasz Pudłocki and Kamil Ruszała, Cracow 2018, pp. 321–347

Orłowski, Hubert *Z modernizacją w tle. Wokół rodowodu nowoczesnych niemieckich wyobrażeń o Polsce i Polakach*, Poznań 2002

Pająk, Jerzy Z. *Od autonomii do niepodległości. Kształtowanie się postaw politycznych i narodowych społeczeństwa Galicji w warunkach Wielkiej Wojny 1914–1918*, Kielce 2012

Pajewski, Janusz *'Mitteleuropa'. Studia z dziejów imperializmu niemieckiego w dobie pierwszej wojny światowej*, Poznań 1959

Pajewski, Janusz *Odbudowa państwa polskiego*, Warsaw 1978

Pajewski, Janusz *Pierwsza wojna światowa*, Warsaw 1991

Płygawko, Danuta *Polonia devastata. Polonia i Amerykanie z pomocą dla Polski (1914–1918)*, Poznań 2003

Pöhlmann, Markus 'Between Manchuria and the Marne: The German Army and Its Perception of the Military Conflicts of 1911–1914', in *The Wars before the Great War. Conflict and International Politics before the Outbreak of the First World War*, ed. Dominik Geppert, Cambridge 2016, pp. 204–229

Procházka, Zdeněk, Ján Lipták, Vladislav Rybecký, Václav Čada, Miroslav Nytra, and Stanislav Mistr (eds.) *Vojenské dějiny Československa*, vol. 2. *1526–1918*, Prague 1986

Proctor, Tammy M. *Civilians in a World at War, 1914–1918*, New York, NY and London 2010

Prusin, Alexander Victor 'The Russian Military and the Jews in Galicia, 1914–15', in *The Military and Society in Russia 1450–1917*, ed. Eric Lohr and Marshall Poe, Leiden, Boston, MA, and Cologne 2002, pp. 525–544

Prusin, Alexander Victor *Nationalizing a Borderland. War, Ethnicity and Anti-Jewish Violence in East Galicia, 1914–1920*, Tuscaloosa, AL 2005

362 SELECT BIBLIOGRAPHY

Pyta, Wolfram *Hindenburg. Herrschaft zwischen Hohenzollern und Hitler*, Munich, 2007

Radojević, Mira and Ljubodrag Dimić, *Serbia in the Great War 1914–1918. A Short History*, translated by Mirjana Jovanović, Belgrade 2014

Rauchensteiner, Manfried *Der Erste Weltkrieg und das Ende der Habsburgermonarchie 1914–1918*, Vienna, Cologne, and Weimar 2013

Retish, Aaron B. *Russia's Peasants in Revolution and Civil War. Citizenship, Identity and the Creation of the Soviet State, 1914–1922*, Cambridge 2008

Rolf, Malte *Imperiale Herrschaft im Weichselland. Das Königreich Polen im Russischen Imperium (1864–1915)*, Göttingen 2014

Roshwald, Aviel and Richard Stites (eds.) *European Culture in the Great War. The Arts, Entertainment and Propaganda, 1914–1918*, Cambridge 1999

Rydel, Jan *W służbie cesarza i króla. Generałowie i admirałowie narodowości polskiej w siłach zbrojnych Austro-Węgier w latach 1868–1918*, Cracow 2001

Sanborn, Joshua A. *Drafting the Russian Nation. Military Conscription, Total War and Mass Politics 1905–1925*, DeKalb, IL 2003

Schanes, Daniela *Serbien im Ersten Weltkrieg. Feind- und Kriegsdarstellungen in österreichisch-ungarischen, deutschen und serbischen Selbstzeugnissen*, Frankfurt am Main 2011

Scheer, Tamara 'Typisch Polen: Facetten österreichisch-ungarischer Besatzungspolitik in Polen (1915–1918)', in *Polnisch-österreichische Kontakte sowie Militärbündnisse 1618–1918*, ed. Claudia Reichl-Ham and Irmgard Nöbauer, Vienna 2009, pp. 233–255

Scheer, Tamara *Zwischen Front und Heimat. Österreich-Ungarns Militärverwaltungen im Ersten Weltkrieg*, Frankfurt am Main 2009

Scheer, Tamara *Die Ringstraßenfront. Österreich-Ungarn, das Kriegsüberwachungsamt und der Ausnahmezustand während des Ersten Weltkrieges*, Vienna 2010

Schuster, Frank M. *Zwischen allen Fronten. Osteuropäische Juden während des Ersten Weltkriegs (1914–1919)*, Cologne 2004

Scurtu, Ioan 'August 1916: Starea de spirit a românilor', *Dosarele Istoriei* 11, 8 (2006), pp. 13–19

Šedivý, Ivan *Češi, české země a velká válka 1914–1918*, Prague 2001

Seton-Watson, Hugh and Christopher Seton-Watson *The Making of a New Europe. R. W. Seton-Watson and the Last Years of Austria-Hungary*, Seattle, WA 1981

Siadkowski, Marcin *Szlachcicen. Przemiany stereotypu polskiej szlachty w Wiedniu na przełomie XIX i XX wieku*, Warsaw 2011

Sierakowska, Katarzyna '"Niech się nasi bracia, ojcowie i matki dowiedzą [. . .], jakich se to wychowali bohaterow". Cierpienie w relacjach żołnierzy Polakow 1914–1918', in *Zapisy cierpienia*, ed. Katarzyna Stańczak-Wiślicz, Wrocław 2011, pp. 267–282

Sierakowska, Katarzyna *Śmierć – Wygnanie – Głód w dokumentach osobistych. Ziemie polskie w latach Wielkiej Wojny 1914–1918*, Warsaw 2015

SELECT BIBLIOGRAPHY 363

Sierakowska, Katarzyna 'Women on War and Women: Polish Lands 1914–1918', in *The First World War on Polish Lands. Expectations – Experiences – Consequences*, ed. Włodzimierz Mędrzecki, Warsaw 2018, pp. 141–159

Simmonds, Alan G. V. *Britain and World War One*, London and New York, NY 2012

Slim, Hugo *Killing Civilians. Method, Madness, and Morality in War*, New York, NY 2008

Sobociński, Jan 'Inwalidzi wojenni i wojskowi w Polsce według pochodzenia oraz przyczyn inwalidztwa', *Praca i Opieka Społeczna* 14, 3 (1934), pp. 313–324

Spoerer, Mark 'The Mortality of Allied Prisoners of War and Belgian Civilian Deportees in German Custody during the First World War: A Reappraisal of the Effects of Forced Labour', *Population Studies* 60, 2 (2006), pp. 121–136

Stibbe, Matthew 'Civilian Internment and Civilian Internees in Europe, 1914–1920', *Immigrants & Minorities* 26, 1–2 (2008), pp. 49–81

Stockdale, Melissa K. '"My Death for the Motherland Is Happiness": Women, Patriotism, and Soldiering in Russia's Great War, 1914–1917', *The American Historical Review* 109, 1 (2004), pp. 78–116

Stockdale, Melissa *Mobilizing the Russian Nation. Patriotism and Citizenship in the First World War*, Cambridge 2016

Stone, Norman *The Eastern Front 1914–1917*, New York, NY 1975

Strachan, Hew *The First World War*, vol. 1. *To Arms*, Oxford, 2001

Teichmann, Christian *Krieg und Ethnizität in Warschau, 1915–1918. Das jüdische Beispiel*, MA dissertation, Universität Leipzig, 2002

Tepora, Tuomas and Aapo Roselius (eds.) *The Finnish Civil War 1918. History, Memory, Legacy*, Leiden 2014

Ther, Philipp *Die dunkle Seite der Nationalstaaten. Ethnische Säuberungen im modernen Europa*, Göttingen 2011

Thorpe, Julie 'Displacing Empire: Refugee Welfare, National Activism and State Legitimacy in Austria-Hungary in the First World War', in *Refugees and the End of Empire. Imperial Collapse and Forced Migration in the Twentieth Century*, ed. Panikos Panayi and Pippa Virdee, New York, NY 2011, pp. 102–126

Todorova, Maria *Imagining the Balkans*, New York, NY and Oxford 2009

Verhey, Jeffrey *The Spirit of 1914. Militarism, Myth, and Mobilization in Germany*, Cambridge 2004

Vermeiren, Jan 'The "Rebirth of Greater Germany": The Austro-German Alliance and the Outbreak of War', in *Untold War. New Perspectives in First World War Studies*, ed. Heather Jones, Jennifer O'Brien, and Christoph Schmidt-Supprian, Leiden and Boston, MA 2008, pp. 215–228

Watson, Alexander *Ring of Steel. Germany and Austria-Hungary in World War I*, New York, NY 2014

Wasti, Syed Tanvir 'The 1912–13 Balkan Wars and the Siege of Edirne', *Middle Eastern Studies*, 40, 4 (2004), pp. 59–78

Weeks, Theodore R. 'Vilnius in World War I, 1914–1920', *Nordost-Archiv* NF XVII (2008), pp. 34–57

364 SELECT BIBLIOGRAPHY

Wehrt, Rudolf von *Tannenberg. Wie Hindenburg die Russen schlug*, Berlin 1934

Weindling, Paul Julian 'A Virulent Strain: German Bacteriology as Scientific Racism, 1890–1920', in *Race, Science and Medicine, 1700–1960*, ed. Waltraud Ernst and Bernard Harris, London and New York, NY 1999, pp. 217–233

Weindling, Paul Julian *Epidemics and Genocide in Eastern* Europe *1890–1945*, Oxford 2000

Westerhoff, Christian *Zwangsarbeit im Ersten Weltkrieg. Deutsche Arbeitskräftepolitik im besetzten Polen und Litauen 1914–1918*, Paderborn 2012

Wettstein, Adrian 'The French Military Mind and the Wars before the War', in *The Wars before the Great War. Conflict and International Politics before the Outbreak of the First World War*, ed. Dominik Geppert, William Mulligan, and Andreas Rose, Cambridge 2015, pp. 176–188

Watson, Alexander '"Unheard-of Brutality": Russian Atrocities against Civilians in East Prussia, 1914–1915', *The Journal of Modern History* 86 (2014), pp. 780–825

Wesener, Katharina 'Internment in WWI: The Case of Thalerhof', in *The Great War and Memory in Central and South-Eastern Europe*, ed. Oto Luthar, Leiden 2016, pp. 111–122

Wolff, Larry *Inventing Eastern Europe. The Map of Civilization on the Mind of the Enlightenment*, Stanford, CA 1995

Wróbel, Piotr *Zarys dziejów Żydów na ziemiach polskich w latach 1880–1918*, Warsaw 1991

Żabko-Potopowicz, Antoni, Marceli Handelsman, Władysław Grabski, and Kazimierz Władysław Kumaniecki *Polska w czasie wielkiej wojny (1914–1918)*, vol. 2. *Historja społeczna*, Warsaw 1932

Zetterberg, Seppo *Die Liga der Fremdvölker Russlands 1916–1918. Ein Beitrag zu Deutschlands antirussischem Propagandakrieg unter den Fremdvölkern Russlands im Ersten Weltkrieg*, Helsinki 1978

Zhvanko, Liubov *Біженство Першої світової війни в україні. Документи і матеріали (1914–1918)* [*Bizhenstvo Pershoi svitovoi viiny v Ukraini. Dokumenty i materialy (1914–1918)*], Kharkiv 2010

Zieliński, Konrad *Żydzi Lubelszczyzny 1914–1918*, Lublin 1999

Zimmermann, Moshe 'A Road Not Taken: Friedrich Naumann's Attempt at a Modern German Nationalism', *Journal of Contemporary History* 17, 4 (1982), pp. 689–708

Zolotarev, V. A. and L. V. Pozdeeva (eds.) *Война и общество в XX веке*, vol. I. *Война и общество накануне и в период Первой мировой войны* [*Voina i obshchestvo v XX veke*, vol. 1. *Voina i obshchestvo nakanune i v period Pervoi mirovoi voiny*], Moscow 2008

INDEX

Abdul Hamid II, 37
Act of 5 November, 302, 330
Adriatic Sea, 8, 49, 59, 131, 185, 339
Aegean Sea, 41, 251, 339
Aehrenthal, Alois Lexa von, 20
Albania, 13, 37, 49, 52, 59–60, 107, 131, 134–135, 143, 294, 297
Albanians, 37–38, 49, 52
Alldeutscher Verband (Pan-German League), 318
Allenstein (Olsztyn), 66–68
Alma-Tadema, Laurence, 307
Anatolia, 46, 56, 144, 186–187
Arendt, Hannah, 19
Argetoianu, Constantin, 145
Asia Minor, 56, 59–60
Asinara Island, 135
Athens, 44, 143–144
Atlantic Ocean, 200, 297
Auffenberg, Moritz, 69
Austria-Hungary, 2, 5, 9, 13, 15, 19–24, 29, 32–35, 37, 40–41, 60–64, 66, 69, 72–74, 82–84, 89, 101, 104, 118, 120, 122, 129, 133, 135–136, 138–140, 145–146, 153–154, 156–157, 165–170, 176–177, 181, 184, 191, 193, 201–202, 207–208, 211–212, 215–216, 218, 221–222, 224–226, 230, 232–233, 235–236, 239, 241, 245, 254, 258, 279, 281, 291, 294, 297, 304, 320–321, 325, 331, 336–341
Austrian Silesia, 226
Azerbaijan, 331

Bad Gleichenberg, 29
Baden, 14
Baernreither, Joseph Maria, 321

Baghdad, 14
Bakończyce, 116
Baltic Germans, 14, 185–186, 331
Baltic provinces, 185
Baltic Sea, 8, 30, 185
Balts, 8
Banat, 120
Barcelona, 16
Basarabescu, Ioan, 147
Báthory, Stephen, 145
Battle at Opatów, 251
Battle of Bunarhisar–Luleburgas, 44–45
Battle of the Bzura River, 78
Battle of Gorlice, 313
Battle of Kirkkilise, 44–45, 49
Battle of Komarów, 69
Battle of Kraśnik, 69
Battle of Mołotków (Molotkiv), 90
Battle of Przasnysz, 1, 5
Battle of the Rawka River, 78
Battle of Slivnitsa, 36
Battle of Stebnícka Huta, 119–120
Battle of Tannenberg, 68–69, 72, 137
Battle of the Masurian Lakes, 68, 246
Beirut, 38
Belarus, 2, 138, 143, 175, 288, 296, 314, 325, 347
Belarusians, 5, 57, 297, 308, 325, 328
Belgium, 30, 33–34, 97, 220, 247, 287
Belgrade, 16, 19–21, 33–34, 44, 63, 83–84, 129–130, 135, 161, 203, 205–206, 246–247, 251–252, 261–263, 267, 285–286, 291, 300–301, 332, 340–341, 345–346
Berbecki, Leon, 141
Berlin, 15, 23, 29, 33–34, 36, 62, 83, 127, 129, 145, 151, 161, 168–170, 174, 176,

365

189, 202, 207, 216, 219–222, 224, 235, 238–239, 287, 295, 298, 313, 324, 349
Bernhardi, Friedrich von, 27
Beroun, 232
Beseler, Hans von, 330, 333
Bessarabia, 144
Białowieża Forest, 297, 299
Bielcza, 275
Bielsk Podlaski, 126
Bieszczady Mountains, 80
Biondich, Mark, 94
Bismarck, Otto von, 14, 320
Black Sea, 8, 47, 147, 251, 323, 339
Bloch, Jan Gotlib, 25–26, 30–31, 57, 193
Bochnia Zamurowana, 234
Bogdanova, Donka, 182
Bohemia, 16, 18, 32, 47, 120, 170, 176, 194, 198, 221, 226, 232–233
Bolimów, 76, 80
Bosnia-Herzegovina, 13, 20, 32, 40, 230, 239, 245, 325
Bosnian crisis, 20
Bosnians, 5, 19
Boubelík, František, 119
Branicki, Ksawery, 253
Brassó (Braşov, Kronstadt), 146
Bratek-Kozłowski, Franciszek, 64
Brătianu, Ion, 144–145, 147
Brentano, Lujo, 320
Breslau, 221
Brest, 174
Brindisi, 134
Brno, 226
Brusilov Offensive, 139, 141–143, 202
Brusilov, Alexei, 28, 138–139, 141–143, 145, 202
Brussels, 345
Brwinów, 205
Bucharest, 4, 37, 55, 57, 143, 145–147, 150–151, 153, 161, 205, 221, 247, 267–268, 285, 290–291, 293, 298, 304, 306
Bucur, Maria, 183, 213
Budapest, 15–16, 18, 29, 36, 156, 162, 168, 170, 198, 202, 207, 221
Bukovina, 18, 76, 96, 140, 145, 153, 170, 197, 211, 226, 248–249, 254–255, 258, 286, 289, 294

Bulgaria, 8, 13, 19, 34, 36, 39–41, 43–44, 51, 53–56, 59–60, 84, 107, 128–129, 135–136, 146, 165, 182, 215, 287, 294, 321, 332, 337–338
Bulgarians, 36, 38–39, 42–55, 58, 112, 129, 147, 187, 294–295, 314, 324, 337–338
Buschan, Georg, 338
Bychawa, 278–279
Byków, 112
Bystroń, Jan Stanisław, 334–335
Bzura River, 251

Cabaj, Jarosław, 273
Carlsbad, 29
Carnegie Endowment for International Peace, 53, 57, 337
Carpathian Mountains, 63, 81–82, 85, 106, 118–120, 123, 138, 145, 150, 164, 187, 233, 315
Çatalca, 47–49, 52, 55–56, 112
Catalonia, 16
Caucasus, 187
Çekmece Bay, 48
Cenov, Gancho, 338
Central Anatolia, 188
Central Asia, 19, 90, 311
Central Powers, 9, 34, 61–62, 74, 78, 84, 104, 107, 120–121, 125, 127, 137, 139, 143–144, 152, 155, 170, 174, 177, 200–201, 210, 231, 264, 268, 292–293, 304, 307, 322, 324, 326, 328, 331, 333, 336–338, 343, 346–348
Čer plateau, 65
Cetinje, 336
Charles I, 216, 221, 233, 349, 351
Chołodecki Białynia, Józef, 204
Chotek, Sophie von, 32
Cisleithania, 15–16, 32, 168, 170, 225, 232–233, 257, 297, 303, 305
Claas, Heinrich, 226
Clark, Christopher, 35
Cleinow, Georg, 322
Constanţa, 144, 147
Constantine I, 50, 55, 143–144
Constantinople. See Istanbul
Corfu, 134–135, 300
Courland, 143, 259, 311, 319, 322
Courtenay, Jan Baudouin de, 57

INDEX

Cracow, 8, 23, 72, 75–76, 157, 161, 171–174, 179–180, 190, 312–313
Crete, 37
Croatia, 20, 32, 230
Croats, 5, 19, 230
Czechs, 3, 5, 33, 93, 119–120, 192, 223–224, 232–233, 320
Czernowitz (Chernivtsi), 139, 186, 190, 226, 249, 252, 260, 263, 285
Czetwertyński, Seweryn, 253
Czetwertyński, Włodzimierz, 253
Czuj, Jan (Jan Borzęcki), 280–282

Dąbrowa coal basin, 299
Dąbrowa Górnicza, 174
Dąbrowski, Jan, 72
Dagestan, 331
Dalmatia, 161
Dankl, Viktor, 69–70
Danube River, 36, 129, 146–147, 150, 152, 261, 291
Danzig, 167, 221
Dardanelles, 38, 120, 137
Dashnak (Armenian social democratic party), 187
Daszyński, Ignacy, 94
Daugirdas, Tadas, 254
Dęblin (Ivangorod), 23, 74, 249
Denmark, 13, 297
Dimitriev, Radko, 48–49, 112
Dnieper River, 191
Dobruja (Dobrogea), 53, 55, 147, 294, 332–333
Dornik, Wolfram, 85
Dowgird, Tadeusz. *See* Tadas Daugirdas
Dragoumis, Filippos, 50
Drina River, 65, 129
Dublin, 16
Dudeşti-Feteşti, 310
Dukla, 123
Dunajec River, 274
Durrës, 49, 134
Durusu Lake, 48
Dyboski, Roman, 157
Dziedzice, 316
Dzierzbicki, Stanisław, 126, 205, 267, 295

East Prussia, 1, 14, 28, 34, 62–63, 65–69, 72, 86, 92, 99, 121, 161, 167, 229, 246–247, 255, 314, 317, 319–320
Eastern Anatolia, 187
Eastern Carpathians, 122, 275
Eastern Front, 2–3, 5, 23, 71, 76, 78, 84, 97, 107, 111, 121, 138–140, 161, 169, 213, 267, 278, 314, 341–342
Eastern Galicia, 69, 71–72, 74, 84–85, 93–94, 111, 140, 153, 165, 201, 203, 225, 232–237, 239, 273, 278, 286, 294
Eastern Thrace, 55, 57, 74
Edib, Halidé, 47
Edirne, 38, 47, 50–52, 55–56
Einem, Karl von, 78
Elbe River, 323
Elbing, 194
Entente, 19, 22, 66, 99, 128, 143, 145, 157, 188, 214, 331
Enver İsmail Pasha, 55, 187
Ephraim, Otto, 299
Ertür, Hafiz Rakim, 51
Estonia, 259, 296, 331
Estonians, 3, 5, 14, 224
Eulenberg, Herbert, 329

Falcon (Sokół) Youth Movement, 228
Falkenhayn, Erich von, 29, 78, 139, 141, 146, 149
Far East, 19, 22
Ferdinand I, 47–48, 128, 144–145, 151
Ferenczi, Sándor, 100
Feteşti, 293, 298, 310
Finland, 2
Finns, 3
First Balkan War, 41, 43, 55, 105, 267, 337
Flanders, 56
France, 1, 15, 19, 22, 24, 27, 30, 34, 37, 43, 62, 83, 97, 121, 128, 134, 144, 164–165, 170, 190, 207, 220, 240, 247, 327
Frankfurt (an der Oder), 319
Franz Ferdinand d'Este, 29, 32–33, 325
Franz Joseph I, 8–9, 15–16, 19, 30, 32, 119, 164, 169, 184, 186, 222, 226, 233, 241, 258, 266, 284, 291, 349, 351
Franzos, Karl Emil, 316–317
Freiburg, 2, 14

368 INDEX

Freud, Sigmund, 100
Frey, Gottfried, 341–342
Friedeburg, Friedrich von, 233
Friederichsen, Max, 333
Friedjung, Heinrich, 20–21, 321
Friedrich, Archduke, 195

Galicia, 18, 21–22, 63–65, 70, 72, 76, 87, 90, 92, 94, 96–97, 117, 121, 124, 129, 140, 170, 184, 197–198, 203, 229, 235–236, 239, 250, 254–258, 268, 276, 279, 283, 289, 311, 314–317, 325
Galician Front, 75, 110
Gallipoli, 1, 8, 58
Gallwitz, Max von, 317
George I, 44
Georgia, 331
Gerlach, Hellmut von, 101, 163
German Empire, 13–16, 22–24, 27–28, 30–31, 33–35, 37, 42–43, 59, 61–62, 77, 80, 89, 97–98, 101, 103–104, 136–138, 146, 153–155, 157, 163, 165, 167–170, 177–178, 183, 189–191, 193–194, 198, 201–202, 209, 213, 216, 218, 220–221, 224–226, 231, 238–239, 246, 258, 267, 287, 293, 295, 297–298, 302–305, 307, 309–310, 318–323, 325, 331–334, 338–340, 342–343
German Reich, *See* German Empire
Germans, 1, 3, 5, 14–15, 20, 23–24, 27, 32, 35, 57, 63–64, 66, 68, 72, 74, 76, 78, 80, 87, 91, 97, 99, 123–124, 129, 139–141, 143, 149, 151–153, 155, 167, 185, 193, 200, 203, 205, 223–225, 227, 237, 240, 247, 250, 254, 259–260, 264, 267–269, 272–274, 286, 288–289, 292, 295–296, 298, 302, 304–305, 307, 309–310, 312, 314, 316, 318, 320–321, 323–326, 328–330, 332, 334, 336, 338–340, 342, 347
Germany, 1
Gertz, Wanda, 182
Goltz, Wilhelm Colmar von der, 42, 44
Gonda, Viktor, 103–104
Gorlice, 8, 122–123, 128, 136, 205, 230, 251, 259, 283–284, 319, 350

Gorlice Offensive, 28, 122, 136, 215, 274, 279, 281
Grajewski, 271
Grand Duchy of Finland, 194, 238, 319
Grand Duchy of Poznań, 315
Graz, 94
Great Britain, 1, 15, 19, 22, 30, 34, 59, 121, 128, 134, 144, 169–170, 202, 207, 221, 240, 307, 321
Greece, 3, 8, 13, 34, 37, 40–41, 43–44, 50, 52–54, 56–57, 59–60, 129, 134, 136, 143–144, 152, 337
Greeks, 4, 8, 38–39, 43, 50, 53–56, 60, 144
Grgjić, Stjepan, 269
Grodno, 285
Grotniki Małe, 228
Grube, August Wilhelm, 315–316
Gryzów, 86
Gulf of Finland, 237
Gumbinnen, 66
Gumz, Jonathan, 94

Haber, Fritz, 77–78
Haberlandt, Arthur, 213
Habsburg monarchy. *See* Austria-Hungary
Habsburg, Joseph Ferdinand, 140
Hadımköy, 46
Hague Conference, 25
Hague Convention, 268, 272, 291
Hague, 245
Hahn, Viktor von, 323
Halechko, Sofia, 182
Hall, Richard C., 55
Hamburg, 141
Hanover, 179
Hartleb, Tadeusz, 307
Hašek, Jaroslav, 9, 84, 212, 233
Healy, Maureen, 173
Hedin, Sven, 137
Hegeler, Wilhelm, 132, 327
Heidelberg, 221
Heiderode (Czersk), 155
Held, Joseph, 197
Helsinki, 2
Herwig, Holger, 169
Herzlodor, 224
Heymel, Charlotte, 316

INDEX

Hindenburg, Paul von, 29, 66–68, 137, 146, 327, 349
Hirszfeld, Hanna, 106
Hirszfeld, Ludwik, 106
Hochwächter, Gustav von, 45–46
Hohensalza (Inowrocław), 334
Hohenstein (Olsztynek), 246
Hołówko, Helena, 223, 227
Hołówko, Tadeusz, 223, 227
Horodenka, 265
Hötzendorf, Franz Conrad von, 19, 21, 28, 33, 62–63, 71–72, 74, 76, 121, 136, 141, 339
Hradec Králové, 221–222
Hungarians, 5, 8, 15, 20, 32, 64, 66, 84, 91, 122, 135, 157, 197–198, 202, 237, 269, 272, 324
Hungary, 15–16, 19–20, 32, 80, 146, 170–172, 202, 218, 236, 257, 332, 349
Hutten-Czapski, Bogdan, 330
Hynek, Jan, 275

Iași, 161, 268, 316
Imre Kertész Kolleg, 9–10
Internal Macedonian Revolutionary Organization (IMRO), 36, 39–40, 55, 187
Ioannina, 50, 52, 56
Iraq, 60
Ireland, 16
Island of Rügen, 238
Israel, 60
Istanbul, 8, 36, 44–45, 47, 50, 55–56, 58–59, 189, 218
Istria, 185
Italy, 18, 22, 34, 38, 41, 43, 60, 128, 134, 139, 184
Iwanowski, 178

Jabłonna, 126
Jabłońska, Helena née Seifert, 114, 123, 163, 178, 207–208, 234, 255–256, 278–279
Jagodina, 129–130
Jałowiec, 252
Jan III Sobieski, 328
Jankowski, Czesław, 162
Japan, 14, 66, 90
Jarosław, 163

Jaworski, Władysław Leopold, 274
Jellenta, Cezary, 177, 205, 210
Jena, 9–10, 153, 221, 299, 306
Jews, 2, 5, 14, 32, 38, 42, 57, 90–92, 111, 114–116, 162, 185, 189–190, 198, 224, 235–237, 239–240, 254–255, 257–259, 265, 268, 276–277, 279–280, 282–283, 289, 292, 294, 298, 306–309, 314, 316–317, 324, 328, 331, 342, 360, 362
Jihlava, 226
Joan of Arc, 183
Jordan, 60
July Crisis, 8

Kafka, Franz, 222
Kakania, 16–18
Kakowski, Aleksander, 227, 250, 340
Kalimanci, 55
Kalisz, 69, 97–99, 272
Kállay, Béni, 325
Kalmykia, 331
Kâmil Pasha (Kıbrisli Mehmed), 47
Kantorowicz, Ernst, 351
Karlovy Vary, 145
Kaunas, 23–24, 254, 259, 261, 299, 319
Kawczak, Stanisław, 70, 72, 85
Kazakhstan, 331
Kennan, George F., 2
Kennard, Dorothy, 149
Kerchnawe, Hugo, 291, 303
Kertész, André, 162
Kessler, Harry, 81, 250, 316–317
Kharkiv (Kharkov), 295
Kielce, 69, 228, 241, 263, 316
Kießler, Emil, 310
Kiev, 161, 285, 303
Kingdom of Poland, 21–22, 62, 65–66, 71–72, 74–75, 78–79, 90, 97, 120, 124–125, 127, 157, 186, 192, 201–202, 209, 223, 228–230, 237–238, 241, 249–250, 254, 259–260, 265, 272, 274, 276, 287–289, 294–295, 297–303, 306–308, 311–312, 314–318, 321, 325, 331, 334–335, 340–342, 345
Kingdom of Serbs, Croats and Slovenes, 3

370 INDEX

Kishinev, 331
Kłoczowski, Józef Dominik, 125
Klofáč, Václav, 233
Knox, Alfred, 79, 121, 125
Kobarid, 2
Kolowrat-Krakowský, Alexander, 215
Komarniki, 233
Königsberg, 14, 23, 167, 190, 194, 221, 312
Konopiště, 32
Korczyn, 269, 277
Korytowski, Witold, 235
Kosovo, 38
Kostyukhnivka (Kostiuchnówka), 141
Kotor, 336
Kovel, 140, 174, 276, 345
Kozłowski, Stanisław Gabriel, 329
Kragujevac, 65, 83, 129, 264
Kraków. See Cracow
Kramář, Karel, 233
Krasicki, August, 163, 207, 265, 275–276, 329
Kraslice, 176
Kraus, Karl, 9, 164, 212
Kraushar, Aleksander, 124
Kreisky, Bruno, 349
Kresna Gorge, 55
Kroh, Antoni, 118–119
Kronenberg, Leopold Julian, 253
Krościenko, 164
Krośniewice, 251
Krupanj, 98
Kruse, Francis, 163
Kruševac, 132
Kubicki, 271
Kumanovo, 49
Künigl-Ehrenburg, Ilka, 219
Kuropatkin, Alexei, 27
Kusmanek, Hermann, 112, 114, 116–117
Kyrgyzstan, 311, 331

L'viv. See Lwów
Łączyński, Ryszard, 276
Landwehr, 207, 267
Lapčević, Dragiša, 129

Latvia, 2, 299, 331
Latvian volunteer riflemen, 186
Latvians, 3, 5, 14, 57, 143, 185–186, 224, 259, 297
Lausanne Conference, 331
Leipzig, 319
Lennhoff, Rudolf, 343
Leonhard, Jörn, 2
Leopold, Prince of Bavaria, 328
Lešnica, 98
Leuven (Louvain), 97–99
Lezhë, 49
Liberal Party of Greece, 144
Liebknecht, Karl, 189
Linsingen, Alexander von, 140
Lipkowski, Józef, 48
Lippmann, Walter, 314
Lithuania, 2, 143, 259, 288, 299, 301–302, 306, 314, 328, 331, 347
Lithuanians, 3, 5, 14, 57, 224, 259, 297, 308, 318, 325, 328
Liulevicius, Vejas Gabriel, 340, 347
Livonia, 173, 223, 306, 322
Lobanov-Rostovskii, Andrei, 251–252
Łódź, 13, 37, 74, 80, 150, 190, 193, 221, 247, 285, 295, 298–299, 303–304, 313, 321, 341–342
London, 30, 36, 52, 219, 222, 224, 327
Lower Austria, 140, 197
Łowicz, 251
Loznica, 98
Lublin, 65, 69–70, 237, 247, 278, 294, 297, 303–304, 308, 313
Ludendorff, Erich, 66–69, 76, 349
Łuków, 272
Luxembourg, 33–34
Lwów (L'viv, Lemberg), 2, 70–71, 74, 83, 114, 123, 138, 167, 174, 190, 201, 203–204, 221, 235, 239–240, 247, 252–254, 258, 260, 262, 264, 268–269, 285–286, 289, 291, 293, 313

Macedonia, 38–40, 43–44, 49–50, 52–55, 60–61, 65, 129, 146, 187, 294–295, 333, 336, 338, 343
Mackensen, August von, 28, 74, 121–123, 128–129, 134, 146–147, 150–151, 205, 299
Madeira, 351

INDEX

Majkowski, Aleksander, 150, 200–201, 226–227, 231–232, 266
Manastir, 38
Manchuria, 27–28, 36, 101
Máramaros County, 72
Mărăşeşti, 183
Marghiloman, Alexandru, 304
Marijampolė, 318
Marne River, 76
Marwitz, Georg von der, 121
Masaryk, Tomáš Garrigue, 21
Masurian Lakes, 66
Mauthausen, 155
Medyka, 256
Memel (Klaipeda), 246
Menczel, Philipp, 263
Michael I the Brave, 145
Middle East, 14
Mielec, 256
Mikhail Alexandrovich, 351
Miletić, Aleksandar, 9
Milukov, Pavel, 351
Misirkov, Krste Petkov, 40
Mitteleuropa, 321
Modlin (Novogeorgievsk), 23–24, 125, 146
Moldavia, 36, 145, 151–152
Molenda, Jan, 311
Moltke, Helmuth von the Older, 24
Moltke, Helmuth von the Younger, 23, 29, 33, 62, 324
Montenegrins, 36–37, 49–50, 131, 336–337
Montenegro, 8, 13, 34, 40–41, 52, 131, 134–135, 143, 218, 294, 300, 306, 312, 332–333, 335, 337
Morava River, 131
Moravia, 16, 18, 20, 120, 170, 176, 194, 198, 221, 226, 232–233
Moravian Ostrava, 232
Mościska, 117
Moscow, 10, 153, 177, 180, 202, 221, 230, 312, 351
Mount Lovćen, 336
Mukhtar Mahmoud Pasha, 45, 58
Murmansk, 137, 157
Musil, Robert, 16, 225

Mütz, Herman, 264–265
Myślenice, 248

Nagel, Fritz, 88
Nagyszeben (Sibiu, Hermannstadt), 146, 149
Narach Lake, 138–139
Narew River, 62, 124, 267
Naumann, Friedrich, 320–323
Nazim Hussein Pasha, 44
Neidenburg (Nidzica), 246
Netherlands, 13, 30, 163
Neudeck (Świerklaniec), 317
Neumann, Józef, 260
Nicholas II, 15, 25, 28, 186, 228, 266, 291, 329, 349, 351
Nida River, 107, 119
Nielsen, Asta, 175
Nikolai Nikolaevich, 223, 237
Njegoš, Danilo, 131
Nonne, Max, 103–104
North Africa, 43
North Sea, 29–30
Norway, 297
Nowa Wieś, 317

Oberhummer, Eugen, 336
Ober-Ost, 288, 297, 299, 302, 325, 340, 347
Obrenovac, 83
Odessa, 221
Olomouc, 226
Olszanica, 163
Opatów, 261
Orłowski, Hubert, 317–318
Ortelsburg (Szczytno), 246
Osowiec, 23
Ostrołęka, 66, 137
Ostrowiec, 316
Ottoman Empire, 8, 13–14, 19, 34, 37–38, 40, 42–44, 53, 55, 58–61, 136, 143–144, 186–187, 189, 215, 337
Ottoman Porte. See Ottoman Empire
Ottoman Tripolitania (Libya), 38, 60

Palestine, 60
Pan-Germanism, 225–226, 318–320, 323
Pan-Slavism, 119, 225
Paris, 10, 36, 219, 222, 224, 327

372 INDEX

Partsch, Josef, 319, 333
Party of Constitutional Democrats, 351
Pašić, Nikola, 82, 106
Peloponnese, 136
Péronne, 1, 6
Peter I, 54, 135
Petrograd. *See* St Petersburg
Petrović, Vukašin, 264
Pflanzer-Baltin, Karl von, 109
Piłsudski, Józef, 69, 71, 228, 235, 283, 314
Pinczów, 107
Pinsk, 139
Piotrków Trybunalski, 249, 261, 271, 307
Plzeň, 180
Pöch, Rudolf, 156–157, 218
Podolia, 316
Poland, 2–3, 5, 10, 165, 255
Poles, 3, 5, 8, 21, 30–31, 33, 57, 59, 107, 127, 141, 143, 157, 164, 201, 223–224, 226–227, 230–231, 235, 240, 253, 257–259, 268, 276, 283, 289, 294, 297–298, 307–308, 316, 322, 324, 326, 328, 335, 342
Polish Legionnaires, 3–4, 71, 75, 86, 90, 107, 119–120, 127, 141, 182, 184, 186, 228, 241, 263, 307, 330, 345
Polotsk, 178
Pomerania, 155, 226, 342
Pontus, 316
Port Arthur, 28
Posen (Poznań), 201, 351
Potiorek, Oskar, 65, 83, 201, 230, 269
Potocki, Józef, 253
Prague, 4, 119, 145, 161, 196, 202, 221–222, 224, 226, 258
Preis, 308
Preusker, Hans, 98–99
Prilep, 336
Pristina, 49
Prittwitz, Maximilian von, 66
Prusin, Alexander Victor, 92
Prussia, 13–14, 22, 178, 184
Pruszków, 250
Prut River, 249, 263
Przasnysz, 1, 76
Przemyśl, 3, 5, 23, 72, 74, 80, 82, 94, 111–113, 115–118, 123, 146, 163,

177, 201, 207, 234, 240, 272–273, 278–279
Przyłęcki, 271
Pszczyna (Pless), 140
Puławy, 328
Putnik, Radomir, 29–30, 50, 65, 82, 129

Radom, 72, 90, 249, 271, 316
Radziwiłłów, 251
Rappoport, Salomon (S. An-ski), 283
Rašín, Alois, 233
Rasputin, Grigory, 351
Rathenau, Walther, 320
Ration cards, 3, 167, 170–172, 298, 304
Rawka River, 79
Redlich, Josef, 155
Refugees, 47, 51, 56, 59, 83, 111, 115–116, 125, 127, 130–132, 134, 162, 167, 170, 174, 183, 188, 191–192, 194, 197, 236, 246–247, 254–255, 268, 279, 295, 320, 350–351
Rennenkampf, Paul von, 66–68, 86, 92, 317
Republic of Austria, 226
Riga, 4–5, 8, 37, 173, 184–186, 190, 194–195, 247, 285, 295–296, 299
Rockefeller Foundation, 307–308
Roda Roda, Alexander (Sándor Friedrich Rosenfeld), 211–212
Rodaun, 212
Rokoszny, Józef, 90, 200, 228, 238, 249, 266, 271, 276, 293
Romania, 3, 8, 13, 28, 34, 37, 43, 53, 55, 78, 104, 143–146, 152–153, 155, 157, 214, 250, 254, 286–287, 289, 291, 294, 296–297, 301–302, 304–306, 309, 311, 326, 331–332, 339, 343
Romanian Carpathians, 122
Romanians, 5, 53, 55, 144–147, 149, 151, 155, 183, 214, 224, 268, 287, 289, 305, 324, 326
Romer, Eugeniusz, 86, 175, 178, 229, 274
Ronge, Max, 93, 239–240
Rostov-on-Don, 297
Ruhr, 180, 221
Rumelia, 36, 57
Russian Empire, 5, 13–15, 19, 22–24, 26, 30–31, 33–36, 40, 61–63, 69,

INDEX

89–90, 101, 108, 121, 125, 127, 137–138, 141–142, 144–145, 152–154, 156–157, 163–165, 174, 176–177, 187, 189–190, 197, 199, 204, 207, 222, 224, 226, 228–230, 239–241, 246, 259–260, 276, 285–286, 294–297, 307–308, 315, 321–322, 326–327, 331, 334, 339, 348–350
Russian Federation, 2–3
Russian Front, 3, 28, 33, 109, 190
Russians, 5, 8–9, 21, 23, 28, 31, 33–34, 57, 62–66, 70–72, 75–76, 78–80, 82, 85–86, 88, 90, 92–93, 101, 107, 111–113, 115, 118–119, 121–122, 124–127, 138, 140–141, 152, 155, 157, 167, 185, 188, 200, 203, 205–206, 208, 227, 233, 235–236, 239–240, 246–247, 249, 251, 253–256, 259–262, 264–266, 268–269, 273, 279, 281–284, 286, 288–289, 291, 293–295, 314, 326–330
Rutowski, Tadeusz, 260, 269
Ružomberok (Rózsahegy), 103
Rypuszyński, Janusz, 264–265
Rzeszów, 284

Saale River, 9
Saarbrücken, 221
Šabac, 66, 98–99
Salonika, 38, 50, 53, 58, 60, 83, 129, 144, 161
Salonika Front, 78, 136, 339
Samsonov, Alexander, 66–68
San River, 72, 74, 113, 123
Sandes, Flora, 182
Sandomierz, 249, 261, 271, 276, 286, 293
Sanok, 123, 164
Sarajevo, 33, 230, 245, 325
Sarajevo assassination, 33–34, 199, 337
Sarıkamış, 187
Sarrail, Maurice, 136, 332
Sassnitz, 238
Sava River, 129, 261, 291
Savov, Mikhail, 55
Schalek, Alice, 212
Schleswig and Holstein, 144

Schoenaich-Carolath, Heinrich zu, 31, 33
Schultz, Arved, 335
Schwerin, Friedrich von, 319
Sea of Marmara, 47
Second Balkan War, 53, 55, 105, 129, 145, 339
Second International, 25, 31
Second Reich. *See* German Empire
Šedivý, Ivan, 232
Seeberg, Reinhold, 327
Serbia, 3, 8, 13, 19–22, 29, 32–35, 37, 40–41, 43–44, 51–54, 56, 59, 61, 63, 65–66, 72, 82–84, 94, 97, 105–106, 128–129, 131, 135, 143, 157, 165, 177, 200–201, 209, 219, 222, 224, 226, 229–230, 232, 250, 255, 264, 267, 269, 286–287, 289, 291, 294, 297, 300–301, 303, 306–307, 311–312, 314, 325–327, 331–333, 337, 339, 341
Serbs, 5, 8, 19, 33–34, 36, 38–39, 43, 49–51, 54, 58, 63, 65, 82–84, 93, 105–106, 120, 129, 131, 133–135, 155, 157, 187, 224, 230, 236, 239, 287, 289, 301, 324, 326, 337
Sering, Max, 319
Seton-Watson, Robert W., 20, 106
Seyfeddin, Ömer, 60
Sheptytsky, Andrey, 269
Shkodër, 49–50, 52, 56, 134
Šiauliai (Szawle), 229
Siberia, 90, 157
Sienkiewicz, Henryk, 307–308
Sighetu Marmației, 72
Skierniewice, 251
Składkowski, Sławoj Felicjan, 75, 88, 91, 95, 101, 106–107, 142, 228, 345
Skopje, 5, 53, 106, 129, 336, 343
Slim, Hugo, 248
Slovakia, 103, 119
Slovaks, 3, 5
Slovenes, 5, 19, 32, 96, 184
Smederevo, 327
Smolensk, 191
Śniatyń, 316
Soča (Isonzo) River, 2–3, 85, 128
Sochaczew, 78
Social Democratic Party of Germany (SPD), 15, 24

374 INDEX

Sofia, 8, 39–40, 43–44, 53–55, 128, 294–295, 338
Sokołowski, Alfred, 346
Solek, Wincenty, 241
Sombor (Zombor), 236
Somme River, 28
Sopot, 226
Southern Dobruja, 146
Spanish flu, 105, 136, 342
Srokowski, Stanisław, 256
St Petersburg, 19, 21, 34, 145, 153, 180, 185, 191–192, 194, 202, 219, 230, 238, 297, 312, 351
Stalingrad, 72
Stallupöhnen, 66
Stanisławów (Ivano-Frankivsk), 63, 140, 240
Starynkiewicz, Sokrates, 192
Starzyński, Roman, 141
Stawino, 272
Stebnícka Huta, 119–120
Steed, Henry Wickham, 20
Stegemann, Hermann, 210
Stepanivna, Olena, 182
Stepanović, Stepa, 65
Stettin (Szczecin), 238
Stochod (Stokhid) River, 182
Stone, Norman, 2
Strausz, Adolf, 338
Stryj Valley, 233
Styr River, 182
Styria, 164
Suceava, 316
Supreme National Committee (NKN), 279–280
Suttner, Kinsky Bertha von, 25
Sweden, 194, 238
Świecie (Schwetz), 341
Świeykowski, Bronisław, 122
Świniary, 229
Switzerland, 15, 331
Syria, 186, 188

Tahsin, Hasan Pasha, 50
Talaat, Mehmed Pasha, 188–189
Tallinn, 161, 285
Tanew River, 69
Tannenberg, 3, 5
Târgu Jiu, 183

Tarnów, 72, 122, 255–256, 261, 264–266, 280–282
Tatarstan, 331
Tatyana Nikolaevna, 192
Teodoroiu, Ecaterina, 181–183
Tertil, Tadeusz, 264–265
Teschen (Cieszyn), 140–141
Thalerhof, 94
Ther, Philipp, 10, 59
Thrace, 38–39, 43–44, 49, 56, 59, 61
Thun-Hohenstein, Franz von, 222
Tilka, Bogislav. See Velburg, Gerhard
Tisza, István, 33–34, 236
Tomaszów Mazowiecki, 237, 316
Transleithania, 170, 202, 232, 236
Transylvania, 144–147, 149–150
Trenčín (Trencsén), 164
Trieste, 176, 184–186, 221
Triple Alliance, 22
Tripoli, 38
Tröbst, Hans, 124
Turkey. See Ottoman Empire
Turks, 8, 36–38, 40–41, 43–44, 46–52, 56, 58, 188–189, 207, 314
Tutrakan (Turtucaia), 55, 146–147

Ukraine, 2, 15, 78, 143, 294, 296, 304, 323, 331
Ukrainian Sich Riflemen, 86, 182, 234
Ukrainians, 5, 8, 14, 21, 57, 94, 157, 182, 195, 198, 224, 235–236, 240, 257, 268, 289, 294, 297, 308, 325, 328
United States of America, 88, 104, 187, 307, 321, 341
Upper Hungary, 165
Upper Silesia, 140, 341
Ural Mountains, 316
Ushlinova, Donka, 182
Ustrzyki, 123

Valjevo, 83
Van, 186, 188
Varna, 332
Vatra Dornei, 76
Velburg, Gerhard, 153, 293, 298–299, 305–306, 309–310
Venizelos, Eleftherios, 143–144
Verdun, 28, 138
Verhey, Jeffrey, 221

INDEX   375

Verkhnyadzvinsk (Dryssa), 175
Versailles, 59
Vido Island, 135
Vienna, 15, 18, 21, 32–34, 83, 93,
  123, 127, 131, 151, 161–162, 168,
  170, 172–174, 176, 180, 186, 191,
  197, 202, 207, 212, 217–219, 221, 235,
  255, 257–258, 298, 300–301, 316,
  324–325
Vilnius, 167, 186, 247, 254, 285, 295,
  302–303, 306, 328–329
Vistula River, 64, 66, 277, 341
Vit, Jan, 112, 117
Vitebsk, 175
Vlorë, 134
Vojvodina, 236
Volhynia, 3, 78, 85, 140–141
Volytsia, 234
Vorarlberg, 15

Wagner-Jauregg, Julius, 103–104
Wallachia, 145
Wallisch, Friedrich, 287, 340
Warsaw, 1, 4, 10, 26, 31, 36, 66,
  74, 79, 124, 126–127, 162, 174,
  190, 192, 200, 202–203, 205,
  209, 218, 221, 223–224, 227,
  247, 250, 253, 258, 260, 267,
  272, 285–286, 288, 290, 292,
  295–296, 298, 302–304, 307,
  312–313, 326, 328–330, 333,
  339, 343–346
Waterstradt, Friedrich, 319–320
Weimar Republic, 313
Weindling, Paul, 348
Weisselberger, Salo, 260
Wenigenjena, 9

Wernic, Leon, 346
Western Front, 3, 28, 76, 78–80, 97–98,
  102, 106, 120, 138, 154, 214, 226
Western Galicia, 76, 95, 279, 294
White Sea, 323
Wieprz River, 267
Wierzchosławice, 261
Wilhelm II, 14–15, 29–30, 34, 62, 222,
  226, 349, 351
Wiłkomierz (Ukmergė), 254
Wilson, Woodrow, 314, 331
Winniki (Vynnyky), 262
Witos, Wincenty, 180, 255, 266,
  274–275
Witte, Sergei, 35
Włostów, 261
Wolbrom, 91
Wolff, Larry, 317–318
Woyrsch, Remus von, 140
Württemberg, 140

Yanushkevich, Nikolai, 258, 268
Young Turk Movement, 37
Ypres, 1–2, 77–78, 80
Yudenich, Nikolai, 188

Zagórski, 173
Zagreb, 8, 20, 141, 230, 346
Zamość, 265
Zamoyski, Maurycy, 253
Zbruch River, 64–65, 71, 100
Zduny, 251
Zeletin, Ștefan, 53
Złaków, 251
Zweig, Stefan, 220–221, 225, 231
Zwoleń, 316
Żyrardów, 76, 78, 250

CPSIA information can be obtained
at www.ICGtesting.com
Printed in the USA
LVHW011048030821
694401LV00005B/357